In Search of Andalucia

In Search of Andalucia

A Historical Geographical Observation of the Málaga Sea Board

by
Christopher Wawn
and
David Wood

Photography by
Michelle Chaplow

The Pentland Press
Edinburgh – Cambridge – Durham – USA

First published in 2000 by
The Pentland Press Ltd
1 Hutton Close,
South Church
Bishop Auckland
Durham
DL14 6XB

ISBN 1–85821-690–7

Typeset in Bell 10/12
by Carnegie Publishing, Carnegie House, Chatsworth Road, Lancaster LA1 4SL
Printed and bound in the United Kingdom at the University Press, Cambridge

To our long-suffering wives Paloma and Anita
without whose tireless encouragement this book
would have been finished in half the time

Contents

List of Illustrations

Maps

Photographs

Between Pages

Key to Conventional Signs

- Provincial Border
- District Border
- Dual Carriageway with Motorway properties
- Dual Carriageway or Main Highway
- Regional Road, some with dual carriageways
- Other roads: Surfaced/unsurfaced
- Railway
- River/Lake/Sea
- Tower
- Castle
- Town
- Church
- Hermitage/Chapel
- Church/Ruin
- Mine
- Burial Ground
- National Park/Game Reserve
- Outstanding Beauty
- Panoramic viewpoint
- Phoenician/Roman settlement
- Hill Fort
- Bridge/Acqueduct
- Ruins
- Mill
- Roman Site
- Spa/Spring
- Camping/Caravaning
- 564 Mountain with Height [metres]
- Tunnel entrance/exit
- Airport
- N W E S Compass Rose
- Pleasure boats/Harbour
- Miscellaneous sights
- Industrial Archeology
- Caves
- Refuge

Acknowledgements

Attempting to climb every hilltop and visit every valley in the province of Málaga in search of tangible traces of its past is not to everyone's taste. Invitations to friends and colleagues to join in the fun of discovery are often met with blank stares, feeble excuses and hurriedly arranged prior engagements. But not always. The authors wish to thank the following who gave generously of their time to help in the enormous amount of fieldwork required for the production of this book. There were days when they were rewarded only with a pitiful pile of stones, but many a stunning view and, we hope, a lot of fun.

Special mention must be made of Richard Dight, whose expertise and knowledge of the area were invaluable. Pat Young, our co-pilot, all but ruined her Fiat in pursuit of the past. Paul Naughton Rumbo for his assistance with the map illustration and art work.

John Swann was the most loyal walker of all, but we cannot forget the sore feet and aching legs of Batty Laura, Steve Brook, Adrian Collister, Mike James, Marilyn Day, George Felipes, Dominic Hawker, the Brothers Haynes (Peter, Andrew and Tom), Charlotte Pederson, Will Bollhorst, Tim Shapland, Peter Stagnetto, Pelu Triay, Stuart Watkins and the students of Sotogrande International School who were participating in the Duke of Edinburgh Award Scheme.

We cannot allow to go unacknowledged the courage of Fiona Elliot-Goddall, who stripped to her bikini and posed in any icy pool on a winter's day; and finally much gratitude is due to Marilyn Morris for adminstrative support beyond the bounds of reason.

Sincere thanks to them all.

Preface

WE LIVE IN THE AGE OF THE INSTANT. It began with coffee, spread via the pizza to eating out, and now, thanks to the digital telephone line and the ubiquitous computer, it has entered into every corner of our lives. Now is all there is.

If the millennium bug fails us, we may well be the last generation to know the joy of slowness, the romance of remote, unreachable places, the mystery beyond the mist. The world has been packed into a plastic box, and each year the box gets smaller. Soon it will be no bigger than a wristwatch, and then a chip to be implanted in our brains at birth. All human life and knowledge instantly available, always on tap in two dozen languages. None of us need ever be alone again.

This book is an unashamed celebration of the world we are leaving behind. A world where a clock which lost half an hour a day was quite accurate enough, a journey beyond the horizon was a journey into the unknown, and life was governed by the seasons and the stars. It is a book of history, and as such it is fitting that it has a history of its own.

It began as a modest MA thesis with the title *Roman Sites in Southern Andalucía.* Chris Wawn, who settled in Gibraltar in the late 1980s, has a lifelong interest in history and archæology. Combining this with the landscape-reading skills he developed during his army years, he felt he could bring a fresh insight into the subject. During his research he was able to discover many sites which had previously been unknown or overlooked.

His notes grew and whenever he could, he tried to pull them together and turn them into the thesis which he intended. But it was not easy. Newly married and with a young family, he was now working in Gibraltar's finance sector and simultaneously following a secondary military career in the Gibraltar Regiment. His notes and his research seemed doomed to lie unread.

The turning point came in 1996. I first met Chris in 1990, when we both worked briefly for the same Gibraltar-based trust company. In mid-1996 he learned that I was unemployed, having been made redundant early in July. Knowing that I had a fondness for writing, Chris suggested that I might like to turn some of my unwelcome leisure time to the collating and typing of the neglected notes.

What began as simple note-transcribing soon altered. I had none of Chris

Wawn's knowledge of the subject matter and, to be candid, very little interest in it. When Chris suggested that I should visit the sites he was writing about in order to absorb some of the atmosphere, I was initially reluctant for two reasons. Beyond my lack of interest, there was also a more practical problem. I do not drive, which made reaching many of the sites difficult if not impossible. The problem was solved when a third member of the team was recruited. Patricia Young, another ex-colleague, had been made redundant at the same time as myself and consequently had time on her hands. More importantly, she was an experienced driver who knew southern Andalucía well. For many months she was my uncomplaining chauffeuse, driving well beyond the call of duty across the face of the countryside in search of the sites which Chris had described. Together we began to learn and, what is more important, to enjoy. Later, when Chris would lead the expeditions in his four-wheel drive 'ain't-no-stoppin'-us-now-mobile', she would often join us. Without her early assistance this book would have died in infancy, and Chris and I would like to pause here briefly to say thank you to Pat – Our Lady of the Pine Cones.

As I visited the sites and began to learn, it was inevitable that my approach to the transcribing of Chris's notes should change. I found it increasingly impossible to be a mere disinterested observer. More and more I would find myself injecting my own style and opinions. As a novice, I brought a dash of irreverence which showed itself in what I hoped were flashes of humour, and a casualness quite at odds with Chris's original vision. We became unlikely collaborators. Each of us was, in a sense, writing a different book. It was as though chalk and cheese had called a truce and bought each other a beer.

The final piece of an intricate puzzle fell into place when Chris asked Michelle Chaplow, one of the coast's best-known and most respected photographers, to complement the text with a set of stunning studies.

The result is this book. It is not the book that Chris Wawn set out to write, nor is it a book that David Wood could have envisaged writing. But writing it was fun. We sincerely hope that you will have half as much fun reading it and that some of you, at least, will be inspired to follow us on to the back roads of Andalucía in search of its past. There's no hurry. Andalucía has waited a long time. It will wait a little longer.

David Wood
November 1999

STOP PRESS
For more information see our website:
www.andalucia com/insearchof

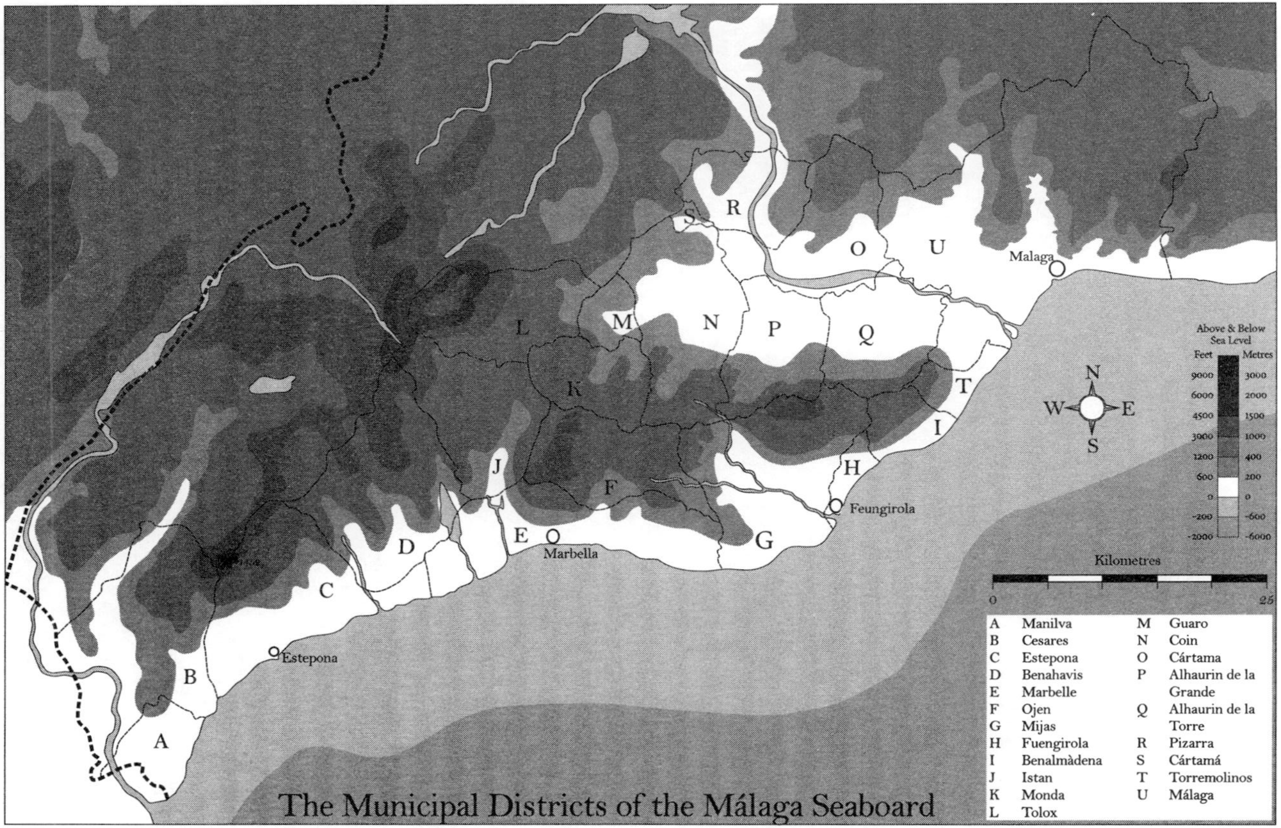

The Municipal Districts of the Málaga Seaboard

Chapter One

Málaga

Historical Background

MÁLAGA HAS A HISTORY RICHER than a Christmas cake. The great bay on the Mediterranean coast where the rio Guadalmedina empties into the sea first attracted the attention of the Phœnicians almost three thousand years ago, and the town they founded there passed in turn to the Greeks, Carthaginians, Romans, Visigoths and, in AD 711, to the Moors. When the Moors reluctantly left, its inhabitants were finally Spanish. The whole history of Andalucía, and of Spain, is written in its streets. In this opening chapter, we shall look in detail at the history of Málaga. As we meander along, it is hoped that the reader will begin to appreciate the bewildering patchwork of influences which have clashed, collided and conspired over more than thirty centuries to make Andalucía what it is today. Only then will the weathered stones that mark the spots where the past still dips its skeletal fingers into the present begin to live and breathe and tell their stories.

We must begin with statistics. They are the essential provisions of our journey, and the sooner we take them on board, the sooner we can be on our way.

But first a word of warning. The Spanish have a confusing habit of giving provinces the same names as their chief towns. If a Spaniard says that he is from Granada, or Seville, or Cádiz, the standard response is to ask, '*Provincia o capital?*' This lamentable lack of imagination may cause us problems from time to time as we try to disentangle one from the other, so we should be on our guard. The province to which the town of Málaga gives its name, and through which we shall be travelling on our journey of discovery, occupies 2,809 square miles (7,276 square kilometres) of the southern Spanish coast. It has an indigenous population of well over a million, of whom around 550,000 live in its eponymous capital. However, these numbers swell enormously during the summer months due to the influx of foreign tourists. In the south it is mountainous (so be prepared for a few strenuous climbs), but its northern half forms part of the Andalucían plain. To the east is the province of Granada, from which it is separated by the Sierra de Alhama, and to the west the province of Cádiz. Close to its western boundary a whole series of *sierras*, those of Ronda, Mijas, Tolox and Bermeja, rise to almost 6,500 feet (1,980

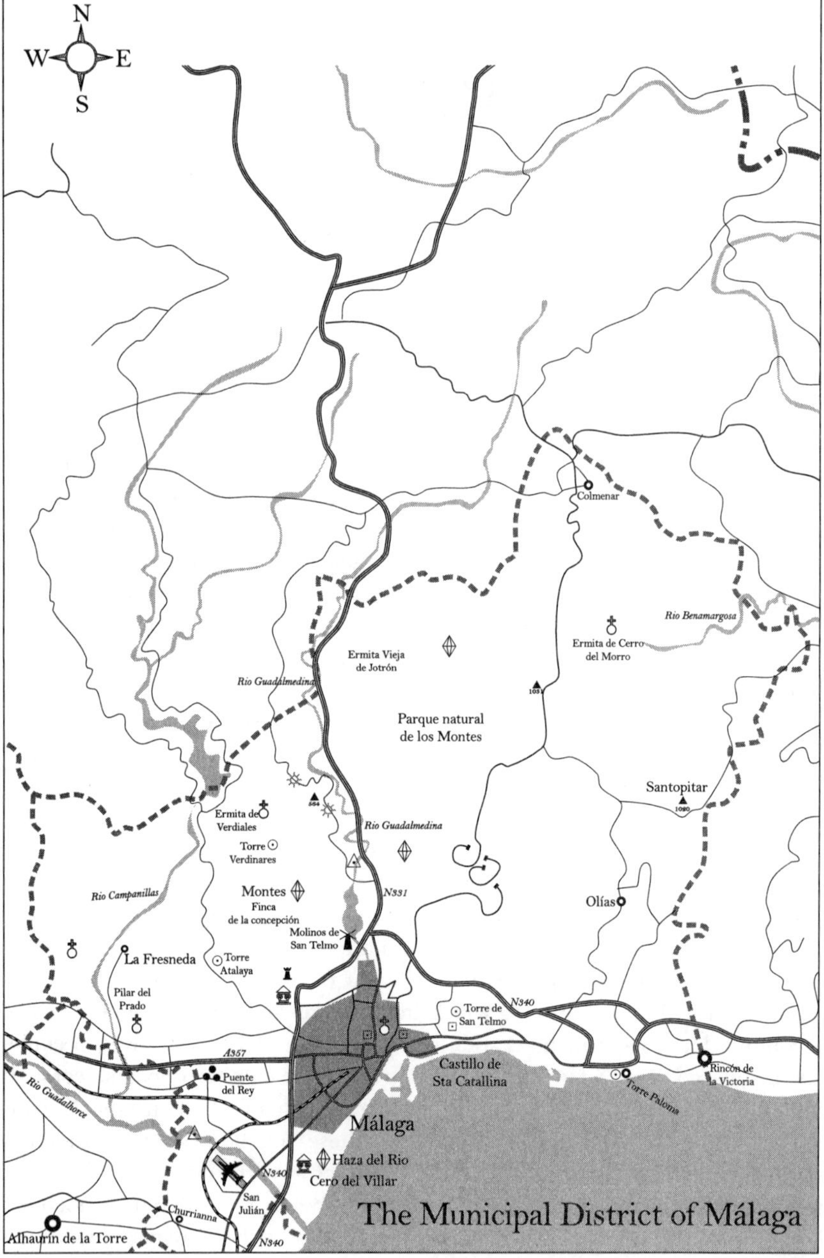

N
W
E
S
Colmenar
Rio Benamargosa
Ermita de Cerro del Morro
Ermita Vieja de Jotrón
Rio Guadalmedina
Parque natural de los Montes
Santopitar
Ermita de Verdiales
Rio Guadalmedina
Torre Verdinares
Rio Campanillas
Montes
Finca de la concepción
N331
Olías
Molinos de San Telmo
La Fresneda
Torre Atalaya
Pilar del Prado
Torre de San Telmo
N340
A357
Puente del Rey
Castillo de Sta Catallina
Rincón de la Victoria
Torre Paloma
Rio Guadalhorce
Málaga
Haza del Rio
Cero del Villar
N340
San Julián
Churrianna
Alhaurín de la Torre
N340
The Municipal District of Málaga

metres). There are many rivers, the two main ones being the Guadalhorce and the Guadiaro. The coastal lowlands and fertile inland valleys of Málaga province have been farmed for thousands of years, producing vegetables, olives, fruit and luscious grapes to make its characteristic wine. Here and there along the way we shall pause to sample them all. For almost as long, the southern mountains have been mined for their rich mineral deposits, notably of iron and lead, though silver and marble have also been important in their time. And readers who can associate such things only with the frozen Siberian wastelands may be surprised to learn that the north of the province has its fair share of salt mines.

As a Spanish seaport, perhaps only Barcelona ranks higher than the town of Málaga in its importance. In addition to the famous sweet Málaga wine, it exports iron ore, dried fruit, almonds, olive oil, oranges, lemons, olives, canned anchovies and more. In turn it imports petroleum, corn, chemicals, iron and steel. Its airport imports tourists. The importation of iron is ironic. The mountains are still brimming with ore, but the mines are gone. In Roman and Moorish times, Málaga exported figs to China, via Baghdad, and, in a surprising reversal of the accepted norm, even sent its woven silks to the East. The rio Guadalmedina, which flows through the city from north to south, was once Málaga's biggest problem as well as one of its greatest assets. During heavy mountain rains it frequently caused severe flooding, until the threat was removed by the construction of the dam at Agujero in 1927.

The Phœnicians may have named their embryonic town for the fish-salting industry (see below), but today it is home to a host of factories producing building materials, fertilizer, textiles and, perhaps most important of all in view of its key location for the tourist trade, beer. For in spite of its continuing industrial importance, the province of Málaga's famously mild climate – a gift from the surrounding sierra beneath which it shelters – has made it the number one destination for sun-seeking holidaymakers and permanent expatriates from the European north. And, of course, its capital town's international airport is the gateway to all the other tourist honey pots along the Costa del Sol.

Málaga was already established as an important seaport town at the time of the Moorish invasion, but it rose to even greater prominence after the disintegration of the Caliphate of Córdoba, when it became the centre of the independent Kingdom of Málaga. The amirs who ruled there called the place, with some justification, 'terrestrial paradise'. It was to remain in Moorish hands for almost eight hundred years until, in 1487 – a momentous year for much of the region, as we shall see – it finally fell to the Christian re-conquerors, but only after it had successfully resisted numerous previous assaults. No-one gives up Paradise without a fight.

After the expulsion of the Moors, more than three centuries were to pass before it changed hands again, if only briefly. It was occupied by the French from 1810 to 1812, during the Peninsular War, also known as the War of Independence.

The name Málaga is a corruption of the earlier form, *Malaca*, which has been taken by some to be derived from the rather obscure goddess *Malake*. Since no-one appears ever to have worshipped Malake, this seems unlikely. It is far more probable that it is related to the Phœnician word *malak* or *malac*, which has associations with the food-salting and conserving industry. The cultural melting pot which Málaga has been through the ages has left its mark in many of the local place names. For example, the fortress of Gibralfaro (see below) bears a name compounded from the Moorish word for a hill, *jebel*, and the Greek term for a lighthouse, *pharos*.

Iberian/Celtic Origins

Man, for good or ill, has been shaping the character of the Iberian Peninsula for at least 200,000 years. Fossils discovered at Gibraltar and elsewhere are proof of that. But it is arguable that human habitation goes back as much as half a million years. Utensils discovered in places as far apart as Algeciras and Madrid, and cave paintings in various parts of the country, certainly make the 200,000 year estimate appear conservative. It is academic. All of that is lost to pre-history and the applied imaginations of archæologists and dreamers.

The first historically recorded inhabitants of the Spanish Peninsula were the Iberians, an Afro-Semitic people who settled the southern part some five thousand years ago, when the country which would one day become Spain was still physically attached to Africa. It would appear that *iber* was their word for a river, and as immigrants from a land that was largely desert, they appear to have been impressed by the comparative abundance of running water, although in truth, none of Spain's rivers is particularly impressive to the blasé modern eye. The river which most attracted them, and along whose banks they made their first settlements, is today known as the Ebro. The name is itself a derivative of *iber*. It is the longest river in Spain, rising near Reinosa in the Cantábrican Cordillera and flowing for 565 miles (910 km) down to the Mediterranean coast, roughly halfway between Barcelona and Valencia. In spite of its length and its impressive outflow, the river is only navigable from its delta to Tortosa, fifteen miles upstream, and then by only the smallest of boats. Nevertheless, it was the fount which watered the earliest stirrings of Spanish civilisation.

Our knowledge of the Iberians comes largely from the writings of Greek scholars and geographers, who were the first to use the terms 'Iberia' and 'Iberian' to describe the land and its people. They mention a number of tribes, of which the most predominant was the Bastetani. The Bastetani lived in Almeria and the mountainous region around Granada. To the west of them were a group of tribes generally lumped together as 'Tartessian', after the name the Greeks gave to the region: Tartessos. Easily the most powerful of these was the unfortunately named Turdetani, who inhabited the valley of the Guadalquivir.

The use of the word 'tribes' is not intended to imply a lack of civilisation. The Iberians developed a highly complex economy. Apart from being accomplished farmers, fishers and breeders of stock, their industrial skills were impressive. They were miners, metallurgists, potters, jewellery-makers, and more than competent producers of textiles and ceramics. Their silver and goldwork was richly ornate. A particularly spectacular and important hoard of dishes bearing religious engravings was found in Tarragona. Nor were they simply good with their hands. They also produced an impressive body of written literature and poetry.

Their walled cities, which were many, and usually built on hilltops for defensive reasons, must have been impressive. In various parts of Andalucía large stone cellars have been found which indicate that the Iberian structures which once stood above them were of considerable size. In some places, notably Tarragona, remnants of Iberian stone ramparts still remain.

However, in spite of their considerable industrial and artistic achievements, the Iberians seem to have been poor warriors. They fought valiantly enough. In fact they were renowned for their ferocious bravery. But the Greek geographer Strabo, in a memorable phrase, said that they 'never learned to hold their shields together'. Potters and poets they may have been, but they could never have invented the chorus line. Their characteristic uncoordinated style meant that a battle with the Iberians was a battle with a hundred or a thousand individuals, never a disciplined army. That made them easy meat for later invaders, who frequently defeated them although far fewer in numbers. In this they may have been helped by another alleged Iberian tradition, which was perhaps a tactic too far. It is said that an Iberian soldier joining the ranks would enter into a solemn oath of blood brotherhood with his chief. The ceremony was no mere symbolic charade. Having sworn the oath, the soldier would defend his leader to the death, and commit suicide in a dramatic explosion of grief and shame if the chief was killed. In this the Iberian recruit goes far beyond his modern counterpart. The practical value of such an arrangement is difficult to fathom. If true, a battle could have been settled by one well-aimed throw of an enemy spear. Kill the chief in the first minute of the fight, and rest on your laurels beneath the trees while the Iberian opposition queue up to throw themselves on their swords. Invaders 1000 – Iberians 0. With hindsight, we can see that the Iberians were always doomed to disappear.

There appear to have been no great ethnic or cultural changes in the Peninsula from the Neolithic era until the arrival of the Phœnicians, Carthaginians, Greeks and Celts. The Phœnicians probably came first, settling the southern coast as many as twelve centuries before the birth of Christ. Beginning around the 8th century BC, Celtic tribes began to move into northern and central Spain. They also settled in Portugal and Galicia, but by and large they left southern Spain untouched. There was inevitably some overlapping, notably in the north-east and Catalonia. In the central regions, the mixture produced a race distinct enough to be dubbed by inspirationally challenged historians as the 'Celtiberians', but in practical terms this influx had little effect on the Iberians in the south. They were absorbing quite different influences. The Greeks had important settlements at Emporion (now Ampurias) on the Valencian coast, and around Alicante. They called the country 'Hesperia' – the land of the setting sun. Further south, the Iberian identity was disappearing under the influence of the Phœnicians and Carthaginians. And one of the key Phœnician settlements was 'Malaka'.

The Phœnician and Carthaginian Periods

The ancient land of Phœnicia covered the whole of modern Lebanon, plus parts of present-day Syria and Israel. The Phœnicians apparently referred to themselves as 'Kena'ani' – 'Canaanites'. The word did not mean simply, 'people of Canaan'. In Hebrew it also meant 'merchants', and this the Phœnicians certainly were. They were, beyond doubt, the greatest merchant travellers of the ancient world. It would not be surprising to learn that every modern travelling salesman story has its counterpart in a Phœnician original. Endless volumes have been written about the Phœnicians, but there may yet be room for another, tracing their influence on the development of the British Music Hall.

They arrived in the area around 3000 BC, possibly from the Persian Gulf, though nobody knows for sure, and for centuries thereafter they sailed their distinctive ships along the Levant coast, up to North Africa and into southern Europe, trading and colonising as they went. Their first settlement was at Tart, or Turt (later Tartessus, Tarshis and eventually Turdetania). The list of goods they brought with them is impressive: cedar and pine wood, fine linen, embroideries, cloth dyed with the famous Tyrian purple, wine, salt, metalwork, dried fish, glass and more. It is probably to the Phœnicians that we owe the invention of glassblowing some time around the 1st century BC. Their alphabet they left as a legacy to the Greeks, and their language developed into Punic, the language of the Carthaginians, which was spoken in parts of North Africa as late as the 6th century AD. Considering their undoubted success as colonisers and entrepreneurs, their subsequent disappearance from the historical record is something of a mystery, but disappear they did. The Phœnicians ceased to exist as a recognisable people some time towards the end of the pre-Christian era. Perhaps they were simply the victims of their own success – putting so much of themselves into the places they visited that they eventually blended into the background like cultural chameleons and became invisible.

As they sailed up and down the coast of Spain, they left small colonies in their wake like drops of paint splashed on to a virgin canvas. Between 770 and 550 BC or thereabouts, the coast between Málaga and Almeria became almost congested with such colonies, particularly in the delta regions of the main rivers. The average distance between the settlements was a mere 4 km

– barely half an hour's walk. The reasons for such a concentration of Phœnician settlers have never been entirely clear. They did not, for example, exploit to any great extent the rich mineral deposits in the mountain regions. (The one notable exception to this rule was silver, which they mined heavily in the sierras around Huelva and Seville.) Obviously by establishing themselves at such strategic river points, they gained access to the interior, which provided increased opportunities for trade. In addition, ships bound for Cádiz frequently had to shelter along that stretch of coast in poor weather. Nevertheless, the sheer numbers and proximity of the Phœnician villages remain puzzling. It may be, of course, that our puzzlement is too profound. While we are seeking explanations that satisfy our intellectual curiosity, we may be missing the point. Perhaps, like the British, the Scandinavians, the Germans, the Dutch and latterly the Russians two and a half thousand years later, they simply decided that they liked it here.

The bay in which Málaga now stands was an obvious choice for a Phœnician outpost, and their first settlement seems to have been in the spot now occupied by the castle of Gibralfaro. Opinions vary as to the date. Some put it as early as the 12th century BC, around the time that the Phœnicians founded Gades (Cádiz), but as much as two or three centuries may separate the two. Unlike their island settlement in the Guadalhorce Valley, which only survived for about 200 years (see Cerro del Villar), the Phœnician town of Malaka was to take root and grow with each succeeding era. The name, having, as it does, connotations with the fish-salting and conserving industry, suggests that the colony was founded for that purpose. However, it is worth noting in passing that the Hebrew word 'malakh', means 'angel'. Could it be that the Phœnician travellers, like the Moorish rulers of Málaga many centuries later, considered the place an earthly paradise?

Malaka, like other Phœnician settlements, quickly became self-sufficient. Though chiefly remembered today as sailors and traders, the Phœnicians were skilled agriculturists, fishers and hunters. From the sea they took tuna, sturgeon, moray eels and anything else unwary enough to stray into their nets. On the land they hunted deer, wild boar and wild cat. In their fields they grew cereals and herded goats and sheep. And in their spare time they could dance, sing and do card tricks. Versatility was the Phœnicians' trade mark.

Malaka had at least a couple of hundred years to settle into its stride before the Phœnicians faced their first major challenge. Their domination of the area was threatened during the 6th century BC when the Greeks moved in and founded their own colony just 50 km to the east, which they called Mainake. In the marked similarity of name there is an impudent whiff of the hopeful imitator inspired to the sincerest form of flattery by a successful enterprise he wishes to emulate and cash in on. 'The Malaka Salted Fish Co Ltd (prop. The Phœnician Brothers)' begets 'Mainake Salt Fish Inc. (a Subsidiary of Acropolis Enterprises)'. It is a business ploy still favoured today, and it inevitably created resentment and friction. The friction eventually festered into war. No-one ever accused the Phœnicians of not knowing how to hold their shields together, and the hostilities were bloodily resolved in their favour. The superiority of Malaka was reaffirmed, and the Greek settlement eventually vanished and is now lost.

In spite of this, the Phœnician star was already on the wane. Between 580 and 550 BC the majority of their trading centres were abandoned and disappeared. The reasons for this sudden collapse of an occupation which had lasted for over two hundred years are complex and inevitably obscure. Carthage and Greece were involved in a struggle to dominate the West – a struggle the Carthaginians were destined to win – and although the Phœnicians' chief port of Gadir (Cádiz) remained independent and untouched by the rivalry for a considerable time, its ties to the smaller colonies along the east coast gradually loosened and snapped. One by one they were extinguished like streetlamps at dawn. Malaka was a striking exception. Now firmly based on the fishing industry which had given it birth, it survived as an important part of the new Carthaginian Empire.

The Carthaginians, or Punics, were closely related to the Phœnicians whom they succeeded. It was almost like the re-launch of a jaded TV show with a new presenter and a redesigned, but still recognisable set. Their base was in North Africa and they were descended from the Phœnicians who had settled there during their dominant period. They had some fresh ideas and, significantly, a new name for the Iberian Peninsula. They called it 'Ispania' – the land of rabbits. This was not intended as an insult to its human inhabitants, but merely as a literal description. The country was indeed generously populated with rabbits, and still is. They had even appeared on early Iberian coins. Unless, of course, the Iberians once had a leader who looked horribly like a rabbit.

When the Romans displaced the Carthaginians, they kept the name, but added an H (the Romans were notorious snobs), and called their new colony 'Hispania'. The Peninsula had finally found the first thing a country needs to turn itself into a nation: it had found itself a name. The upstart H was eventually discarded, and España was born.

The Roman Era

By the middle of the 2nd century BC, the Carthaginians were beginning to feel the might of the growing Roman Empire. In the First Punic War (264–241 BC) they lost control of the strategically important island of Sicily. In Spain they remained strong, but continual conflict with the Romans eventually led to the Second Punic War (218–201 BC) which ended with their expulsion from the Peninsula. Oddly enough, the most well remembered story of the war concerns not a Roman, but a Carthaginian. It was during this campaign that Hannibal and his famous elephants crossed the Alps from Spain into Italy and dealt the Romans a number of severe blows before Hannibal was himself defeated in 203 BC and forced back into Africa. The Romans, under Publius Cornelius Scipio (Africanus), pursued him and delivered the *coup de grâce* a year later. Hannibal's father, Hamilcar Barca, had himself been a fine general, and gave his name to the city of Barcelona.

After the loss of Spain, the Carthaginians were all but finished. The final act of their tragedy came in the Third Punic War (149–146 BC), when Carthage itself was seized and totally obliterated.

Rome divided Spain in two. The east Coast became Citerior (Nearer Spain), and the southern part was called Ulterior (Further Spain). Later, the Emperor Augustus renamed the greater part of Ulterior 'Baetica'. The name was taken from the river Baetis (now the Guadalquivir).

And so 'Malaka' became 'Malaca' and settled down to life under the Romans. In practice, things changed very little. The Romans were content to let the town carry on much as it was, and allowed it a great deal of autonomy. Pragmatically, the Punic population shrugged its communal shoulders and adapted to the New Age. In tune with the philosophy that a rose is a rose is a rose, they tacked on Roman names to their old gods – Tanit, for example, became 'Juno' – and went on living and worshipping much as they had before. Things did not begin to change radically until the arrival of Christianity in the 1st century AD.

The extent of the town's autonomy, together with its legal rights and privileges, within the limits set by the Romans, were formalised by the emperor Titus in the *Lex Flavia Malacitana*. This treaty was immortalised in bronze, and the inscription can now be seen in the National Archive Museum in Madrid. It was a mutually beneficent arrangement – neither side was looking for trouble – and Malaca thrived as well under a Roman sun as under a Punic, Phœnician or Iberian one.

All this is not to say that the centuries of Roman rule were an idyllic interlude. Christianity had arrived to upset the applecart around the middle of the first century. St Paul had identified Spain as a target for conversion in his Epistle to the Romans, and in AD 62, like the boss of any great corporation hoping to expand, he visited the country to set the wheels in motion. Returning to Rome after his fact-finding mission, he gathered together an evangelical task force and sent them to Baetica, where they set up their first mission close to Granada, at Guadix, now famous only as the home of some of Europe's last remaining troglodytes.

It cannot be said that Christianity flashed across the land like a bolt of white lightning. The establishment of the Church was steady and strong, but it was to be more than two hundred years before the Spanish bishops could hold their first Council at Elvira, in AD 300. Among those attending was Patricius, Bishop of Málaga. Throughout this time, the Christians had been the subject of frequent repression, and had had to suffer more when the Emperor Diocletian instituted their last ruthless persecution in AD 303. The Christian citizens of Malaca were not immune. The side doors of the cathedral bear effigies of Saint Cyriacus and Saint Paula, two Malagueñans who were put to death, along with thousands of others throughout Spain, during the Emperor's vicious campaign. Spain has a particular affinity with martyrs and martyrdom, as a cursory glance at the effigies in any church, and a check on the apparently endless list of celebrated saints' days will show.

To paraphrase and go beyond the old adage about greatness; some are born martyrs, some achieve martyrdom, some have martyrdom thrust upon them, and some just go out and grab it by the tail. Into the latter category we must put one of Spain's earliest Christian martyrs, St Eulalia. While still little more than a child, Eulalia is said to have burst her way into the council chambers in Mérida yelling, 'The old gods are worthless! The Emperor himself is nothing! The old gods are nothing because they are made by human hands! The Emperor is nothing because he worships them!'

After recovering from the shock of having their learned deliberations so rudely interrupted, it might have been hoped that the magistrates would have sent for the child's mother and instructed her to keep her impetuous daughter away from their chambers during working hours, and under stricter control. Instead, they chose the more authoritarian option of trussing her up and tearing her body apart with red hot pincers. Eulalia, it is said, reacted to the punishment by singing happily throughout. Martyrdom is clearly not what it used to be.

The Romans did build a number of important public buildings in Malaca, including an impressive theatre close to the site of the later Moorish Alcazaba. This, as is noted elsewhere, came to light only in the 1950s. There was a triumphal arch with carvings on the keystone devoted to the youthful goddess Victoria, depicting her with wings and wearing a pleated gown.

A shrine has also been found dedicated to Venus, the goddess of gardens and beauty. Although we now think of Venus as a 'Roman' goddess, she played no part in Roman worship in early times. She became absorbed into the religion of the Romans only around the time of the Second Punic War, when the long-established cult of Venus Erucina was adopted from Sicily. In time she came to be identified with the Greek goddess Aphrodite, but how and why remains obscure. With no myths of her own, she pilfered those of Aphrodite until the two goddesses became inextricably linked and worship of one was *de facto* worship of the other. Her cult was to achieve its greatest importance at the time of Julius Caesar. His clan, the Julia, claimed descent from Iulus, son of Aeneas, and since legend proclaimed Aeneas the son of Aphrodite, this conferred divine origin on Julius Caesar and his relations. He dedicated his temple to Venus Genetrix, and she was known by the name Genetrix until the death of Nero in AD 68. Despite her close connection with the Julio-Claudian dynasty, her popularity far outlived its demise.

Some important Roman mosaics have also been discovered in Málaga, and they can be seen in the *Museo de Bellas Artes* in calle San Agustìn. The building which houses the museum is itself an old palace, as we shall see.

During the Roman occupation, the town's economy was firmly based on the fish sauce industry and this delicacy was exported to all parts of the Empire in its distinctive *amphorae.* It was not, however, a one-product town even then. It was already exporting locally mined and quarried metals and marble. But the Romans found Malaca an increasingly expensive city to maintain, and by the time they abandoned their theatre and their other works to history in the dying years of the 3rd century, it was already showing signs of decay.

In a curious pre-echo of what was to come, invading Moorish tribesmen, pre-Moslem Berbers, had established communities in the hills and mountains behind Málaga as early as AD 171–173 – the very height of Spain's Roman occupation. To some extent they were fleeing Africa due to the gradual northern expansion of the Sahara desert. The fertile north was a highly prized wheat-growing area, but as the desert crept inexorably closer, the Romanised population living there came under constant pressure from the nomadic Saharan tribesmen. During the years to AD 210 the Moorish refugees consolidated their presence in Andalucía, and although the cities away from the mountains remained solidly in Roman hands, the area did experience some destabilisation. Finally, irritated beyond endurance, C. Vallius Maximianus declared military law, and the troublesome Berbers were ruthlessly eliminated. They went, but they would be back.

The idea that history is a gradual progression along a narrow, winding road which passes in turn through the Past, the Present and on into the Future is a hopelessly simplistic one. Trying to disentangle the millions of strands which make up the historical thread is like staring into a melting kaleidoscope whose pattern pieces, large and small, are constantly moving in ten different directions at differing speeds. All history is to some extent simplified, and necessarily so, just as all written history is, despite the best intentions of the historian, selective and subjective. No man can keep his eye on all the pieces in the kaleidoscope at the same time, or make their patterns satisfyingly simple. Gibbon took several volumes and millions of words to describe *The Decline and Fall of the Roman Empire.* Here we must attempt to write its obituary in a few brief sentences.

The expanding Mongol population was pressurising the tribes of the Russian Steppes, and they in turn pushed the Vandals, the Visigoths and the Franks further and further towards the boundary of the Roman Empire on the Rhine. It was like boiling a kettle without an outlet for the steam. An explosion was inevitable, and it finally came around AD 410 when the Roman frontier was breached and the Germanic population broke through.

The first Germanic wave to wash across Spain was comprised of three tribes: the Suevi, the Alani, and the Vandals. All three left a trail of havoc wherever they passed, but the Vandals did it with such thundering exuberance that their name has become a byword for mindless destruction. After smashing to bits everything that lay in their path, they paused for breath and settled in the south. It was a brief respite, for only a few years later the comparatively civilised Visigoths dislodged them. The Vandals moved on, with fresh boots and hammers, to terrorise North Africa and Italy. Behind them, the Visigoths settled into Spain and began to pick up the pieces.

The Visigoths and the Byzantine Empire

The Germanic inrush which swamped the Empire in the early years of the 5th century was, it must be remembered, a far more complex affair than our simplified outline above might indicate. The Germanic tribes had enjoyed an almost symbiotic relationship with the Roman Empire for more than a century before the great bubble burst. And ironically, their strength within the Empire had grown steadily since the first Christian Emperor, Constantine, had enthusiastically recruited them into his army due to their reputation for ferocity and valour.

The Visigoths were one of two branches of the Germanic Goths, the other being the Ostrogoths. The Ostrogoths, to the east, built and lost an empire of their own, but their story belongs to another book.

The Visigoths (the name meant 'valiant people') first encroached on the Roman Empire in the 3rd century, when they took the province of Dacia, in east central Europe. In the 4th century they were allowed to live within the Empire, but they tired of the petty impositions of Roman officials, as people noted for ferocity and valour are prone to do, and rose in revolt. They scored a victory at Adrianople in 378, but four years later their rising was put down by the Emperor Theodosius I and they were forcibly settled in the north Balkan peninsula province of Moesia. Obviously it couldn't last. Once a warrior, always a warrior. Moesia was only a resting place; somewhere to lick their wounds while they planned their revenge. They stayed there, sullen and resentful, until the beginning of the southward drive which culminated in the sacking of Rome and of Spain in 410.

From 418 until 475, by arrangement with the intimidated and punch-drunk Romans, they held the Roman province of Aquitania Secunda (in Gaul), but as the Romans became progressively weaker, the Visigoths had less and less need of treaties and confederacies. In 475, the Visigothic king Euric swept them aside like the scattered residue of yesterday's party and declared himself independent of Rome. The Romans were powerless to do anything about it, and Euric was left as the ruler of both Gaul and Spain. Gaul was lost in 507 when its king, Alaric II, the son of Euric, was killed in battle by the Franks, but they were to hold on to Spain until it fell to the Moors more than two centuries later.

Málaga had fiercely resisted the invasion of the Visigoths, just as it was to repel several attempts at conquest by the Christians in the future. And, as we shall see, it was to pose particular problems during the years of the Byzantine invasion.

When the Visigoths finally overcame Málaga's resistance, they entered a town which, despite its doggedness, was more than half deserted, even though it had been the seat of a Roman bishopric and became in turn the seat of a Visigothic one. Although of Germanic origin, the Visigoths had lived within and close to the Empire for a long time, and had become considerably

Romanised, so there was no great cultural shock. They easily adapted to the Roman way of life. The Roman agricultural system, dependent upon the small landholders, had survived in Málaga and little changed there beyond the name of its masters. Málaga had seen it all before.

That is not to say that there were no fundamental differences between the two societies. The Visigoths had no time for emperors. Instead, they had an elected king who ruled with the help of an assembly consisting of free men who were eligible to go to war. This presumably meant that the lame, the asthmatic and the congenitally short-sighted had no vote, but democracy must begin somewhere. Their religion was Arianism, a Christian heresy dating from the early years of the 4th century, which taught that Christ was not divine, but a created being. Of such wafer-thin nuances of interpretation are great conflicts made. The Visigoths did not, however, impose their customs and religion on the people of their new colony. Instead, they operated a form of cultural apartheid, leaving the Hispano-Romans to continue largely as before, while maintaining minority rule by controlling the military power. But though they tolerated their new subjects, they certainly did not want their sisters to marry one. A ban on marriage between Visigoths and Hispano-Romans was not revoked until late in the 6th century. They considered themselves a noble elite among comparative barbarians, and their numbers in the Peninsula never rose much above 200,000. This 'us and them' attitude did not stop the Visigoths from constantly fighting among themselves and assassinating kings almost reached the status of a national sport. During the two hundred years or so that they were to rule Spain, they managed to elect and subsequently murder more than thirty. Only the odd one or two lived long enough to die in their beds.

Sadly, from the point of view of the Roman scholar and the seeker of solid remains, the Visigoths disdained bathing. In their opinion, the Roman habit of soaking the body in hot baths – *thermae* – was a decadent one which led inexorably to effeminacy and effeteness. Roaring their scorn in deep, manly voices, they destroyed the Roman baths wherever they found them. Bathing did not become fashionable again until the coming of the Moors.

For some time, certain parts of the Peninsula stayed stubbornly outside Visigothic control. The Suevi held on to Galicia, and then, as now, the mysterious Basques were fiercely independent and violently resisted any outside interference. But both were eventually subjugated during the reign of the greatest of the Visigothic kings, Leovigild (568–586). He adopted much from the old Roman system and ruled the province from his capital, Toletum (Toledo).

Leovigild was concerned at the growing number of Visigoths who were converting to the Catholic faith, and for the first and only time in the Visigothic era, there is evidence of some persecution. His son Heremenegild, at that time in charge of Baetica (Andalucía), had married a 13-year old Merovingian princess who, because of her Catholicism, was badly abused by the Royal court in Toledo, and not only verbally. On one occasion the Queen Mother grabbed her by the hair, knocked her down, kicked her until she was covered in blood, and, shrieking like a banshee, ordered that she should be stripped naked and tossed into a fishpond. Diplomacy had not yet achieved the status of a fine art. It was more than Heremenegild could take. In response he instantly converted to Catholicism himself and rose in rebellion against his father. The war went badly, and in February 584, after a heavy defeat, he sought sanctuary in a church in Córdoba. Leovigild sent another son, Recared, to talk him into leaving his refuge. He did so and threw himself on the mercy of his father, only to be sent into exile, first at Valencia, and then at Tarragona. Nevertheless, he stubbornly refused to recant his new Catholic faith. There was only one thing to do. These were, after all, Visigoths. In 585 he was poisoned by a Goth named Sisbert, probably on the orders, or with the collusion, of Leovigild himself.

In 580, five years before Heremenegild's death, at a Synod of Arian Bishops called by Leovigild, some aspects of Byzantine religious ceremony had been introduced into the Arian church, and the unpopular stipulation that Catholics joining the church should first be re-baptised was removed. If this apparent ambivalence strikes the reader as confusing, as it inevitably must, it should be remembered that Leovogild's persecution was not of Catholics *per se*. Like other Visigothic leaders, he was indifferent to the beliefs and practices of the Hispano-Roman population. They could worship who, what and how they chose. His concern was with Goths who had let the side down by taking the Catholic faith. By bringing the two faiths a small step closer together, if only superficially, he hoped to make it easier for the heretics to admit their error and revert to the true religion.

But it was too late. Catholicism among the Goths was spreading faster than a new joke. Leovigild died in 586, to be succeeded by Recared, who had followed his murdered brother Heremenegild into the church of Rome, but had adroitly avoided imprisonment and the visit of an official poisoner. Times were changing. Recared was a pragmatist. He bowed to the inevitable and made Catholicism the official state religion. This removed the greatest barrier between the two social groups, and a deep loyalty to the Visigothic monarch took root among the Hispano-Roman majority.

While all of this was going on, the Visigoths were fighting another, less spiritual, battle against Rome. For Spain had not quite heard the last of the Romans, or at least of the Byzantines.

The Byzantine Empire was the Eastern successor to the Roman Empire in the West. It came into being around the year 330, when Rome's first Christian emperor, Constantine I, moved the capital from Rome to Byzantium (subsequently Constantinople, and now Istanbul), but only developed a truly individual identity after the final fall of the Western Empire in the 5th and 6th centuries.

Under the Emperor Justinian, who succeeded to the title in 527 and ruled for 38 years, a determined effort was made to regain much of the lost Empire.

In Spain, his efforts were aided by the traditional discord and rebellion among the Visigothic rulers, who, as we have seen, spent most of their time killing each other. In 551 a nobleman, Athanagild, rose against the incumbent but weakened king, Agila, and established himself in Seville. In pursuance of his campaign, this witless buffoon called on the Byzantine Emperor, Justinian, for help. Not surprisingly, Justinian was only too pleased to lend a hand. He had been preparing to send an expedition to Spain in any case. His forces arrived in the summer of 552, and with their help Athanagild defeated Agila's army. Three years of confused fighting followed, before the Visigoths belatedly realised that they had taken a viper to their bosom and that their internecine squabbling was doing Justinian's work for him. Accordingly, and characteristically, they resolved the issue by assassinating Agila at Mérida, and formally placing Athanagild on the throne. This was Athanagild's cue to renege on his promise to grant territory to his Byzantine allies of convenience, and so began the long struggle to force them once again out of Spain.

The historical record of this period is somewhat confused, largely because, since it was ultimately a grand failure, Byzantine chroniclers virtually ignored their Spanish adventure. If the Visigoths wrote epic accounts of it, we have yet to find them. However, we can be sure that Málaga was among the cities definitely held for a time by Justinian's forces. Indeed, during its years as a Byzantine enclave, Málaga exported marble and stone for the construction of what was to become arguably the greatest church in the world – the *Sancta Sophia* in Constantinople. However, it is unclear whether the Byzantines ever occupied the entire diocese of Málaga, or whether parts of it were recaptured during the anti-Byzantine campaign of Leovigild between 570 and 572. Certainly, by the year 619, when Visigothic Bishops met in Seville for their Second Council, the city and province were once again fully in Visigothic hands. The final blow had been dealt by King Sisebut (612–621).

The confusion arises because, at the Second Council, Málaga had been represented by its new Bishop, Theodulf. He proposed successfully that his see be restored to its pre-Byzantine state. For some time it had been fragmented, with parts of it being given to the sees of Astigi (Ecija), Illiberris (Granada), and Cabra. The Council, presided over by Isidore (later St. Isidore), Archbishop of Seville and one of the era's greatest historians and writers, returned the various sees to Málaga 'just as those who become captives by barbarian ferocity recover their former possessions on their subsequent release'. This suggests strongly that the city of Málaga had indeed remained in Byzantine hands until it fell to Sisebut.

Athanagild's efforts to eject the Byzantines were largely futile, but they were carried on with greater fervour and more success by Leovigild, who succeeded him as king in 568. As we have noted above, it is believed by some that Leovigild re-took Málaga during his energetic campaign of 570–572, but the record of this is not precise, and it seems more likely that he captured most of the province of Málaga, but that the city itself remained under Byzantine occupation for some time afterwards. Visigoths were notoriously poor at conquering walled cities. Every time they came upon a walled city, their faces fell and their generals resigned. Another reason for believing that

Málaga succumbed somewhat later than Leovigild's time is the fact that it was left virtually intact after its capture. The Goths, like other Germanic peoples, had a petulant habit of reducing captured cities to rubble to prevent them falling once again into enemy hands. A little like setting fire to one's new home to thwart the intentions of burglars. Cartagena, another Byzantine stronghold in Spain, was reduced to a whisper of dust in the wind. The fact that Málaga was not similarly destroyed may have been a clumsy administrative oversight (it was certainly not a deliberate act of compassion), but more probably indicates that by the time of its taking, the Byzantine forces were so weakened that they were no longer considered a credible threat.

In spite of Leovigild's successes, it was not until the reign of King Swinthila (621–631) that the Byzantine enclaves were finally eradicated. From that moment on, the whole of Spain, without exception, was under Visigothic rule. But History was once again flexing its muscles for change. As the 7th century came to its end, the Visigothic monarchy entered a particularly turbulent period. King Wamba (672–680), an able enough reforming king, was violently deposed, as was the Visigothic custom, and those who followed him faced increasing unrest. They looked for scapegoats and, like others before and since, found a convenient one in the Jews, whom they had attempted to enslave and convert to Christianity. As so often throughout their bloody and tragic history, the Jews became victims of vicious persecution. So vicious, indeed, that however curious it may appear to modern eyes, the Jews actually welcomed the arrival of the Arabs in 711, and lived peacefully with them for a long time thereafter.

When King Witiza (700–710) died, his wish was that his son should succeed him, but by now the kingdom was completely fragmented into competing factions. Ignoring Witiza's son, the council elected, instead, Roderick, Duke of Baetica. A chronicler of 754, obviously not a Roderick supporter, describes his ascent to the throne as 'usurpation at the exhortation of the senate'. Witiza's family, if the legend is true, then made one of the most monumental and far-reaching decisions in Spain's, and the world's, history. Seeking allies to overthrow Roderick, they turned for help to Tariq ibn Ziyad, the Moslem governor of Tangier. They had learned nothing from Athanagild's blunder with Justinian. A second persistent and far more romantic legend has Roderick seducing the daughter of the Spanish governor of Ceuta, Julián, and bringing retribution on his head when Julián himself allied with the Arabs to bring him down. Whether either or neither of these stories is true has long since lost its relevance. Invited or not, Tariq landed at Gibraltar with his troops in 711 and easily defeated and killed Roderick in battle near the rio Guadalete on July 19th.

It has to be said that Roderick did not make himself an inconspicuous target. For centuries afterwards, marketplace storytellers held their audiences spellbound with tales of him watching the battle while wearing his gold crown and a heavily embroidered silk robe, and stretched out on an ivory carriage drawn by two white mules. It was the best that kings could do in the days before the invention of the long, black, armour-plated limousine. Not surprisingly, the invaders spotted him. Having drawn their unwelcome attention, Roderick leapt unregally from his carriage and attempted to flee on a fast white horse, only to fall off and drown in the river. The horse was no less sumptuous than the carriage, being decked out with a golden saddle encrusted with rubies and emeralds, and a mantle of gold cloth.

It was widely believed among the Goths that the Moslems had no desire to seek long-term territorial gains in Spain. They thought that they would be satisfied after a spree of looting and pillaging, and return home singing the praises of Allah, perhaps vowing to return for a fortnight each July. Every victorious army deserves at least one good loot and pillage. Needless to say, the Witiza family plan, if it existed, spectacularly backfired. Having disposed of Roderick, the Moors swept northward with little resistance, and Spain readied itself for eight centuries of Arab rule.

Oscar Wilde once said of Truth, that it was 'never pure, and seldom simple'. He might have said the same of History. There is much to be said for the cynic's view that history is composed in equal measure of opinion, hearsay, legends and lies. Certainly the man or woman who sets out to write authoritatively about events which happened centuries before he or she was born is handicapped by having to choose between the invariably opposing views of earlier writers who, even if they were there, saw things through individual and subjective eyes. Ask three friends to describe the events of a single shared day, and you will be rewarded with three different stories. Ask three enemies to do the same, and you will hear three different lies.

But the search for the holy grail of objectivity goes on, and the clear-eyed chronicler loves nothing more than a good, firm date and a decisive incident on which to hang the hinges of his narrative. He seldom gets either. July 19th, 711 offers both, and historians have settled on it like flies on a lidless pot of jam at a picnic. The defeat of Roderick neatly divides 'Visigothic Spain' from the Moorish era. To some extent this is, of course, true. But History loves loose ends and unfinished symphonies. Roderick did, in fact, have a successor: a certain Achila, who reigned for another three years in almost totally unchronicled obscurity. A few coins bearing his name have survived, minted at Narbonne, Gerona and Tarragona, but the details of his life are otherwise an impenetrable mystery. Some have argued that his 'rule' was actually contemporary with that of Roderick and that he was an alternative king proclaimed by supporters of the Witiza faction. That may be true, but since no army ever occupied a nation without provoking resistance, it seems more likely that Achila and his men represent the last heroic but hopeless stand against the closing of their chapter and the opening of the next, a small and isolated fire that burned briefly in the hills and was gone.

One person who clearly held no hard feelings against Spain's Arab conquerors was Roderick's widow, Egilona. He hardly had time to hit the water and get his robes wet before she threw off her black shawl and married one of the country's new Arab governors – a son of their leader, Musa.

For though Tariq ibn Ziyad's landing at Gibraltar was a decisive moment, and he was prominent in the conquest of Spain, he was not the Moslem ruler. He had been placed in charge of Tangier by his superior, Musa ibn Nusair, who after the conquest set up court in Seville. He was later disgraced after being accused of corruption. It was alleged that he had misappropriated a disproportionate amount of the loot for his own ends. Times change, but some things are forever constant. It is almost comforting. The charge could have meant execution, but he escaped with a heavy fine and much bribery. Suddenly the mists clear, and history becomes a shining mirror in which we see the reflection of ourselves.

Moorish Málaga

The term 'Moor' is derived from the Latin *Mauri*, and was originally used by the Romans to describe the inhabitants of their province of Mauretania, which on a modern map would cover the western part of Algeria and the north-eastern part of Morocco. It should not be confused with the present-day Islamic Republic of Mauritania which is situated in the great Sahara region between Morocco, Senegal and Mali.

The *Mauri* were semi-nomadic Berber herdsmen who were ruled by a king. At some point in the late 2nd century BC, the kings became vassals of Rome, and in the 1st century AD the Romans went one step further and annexed the country altogether. They divided it into two new provinces: Mauretania Tingitana, with its capital at Tingis (Tangier), and Mauretania Caesariensis, whose capital was at Caesaria (now Cherchell, in Algeria). Still later, towards the end of the 3rd century, they turned the eastern part of Caesariensis into yet another province: Sitifensis. It is clear that Rome produced as many bureaucrats as it did warriors.

Despite this, the influence of the Romans was always concentrated in the coastal regions, and made little impact inland. When the Empire crumbled, Mauretania was left virtually independent, until it was conquered by the Arabs in the 7th century.

It is perhaps unfortunate that, just as the word Moors has come to have a much wider and more generalised meaning than it originally had, so the term Arab outgrew its original application to the people of the Arabian Peninsula and came to describe virtually all Arabic speakers. Consequently, and certainly in the context of Islamic Spain, the two terms are now virtually synonymous. While this may be a point of merely academic interest, it does disguise the fact that the origins of the two people were quite distinct. The Berber *Mauri* were of Caucasian origin, while the Arabs who conquered their nation and went on to conquer much of Spain were Semitic. The Moors became 'Arabs' only after their subjugation to Islam.

The Islamic faith, founded by the Prophet Muhammad in the 7th century AD, took root firmly and quickly in Syria, Iran, Mesopotamia and Egypt.

Byzantium was caught on the hop by the rapid rise of the new religion, but rallied to put up some kind of defence. The conflict lasted for several decades, and a detailed history is not possible within the confines of the present volume, but suffice it to say that by the time that Tariq ibn Ziyad landed at Gibraltar and swept on into Spain, the whole of North Africa was under Islamic control. Islam's northward advance was halted in 732 at Poitiers, in the south of France, by Charles Martel, popularly known as 'Charles the Hammer'. Later French kings who shared his given name were often less lucky, attracting epithets such as the Bald, the Simple and the Fat. One begins to understand the readiness with which the French seized upon the idea of Revolution.

The Arabs called their new country *al-Andalus.* The name is said to have derived from *Vandalusia,* meaning 'Land of the Vandals'. Since the Vandals were long gone, and their tenure in the Peninsula had been short, this must be taken as a tribute to the memorable ferocity of their hooliganism. A second possible translation, given the dazzling brightness of the Spanish sun, is 'land of light'. The name *al-Andalus* was originally applied to the whole of the Peninsula, but in time it came to categorise only the southern province which roughly corresponded to the Roman Baetica, and is now Andalucía.

The Moors, in contrast to the Visigoths and the later Christians, took control of Málaga with considerable ease. After a successful battle south of Córdoba, the Islamic army split up near the town of Ecija, and it was one of Tariq's lieutenants, Mugaith ar-Rumï, who marched on and overran Málaga and Córdoba. Tariq himself went straight for the jugular – the Visigothic capital of Toledo. They were unstoppable. Historians down the years have turned the rapidity of the Moorish conquest of the Iberian Peninsula into a mystery which they have expended millions of words in attempting to solve. It is a futile exercise. From time to time history yawns, turns over in its bed, and wakes up ready for change.

Moorish rule was to survive relatively unchallenged in Spain for 640 years, although there was almost constant internecine squabbling. Unlike the northern and eastern parts of Andalucía, which after the Moorish conquest were dominated by Takurunna Berbers, Málaga was settled by Reyyo Arabs, who developed it into an important Islamic centre. Such Christian outposts as remained were confined to the mountainous regions behind the city.

It has to be said that, unlike the later Christian re-conquerors, the Arabs pursued a policy of tolerance towards the established religion. There was no orgy of church burning to match the wholesale destruction of mosques which was to come. The worst that their Christian citizens had to endure was a special tax and some inequality in the eyes of the law. That is not to condone discrimination, but it was better than being killed or ejected from their homes and left to roam the mountains. Many Christians avoided this petty persecution by conveniently adopting Islam, which may not have fooled Allah, but was good enough for his earthly representatives.

Málaga continued its development under the Caliphate of Córdoba, which was founded in 929 when Abderrahman III broke the nominal link with

Damascus and declared himself independent. In the succeeding years, Málaga became a key naval base from which to defend the coast against the frequent Viking raids which plagued the Peninsula between the years 966 and 971. Indeed, as early as 859, Algeciras had been sacked by these northern pirates and its mosque burned to the ground. Clearly the pirates were Christians on a practice run.

Málaga is proud to be known as the birthplace of possibly the greatest artist of modern times, Pablo Ruiz Picasso. Another great artistic son is relatively forgotten – the Hebrew poet and philosopher, Solomon ben Yehuda ibn Gabirol, better known (but only just) by his Latin name of Avicebron. He was born around the year 1021, during a turbulent period for southern Spain. Berber uprisings were everywhere and his parents fled south from Córdoba after Berbers had taken control. Ironically, Málaga itself was later to fall briefly to a Berber general who ran it as a satellite state. The revolts raged for over twenty years, beginning in 1008 and fizzling out in 1031. Although ibn Gabirol was to leave Málaga at the age of ten to receive his higher education in Saragossa (Zaragoza), he continued to sign his works for the rest of his life as 'al-Malaqi', the Malagueñan. He had achieved worldwide fame by the age of sixteen and his major work, the *Keter Malkut* (Crown of the Kingdom) has often been compared to the psalms. Even so, it had to wait 900 years before it was finally translated into Spanish free verse in 1965 by the Italian born Malagueñan, Angel Caffarena, at the urging, surprisingly enough, of Málaga's Jewish community.

With the disintegration of the Córdoba caliphate after the fall of the Ummayads, an independent caliphate was established in Málaga by the Banu Hammud family, which was to extend its influence in time to Granada, Jaén and Carmona. For thirty years it was ruled by the scholarly and benevolent Idris II, who was himself a poet, though of far lesser stature than ibn Gabirol. Idris made his kingdom a place of refuge for those fleeing the more oppressive amirs who ruled elsewhere, and each Friday he would go to the gates of the Alcazaba to distribute alms to the poor. Nevertheless, his court was no less immune to the apparently unavoidable skullduggery and intrigue which was so characteristic of the time, and in 1046 he was ousted by one of his cousins, who was probably sick of him giving the family's money away. To avoid the shedding of blood, not least his own, Idris took refuge in one of the fortress towers. By the time he was talked into coming out, or the door was knocked down, or a window breached, or a fresh key obtained (history is vague on the subject), tempers had cooled, and any plans which his cousin may have had to execute him were forgotten. Instead he was banished to Tangier. After a while he returned to Spain, but rather than march boldly into Málaga and demand the return of his throne, he waited patiently in Ronda for four years until his upstart cousin died, whereupon he returned peacefully to pick up the reins. There being no better candidate, he got his old job back, and kept it until his death in 1056.

The Hammud caliphate did not long outlive him. Only a year after his death, the Berber chief Badis-ibn-Habbus swept in from Granada and dethroned Idris' successor, Muhammed al-Musta'li. One thing about being a court chronicler in those days: the ink on your quill never got dry.

There was more deposing in 1090 when the incumbent ruler, Tamin, along with his brother Abd Allah of Granada, was kicked out and exiled to Morocco by Yusuf. The brothers had failed to give Yusuf sufficient support in his fight against the Christians, and Yusuf was a notorious sulker. Relations between the Moslem and Christian communities in and around Málaga became steadily worse and the Christian bishop, Julian, was thrown into prison by the Almoravid authorities in 1110 and left to rot – a fact which might have been lost to history had it not been mentioned in a papal letter to Málaga's Christian community seven years later. At the time of the letter Bishop Julian was still being held, and had probably abandoned all hope of release. In spite of their troubles, Málaga and Málagueñans had a reputation for light-heartedness and gaiety (possibly not shared by Bishop Julian) which has survived to this day. Writing of the town's night life in the 11th century, Ahmad-el Yamani declared, 'people sing so much that strangers find it impossible to sleep at night'. Even today, Málaga's annual fiesta is considered the best in Andalucía, if not the whole of Spain. But strangers no longer seek sleep. They come by the thousand to sing as long and as loudly as their hosts.

The middle of the twelfth century saw a widespread rebellion in Andalucía against the fanatical North African Almoravides. This dedicated Islamic sect had crossed the Straits of Gibraltar in 1086 in response to a request for help from the Arab rulers in Spain. The Arabs had panicked after Toledo had been seized by the Christians in 1085. It was not a wise move, for these ruthlessly committed Berbers instantly imposed their will on the divided Moorish kingdoms. It was like buying a Rottweiler only to have it leap at your throat and trap you in your own kitchen. In the midst of this self-inflicted unrest, Málaga once again declared itself an independent kingdom under its ex-Cadi, ibn Hassur. However, his own dictatorial excesses made him extremely unpopular and in 1152 he committed suicide, though whether this was due to depression because nobody liked him is unclear.

A year later the equally fanatical Almohades, who came, like the Almoravides, from North Africa, grabbed the town and turned it into a base for their impressive fleet. Their fanaticism, happily, was soon softened by the warm Spanish sun, and although their stay in Spain was short, it was characterised by an intellectual freedom which was to leave its mark well beyond their going. Their tenure spanned three-quarters of a century, but as their star waned in 1228, King ibn Hud of Murcia decided that it was his turn to rule the town and he promptly captured it and remained in power until someone got heartily sick of him a few years later and resolved the problem by murder. Thereupon, Málaga passed to the Nasrid dynasty of Granada.

While the Moors were kicking Málaga around like rowdy urchins playing football in the street, the power in Léon and Castile was in the hands of the tenth in a long line of Alfonsos. This one, who came to the throne in 1252, became known, with reason, as Alfonso the Wise. He was a progressive law-maker and a sincere patron of literature and the arts. Naturally he could not allow that to stop him taking on the Moors whenever he got the chance, and he managed the token 'liberation' of the rebuilt Cartagena and Cádiz. Málaga eluded him, but his influence lives on there in a curious way. It has been traditional in Spain since time immemorial to entrust the naming of animals to dyslexics. Thus the tuna fish has become *atún*. Should you inadvertently ask your Málaga waiter to bring you a *tuna*, do not be surprised if he brings you several, dressed in balloon breeches and black stockings, playing guitars, mandolins and violins, and clicking castanets. *Tunas* are male students from Málaga university, who augment their meagre resources by appearing suddenly to serenade startled diners. Their right to do so without hindrance goes back all the way to Alfonso the Wise, who banned begging, but allowed poor students to sing and play in this way, so long as they dressed in this exotic uniform and wore armbands to distinguish themselves from ordinary beggars. Whether this led to a flourishing trade in balloon breeches and armbands on the beggars' black market is undocumented.

The Christians made their first serious, though unsuccessful, attempt to win Málaga in 1351. The attack came from the sea and many Christian lives were lost in the fiasco. They went away to lick their wounds and left Málaga to its Moorish masters for the best part of another century. Beginning around the year 1435, they tried time and again to drive the Moors out, but time and again they were repulsed. One massive defeat in 1483 left the Christian armies in total disarray and many of those who were not killed found themselves prisoners. It was four summers later, as we have seen, that the Christian onslaught finally bore fruit. Having lost too many men by frontal assault, they decided this time on a siege and a little devious political exploitation of the divisions among the rival Moorish factions.

A civil war was raging between the Sultan Muley Hacén (Abdul Hassan Ali ibn Sa'd) of Granada, and his brother Abu 'Abd Allah Muhammed, who made life much easier for westerners whose tongues were unused to such exhausting eastern gymnastics by adopting the name of El Zagal (*az-Zaghall*) – 'the shepherd boy'. It was a surprisingly modest nom-de-guerre for so valiant a warrior.

In 1481, Muley Hacén reneged on his reluctantly entered into agreement to pay annual tribute to the Catholic Monarchs, and in surly mood snatched control of the fortified town of Zahara. The inevitable hostilities went badly for him, and two years later his son Boabdil (Muhammad Abu 'Abd Allah) rebelled and claimed the throne for himself. Muley Hacén instantly decided that his brother wasn't such a bad old stick after all, and took refuge in Málaga with El Zagal, who had been having better luck against the Christians in the mountains.

El Zagal had once formed an ill-starred. opportunistic alliance with the inept and eccentric Christian king of Castile, Henry IV. Since the people of Málaga were firmly on his side, he and his court took up residence in the

Alcazaba. Henry's disastrous, strife-torn reign ended, mercifully, in 1474, but El Zagal remained firmly in control of Málaga and began fighting the Christians again. It was something to do. From his new base in the town, Muley Hacén, with the assistance of the Zegries, or 'border people', successfully regained his capital. It was the moment El Zagal had been waiting for. As soon as his brother Muley was back on the throne of Granada, he moved in and took it from him. This was not a happy family.

The Christians, now ruled by the altogether more able Ferdinand and Isabella, were in the full flood of their re-conquering zeal, and although their attempt to capture Málaga was ruinously repulsed by El Zagal's troops at the battle of Axarquia, to the east of the city, they did manage to capture Muley Hacén's son, Boabdil, at Lucena. The price of his freedom was high. In return for the Christians' help in the recovery of Granada (where his deposed father still had control of the Alhambra), he must agree to hand over to Ferdinand and Isabella all parts of his kingdom currently held by El Zagal. This agreement was formalised by the Pact of Córdoba. Faced with the treachery of their respective son and nephew, Muley Hacén and El Zagal once again ceased their fraternal squabbling, dusted themselves down, and turned their combined hatred on Boabdil instead. Boabdil scuttled away to asylum in the Catholic court. He came out again only after his father died in 1485 when, assisted by the people of Albaicin, he took control of the Alhambra himself.

Meanwhile, ostensibly to 'win back Granada for Boabdil', the Christians had attacked and subdued first Ronda, then Loja, and eventually Vélez-Málaga, close to Málaga itself. El Zagal attempted to regain control, but this time it was he who came off worst, and in 1487 he fled to Guadix, where he still had a few loyal fans. After that it was an easy task for the Christians to take the fortified hill villages of Comares and Montemar and thence to lay siege to Málaga. From his refuge in Guadix, El Zagal sent emissaries to North Africa and Egypt to beg help from their kings, but it was all too late. The siege, by both sea and land, was cruel and relentless. Ferdinand was determined at all costs not only to punish Málaga with all his might, but to use his punishment as an example to other towns which might foolishly consider resistance to his unstoppable army.

After three months of desperate fighting and growing starvation, there were, unsurprisingly, many renegades in the city ready to betray it. One of them, a merchant called Alí Durdux attempted to negotiate a reasonably bloodless end to the siege. It is not clear on exactly whose behalf Durdux made his approach, but it was in any case futile. Ferdinand had Málaga by the throat and was not going to let go until the last ounce of life was squeezed out of it. The inevitable ignominious and unconditional surrender finally came on August 18th 1487. (It is to celebrate this event that the famous and unforgettable Málaga fair is held each year in that month.) The incoming Castilian soldiers and officials were, alas, Christian in name only, and after the obligatory burning down of the mosque (to be replaced, of course, by a cathedral), they immediately set about the systematic enslavement, abuse, murder and expulsion of the defeated and demoralised people. There was one glaring exception. Alí Durdux and his family were not only allowed to live, but to remain in Málaga. Clearly his attempted betrayal of the town, though rejected by Ferdinand as unwanted and unnecessary, was well rewarded.

The long rule of the Moors in Spain was all but over. El Zagal capitulated in 1491. He delivered what was left of his lands to the Catholics and went into exile at Tiemcén. Only Boabdil remained, isolated and impotent in besieged Granada. That city's population became polarised – one faction wanting to fight on, the other wanting to face reality and admit that all was lost. By the end of the year, Boabdil accepted the futility of resistance. To forestall any possible disturbance, he allowed Castilian troops to enter the Alhambra quietly and unopposed on the night of January 1st. The next day, January 2nd 1492, he surrendered Granada to Castile. The glory that was Moorish Spain was gone.

The Christian Period, 1487–1800

Though we have dated the start of the Christian period from 1487, the fall of Granada and the final expulsion of the Moors from Spain did not come, as noted above, until 1492. This underlines the point that 'The Re-conquest', *La Reconquista,* is not 'an event' which can be fixed on a single year, or even in any meaningful sense within a single century. It was not merely a fifteenth century crusade. It had begun as early as 722, only eleven years after Tariq ibn Ziyad's arrival in Gibraltar. In that year a Visigothic nobleman, Pelayo, defeated the Moors in battle at Covadonga, and founded the Christian kingdom of Asturias. From that point on, the Christian war to recapture Spain was waged on and off, with varying amounts of intensity and success, for almost 800 years. 1492 was the end of a very long road. It is surely apt that the year is forever linked in the popular mind to Columbus' discovery of the New World, for back in Spain, Ferdinand and Isabella were at last the undisputed monarchs of a new world of their own. Little is known of Pelayo's life, but in memory of his famous victory, the heir apparent to the Spanish throne is known to this day as the Prince of Asturias.

In Málaga, the triumphal persecution and dispossession of the Moors which followed the Christian conquest of the city and its hinterland resulted in rapid economic decline. The virulence of this persecution should not be underestimated. In many ways the final capitulation of the Moors in 1492 was merely the beginning of the new Spanish order's determination to eradicate them from the landscape. They embarked on a policy of ethnic cleansing which sailed perilously close to genocide. History tells us that the century which followed was littered with constant Moorish rebellions, but it is difficult to avoid the conclusion that if the rebellions were real, and not latterly invented pretexts for Christian 'reprisals', the Moors had much to rebel about. One such rising, if we are to take the historical record at its word, began in las Alpujarras in 1568, rapidly spread to the province of Málaga, and was put down with crushing severity by the Christians. The climax came at el Peñon de Frigiliana, where over two thousand *Moriscos* (Christianised Moors), including women and children, were slaughtered. Those who survived were either expelled or taken into slavery.

As fast as the Moors were expelled from their homes, Christian immigrants moved in to take them over. In the years between 1485 and 1498, it is estimated that as many as six thousand Christian families moved into Málaga province, two thousand of them into the capital itself. It should have presaged an age of great expansion and prosperity, but although the years from 1500 to 1659 were the golden age of Spain's imperial glory, very little of the wealth being generated by its new American colonies reached Málaga. The central authority was far more concerned with attempts to convert the remaining 'heathen' Moors to Christianity although, as we have seen, this was no guarantee of better treatment. What time and money was left on its hands was largely used to establish religious houses to oversee the Catholicisation of the newly conquered lands. The town of Málaga was no longer fashionable. It was the dowager duchess of a fallen dynasty, still swaddled in its threadbare robes, but no longer welcome at court. It did not receive the Christian king's favour, and the fawning nobility deserted it in great numbers. As a result, Málaga today is no great treasure house of classic Andalucían Christian architecture.

Nevertheless, Málaga did remain an active port with some commercial success as the region's administrative centre. There was an influx of lesser, or at least less sycophantic, nobles, and a new artisan class who rented property and spent their money in the town, but this hardly compensated for the lost income. In addition, the previously flourishing agriculture in the surrounding countryside largely disappeared as the terraced hillsides were gradually abandoned and given over to hunting reserves. Thus Málaga ticked along quietly and unspectacularly while most of the new wealth went to the rapidly expanding Seville and Cádiz.

One lucrative trade which did continue in Málaga right up until the 1600s was that in slaves. Captured Turks, North African Berbers and indeed Moriscos were bought and sold there.

Like most great seaports, Málaga was always at risk from diseases carried in by sailors who had travelled from exotic parts. It was one such sailor who is said to have started the disastrous epidemic of bubonic plague which devastated the town in 1637. As news of the infestation spread, many towns, including Granada, cut off all contact with it. Vinegar, for reasons which are difficult to fathom but which were no doubt warmly welcomed by vinegar producers, was believed to be an effective anti-plague weapon. The streets were covered with awnings which had been soaked in it. Nevertheless, people stubbornly continued to die in their thousands, not only from the pestilence, but from starvation. It was said that dogs were eating the bodies of children dead or dying in the streets, and as a result the keeping of dogs and, to be on the safe side, cats, was forbidden. The logic is not readily apparent. Was it considered more acceptable, more dignified, for the bodies simply to rot or be eaten by rats? Here, surely, is a fine example of the human mind's inability to operate effectively under exceptional stress. Yet who could wonder at it? As many as forty thousand people are said to have died in the outbreak.

As a last desperate measure, the dwindling band of survivors threw in the scientific towel, poured their vinegar down the sink, and turned to religion. They decided to call on the Virgin of Victory for help. She was carried in procession to the convent of St Francis on July 9th. The whole of Málaga knelt beside the route and in the church, praying and scourging themselves so heavily that the floor became covered in blood. Whether due to the power of faith, divine intervention or mere coincidence, it was a turning point, and gradually the plague subsided. It might easily have wiped the town out completely, but somehow it pulled itself together and began to live again.

The late 16th and the 17th centuries were difficult and tragic times for Málaga in many ways. The plague was not the only disaster which it had to face. There were catastrophic floods in 1580, 1621 and 1661, which took many hundreds of lives. The flood of 1661 also destroyed the Roman bridge of Santo Domingo. Hundreds were also killed in two explosions at a plant manufacturing gunpowder which stood close to la Atarazana in the Plaza de Arriola: the first in 1595, and the second in August of 1618.

In 1656, an English fleet arrived in the harbour determined to raid and sack the town, having formed an alliance with the French against Spain. Málaga must have been happy to see the 17th century end, but the 18th was still in its infancy when it was the scene, albeit indirectly, of violence once more.

On the same day in 1704 that Marlborough was winning his dukedom at the Battle of Blenheim, a fierce sea battle was raging off the Málaga coast. Admiral Sir George Rooke had seized Gibraltar on August 4th, ostensibly on behalf of the Hapsburg pretender to the Spanish throne, and in an attempt to repel the invaders, a French fleet had sailed towards southern Spain. Rooke sailed north to intercept them and they met close to Málaga on August 24th. Numerically the two fleets were evenly matched – one consisted of 50 ships, the other of 51 – and although neither side managed to sink a ship, damage and losses were great. The French fleet suffered 3,048 casualties, against 2,719 suffered by Rooke. Oddly, the French considered this a great victory and sailed back to Toulouse the following day singing their lungs out and proclaiming it as such. Rooke, for his part, sailed back to Gibraltar and on to England where, unlike Marlborough, he received little public recognition and no great reward.

1704 was also the year that Fr. Francisco de San José became Bishop of Málaga. Christianity had by then been firmly established throughout Spain for more than two centuries, and the Church had grown into an immensely powerful pillar of state. Francisco de San José seemed determined not to allow that to go to his head, and his fanatical pursuit of simplicity begs the question of how close apparent saintliness can often be to mental instability, or outright madness.

The son of the Count of Santo Firmio, he turned his back on his famous name and his wealth at an early age to become a Franciscan friar. So far so good. The Franciscans observe a vow of poverty, but they tend to do it discreetly. When he became Bishop of Málaga, Francisco was determined to shout his humility from the rooftops. He rode around town on a mule, wearing the simplest of wooden crosses around his neck and giving away everything he owned to the poor. Since this included money, jewels and fine clothes, we must assume that at some point he had reclaimed his inheritance in order openly to squander it. But giving away his private wealth was not enough. The wealth of the Church must go too. Out it went, including his silver bishop's staff.

Desperate to find something else to give away, he decided on his food. After exhausting his worldly goods, and giving away his final crust of bread, the destitute bishop started knocking on doors and asking for some of it back. The people of Málaga had the curious luxury of a bishop who was also a beggar. One wonders if the man to whom he gave his silver staff used it to chase him away.

Piety, like all virtues, and every vice, can be overdone. When Francisco de San José died, he owned nothing worth making a note of. He may have felt spiritually pure, but what lasting benefit his eccentricity bestowed on the people of Málaga is hard to determine.

Every action begets a reaction, and Julio Alberoni, who followed Francisco de San José into the bishop's chair in 1717, was so outrageously worldly and devious that he comes almost as a relief. A born political intriguer, his eye was forever on the main chance, and he used his position in the Church to become powerful and wealthy. In this, he and Francisco de San José were polar opposites. The fact that they could co-exist and both reach high office paints a picture of a Church in which the spiritual and the temporal had become inextricably entwined. The ordinary people hardly cared. They respected their bishops, but they worshipped only their God.

Málaga, 1800–1930

One bishop who did gain almost universal respect in Málaga was Bishop Molino Lario, a tireless worker for the town, who was to a great extent responsible for the upswing in its commercial life and prosperity in the dying years of the 18th century. Largely through his efforts, the port gained a new wharf, and communication with the interior, in particular with Antequera and Velez-Málaga, was dramatically improved. Málaga forged new trading links with America, and began vigorously to export the natural products of the province. It seemed that nothing could stop the town's rapid progress towards becoming one of Spain's major ports. But, as always, there was a hitch. Whichever malevolent god had cursed the Phœnicians' favoured spot decided to wave the halt sign again in 1803. This time the chosen instrument was yellow fever. The epidemic raged for a year, leaving Málaga once again devastated. It was to be another thirty years before things were 'on the up' again.

Though the complex historical strands which led to the Peninsular War, the War of Independence (1804–14), are well outside the scope of this book, a brief resumé is necessary to explain the French occupation of Málaga between the years 1810 and 1812.

Charles IV had succeeded to the Spanish throne in 1788, but he was a weak, vacuous king with a shrewd and ambitious wife, Maria Luisa, who dominated and despised him. She made no secret of her infatuation for a handsome, if slightly overweight, officer from the minor nobility, Manuel de Godoy. The French Revolutionary and Napoleonic Wars which were seething in Europe made it impossible for Spain to remain neutral, but neither alliance with France, nor with the anti-Revolutionary coalition led by Britain, offered much security.

Into the vacuum created by this lack of a coherent foreign policy stepped the unskilled and uncertain Godoy, who, under the Queen's influence, became Spain's prime minister in 1792, at the age of 25. He too could not define a suitable role for Spain amid the turmoil, but a declaration of war against France became inevitable with the execution of Louis XVI in 1793. Although the war was initially popular, it proved disastrous. In 1794 the French occupied Bilbao, San Sebastián and Figueras. Godoy, afraid that the example of the French might incite similar revolutionary fervour in Catalonia and the north, and convinced in any case that the true enemy of Spain was Britain, decided on alliance with France. This was formalised by the Treaty of San Ildefonso in 1796.

It was a glaring blunder. It ensured war with Britain and cut Spain off completely from America, where its colonial markets were eagerly snapped up by Britain and the emerging United States. Godoy, it is true, masterminded a successful invasion of Portugal in the War of the Oranges (1801), but after Nelson's victory over the Franco-Spanish fleet at Trafalgar in 1805, Spain had to seek some rapprochement with the allies. Godoy was now heartily disliked by almost all sections of Spanish society, which should cause us no surprise. He signed the Treaty of Fontainebleau in 1807, by which Napoleon and the Spanish agreed to the conquest and partition of Portugal. Godoy, it is said, hoped to be given part of the country as his private principality.

His hopeless naïveté was immediately exposed once again when the French troops making towards Portugal occupied the fortresses of northern and central Spain and demanded territorial gains in Spain itself. Napoleon was totally disenchanted with the idea of both Godoy and Spain as allies, as well he might be. The prime minister and the ineffectual Charles IV, still Spain's leader in name, if not in substance, were constantly intrigued against by Charles' son, Ferdinand, Prince of Asturias, and Napoleon decided that the only solution was direct intervention in Spanish affairs.

When supporters of Ferdinand rose in revolt in Aranjuez on March 17th 1808, it gave him his cue. The rebels compelled Charles to abdicate in favour of his son, and also insisted on the sacking of Godoy. Napoleon went further. Summoning the ousted king and Ferdinand, now Ferdinand VII, to Bayonne a couple of months later, he gave them both their marching orders and handed the Spanish throne instead to his own elder brother, Joseph. The Spanish royal family went into exile on May 2nd.

Poor old Joe could never do anything right as far as his brother was concerned. His disdain, however, did not prevent him from dragging Joseph into his schemes at every opportunity. Trained as a barrister, Joseph became embroiled in politics largely at Napoleon's insistence, but by 1799 he had had enough and retired into the background. It could not last. While he was off campaigning in Germany in 1805, Napoleon needed someone to take charge of his government in France, and Joseph was the natural choice. A year later the little Corsican switched his attention to Italy. He invaded Naples and kicked out the Bourbons, who fled to Sicily, where they lived in exile under British protection. Naples was short of a king. Step forward, Joe Bonaparte, your brother needs you. Joseph was crowned King of Naples on March 30th 1806, but Napoleon was, as usual, unimpressed by his performance. Nevertheless he was his brother and he would give him another chance. Thus, in 1808, it was he who was chosen to assume the crown of Spain. King Joseph arrived triumphantly in Madrid on July 20th.

This move was not without support in Spain, but the strength of that support was overestimated by the egotistical French emperor. He had quickly put down a rising in Madrid early in May, but the brutality with which the occupying French troops murdered the patriot leaders incensed the Spanish, and sporadic local risings met with greater success. In Málaga, the people took revenge by seeking out and killing anyone who was unlucky enough to be French and in town – including the French consul. Only weeks after Joseph's accession, he was forced to leave the country rapidly after a significant success by the Spanish resistance at Baylen.

Napoleon decided on a full-scale invasion, and within a year he held the greater part of the Peninsula. Joseph was reinstated, but kept very strictly under his brother's control. Four times he tried to abdicate, and four times he was told to buckle down and do the job with more vigour. To Napoleon, vigour meant brutality. Málaga felt the cutting edge of his anger. When his troops had approached the city, they had been met by a mob wielding all manner of makeshift weapons – spades, sticks, knives. Hopelessly outclassed, they were brushed contemptuously aside by the French, who went on to sack the city with merciless cruelty.

Spain might still today have been part of a greater France had it not been for the British. Led by the Duke of Wellington, they marched from Portugal with the aid of Spanish guerillas and eventually ousted the French after their victory at the Battle of Salamanca on July 22nd 1812.

In 1814, assisted by elements of the army who objected to the liberalism which was the hallmark of the Constitution of Cádiz, Ferdinand returned from his exile in France to become an absolute monarch. The Constitution had been written in 1812, towards the end of the Peninsular War, by a Cortes raised in that city. It severely limited the power of the monarchy and laid out rules for a new single-chamber Parliament without privileges for the nobility and the Church. Conservative opinion was predictably against it, and eventually the army intervened. The reinstated king's repressive rule sparked many rebellions, and Málaga featured heavily in that led in 1831 by General José Maria de Torrijos. Torrijos and other Spanish liberals had moved to London a couple of years earlier to plan what they hoped would be Ferdinand VII's overthrow, but although they drew support from the likes of Tennyson and Carlyle, they could not raise sufficient funds to mount a convincing expedition. They never numbered more than a few dozen – certainly less than a hundred – but to Carlyle and other young English romantics they became symbols of heroic resistance to tyranny. There is a distinct foreshadowing here of the International Brigade which was to fight against General Franco in the Spanish Civil War a century later.

One of the English converts to the Torrijos cause was John Sterling, a young man just down from Cambridge. His father, Captain Edward Sterling, had a house in London at which Torrijos was a regular guest. It was Sterling who introduced the rebellious Spaniard to Carlyle, Tennyson and other prominent intellectuals. Gradually firm, if impractical, plans for an expedition were made, but there remained the problem of finance. It was solved, once again, by John Sterling.

Sterling had an Irish cousin, Lieutenant Robert Boyd. Boyd seems to have been a born adventurer. He held a commission in the Indian Army, but resigned after receiving an inheritance of four thousand pounds and returned to England with vague ideas about buying a ship and beginning a new career as a privateer in the Philippines. Sterling had a better idea. He approached his cousin and persuaded him instead to spend the money on the charter of a small ship in which the conspirators could sail for Spain. In return, after the inevitable overthrow of Ferdinand, Torrijos would make Boyd colonel of a Spanish cavalry regiment. With the bargain struck, the plot moved into high gear, and the combined Spanish and English brigade readied themselves for the off. At this point, curiously, John Sterling withdrew from the expedition after suddenly becoming engaged to be married. A few days later, in response to dark rumblings from the Spanish Envoy in London, the British authorities seized the ship and prevented it from sailing. Obviously the rebels had a spy in their midst.

Nevertheless they had gone too far to turn around, and one by one they made their way to Gibraltar where they re-grouped in the summer of 1830 to try again. Tennyson was part of the conspiracy, but he and another Englishman, Arthur Hallam, had gone to the Pyrenees to deliver funds to other similarly-minded rebels in the north. Back in Gibraltar the conspirators made half-hearted attempts to kick-start their intended revolution. They attacked the neighbouring town of La Línea (even holding it for a few hours), and then San Roque and Estepona, each time hoping for support from Spanish sympathisers, but this did not materialise. Paradoxically, despite the harshness of his regime and the frequent revolts, Ferdinand enjoyed considerable popularity among the masses. The actions of Torrijos and his men were placing severe strain on Anglo-Spanish relations and the English, including the Madrid envoy, Addington, and the Prime Minister, Lord Palmerston, were anxious to see the back of them. It looked for a while as though time alone would wipe them out. Many English members of the party began to tire of their romantic adventure. They spent their money on wine, women and song across the border in Spain and then drifted home. But the hard core, including Robert Boyd, lingered on the Rock for eighteen months, becoming steadily more of a nuisance. The authorities decided it was time to act.

They first tried bribery, offering the troublesome idealists British passports and voluntary resettlement anywhere in the world except, of course, Spain or Gibraltar. Staunch commitment to an idealistic cause is always an unfathomable mystery to the diplomatic mind, and when the offer was predictably declined, official patience wore thin.

Out of the blue, a letter reached Torrijos from Málaga, purportedly written by his second-in-command, Viriato, but almost certainly a forgery. It assured the rebel leader of the support of 2,500 troops from the town's garrison, and immediately he and his band set sail. It was November 30th 1831. At Fuengirola they were fired on by the coastguard captain, whom they had previously looked upon as a supporter. They should by now have been deeply suspicious, but blinded by zeal they put to shore and climbed into the hills to begin their march on Málaga. On December 5th they stopped at Alhaurin de la Torre for rest and refreshment, and were immediately surrounded by forces led by González Moreno, the Governor of Málaga, and forced to surrender.

They were taken to Málaga's Carmelite monastery and imprisoned there while the Governor waited for instructions from the Secretary of Defence in Madrid. The presence of Robert Boyd amongst the rebel captives was belatedly reported to the British Consul, William Mark, but he was not allowed to see him. The word from Madrid was brutally unforgiving. All fifty-two prisoners were to be shot immediately, including the 15-year old cabin boy who had known nothing of the conspiracy. Accordingly, just a week after their capture, they were taken to the Playa de San Andrés and executed. Robert Boyd gained the unwelcome distinction of becoming the first person to be interred in Málaga's British Cemetery, the story of which is told below. Like many a rebel before and since, the name of Torrijos outlived the tyranny which took his life. A commemorative obelisk raised to his memory and that of his comrades was erected eleven years after their deaths in the Plaza de la Merced, and just down the road from the cemetery where his friend Boyd lies, his name is perpetuated in the Plaza del General Torrijos.

Addington composed a formal but limp and unconvincing letter of protest to the Spanish, in which he cravenly acknowledged that the British citizen Boyd deserved to be shot, but feebly complained of the lack of a trial first.

It is the reaction of the chief British conspirators which strikes us as most odd. The rising may have been hopelessly impractical and doomed from the outset, but the rebels were fighting for a just cause, and, as rebels often do, they had died for it. No-one connected with the conspiracy need have felt any shame. Some might even have been expected to wear their involvement as a badge of pride. Yet only Carlyle ever wrote about it in any depth. Tennyson never referred to it at all, and John Sterling forever afterwards forbade the name of Torrijos to be mentioned in his presence. Why Torrijos? Why not Addington? King Ferdinand? The Governor of Málaga? This seems deeper than simple guilt at involving an adventurous cousin in a fateful enterprise. Any reading of the Torrijos/Boyd story leads inevitably to the conclusion that the rebels' every move was known to both the British and Spanish governments. Was there, perhaps, a more sinister reason for such reticence, and Sterling's apparently bottomless and bitter remorse?

By now the true revival in Málaga's fortunes was well underway. The wine industry and sugar production along the eastern Costa del Sol had really started to develop and prosperity was once again on the horizon. Perhaps 'redevelop' would be a better word, since Málaga's rich, sweet Moscatel had long been famous. It was known to the Romans as *Malacena vinum* and to the Arabs as *sharah almalaqui*, or Málaga syrup. This quaint euphemism was a neat way of avoiding their guiding Prophet's prohibition on the consumption of alcohol, and many an otherwise devout Moslem drank it with a clear conscience, if not a clear head. In his *Historia de Granada*, published in 1843, Miguel Lafuente tells the story of a dying Malagueñan Moslem who called on Allah to ensure that Paradise, to which he felt sure he would shortly be heading, had but one thing in abundance: delicious *sharah almalaqui*. (Incidentally; although the word 'sherry' is universally accepted as a corruption of 'Jerez', is it not at least as likely that it derives ultimately from the Moorish *sharah*?)

To survive, the industry had to fight off two potentially lethal threats in the nineteenth century. The first, and most serious, was an infestation of the vines by the tenacious phylloxera, an all-consuming species of plant louse with a penchant for the unfermented grape. Secondly, sweet wines fell out of favour as the dry varieties grew more popular. Today, both vines and sales are healthy once again.

The engine of revival, however, was not fuelled by wine alone. Following the death of Ferdinand VII in 1833, Málaga made use of the new freedom by opening up its port to the process of industrialisation and in so doing, finally took its place at the heart of Spain's economic life. These were the white hot years of the industrial revolution, and Málaga was perfectly placed to take advantage of them. In nearby Marbella and Ojén, Manuel Agustín Heredia had opened his two iron foundries, *El Angel* and *La Concepción* (see Ojén), and in 1846 he joined the Larios family from Rioja in setting up, in Málaga, the textile company, *Industria Malagueña, S.A.* Work and wealth were suddenly plentiful. Somebody had to look after the money, and the man who assumed this onerous task was a certain Señor Loring, who stepped forward to join the already formidable Heredia/Larios partnership in giving Málaga its final badge of financial respectability. They gave it its own bank - *el Banco de Málaga.*

Chiefly because of its beneficial climate, Málaga became a favourite foreign residence for wealthy English invalids from around the middle of the 19th century. However, if the observations of Lady Louisa Tenison, who visited it in 1850, are anything to go by, it had very little else to offer besides fine weather. 'Society there is none', she wrote, 'and with the exception of the theatre, there are no amusements whatever which could contribute to make time pass agreeably, and no objects of interest to attract the attention of the traveller.' The chief meeting place for all levels of society, Spanish and foreign alike, was the Alameda, where people would stroll in their best clothes each evening and at weekends. But even that did not entirely please her ladyship. She complained that during the drier months it frequently became very dusty.

Indeed, Lady Tenison was profoundly unimpressed with Andalucía in general. In her opinion, the accommodation at the inns was bad, and the cookery still worse. So far as she was concerned, the place was frequently unbearable. What perverse desire for martyrdom, we wonder, made her stay?

Rising and Revolution, 1931–1938

The infrastructure of Málaga suffered massive destruction during the Spanish Civil War of 1936–1939. The writers of many Spanish guide books still find the issue too sensitive to dwell on, but a brief history of this period is essential to some understanding of the decline of Málaga's rich heritage, which was left in great neglect for many years after the war.

The Second Republic, which displaced the Monarchy, was declared on April 14th 1931. Anti-clericalism was rife, and organised church burning began almost a month later, on May 11th, in many major centres of population. Málaga was a hotbed of the anarchist movement and few of the churches in the city escaped its attention. The authorities, such as they were, did little to prevent the destruction, and a great many religious buildings suffered before some degree of political stability was restored amongst the various factions, although the communists, trade unions and anarchists continued to disagree on some social issues. Which of them should be in charge, for example.

Málaga suffered a further period of devastation at the outbreak of the Civil War. On July 19th, 1936 the Spanish army units stationed in Morocco revolted and the rebellion, led by Francisco Franco Bahamonde, who had distinguished himself by becoming Spain's youngest general, quickly won over a number of cities including Seville and Granada. A small pro-Franco rising in Málaga, on the other hand, quickly fizzled out and the city remained fiercely loyal to the Republic.

With the help of Adolf Hitler's Junkers 52 transport planes, which were able to ferry 500 men a day, the army of Africa was in Seville by August 5th. Franco flew to the city the following day to begin his battle against the Republic. With the failing of the rising in Málaga, and the Civil Guard remaining staunchly Republican, various militia groups began to form. The Popular Front was a strong force, whose activities were felt all the way down the coast to San Roque, which was, by this time, under semi-Nationalist control. Their preferred tactic, brutal but viciously effective, was simply to round up all political opponents and clergy and execute them. In Málaga alone this resulted in the deaths of 2,500 people out of a total population of 100,000. Churches were burned, private houses were looted, and the fashionable district of La Caleta was completely destroyed. There is no hatred quite so violently mindless as that unleashed by civil war.

Málaga began to behave as a separate republic from the rest of Spain and further disintegration followed as the various militias inevitably fell out with each other. The city was ostensibly under the command of General Martínez Monte and a Russian adviser, Major Meretskov (later to become a Russian marshal), but the split in the military organisation led to bad discipline, low morale and frequent brutality within the ranks.

The anarchists revelled in inflicting damage on the city and the surrounding area, especially to buildings which were associated with the old order, and their ferocity was not restricted to objects of stone. In Ronda their habit of throwing priests and political opponents over the bridge and into the gorge 300 feet below was vividly described in Ernest Hemingway's *When Eight Bells Toll.* They also clashed with the Socialist Agricultural Union, the FNTT, in the rural *pueblos* around Málaga, often just pushing them aside to rob the smallholders.

Between August and October of 1936 the main group of the Nationalist Army in the south left Seville and moved north to Merida, Toledo and eventually the outskirts of Madrid. A much smaller force under the command of General Varela marched to Granada to relieve the town and then on to Ronda, which fell to the Nationalists on September 16th. General Varela took pueblo after pueblo on his criss-cross march across the northern roof of Málaga province, meeting little or no resistance.

At the start of 1937 the Nationalists controlled everything from the south of Estepona, inland to Ronda and onwards to Granada, leaving only a coastal belt of land 20 km long in Republican hands. Málaga and its hinterland were protected by a mountain chain which had presented a formidable obstacle to the advancing General Varela in the previous August, but before he could take on the unwelcome challenge, he was called north to Córdoba. Nevertheless, the fact that Málaga was now almost entirely isolated resulted in a further severe loss of morale and infighting among the Republican groups. The city came under aerial bombardment and yet more sections of the town were destroyed or badly damaged. Even the commander in Valencia grew disenchanted with his comrades in the besieged town and wrote them off with the dismissive words, 'Not a rifle or a cartridge more for Málaga'.

The Nationalist colonel, the Duque de Sevilla, a cousin of the ex-king, was given the task of starting an offensive on January 17th 1937. His troops moved up the coastline and met so little resistance that only three days later they had taken Marbella. A second thrust to the north of Málaga took the town of Alhama during the same period.

The Málaga command inexplicably failed to realise that a major assault was coming even though refugees were flooding into the city, with many of them being billeted in the cathedral. On February 3rd 1937, nine battalions of Italian blackshirts started to advance on Málaga from Ronda and Antequera supported by a hundred aircraft. Both of these mountain advances encountered fierce resistance and the fighting soon produced panic when it became clear that the Almeria corridor to the coast might be cut. In practice, however, the road had already been blocked by the Republicans themselves when they deliberately flooded it at Motril during a general retreat. From the Nationalist point of view, the cutting of the road was a problem, since they had no wish to fight a desperate and undisciplined army in an urban environment.

During the time of this general retreat, further naval and aerial attacks inflicted continuing damage on the city. The bombardment was deliberately designed to increase the swelling panic.

On February 7th the Italians reached the outskirts of Málaga, opening the way for the Spanish forces under the Duque de Sevilla, who entered the city the following day.

The first act of the victorious Nationalists was to round up all the prominent Republican sympathisers. An English volunteer ambulance driver fleeing to Almeria left a harrowing account of the flight. Pursued relentlessly by Nationalist troops, as many as 4000 refugees died in skirmishes, from starvation, or as a result of summary execution when caught.

They left behind a city in ruins.

Present-Day Developments

Although the wine-fuelled revival of the early 1800s did something to restore Málaga's fortunes, its real renaissance has only happened in the last half-century. As in so many places on the Costa del Sol, the story is an everyday one of tourists. As Spain, especially the Costa del Sol, grew and grew and grew as the favoured destination of sunseekers from the north, Málaga grew with it. Since the early 1990s there has been a huge investment in its infrastructure. Spurred on by the improvements in nearby Marbella, its beaches and promenades have been upgraded and many of its monuments restored. Repairing the damage of the Civil War has not been easy, but the authorities have certainly tried.

Málaga, like every other town and city on earth, is a living entity. The centuries have seen it blossom and wither and bloom again like some seasonal flower. Each succeeding age believes that, with its dawning, history has reached a plateau: that all boundaries are drawn, and that all will forever remain more or less as it is. And every age is wrong. The world will continue to change, as it has always changed, and Málaga, and the Costa del Sol, and the country our own age calls Spain will change with it. Were we to wake a thousand years from now, we would be as lost as a Roman finding himself suddenly in the departure lounge at Málaga airport. Which of today's stony fingers will survive to write their stories in the dust of centuries yet unborn we cannot know, but that there will be some we can be sure. And somewhere amid the ruins of our long-vanished world, there will be people striving to read them.

Chapter Two

Málaga, the City

Málaga's Historic Monuments
Muralla Nazari and Muro Portuario

HISTORY HIDES EVERYWHERE in Málaga. The visitor arriving by car, armed with guide books and maps, and anxious to get to the Alcazaba, the Gibralfaro and the Cathedral would be well advised first to find a parking space in the town's underground car park, which has many entrances in the Alameda Principál. Not simply because it provides a safe haven for the vehicle while he is out exploring the town on foot, but because in the very car park itself he will find two solid pieces of Málaga's past.

The port has been much enlarged over the years, and though the car park is located several hundred yards from the jetties and the harbour, the *muro portuario,* a stretch of which is preserved within it, once formed part of the harbour wall. (*Muro portuario* means, simply, 'harbour wall'.) Nearby, a second stretch of wall, the *muralla nazari,* is also in a good state of preservation. Though the name *nazari* indicates an Arabic origin, and the port wall is officially dated to the 18th century, both walls definitely display Roman characteristics, especially in the surviving bastions.

During 1998, efforts were being made to restore the walls and to turn them into an attractive feature of the car park, such as would draw the attention even of visitors who knew or cared little about their history. As a first step, black tiles have been laid around them both on the ground and in the ceiling, giving the impression of water. The ground looks wet and slippery, and the dryness of the tiles comes as a surprise. Up close, the two sets of tiles act as mirrors, giving the area around the walls an illusive depth at odds with the rest of the parking lot. A pedestrian exit ramp leads from the walls to the street, and this has been lined with display cabinets. When the restoration of the walls is complete (and the walls are so finely preserved that there really seems little for the authorities to do), these will be used for historical exhibits. It is to be hoped that a few people, anxious for the pleasures of the city, will pause to look.

The Alcazaba

As you leave the car park, the massive fortress of the Alcazaba will attract your attention. Built on the ruins of an earlier Roman fortress, this magnificent Arabic structure, which, along with Gibralfaro, dominates the city of Málaga, was begun during the reign of Abderrahman I around 756–780 BC as a defence against pirates, but not fully completed until its rebuilding three centuries later by the Granada king, Badis Al-Ziri. The work lasted from 1057–1063 and, as so often, the pragmatic Moors made use of whatever the Romans had left them. Roman traces remain throughout the building, including marble pillars used to hold up characteristic Arabic horse-shoe arches. The fortified causeway, or curtain wall, which connects it to Gibralfaro, was built in the 14th century by the Nasrid ruler, Yusuf I. At the time of writing, the structure is once again undergoing extensive restoration, making much of it inaccessible to visitors, but this should be rectified before too long. The Alcazaba in Seville and the world-renowned Alhambra in Granada are both more famous, but their counterpart in Málaga was already almost three centuries old before either of those was built. Even in its present (1998) restricted state, the fortress has a distinct feel of the Alhambra, and visitors to Andalucía who are unable to reach Granada could do far worse than to pay it a call.

The Alcazaba was used as a residence by the city's governors, and was defended by a triple enclosure of walls and towers, interspersed with gardens and small patios. The poet Ovando Santaren, writing of it at the height of its splendour, tells us that it had no less than 12 gates and 110 towers. How he would have wept if he could have seen it in the early years of the twentieth century! After the Christian conquest it was allowed to fall into decay, and over the years it became a kind of shanty town inhabited by squatters and the destitute poor. They built rough shelters wherever they could find room, and splashed whitewash over the remnants of its original stucco work. It became a ruin lying among filthy streets like a carelessly discarded bag of festering rubbish rotting in the sun. This situation continued well into the 1930s, when the authorities finally moved in to tear down the shacks, evict their inhabitants, and commence the restoration work which ultimately returned the Alcazaba to the state we see it in today.

Entering the castle, the visitor is immediately struck by the extensive use of Roman columns and capitals in its construction. To emphasise this, other Roman pieces and inscriptions have been laid beside the pathways, giving the impression of an alfresco museum. Not all of the exhibits are Roman. The selection is eclectic, even including an inscribed stone sarcophagus from 1808. This first walled enclosure, known as the *Recinto Inferior*, is reached by way of a gate known as *Torre del Cristo*. For many years this part of the castle was used as a chapel. The *Recinto Inferior* completely surrounds the second walled enclosure, the *Recinto Superior*, from which it is separated by the *Patio de Armas*. Today it is less belligerently a garden, with a bastion on its southern extremity which once defended the coast. On its eastern side there is an exit leading towards the fortress of Gibralfaro.

The second walled enclosure, the *Recinto Superior*, was strongly defended on both sides. Its western face is the site of the *Puerta de los Cuartos de Granada* (the Granada Rooms Gate) – the only access to the *recinto*. This has been much restored and is now in impressively excellent condition. The same cannot be said of its eastern defence, the *Torre del Homenaje* (Tower of Homage) which is still there, but in a state of ruin.

Within the final enclosure is the palace, *El Palacio*. This dates from the 11th century, though parts of it were added in the 13th and 14th. There are numerous Moorish dwellings to be seen, although during the ongoing restoration work these are not open to the public. The palace is quite extensive, with arches, towers and original marble columns. When the whole site is finally reopened to visitors, there is no doubt that it will be as great an asset to Málaga as the Alhambra is to Granada. Sadly, there is no Washington Irving on hand to mythologise it with his *Tales of the Málaga Alcazaba*, but that should not deter the reader from visiting it. This is a fine, atmospheric building which can only improve with time if the authorities persevere quickly with its restoration, and maintain their determination not to allow it to fall into ruins again.

The gardens and terraces of the Alcazaba, as noted above, are now either restored or semi-restored, and a cobbled path leads you lazily through them to the eleventh-century palace. Inside you will now find a small archæological museum. Among its exhibits are fragments of Roman pottery and statues from various sites around the province, including Lacipo (see Casares) and the Villa del Rio Verde (see Marbella).

Another impressive and important part of the exhibition is undoubtedly the Arab work contained in the pavilions and galleries of the *Cuartos de Granada*. It is heartening to see such concentrated efforts being made to make Málaga's history come alive to a new generation in such an accessible way. At present, entrance to the castle is from 9:30am to 8:00pm except on Tuesdays, when, inexplicably, it is closed.

The Fortress of Gibralfaro

Now standing close to a state-run hotel, or *parador*, the fortress as we see it today dates from Moorish times, although it has existed in one form or another since the Phœnician era. Graphic evidence of its age and importance came to light after heavy rains and landslides in 1996 uncovered human remains just to the south of the castle. The following year, an archæological team led by Juan Antonio Martín and Alejandro Pérez-Malumbres discovered a dozen tombs dating from the late Phœnician period in an area covering approximately 40 square metres. The hillside site was in an excellent state of preservation, and as this book goes to press, the investigation is an ongoing project which promises to be one of the most exciting archæological finds in Málaga for some considerable time.

The castle's probable original use was as a lighthouse, since its name, deriving from *Jabal-Faruk* or *Jebel al Faro*, means literally 'lighthouse hill', or mountain. Some time after AD 929, Abderrahmán III built what is effectively the present-day structure on the site of the Phœnician and Roman remains, although Yusuf I enlarged it somewhat in the early years of the 14th century. He connected it to the Alcazaba by a double curtain wall (*chemin de ronde*). It is possible to walk from the Alcazaba to the Gibralfaro fortress via the wall, up through the pine woods and tropical gardens, and thus combine a visit to both historic places. Alternatively, Gibralfaro can be reached by road from the opposite direction. The fortress is 426 feet above sea level and is justly famous for its stunning views of the town, the Alcazaba, and the 19th-century bullring below.

Lest we conclude that the Moors spent all of their time building or rebuilding fortresses, it should be noted that while Yusuf was overseeing the reconstruction of the Gibralfaro, a sufi holy man (*santón*) was founding the first university (*madraza*) in Spain at the western corner of Málaga's great mosque. The site is, of course, now occupied by the cathedral. An echo of the rich vein of earthy Spanish cynicism about clerics can be caught in the fact that *santón* has a second meaning. It also means 'hypocrite'. Perhaps that cynicism extends to universities also. These days, *madraza* is used to describe an overly protective mother.

In July, 1998, Mayoress Celia Villalobos officially opened the Gibralfaro archæological museum, housed in what was once the castle's gunpowder store. A sister to the museum in the Alcazaba palace, this one is devoted mainly to the castle and the city after the Christian reconquest of 1487, although a model of its old Arab fortifications is included. The gunpowder store replaced the church of San Luis, which in its turn had superceded the old mosque. The church was destroyed by French troops during the War of Independence. The exhibition includes pieces from virtually all the successive periods of Málaga's history and pre-history, while concentrating heavily on the 18th century.

Entrance to Gibralfaro is free, although an inevitable *varilla*, or stick man, is on hand at its roadside entrance unofficially to demand a small payment for his unnecessary assistance in helping drivers to park. This thinly disguised form of begging is common in Spain, and it is usually better to hand over a hundred pesetas than to take umbrage and make a fuss. Once inside, a walk around the fortress's walls is a fascinating and rewarding experience. It is clear that development of the internal architecture continued even into our own century, but there is still a satisfying feeling of homogeneity.

Roman Theatre

The Roman Theatre, situated at the main entrance to the Alcazaba, was first excavated in the early 1950s, and is the only genuinely Roman structure still to be seen in the city. Its existence came to light by chance during excavation work on another building. At the time of its discovery, a quarter of the site which it occupies was concealed beneath the *Casa de Cultura.* Hardly pausing to toss a coin, the authorities recently tore down the modern building so that the theatre could be properly uncovered, and the emergent structure is undergoing extensive restoration. Most of the site can be seen easily and effectively from behind the protective wire mesh fence which separates it from the road. Unfortunately, as is so often the case in Spain, the restoration work is proceeding at a snail's pace and no date has yet been fixed for opening it properly to the public. In spite of that, the ruins are quite imposing, as well as being unique in the area. With a little imagination on the part of those responsible, the combination of the Alcazaba, Gibralfaro and a fully excavated and well-maintained Roman theatre could certainly become one of the most impressive and well-visited historical sites in Southern Spain.

Puerta de Atarazanas

This marble Moorish gateway, 64m high and 7m wide, is now the entrance to the city's main market. The horse-shoe arch is flanked by two coats of arms bearing the Moslem inscription, *Le Gali Ille Alah* (Only God Conquers). The Atarazanas, to which the gate was once the entrance, was an immense fortress that incorporated a shipyard and an arsenal. (The word *atarazana* means simply, 'dockyard'.) Now only the gateway remains, the sole surviving fragment of the walls which once surrounded the mediæval town. The Atarazanas must have been a magnificent sight in its heyday. The Spanish diplomat Ruy González de Clavijo, who died in Madrid in 1412, left a short but memorable description in his account of his travels to the court of the Turkish conqueror Timur (Tamerlane) in Samarkand. At the start of his journey, his ship spent five days in Málaga harbour unloading jars of oil and other merchandise. Clavijo did not go ashore, but he must have spent many hours on deck gazing at the town.

> The said Málaga has a town in a hollow, one part of which is on the coast; and on a headland is a castle. And outside the town is another castle which is called the alcazaba, and from one castle to the other there are two walls, one close to the other. And below, on the other headland outside the town on the other side, are some tarazanas. And then near them there is a wall with towers running alongside the sea. And within this enclosure there are many beautiful gardens, and above these gardens and the town, are some high mountains in which there are villas and orchards. Between the sea and the enclosure of the town there are a few merchants' houses. And the town is very populated.

Of the countless people who pass through it each year, it is doubtful that one in a thousand is aware of the gateway's history, or would care if they knew, but at least it is there.

The Cathedral

It is impossible to see the exterior of Málaga's cathedral as its long list of designers, architects and builders intended. Cathedrals should stand in glorious isolation so that the splendour of their architecture overwhelms the approaching visitor – believer and non-believer alike. Unfortunately, since it was built or, as we shall see, semi-built, the area around the cathedral has become so congested that it is virtually hidden among the surrounding streets until you arrive on its doorstep. With no real chance to step back and admire the building properly, the visitor is condemned to stand too close and crane his or her neck to stare upwards. The effect is dizzying and curiously claustrophobic.

Like so many churches and cathedrals that we shall visit on our journeys through Andalucía, Málaga's cathedral is built on the site of a mosque which was deliberately destroyed by the victorious Christians after the reconquest. Before its construction, the site was occupied by a Gothic church, of which only the portal of the *sagrario* (sanctuary) remains.

Work on the cathedral began in June of 1522. The original architect, one of the most brilliant of his time, was Diego de Siloe of Granada. He worked on the building until 1525, when he was called home to oversee another project. Without his guiding genius to keep a steadying eye and hand on the progress of construction, the building concept lost much of its direction. A succession of other architects came and went over the years. The Toledan, Maestro Enrique in 1528, D. de Vegara in 1563, and later his son, de Vegara the younger, in 1582. It was he who designed the capilla-mayor and who started work on the *coro* in 1592. Seventy years from the laying of the foundation stone to the first day's work on the *coro.* Modern-day travellers, dismayed at finding their Spanish holiday hotels unfinished, may at least take comfort in the knowledge that they are living witnesses to a long and proud tradition.

On August 31st 1592, the building, though still far from finished, was finally consecrated.

In fact, the building was never finished, and Malagueñans refer to it wryly as *La Manquita,* the little one-armed lady, since only one of its planned two towers exists. This was completed, if the inscription upon it is accurate, on August 3rd 1779. 257 years in the making, but one of its towers was finally up. As any good Spaniard will tell you, quality workmanship should never be rushed. A subscription was raised in 1782 to build the missing second tower, but then, as now, money donated to such causes had a habit of disappearing like a card in a conjurer's hand, and for one reason or another the tower was never built. The unconvincing official story is that halfway through the job, work came to a grinding halt as the result of a Royal Decree which sent the money instead to the victims of an earthquake in Mobile, Alabama. The spin doctor responsible for that one deserves the coveted Aesop Award. It does seem, however, that around 400,00 *reales* of the amount raised was channelled to North America to assist the colonists who were struggling to throw out the British. When, as it occasionally does, the non-completion of the second tower made the news again in early 1997, the Sons of the American Revolution sent a delegation to Málaga to thank the city for its help. They presented a bronze plaque to the cathedral to express, in both Spanish and English, their gratitude, and to explain to visitors why the tower was never built. This you will find proudly displayed on the outside of the building. Perhaps the people of Antequera should do the same, since more of the money is said to have been spent on the construction of a road to the town.

Before that, in 1680, a century and a half's work was almost obliterated when the building was itself partially, and aptly, destroyed by an earthquake. This apparent act of irritable displeasure at the slow progress on the part of the Almighty must have caused widespread dismay, since it was not until 1719, almost forty years later, that the builders eventually found the heart to begin again. They had a problem. All of the original designs had been lost, and the new architect, Bada, fell back on a plan of his own, which he mixed liberally with another by the architect, Acero. Bada worked diligently until 1756, when he was succeeded by A. Ramos. When Ramos eventually gave up, that seems to have been that. The building, still uncompleted after almost three centuries of work, was left as it was.

But what there is is well worth seeing. Having been knocked together sporadically over such a long period of time, the cathedral offers a kind of sampler of changing architectural styles from the Gothic to the Baroque and everything in between. The fine altar is made of Italian marble with agate columns, and the choir reliefs are considered by many to be among the greatest works of the Granada sculptor, Pedro de Mena (1628–88).

The chapels around the sides each have something interesting to offer. One – the first to be seen on the right as you enter – has a crypt beneath its altar in which are buried the remains of those who died at the hands of the Reds when they ruled the town in the early days of the Civil War. The chapel is known as the *Capilla de los Caidos* (Chapel of the Fallen). It is renowned for the *Dolorosa* carved at the foot of its crucifix by Pedro de Mena, and considered by many to be his masterpiece.

Those visiting Málaga's cathedral for the first time may be surprised to learn of the existence of a patron saint of throat diseases. Not, as might be expected, St Veno or St Benylin, but a certain St Blas, or Blaisius. There is a chapel dedicated to him and on his Saint's Day it is possible to buy blessed bread rolls from the cathedral, which the faithful believe to cure and prevent throat infections. We should be grateful, perhaps, that there is no similar shrine dedicated to the patron saint of trumpets (St Vincent Ferrer), of hatchets (St Adjutus), or of any of the four patron saints of frogs (Huvas, Rieul, Sinorina and Ulphia). Sadly, there appears to be no patron saint of frogs in the throat. St Blas, incidentally, is no dull specialist. Aside from throat disease sufferers, he is also the patron of stonecutters, woolcombers, woolweavers, sick cattle and, ironically, builders. Maybe his prominent presence in a building that was never finished is saying something to us that we simply cannot hear.

More work by Pedro de Mena can be seen in the chapel of *Nuestra Señora de los Reyes* – Our Lady of the Monarchs. These are sculptures of the cathedral's sponsors, Ferdinand and Isabella, in the act of praying. The chapel also includes a statue which, legend has it, was carried by the Catholic Monarchs on their campaigns. In addition, there is a head of Christ on the altar's urn which has an interesting history. It was originally in Oran, Algeria. This town, now the capital of Oran province, was founded by traders from Andalucía in the early part of the 10th century to facilitate trade with the North African hinterland. During and after the Christian reconquest, a great many Spanish Moslems fled to Oran to escape persecution and enforced conversion to Christianity, and the town rapidly became a notorious centre of piracy. In an attempt to put a stop to it, the Spanish occupied Oran in 1509 and held on to it against all opposition until it fell to the Turks in 1708, only to revert to Spain in 1732. (For the final 130 years or so before the Algerian revolution in 1962, it was in the hands of the French.) However, Spain's control was always hanging by a thread due to frequent pirate raids, especially by the Berbers, and to avoid possible profanation of the image by the Arabs, it was removed and taken to Málaga.

Though the word *jubilee* has come to refer to virtually any great celebration, it has specific significance in both Hebrew and Roman Catholic religious observance. To the Jews it signifies every fiftieth year, which is dedicated to commemorating the deliverance from Egypt. In Catholic tradition it refers to a period of time, usually a year, declared at regular intervals by the Pope, during which indulgences are granted to penitents. Pope Boniface VIII proclaimed the first jubilee in 1300, and declared that it should be repeated at intervals of 100 years. However, no doubt due to popular demand, this was gradually whittled down in stages until, in 1470, it was set at 25 years by Paul II. Originally, to receive the indulgences of the jubilee, it was necessary for the penitent to travel to Rome. This tiresome requirement was scrapped in 1500, much to the relief of the lame and the lazy. In the chapel dedicated to St Francis of Assisi it was once possible to obtain indulgences granted under the hard-to-pronounce but widely popular jubilee of Porciúncula. (Incidentally, the full Spanish name of the American city of Los Angeles is, *El Pueblo de Nuestra Señora la Reina del Los Angeles de Porciúncula* – the Town of Our Lady the Queen of the Angels of Porciúncula. It was founded when a Spanish missionary expedition pitched a riverside camp on the site the day after celebrating the jubilee. The river also became the Porciúncula.)

The chapel of Santa Barbara features an early 16th-century Gothic retable, which is noted as the most beautiful in Málaga.

There are other equally interesting chapels, but perhaps the cathedral's most impressive feature is the magnificent choir, containing over a hundred stalls and 58 carved wooden figures, forty of them by Pedro de Mena. The remainder are the work of José Michael and Diego Fernández. There is an

The Alcazaba, once the residence of Málaga's Moorish governors.

The Gibralfaro still dominates the city skyline.

The Roman Theatre, built in the shadow of the fortress.

Málaga's Cathedral, *la manquita*, was never completed.

The Bishop's Palace.

The tomb of William Mark, founder of Málaga's English Cemetery.

Los Baños Hediondas are still usable today.

The pueblo of Alhaurin el Grande.

Molino Morisco de los Corchos – still working after 500 years.
Inset: Visitors are always welcome at the Moorish Cork Mill.

Alhaurin de la Torre

El Retiro – Jewel of Alhaurin de la Torr

The trains are gone, but the station remains (*La Alqueria*).

La Alqueria is rich in Roman remains.

Benahavis

Benahavis was built into the castle walls.

The Town Hall, Benahavis.

Torre Estoril – now one of the hazards o the golf course of *L Arqueros.*

Montemayor once dominated the country around Benahavis.

The view from Montemayor.

upper and lower row of stalls, with the upper row's lecterns forming the back of the row beneath. In the centre of the upper row is the bishop's throne, behind a red marble lectern.

Pedro de Mena was a famous and much sought-after artist in his day. He had his workshop in Málaga, and by all accounts ran it along the lines of a modern factory. His wooden images are to be found in churches and cathedrals all over the south of Spain. The carvings in Málaga Cathedral, which are to be found in the chapels as well as the choir, were completed around 1658–60, and are said to have cost a thousand *reales* each. Many students of de Mena rate his work in Málaga Cathedral as his finest, and the delicacy of the carving is certainly striking. They are executed chiefly in mahogany.

The cathedral boasts not one, but two mighty organs with, between them, four thousand eight hundred and eighty-eight pipes. They were built in 1871 by Julián de la Orden, who was so proud of them that he requested, and was granted, a room in the tower where he could live close to them forever. He died at the end of the century, presumably profoundly deaf.

There is much to hold the interest in Málaga Cathedral: Pedro de Mena's carvings, the choir, a plethora of paintings and sculptures by renowned artists, a fine high altar. And like all consecrated buildings, it provides a cool, quiet refuge from the sun and the crowds. However, like many ancient buildings in modern, traffic-choked cities, it is visibly suffering as the millennium approaches. Even the local pigeons have been denounced as unwitting villains in its crumbling, dingy distress, and in many of the town's shops you will see pink cathedral-shaped collecting boxes as another effort is made to raise funds for its repair. No-one, it seems, still harbours hope for that second tower.

La Plaza del Obispo

Beside the cathedral is the *Plaza del Obispo* (Bishop's Square) which is the setting for the Bishop's Palace. Whether earthly representatives of a saviour born in a stable should live in palaces is a moot point on which we shall not dwell. Let theologians debate it. The palace is certainly a fine 'des. res'. It has a superb façade incorporating a doorway with six red stone pillars, above which is a balcony perfectly suited for standing on to bless the huddled masses beneath. Aspiring Popes could practise there for hours. Over the balcony is a recess containing a marble statue of Our Lady of Sorrows.

In the centre of the square is an old, though not particularly notable, fountain. In earlier times, when the Bishop's Square was a popular commercial centre, the fountain was used as a drinking trough for horses. It was, in fact, a very lively place with a number of well patronised inns. Perhaps successive bishops, anxious to practise their blessings in peace, found such riotous company incongruous. For whatever reason, the square gradually declined as a trading centre and is now relatively peaceful.

The Sagrario and Puerta del Sagrario

The past is an incredibly stubborn stain to remove. Ultimately, Time destroys everything in its relentless path, yet some monuments melt away like ice in the sunshine, while others rot as slowly as an old man's tooth – defying the years with heroic determination. Visigothic Málaga has slipped beyond memory into the historical abyss. All, that is, except for the *Puerta del Sagrario.* Though sorely ravaged by the passing of the centuries, as it has every right to be, the old gate to the shrine deserves a mention as the only remaining Gothic monument in the town.

They began building the church of the Sagrario itself in the early years of the 16th century, during the tenure of Málaga's second bishop, Diego Ramirez Villaescusa. He was long gone by the time it was completed, so bishop César Riario was the lucky one who got his coat of arms incorporated into the decorations. The ornate high altar has twenty-seven statues and apparently endless finely carved reliefs. The Assumption of Our Lady takes pride of place, but there is also a Calvary with Our Lady and St John, and a superb Descent From the Cross. As in so many places of religious devotion, one can only stand and wonder at the endless hours of patient craftsmanship, more often than not by unknown artists, which resulted in these masterpieces. Some have attributed the reliefs in the church of the Sagrario to Alonso de Berruguete, arguably Spain's most important Renaissance sculptor, but ultimately it is almost irrelevant. These images spring from the soul not of a single man, but of a whole people. The artist is merely a tool.

The two other retables in the church are a relative anti-climax, though not without interest. One contains an excellent image of St Sebastián, and the other a statue of St Joseph.

Museo de Bellas Artes

While in the vicinity of the cathedral, take the opportunity to stroll the short distance to the calle de San Augustín and visit the *Museo de Bellas Artes.* The superb mansion house which now bears the name dates from the 16th century, and is notable for its excellent tiling and *mudejár* windows. In its centre is a beautiful patio which is almost as much a work of art as any of the museum's more conventional exhibits. There are sculptures by Fernando Ortiz and Pedro Manor, but its best exhibits are hanging on the walls. It is interesting to compare the styles of the two great 17th century Baroque painters, Francisco de Zurbarán and Bartolomé Esteban Murillo. Murillo was the more popular. Indeed, he was arguably the most popular Spanish religious artist of his time. Born in 1617, and baptised in Seville on January 1st of the following year, he started painting in a subdued, conservative style which underwent a radical change after he visited Madrid in the 1650s, and met Velázquez. After that his paintings were increasingly romanticised, idealised, and full of the heavy sentiment that we tend to associate with religious art of the time. Zurbarán was almost twenty years older than Murillo, and his paintings of monks and other religious subjects were, for the most part, far more realistic and uncluttered. At least, that was true until the late 1650s when, perhaps inspired by, or jealous of, the great popular success of Murillo, he began to paint in a style broadly similar to that of the younger man. He died in 1664, leaving his rival to paint on for another 18 years. Examples of both men's' work are in the museum.

However, what most people come to see are the sketches on show by the young Picasso. Pablo Ruiz y Picasso is undoubtedly the most famous painter to have been born in Málaga. He is to art what Louis Armstrong is to jazz, and John McEnroe to tennis – the one name that people who know nothing else about it know. He was born in Málaga on October 25th 1881, and his achievements in painting, sculpture, ceramics and much more are far too vast to be adequately described in this book. His first teacher, the comparatively little known Antonio Muñoz Degrain, is also represented in the museum's collection. Either before or after viewing the exhibition, you may wish to pause in the *Plaza de la Merced,* just to the north, and see not only the memorial to General Torrijos and his ill-fated companions, but also the house where Picasso was born. Please note that sadly, like so many similar places in Spain, the museum does not open its doors at weekends. If you wish to pay it a visit, it must be on a weekday between the hours of 10:00am and 1:30pm, or 5:00pm and 8:00pm.

Museo de Artes y Tradiciones Populares

The Costa del Sol has become so synonymous with the excesses of tourism and intense pleasure-orientated urban living that it is sometimes difficult to imagine life on the coast before the coming of the karaoke conquistadors. Marbella, Fuengirola and other places have turned from tiny fishing villages into pulsating cosmopolitan infernos in little more than a generation or two. Málaga itself, despite being at the centre of the ever-spinning wheel, has avoided most of the wilder aspects, and if you wander to the banks of the Guadalmedina river to the west of the city, you can spend a tranquil half-hour at the wistfully named Museum of Arts and Popular Traditions, peering back through time to a world where a tourist was a man from the next village whose donkey had got lost in the mist. The museum, with its collection of fishing and farming tools, its dusty *bodega,* and so on, is situated in an interesting 17th century coaching inn which would be worth a visit in its own right. Unlike the *Museo de Bellas Artes,* the *Museo de Artes y Tradiciones Populares* is open both weekdays and weekends from ten in the morning until one in the afternoon, when, in the true spirit of popular tradition, everyone goes off for a siesta until five o'clock, when they reopen the doors until eight.

Málaga's Churches

Devotees of religious buildings are spoiled for choice in Málaga. One might be forgiven for thinking that after the cathedral and the Sagrario there was little else to see, but that is far from the truth.

Take, for example, the church of *Santa María de la Victoria,* Málaga's patron, which you will find at the end of *Compás de la Victoria* (a continuation of the street that bears the same name). The church was built on the site supposedly occupied by the tent of King Ferdinand towards the end of the siege which finally brought the Moors to their knees. The railings, they say, were made from the chains of prisoners liberated by the victorious Christians as they swept in shouting ferociously and cutting off Arab heads. It is a legend as likely as the tale of the cow that jumped over the moon, but it has lasted well.

The moment the town was declared taken, Ferdinand's tent was rolled up and a shrine put in its place. Ultimately the shrine became the church and an image sent to the Catholic Monarchs for luck at the onset of the attack by Archduke Maximilian of Austria was placed behind the altar, where it remains.

The extravagantly decorated altar shrine, in which the statue of the Virgin is supported by three decidedly weary looking angels, is the work of a certain Lurinzaga, who laid down his chisel with a satisfied sigh in 1695. The baroque fussiness is repeated in the carvings which decorate the crypt, where lie many generations of the Condes de Buenavista. Religious sculptors have long had a penchant for the macabre, and in the crypt this is given full rein, with depictions of skeletons and bodies galore.

The crypt of the church of San Lazaro, a little further down *calle de la Victoria,* cannot boast a collection of counts. It used to be a leper-house, and it is the victims of the ancient dreaded disease who are buried there. There is a horrific poignancy in the fact that the tombs were decorated in an unskilled but moving way by other lepers waiting their turn to die. No Lurinzaga for them. The church is also the scene of a curious rigmarole each year during Holy Week. The carved figure which is carried through the streets in procession is too large to pass through the church door, so year after year a man comes along and solemnly knocks down part of the wall. When the procession ends, and the statue is safely back inside, he solemnly puts it back again. Is the ceremony, we wonder, accompanied by some specially commissioned hymn?

The church of Santiago is in the Plaza de la Merced at the entrance to *calle de Granada.* Unfortunately, much of the interior was destroyed by fire in the fiercely anti-clerical months of 1936, but the fine *mudejar* tower dating from 1545 survived. There is also an 18th century retable behind the High Altar which weathered the flames surprisingly well.

Roughly contemporary with the church of *Santa María de la Victoria* is the church of *Los Mártires.* At the time of writing, its tower is celebrating its

450th anniversary, having been built in 1548. Two notable 18th century images in the church are Our Lady on the Mount of Olives, and Our Lady of the Sorrowful Conception, by Fernando Ortiz. A gypsy sculptor. Juan Vargas, contributed a statue of Jesus, which is carried annually in procession by gypsies on the Monday of Holy Week.

The final church of note in Málaga is the church of San Juan, which grew out of a chapel established by the Catholic Monarchs like a loaf rising in an oven. At the entrance there is an intriguing 17th century statue by Pedro de Zayas depicting the Holy Christ of the Blind Souls. And thereby, of course, hangs a tale. As the Christians consolidated their grip on Málaga after the reconquest, those Moors who had miraculously escaped death were robustly encouraged to embrace Christianity and become *Moriscos.* Given the choice of that or a taste of cold steel, many did so. To administer this mass conversion to the Christian team, the Catholic Monarchs sent in squads of teachers to explain the differences and help the choir learn their new songs. The Arabs were eager to get the T-shirt, the badge and the scarf, but on one point they were adamant. The infidels must not gaze upon the beauty of their women, and they insisted that any teachers sent to instruct the womenfolk must be blind. (This was presumably before some unsung genius of the Moslem world had the inspiration of the veil.) 'No problem', said the Christians, promptly blinding a few.

Like so many legends and oft-repeated stories, this one is inherently incredible. The conquering Christians were not noted for their pious respect for Arab custom, which they were in any case determined to eradicate. The directive for the Moors to convert to Christianity or get out was an ultimatum, not a request. The routed Moors were in no position to make provisos or demands. But it is an appealing story and it captured the hearts of the public.

A character in Agustín de Rojas Villandrando's novel, *El Viaje Entretinido* (The Pleasant Voyage – 1603), takes refuge in the church of San Juan after killing a man. Some say the story is autobiographical and that the refugee was Rojas himself, but if so the affair quickly blew over. Shortly after the appearance of the book he married and became a civil servant in Zamora. That may, of course, have been the sentence of the court.

The English Cemetery

When William Mark arrived in Málaga in 1816 to take up his post as the new British Consul, he was astonished and horrified to learn that in Spain, burial in consecrated ground was reserved exclusively for Catholics. Protestants were buried without rites, and in Málaga such burials were bizarre. The bodies of dead Protestants, regardless of nationality, were buried upright on the seashore under the supervision of local guards, and invariably at midnight. One can imagine it as the opening scene of some 1960s Hammer horror film.

Not surprisingly, the bodies frequently attracted the hungry attention of stray dogs or were swept out to sea. It was all very strange.

This blatant religious discrimination first aroused British concern in the mid-1650s, when Oliver Cromwell's envoy, Ascham, was assassinated in Spain and buried without ceremony. Cromwell insisted on a paragraph being written into a subsequent commercial treaty between the two countries, which placed a duty on the Spanish authorities to provide a decent burial ground for British subjects who died in Spain. As we have seen, this article was completely ignored and the separate treatment of Catholic and Protestant dead continued at the time of Mark's appointment more than 150 years later. He determined at once to secure a plot of ground where expatriate British subjects could be properly buried.

The next logical move might have been to raise the matter with the Governor of Málaga. This blinding inspiration, however, did not strike William Mark until more than twenty years later, when he dreamed that he saw the Governor, General José Mansó, standing beside the brand new cemetery. He went hotfoot to the Governor the next morning and the General immediately called the Board of Health and arranged for a suitable site to be provided. So readily was this granted, and with so little fuss, that one is compelled to wonder why it took Mark so long to get around to the obvious. His years of struggle might have been expected to follow a confrontation with the Spanish authorities, not precede it.

Nevertheless, Mark had his cemetery, and the granting of the land was ratified in 1830 by a royal order of Ferdinand VII. It was in 1831 that the cemetery received its first tenant: the hapless 26-year old Robert Boyd, executed along with his fellow Torrijos rebels on San Andrés beach.

Today the bodies of many nationalities lie in the British Cemetery alongside Boyd and its founder, William Mark. It is easily found, just a short walk east of the bullring along *Avenida de Priès*, close to the Hotel Miramar. Fittingly, carved lions lounge over the gate, and at the entrance is a small Anglican church. The cemetery is neat and well-kept, just as Mark would have wanted – a tiny corner of England in a foreign land that existed long before the English colonised so much of the Málaga seaboard.

Málaga Park

Though only a century old, the park more than deserves its mention in this book. It is situated on land that was once the old port of the city. The winter rains which fell on the mountains would bring down mud and soil, which settled on the port and gradually obliterated the ancient quays and silted up the harbour. As the depth of the water diminished, the quays were extended southwards, leaving behind a wide stretch of land reaching from the harbour to the Alcazaba, covered with rich, fertile soil.

In September of 1896, urged on by her Malagueñan prime minister, Antonio

Canovas de Castillo, Queen Maria Cristina broke her holiday in San Sebastián to sign the order which led to the park's development. This may seem curious, but the matter was urgent. The land was then owned by the port authority, which had considered selling it to pay for the port's extension. The Queen's decree handed it over to the municipality. It also required that a project be created to make use of the land, and specifically demanded the building of gardens, streets and walking areas as well as the extension of the main Alameda in the direction of the *Paseo de la Fareola.* Designs flooded in for the project, and a short list of three was drawn up. The eventual winner was the plan submitted by Joaquín de la Rucoba.

Although Málaga was then basking in the distant glow of a former glory, its 125,000 inhabitants were still proud of their city, and the result of their efforts was a fine adornment to it. It is not large when compared to London's Hyde Park, or New York's Central – covering just 38,000 square metres – but what it lacks in acreage it certainly makes up for in variety. Here it is possible to see species of trees and vegetables unique in Spain, and even in Europe. One of the latter is the 'bottle tree', also known as the 'drunken stick', which stands in the *Plaza de la Marina.*

As you wander around the park, you will see many rare arboreal wonders. There are Japanese quince trees, tulip trees from Gabon, syringas from Greece and many more. Over 160 species are represented. There are also fountains which, according to venerable custom, are occasionally uprooted (unlike the trees), and moved from place to place. Here and there, monuments have been erected to distinguished Malagueños, including the writers Arturo Reyes, Rubén Dario and Salvador Rueda, the painters Muñoz Degrain and Bernardo Ferrándiz, and the war hero, Commander Benitez. Ironically, the man who was chiefly responsible for the park's existence, Antonio Canovas de Castillo, had to wait until 1975 before posthumously receiving the honour.

By the second and third decades of this century, while the Alcazaba was still an eyesore in the middle of a deplorable slum, the park had become the social heart of the city. It was the place to *pasear*, to picnic, to meet. Its social bustle has declined with the years, but none of its splendour has been lost. It has earned a deserved reputation as one of the botanical treasures of Europe. In 1996, councillors from the local *ayuntamiento* petitioned the Andalucían Government to designate it an asset of Cultural Interest as an Historic Garden.

Sub-Districts of the Municipal of Malaga

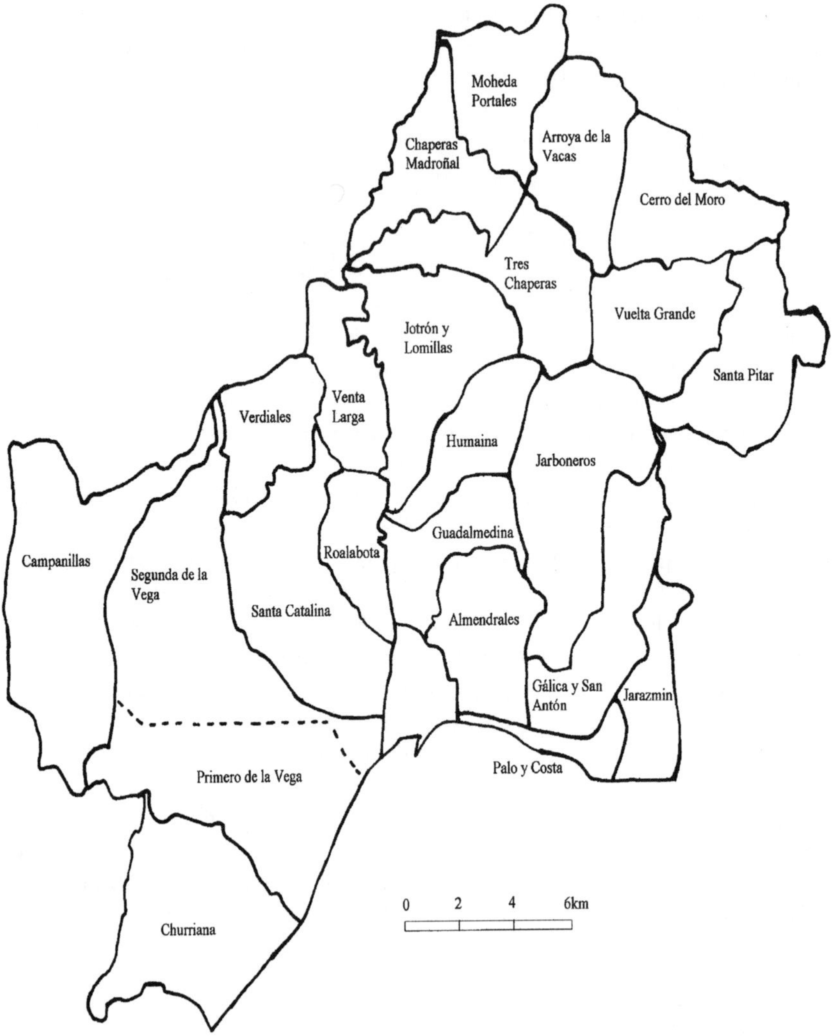

Chapter Three

The Municipal Subdistricts of Málaga

TO ALL BUT A HANDFUL of the millions of tourists who pass through it each year, Málaga is merely a crowded airport and a city of which they are vaguely aware as they head for their holiday hotels in Torremolinos and elsewhere. We have seen that there is considerably more to Málaga than this. Within its municipal boundaries are no less than 23 separate districts, ranging from the messy urban sprawl of Campanillas in the west, to sparsely populated semi-wildernesses in the mountainous north. Some, such as *Cerro del Moro*, now contain only a handful of people, but most were once heavily populated enough to have developed a recognisable identity.

Most of the mountainous region, stretching northwards to Granada, is now the *Parque Natural de Montes de Málaga*. It was not always a haven of peace. In former times the park area was important as a centre of silver and lead mining, and the hills within it are still liberally dotted with ruined and deserted farmsteads. In the early 19th century an attempt was made to re-populate and re-vitalise the mountains. Purpose-built farmsteads were created near springs and suitable wells, and since they were known as *lagars* (winepresses), we can see that the new men came not to burrow into the ground in search of silver and lead, but to distil the golden syrup of the grape. For a while things went well. An 1896 study reported an average of between two and four *lagars* per square kilometre. And then, as things do, it all began to unravel and fall apart. The twentieth century was underway and screaming for attention. Mountain farmsteads were as out-of-date as pack mules, ruffles and snuff. Young men wanted to feel the pulse of change in their veins, and suddenly mountain air smelled not of the sweet joy of an ordered life, but of stagnant water and decay. First as a trickle, and then as a flood, they moved away. Now their ancestors' homes – the lucky remembered ones – are no more than names on a map and ruins on the ground.

An interesting history has been written of the rise and fall of these homesteads, though only a handful are touched on in the present volume.

Should you wish to visit the park, you should be prepared to do so on foot, since its interior is difficult to reach by vehicle, although camping is permitted at a site known as *Camping del Torrijo*, which you will find on the Puerto del Leon road.

Campanillas

Campanillas is an industrial dormitory town. It used to be an industrial dormitory village, but it has inevitably spread like the waistline of a middle-aged man who loves food and hates exercise. Though a distinct entity in its own right, it is administered as a sub-municipality by the city hall in Málaga. This may not always be the case, and a future edition of this book may have to give it a chapter of its own, but for the time being it remains merely a footnote to the great city.

Four other rapidly expanding communities form part of this sub-district. The only true rural life still to be found is in the northern area of *Cerro de las Viejas,* based around two 19th-century *lagar* farmsteads. Its anachronistic lifestyle, in sharp contrast to the fast-lane activity all around it, lends a sad irony in the fact that *Cerro de las Viejas* means 'hill of the old women'.

Drive off the new highway into Campanillas, and the first feature which will attract attention is a large complex with a tower and a barn. There is an unmistakable ghostly air about it which recalls shivery moments from late night films. One can easily imagine Christopher Lee or Peter Cushing lurking in its darkened corners. In the 19th century the buildings housed a religious community, but within the last decade it has been abandoned and is now falling rapidly into decay, taking who knows how many secrets with it.

As you drive towards the town centre, turn right at the church, which also dates from the 19th century. Campanillas (*Little Bells*) is not a pretty place. In essence, it is like a grime-covered urchin scuffing his shoes on the pavement, but look above and you will see a very odd rock formation brooding over the area. It is the dominant feature of a hill appropriately called *Torre* (tower). The hilltop, standing 209 metres above the Guadalhorce flood plain, is difficult to visit, since there is no pathway to the summit. The best way to make your approach is to park your car beside the quarry on the minor road and make your way up on foot as best you can.

The outcrop was certainly used as a look-out post by the Moors, who took advantage of its position in line of sight with Cártama, Puerto de la Torre and Málaga itself. Today a flag flies proudly above it, though whether this was raised to celebrate a successful but arduous climb is hard to tell. Despite its undoubted use by the Moors, no substantial fort seems to have been built on the hill.

The same cannot be said of nearby *Cerro del Conde.* Here a definite hill fort existed. Follow the track road to Puerto de la Torre until you reach the crossroads a little to the north of the hamlet of La Esperanza. During the rainy season you will have to ford the river, but once spring is past and the land is dry, you can, with a suitable vehicle, drive along the parched riverbed itself. Look for a flat-topped hill buttressed by sandstone cliffs. The 193 metre-high *Cerro del Conde* was once the site of an Iberian hill fort which traded very successfully with the Phœnicians, whose nearest colony was 6 kilometres away, close to Los Chopos, the site of the old *Puente del Rey.* 'Chopo', incidentally, is the name given by the Spanish to the black poplar tree, but it is also a slang term for a rifle. Driving through the rather seedy area today, the two meanings mingle strangely. The village may have been named for the trees, but now its mean streets definitely whisper 'rifle'.

The Iberians of Cerro del Conde were not restricted in their dealings to the Phœnicians of the Los Chopos area, since there was at least one other similar colony across the rio Guadalhorce at Zapata.

Churriana

Churriana is a good example of how the swamping tide of progress and urbanisation need not necessarily eat away at the rural heart of a community. Forty years ago, in common with both Alhaurins, Churriana was an isolated, self-contained village of agricultural workers, lost, and happy to be so, in the Málaga hills. Today its neat little *mirador* (viewing balcony), where both young and old come to meet, looks down on the busy runways of Málaga airport. Day after day, dozens of planes carry thousands of tourists in and out of Spain. Most of them are blissfully unaware of Churriana's existence. They come to swim, play golf and soak up the sun in Torremolinos, Marbella and Fuengirola. It is understandable, since Churriana has little of interest to offer them.

Yet whereas Alhaurín el Grande is now a fair-sized town and Alhaurín de la Torre has become a sprawling urban mass which shows no sign of slowing the speed of its unruly expansion, Churriana has miraculously retained the sleepy, timeless air of a true village. The mountain railway used to pass through here, but that has now gone, leaving only the station house to mark its passing. There is a wry irony in the fact that since the disappearance of the trains, the building has become the headquarters of the local cycling club.

There are no grand ruins to see. The sub-municipal district of Churriana never rated a castle, and most tourist guides ignore it. But it is worth visiting if only to stand for a while on the *mirador* and watch the aeroplanes come and go, and wonder at the resilience of its tranquillity when all around is bustle and noise and life in the fast lane. But the fast lane hates a slowcoach. In 1998, Churriana was chosen as the first place in Spain to experiment with the looming pan-European currency, the Euro.

Cortijada de San Isidro

On the north side of Málaga Airport, like a stubborn piece of rural grit beneath an uncut urban fingernail, is the *Cortijada* (farm estate) *de San Isidro.* To find it, simply follow the signs which direct you to the NCP car parking facility.

Before the building of the airport, this must surely have been one of the most imposing farms in the area. The main buildings are grouped into two, each set with its own arched entrance leading into a courtyard. The arches, built of brick and still in good repair, are well over a century old. When *San Isidro* was in its heyday, the arches would have had thick wooden gates to keep out unwelcome strangers at night.

Although *Cortijada de San Isidro* is currently being developed as a small and rather exclusive housing estate, there is still some residual farming activity here. The yard beyond the first arched entrance is now filled with parked cars, but a short walk away the second and, it would seem, slightly older, arch is the gateway to a much more rustic scene, complete with stables and the kind of farmyard smells that either flood the senses with warm nostalgia or send you reaching for your handkerchief. From behind a grilled window your approach is watched by a squad of wary chickens, who noisily alert the residents to your coming. San Isidro has compromised to survive. The enemy (out-of-towners, NCP) are literally within the gates, and the constant sound of aircraft coming and going is an inescapable reminder that the reprieve is not absolute, but merely a sentence suspended. Whether the rustic smells will still hang over *Cortijada de San Isidro* a generation hence, and the chickens still be warily on guard, is unlikely. But with luck the buildings and the arches will survive, and where stones survive, history lives.

Cerro del Villar (Salduba)

Spain was important to the Phœnicians, not least as the source of the shellfish which provided them with their highly prized purple dye. In 1100 BC they founded the town of Gadir (Cádiz) and went on to found other settlements along the Spanish coast, including some close to Málaga.

Yet today little physical evidence survives of this mighty trading empire. Even Cádiz itself provides virtually none. Should we be surprised? As was demonstrated by the Roman destruction of Carthage, later civilisations were ruthless in their deliberate obliteration of the Phœnicians and their works. The question we should ask ourselves is 'why?'

The paucity of Phœnician remains makes Cerro del Villar particularly important, even though there is little left to see, and the visitor must consequently resort frequently to imagination. The site can be found south of the rio Guadalhorce close to Málaga airport. Look for the old railway bridge across the river. The community shared the name '*Salduba*' in Roman times with the settlement which once existed on the site of present-day Estepona. This particular Salduba did not develop as a settlement, probably due to the proximity of Malaca (Málaga), but as more of an industrial and service centre.

There is, we must stress, no absolute certainty that this *was* the site of

Salduba, but there is no doubt at all that Cerro del Villar was an important site to the Phœnicians, who maintained a whole network of closely packed settlements in eastern Andalucía for about two hundred years, beginning around the 8th century BC. When the remains of this earlier settlement were first discovered, they were initially thought by some to be the lost city of Mainake, built in the 7th century BC by the similarly named Phocians from central Greece. The remains of Mainake are widely believed to lie in the general area, but have yet to be identified. However, it soon became clear that the settlement pre-dated the arrival of the Phocians by at least a century and therefore had to be Phœnician. Although situated today on a rather undistinguished hill, the site in Phœnician times was an impressive island in the estuary of the rio Guadalhorce. Cerro del Villar is unique in being the only known instance of a Phœnician island settlement. Geographical changes over the past two millennia have not only changed the course of the Guadalhorce, but have left Cerro del Villar stranded some distance from the coast.

Excavations soon showed the site to be much larger than originally thought, covering more than thirty acres instead of the estimated five. The layout of the town was surprisingly modern, featuring plazas, rectilineal streets and a clearly well thought out town plan. It is thought that at its height it was home to at least a thousand people. Today such a place would qualify as no more than a village, but it must be remembered that three thousand years ago the population was much smaller and more widely scattered in small rural groups. Wherever a thousand people gathered together to live and work, you had a thriving town. Many of those who gathered at Cerro del Villar were, if we are to judge by the apparent sumptuousness of their houses, very wealthy. Several of the larger villas contained up to nine rooms and were built around central patios.

There is no evidence of the smelting of metals here, and indeed the nearest iron mine is 40km away in the *Sierra Blanca de Marbella*. It is far more likely – and this is emphasised by the discovery of several stone querns, or hand-mills – that this was an agricultural and cereal-growing community. Goats and sheep would have been domesticated and in addition there would have been ample hunting, the quarry being deer, wild cat and wild boar.

The possible fate of Cerro del Villar became a subject of controversy in late 1997 when work began on the construction of a huge channel intended vastly to increase the amount of water which the rio Guadalhorce could safely handle. Eight years before, the river had flooded and caused extensive damage to the surrounding countryside. The digging of the channel was widely welcomed, but some ecologists called for the project's abandonment because of potential damage to Cerro del Villar. The authorities, with the bland complacency for which authorities are renowned throughout the world, dismissed their concerns as misguided and unnecessarily alarmist. It is to be hoped that on this occasion they are right.

Guadalmedina and Humaina

These rural districts lying between the Guadalmedina river and the road that leads to *Puerto del Leon* contain an interesting trackway which leads to some abandoned and ruined farmsteads. You will see the river opposite the gardens of *La Concepción*, by the turn-off at km 553.5.

Two sites, at least, are worth a mention and a visit. They are each ruined mills, *Molino de San Telmo* and *Molino del Inca*, and the best way to see them both is to follow the course of the Aqueduct of San Telmo. This is also known as the *Molino Lario*, after the bishop who was responsible for initiating its construction towards the end of the 18th century, and it was the first to bring water to Màlaga. The architect responsible was once again José Martín de Aldehuela, and enough of it remains in decent condition to make a visit more than worthwhile.

At one time it was possible to reach the start of the aqueduct directly from the Las Pedrizas road, but this is no longer the case, and currently the best place to gain access is from the old road leading to Casabermeja.

Look for the venta, *El Túnel*, and a short way beyond that you will see a fine rural house. Travel a further 200 metres and you will reach the chapel of San Isidro. To the right – its start marked by yet another venta, *Las Pitas* – is a road which descends towards the rio Guadalmedina. Just a few minutes walk along the road will bring you to the ruins of *Molino del Inca*. It is a brick construction with fine arches still in an excellent state of repair, and from there it is a simple matter to follow the aqueduct along the course of the river. The majority of it remains as it was when it was built, although naturally enough some parts have withstood the ravages of time better than others. In one spot, however, one damaged span has been reconstructed in concrete, with no consideration for the aqueduct's history or æsthetic appearance. Obviously the work was carried out for sound commercial and utilitarian reasons, but it does bring a jarring note to the otherwise unadulterated brickwork. Among the best preserved parts are those where the sediment was purged from the water before it passed on, comparatively purified, to Málaga. Here, particularly in the spring and autumn, there are pools which teem with wildlife, including frogs and even turtles.

As you walk on you will pass the ruins of several more mills, but the other major one of note, *Molino de San Telmo*, comes almost at the end of the aqueduct, and your ramble. It is both an inspiring and slightly depressing spot, since there are two very contrasting features, besides the mill, immediately to catch the eye. One is the magnificent bridge which spans the *arroyo Hondo*, and the other is the almost inevitable rubbish tip piled high with discarded junk of all descriptions. We gaze in awe at the bridge, and disgust at the rubbish. We are here too soon. A thousand years from now, future generations of archæologists will unearth that very same tip and look upon it as a treasure house.

Jaboneros, Almendrales and Gálica y San Antón

Soap, almonds, a Gallic woman and Saint Anthony. Rural life in a nutshell. They could be the scribbled notes of some radio producer intent on creating a Spanish version of *The Archers.* In fact, the most interesting feature within these three associated districts is the small pueblo of *Ollas,* which stands 422 metres above sea level. The mundane utility of the place is captured in its very name, which means merely pots and/or pans. If we wanted to be kinder we might at a pinch translate the word as 'kettles'. Or, on fine days when the mountain sun paints every blade of grass as clearly as a Canaletto, we might take the name as being a truncated version of *ollas de río* and give the village the much more evocative name of 'pools', or even 'whirlpools'. Access is from *El Palo* or *Puerto del Leon.* It is surprising that this venerable old community has not been granted its own municipal status, since that honour has been bestowed on the even smaller pueblo of *Totalan.* A lone road leads from *Ollas* to the latter village, which has its share of interesting ruins but is outside the scope of the present volume, falling within *Axarquía.*

Ollas, meanwhile, is a wordless encapsulation of the recent history of the hills. Its simple church still stands, serving the 25 or so houses that make up the village. But the school house is closed, and only the cemetery is continuing to expand.

Though the word is derived from jabon – soap – Jaboneros is named for a lagar complex. It is to be hoped that the association of soap with the wine was not indicative of its flavour. If so, the authors might need radically to revise their views on the decline of the industry. The vicinity of *Jaboneros* is generously dotted with abandoned *lagars,* but only one has survived in its original state: *el lagar de los Llanes.*

Also still standing, and with its own small chapel, is *el Cerrado Victoria,* while in nearby *Gálica y San Antón,* the best preserved of the homesteads is *la Antigua.*

Jotrón and Lomillas

To reach this very remote district, look for km 546 on the Granada road, by the *Venta de Medina.* From this spot, a dirt track leads off to the right and crosses over the river. 2 km along the track you will find the *Ermita de Jotrón,* which was once effectively the parish church for about 11 homesteads. Easily the most important and impressive of these is *Lagar de Jotrón.* Important and impressive, but inevitably now in ruins. Its striking entrance tower has survived, but the buildings themselves are windowless and roofless. The farmstead is a kilometre east of the chapel, but it can also be approached along a track beginning at km 548 on the Granada road.

Other *lagars* in the district are, or were, *la Torre, Borondo* and an interestingly named community of five houses, *Casilla de los Frailes.* Meaning literally, 'the Friars' hut', this must presumably have served at one time as a kind of monastery, but may also be the site of a lost Moorish settlement.

La Vega

La Vega – the fertile plain – lies on the northern side of the río Guadalhorce, and is the largest of the sub-municipal districts of Málaga. It is split effectively into two – the first and second *vegas,* of which the first is the more fertile. This is the area described in Marjorie Grice-Hutchinson's book, *Málaga Farm.* Mrs Grice-Hutchinson lived and farmed here in the 1950s. She would certainly not recognise it today. More than four decades of rapid and immense change continue apace with the construction of a deep, straight outlet to carry the waters of the Guadalhorce to the sea. An area which once contained a marsh of great natural and scientific interest will disappear as the water table drops to feed the new cut. Progress is a ruthless predator and as it eats its way across the marshland, the old railway line and bridge will also vanish.

Flooding has always been both a benefit and a problem in *la Vega,* and those who ignored its power did so at their peril. The old bridge, *Puente del Rey,* now in ruins, once spanned the lowest river crossing point on the ancient Málaga to Cádiz road before the coming of the mighty N–340. Twisted piles of masonry on either side of the rushing water are all that now remains. The bridge itself has been washed away many times. The last time it happened, there was simply no point in replacing it, and the bridge and the road of which it formed part were shunted into an historical siding and forgotten.

To find it, turn off at km 7 on the Campanillas road and drive through the rough and run-down area of Los Chopos, over the railway line, and down to the river. You will need to hack your way through much jungle-like undergrowth to get to the river's edge and the rubble. 'The King's Bridge' is dead, long live the N–340. The bridge, some 400 metres in length, once formed part of a road which led around to the far side of Málaga airport and on to Churriana and Torremolinos.

Palo y Costa and Jarazmín

These two districts cover the eastern coastal area of Málaga. *El Palo* has followed the clichéd Costa del Sol path and ballooned from a fishing village to a prosperous suburb of its parent town, from where wealthy Málagueñans commute on weekdays and don't at the weekends. But it is not all luxury villas and sleek cars. There is history here too, if you know where to find it, though it is frequently hidden more carefully than a villa owner's wall safe. Take, for instance, the *Castillo de Santa Catalina.*

Castillo de Santa Catalina

Drive or walk one and a half kilometres east of Málaga's bullring, along the coastal road close to *Arroyo de Fasara,* and the modern urbanisation road system will lead you to the castle. But you will scan the skyline in vain for turreted towers and mighty stone walls. What is left of the building is now on private land, and its ruins have been incorporated into a landscape garden. However, its outer walls can be seen from the main road and if you find yourself a good enough vantage point, you will also be able to make out the old keep, which has clearly Moorish origins. Obviously the castle once commanded the approach to Málaga and would have acted as a good solid buffer. The outer walls are largely of later Christian construction and would have been defended by primitive cannon. From here a road leads to the equally elusive *Ermita de San Cristóbal.*

Ermita de San Cristóbal

The hill on which the hermitage stands has had various names. For a long time, beginning in the era of the Catholic Kings, it was known as *Cerro de San Cristóbal,* due to the presence of the hermitage. When this was abandoned, the hill quickly gained the name of *Monte Victoria.* King Ferdinand once had estates nearby, and the church of *La Virgen de la Victoria,* built and named with a flourish of triumphalism after the fall of Málaga in 1487, remains there today. However, over recent decades the hill has acquired the popular name of *Monte de las Tres Letras,* thanks to the three large letters which have been visible on its steep sides since someone decided to use it as a kind of natural billboard. The letters were originally *J. A. C.*, but these were succeeded by *C. N. T.* (the initials of one of Spain's largest trade unions – the *Confederación Nacional de Trabajores*), and subsequently others.

Further along the coast in the direction of *El Palo* is *Torre de San Telmo,* and stranded among the cement factory chimneys close to the boundary with *Rincon de la Victoria,* is *Torre Paloma.*

Torre Paloma and the Old Veléz Road

The shoreline of the Costa del Sol is studded with the remains of mediæval watchtowers, most of them built in the 15th century, although frequently on the sites of existing Moorish constructions. A giant could walk the whole of the coastline using them as stepping stones. This particular round tower stands by the sea at *Peñon del Cuervo.* Take the N–340 as far as the port of El Candado, and you will see a narrow road running between the port and a petrol station. This will lead you to the beach.

There is a curious mixture here of the old and the new, or at least the not-so-old, since, as well as the ancient tower, there are vestiges of the former coastal tramway and tunnel system, and looming over everything like a great, greedy ogre demanding tributes from the village, is an enormous cement works, with the aptly ironic name of Goliath (*Goliat*). It is impossible to avoid its influence. The entire village is coated with a fine layer of grey dust, and a few minutes in the vicinity are enough for it to find its insidious way into your eyes and the back of your throat. The coastline is beautiful and the people appear content, but it would be interesting to learn the local statistics for chest ailments and diseases of the lung. Perhaps the villagers are simply used to it, for it is clear that this has been an industrial site of one kind or another for a long time. Close to the cement works are a number of redundant 19th century lime kilns, and the evidence of former limestone quarrying is all around.

There are a number of caves along the shore at this point, and some of them have yielded important traces of Paleolithic occupancy. Sadly, virtually all of the evidence has now been destroyed.

Across the ghost of the vanished railway line, directly opposite *Peñon del Cuervo* in *Arroyo del Judio*, and forming part of the old road to Vélez, is an interesting bridge. In its present form it was constructed in the last century, but it has a long history extending as far back as 1786, and the reign of Carlos III. It is easy to find – simply drive a little way along the road which winds its way inland behind the cement works. But the experience is not a happy one. To reach the bridge and what remains of the road, you will need first to scramble over mounds of rubbish and discarded earth from industrial diggings. There is an almost tangible air of melancholy hanging over the place. This, it takes an effort to remember, was once the chief road in and out of Málaga. Generations of traders and countrymen on their way to market passed along it. In its time it saw every facet of human life: laughter, tears, anger and love. It baked in the inferno of countless Andalucían summers, and shivered under endless winter rains. Now it is forgotten and left to rot, as only yards away the new highway thunders ceaselessly with monstrous metal carts the old road's builders could only have imagined in their nightmares.

A fine archway is still visible, but the area is overgrown and dirty and strewn with rubbish. It is almost as though yesterday has been placed in the stocks like a withered strumpet and the ignorant of the town invited to taunt her with their insults and their well-aimed refuse. All around there is evidence of digging and destruction, and there is a brooding feeling that soon even the little that is left will disappear. It is said that we cannot move into the future until we let go of the past, but it is difficult to watch the past slipping away before our eyes without shedding at least a few regretful tears.

Santa Catalina and Roalabota

Except for where they encroach on the outskirts of Málaga, these areas are totally rural, and are centred on *Alcuza* at an altitude of 543 metres. Access to the region can be gained via a track which leads out of Puerto de la Torre and on to Verdiales. The most interesting features are to be found near the central town itself.

El Cerro de la Tortuga

This rocky mesa top outcrop, set on a slight incline 300 metres above sea level, was the site of an Iberian-Phœnician temple and necropolis complex. Situated on the Almogía road near to the ruined *Torre Atalaya* (Gr. Sq. 7066) 4 km from the Phœnician colony of *Malaka* and 7 km from the inland colony of *Cerro del Villar,* this consecrated hilltop dominated the surrounding area. Excavations have suggested that the site was founded between the 6th and 4th centuries BC and remained in existence until the 1st century BC, when the Romanised culture absorbed many of the local traditions.

Various phases of excavation since the 1960s have enabled us to reconstruct the complex, at least on paper. The site consisted of a temple surrounded by approximately six buildings with additional extensions. The style of construction was no further advanced than that of the late Bronze Age and consisted of a well-built wall base 3–4 feet high supporting timber and plastered clay walls topped by a thick reed roof.

The site has also yielded numerous ceramic items painted in a distinctive Iberian style. Important epigraphs and scratchings have also been unearthed, some of which suggest Phœnician writing. There are also drawings of animals, including an elephant. Elephants were abundant at that time in North Africa, but there is little evidence that they were wandering freely in Spain. We may tentatively conclude, therefore, that either the painter or his model was in exile.

During the excavations, munitions from the Spanish Civil War were uncovered. This should come as no surprise since the outcrop occupies a dominant position from which the southern approaches to the suburbs of Málaga could be protected. The mesa top would have played an important part in the defence of the city during the Nationalist advance of 1937.

To reach the site of the Phœnician temple and necropolis, aim for the east of the city and the new Málaga dual carriageway by-pass. At junction km 245, turn left and head for the small suburb of Teatinos. From this point you will easily see the prominent limestone mesa hilltop of *El Cerro de la Tortuga* (Turtle Hill) as well as the Moorish tower, *Torre Atalaya.* The only access to the Cerro is via the river bridge immediately to the west of the suburb. You will find it between two residential complexes. The steep waste land, climbing approximately 120 metres in half a kilometre, leads directly to the limestone outcrop and a final quick scramble up the rock face leads you to the mesa hill top itself.

You are more likely to be initially impressed by the views rather than the ruins. The spot commands an excellent view of the city of Málaga and its cathedral, and also in line of sight is the Moorish fortress of *Castillo de Gibralfaro.* 11 km to the south are the cliffs of Torremolinos. *Cerro de la Tortuga* was the last high ground before the cliffs, in the now silted up estuary of the Guadalhorce. Only the Phœnician island settlement of *Cerro del Villar* (see Torremolinos) has been found in what was once a vast open waterway.

In spite of the great age of *Cerro de la Tortuga*, numerous excavated walls remain to be seen, along with some primitive rendering. A natural crack in the hilltop seems to have been made use of to form the rock walls of a building, and at the highest point a large deep pit can be found that was once part of the main temple itself. Below the southerly rock face is a large overhang which may have been linked to the deep pit.

It is interesting to note that when the Moors built their lookout post to protect the city and the estuary, they chose a hill top 2km inland. (See Torre Atalaya.)

Torre Atalaya

A suburb called *Puerto de la Torre* has grown up at the base of the hill on which this mediæval construction stands. Though in ruins today, two of its sides are intact and still manage to dominate the landscape. To visit the site, head for *Puerto de la Torre*, but avoid the modern road into the 'Puerto' cutting, since this leads directly into the suburb. Take instead the road to the left and park your car once you have turned the corner.

Be well prepared, for this is not a gentle climb and in parts it becomes an exhausting scramble, although the hilltop itself is gentle enough and not an outcrop. The views are in the main similar to those of the Phœnician temple site, but Málaga itself cannot be seen. This place undoubtedly helped to protect one of the inland approaches into the city during the Moorish and subsequent Christian periods.

La Concepción

Lovers of fine gardens should not miss a visit to *La Concepción*. It is well signposted and easily found, just off the new bypass junction with the Granada road and close to a large dam. The gardens were the mid-19th century brainchild of the Marquis and Marchioness of Casa Loring, who set out to recreate the feel of a tropical forest in continental Europe. How well they succeeded is apparent within minutes of the visitor's arrival. Like all great gardens, La Concepción must be seen and experienced. No amount of description can satisfactorily convey the kaleidoscope of colours and smells amid the whispering silence. No mere list of plants, no plan of the meandering pathways, no dry catalogue of trees can even come close.

La Concepción was an immediate triumph. By the end of the 19th century it was already a firm fixture on most tourists' itineraries. In 1943 it was officially designated a garden of exceptional historical and botanical interest and in 1990 ownership passed to Málaga City Hall. The authorities, without a green finger between them, wisely passed it into the care of experts. The independent *Patronato Botánico Municipal 'Ciudad de Málaga'* scientific organisation happily took the reins. Under its auspices, the gardens were formally opened to the public on June 21st 1994. Among its many visitors are around 30,000 schoolchildren each year, for the regional government considers it important to foster environmental awareness. The children are not merely talked at. In one winter alone, 42,000 of them were involved in a reforestation project.

Nor is that all. Within the gardens there is a school where youngsters can learn the secrets of gardening, nursery gardening, irrigation installation and, oddly, bricklaying.

Except for members of the Association of Friends of La Concepción, who have the privilege of enjoying the gardens at their leisure, visits are restricted to guided tours lasting roughly an hour and a quarter. The gardens are open all year round with the exception of Christmas Day and New Year's Day. Opening time is 10:00am, but closing time varies from 5:30pm in the winter to 9:00pm in the summer. The last tour each day commences one and a half hours before closing time.

Verdiales

This very rural district contains approximately seventeen homesteads, the ruins of a Moorish lookout tower, and an inevitable hermitage church.

There are times when it seems that the history of Spain is an endless story of people wishing to flee the pressures of contemporary life and to seek solace in undisturbed religious contemplation. Certainly in this part of Andalucía it is sometimes difficult to toss a stone into the air without it coming down on a ruined hermitage. The particular refuge at *Verdiales*, and the tower which stands close by, are located on an ancient route which links the Casabermeja road in the north to the head of the Guadalhorce river, west of Málaga. The track can be found at km 24 on the Málaga-Casabermeja road, and to drive along it you will need to have a good off-road vehicle. Hikers can leave their transport at the start of the track and enjoy a long walk through scenery from a landscape painter's dreams. It runs due south along a ridge which starts 500 metres above sea level and rises a further 100 metres in the 3 km you will need to drive or walk to reach the Moorish tower. A thousand feet below, the traffic hurries purposefully by along the modern highway – its noise and choking fumes both sucked away and lost in the silence of the hills. At times it is possible to forget the car rattling about you, or your feet trudging mundanely along the path, and imagine yourself flying free above the world. Follow the track to its natural conclusion, and eventually you will emerge on the far side of Málaga.

The terraced hills are clear evidence that this has been heavily cultivated land since at least the time of the Moors. Today the whole area is contained within a national park, and the pathside is liberally dotted with old country houses – *fincas* – not all of them deserted. One which is has the poignant message *NO ROBAR* (Don't steal) daubed on the wall beside its ever-open door.

Each building has been numbered by the authorities and bears a blue metal plaque giving its details. This is true even of the hermitage, which you will pass as you make you way to what remains of the Moorish watchtower. The hermitage, happily, is not in ruins, or at least not entirely so. The right hand side of the building has lost its roof and the shells of the rooms it once sheltered are now open to the elements and overgrown. In spite of this, it is a very striking building with an almost triangular facade rising to a sharp point, which, no doubt deliberately, directs our attention to Heaven. Except for the ruined portion on the right, it has a fine tiled roof, and is set in a spot of exceptional beauty. Sadly, though perhaps with reason considering the heartfelt plea written across the face of our abandoned finca, the door to the roofed section is securely locked and it is not possible to enter. There is a barred but glassless window on the left hand side of the building through which you can peer into a room jammed with piled chairs, stepladders and the broken remains of wooden cabinets. The hermitage, it would seem, has become little more than a lumber room.

Even with the modern world careering on its crazy and temporarily forgotten way in eerie silence a thousand feet below, it is difficult genuinely to grasp the sheer remoteness of places such as this in earlier times. We can drive up from the valley and return to our homes or hotels in an afternoon. For those who built and lived in this building, it was as far from the bustling streets of Málaga as the far side of the moon. Clearly it was a place designed for the contemplation not only of the mysteries of heaven, but of earthly beauty and natural wonders. In our comparatively godless times, we too often forget that the two were once considered to be inextricably linked. The natural world was the work of God, and the study of one brought us inevitably closer to the other. Science and religion have, to a great extent, gone their separate ways and we leave it to the reader to decide which path, if either, leads us closer to contentment and the truth.

Leave the hermitage behind, and walk on along the track to the stump of the ruined Moorish tower, and you will be rewarded with a view of Málaga which, even on an indifferent day, will take your breath away. On a day when the air is clear and the sun is shining on a sea made from silvered glass, it is almost beyond description. From here the defenders of the Moorish kingdom had commanding views of the entire valley, and the tower stands in direct line of sight to Málaga castle. News of any hostile approach could be transmitted immediately by beacon.

Most of the tower is gone. Like so much that the Moors left behind them, it would have been deliberately destroyed by the conquering Christians. What remains is a defiant, solid stump which still stands guard over the valley like a faithful dog which will not leave the grave of its master.

Montes de Málaga

Under this convenient heading we can throw together a number of regions:

Chaperas-Madroñal, Moheda Portales, Arroyo de la Vacas, Tres Chaperas, Cerro del Moro, Vuelta Grande and finally *Santo Pitar.*

Together they form a vast and sparsely populated rural area, which is far too great to be explored in a single day, or even two. However, *Puerto del Leon* does have a camp site, so those wishing to pitch their tents and take their time can certainly do so. And those without tents and a fear of ghosts might be even more adventurous and spend their nights in one of the numerous ruined *lagars.*

Five kilometres north-west of the pass and camp site is yet another ruined hermitage – the *ermita del Cerro del Moro.* Arab dwellers in Christian hermitages were never more than a piquant novelty, so we can be reasonably certain that the hermitage replaced a long forgotten mosque. To the north of the Málaga boundary, in *Casabermeja, Colmenar* and *Comares,* are a number of prehistoric monuments. There is always the next hill, the next valley, the next town along the road. But this book is about the province of Málaga, and though boundaries are at best inventions and at worst mere aberrations of the human mind, here we must stop.

Chapter Four

Alhaurín el Grande

Historical Background

THE SIERRA DE MIJAS had human inhabitants long before it had a name. In the forested areas south-east of what is now the village of Alhaurín el Grande there are traces of Neolithic occupation – the first stirrings of Man's need to settle down somewhere and make himself a home. The old hunter-gatherer cultures were giving way to fixed settlements with a surprisingly high degree of sophistication in farming, animal husbandry, and even religious thought. But if these people felt the need to give each hill, each valley, every part of their gods' creation a name, they lacked the means to pass that knowledge on, and their words are as lost as the smoke from their long-dead fires.

As towns and villages grew more permanent, they needed names simply for people to know where they were. This may seem like a fatuous observation, but consider the fundamental conceptual shift that is involved in the move from a nomadic to a settled existence. The wandering hunter-gatherers, living and moving across the land in small family groups, would have felt as one with the world around them. Their territory, whether they were hill folk, valley people or plains dwellers, was the Universe. They travelled across it knowing only that this spot was good for hunting, that one for water, and that they should beware of the forest beyond the hill, for there there be tygers. The coming of the fixed settlement changed all that. For the first time certain parts of the land became individual and significant in human terms. It was necessary to codify that concept in order to make meaningful communication possible. To a nomad, the question, 'Where are you from?' has no meaning. A man from a town or village, when asked the same thing, could hardly be expected to embark on a long and tedious geographical description of its location. It was far easier to give it a name. The practice is so universal, and so taken for granted by us today, that we have forgotten what an extraordinary evolutionary advance the concept was. It was the intellectual equivalent of the invention of the wheel or the taming of fire. For good or ill, in pride or insufferable arrogance, the giving of names was Mankind's way, not only of making sense of his world, but also of laying claim to it and all that it contained.

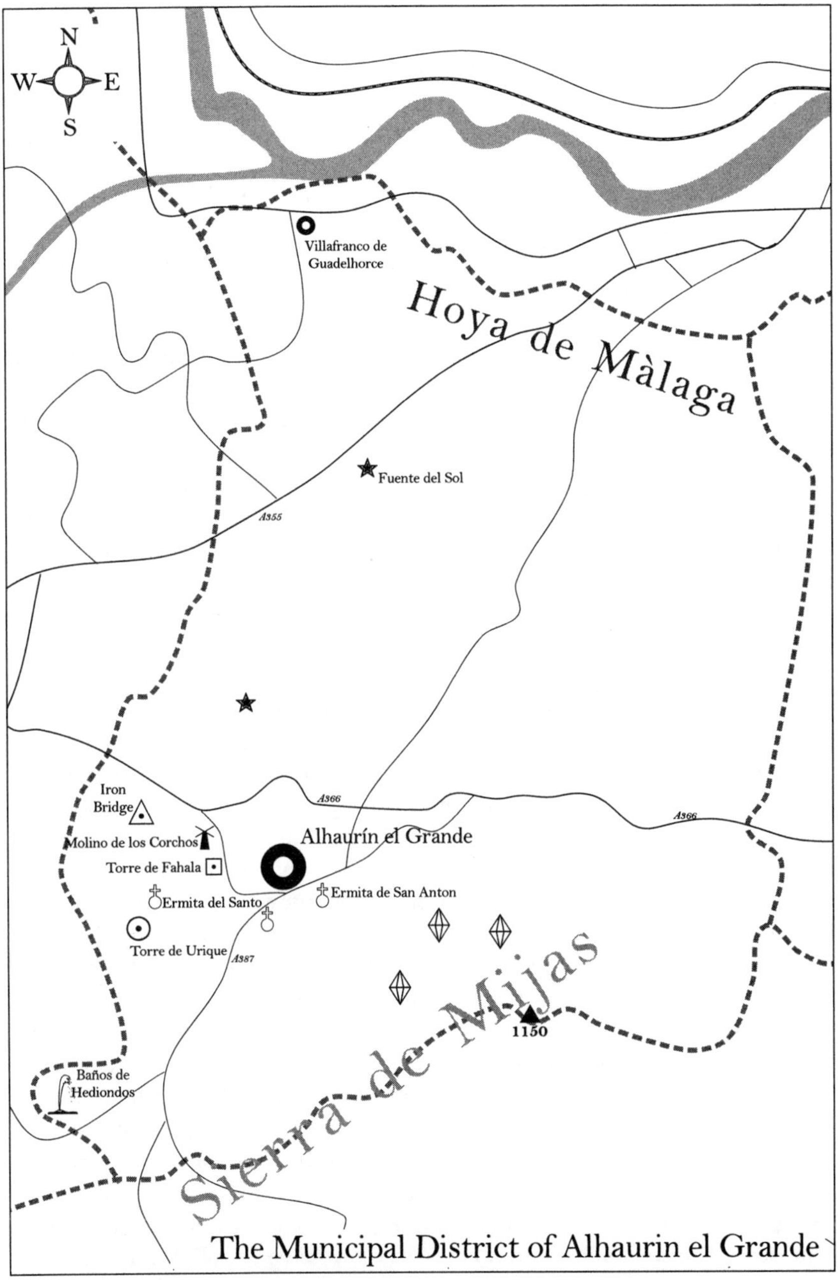
N
W
E
S
Villafranco de Guadelhorce
Hoya de Màlaga
Fuente del Sol
A355
Iron Bridge
A366
A366
Alhaurín el Grande
Molino de los Corchos
Torre de Fahala
Ermita de San Anton
Ermita del Santo
Torre de Urique
A387
Sierra de Mijas
1150
Baños de Hediondos
The Municipal District of Alhaurin el Grande

Place names often survive long after those who bestowed them have gone, and the reason for the naming with them. Close to Alhaurín el Grande, for example, a bare hilltop carries the name *El Castillo.* Along with *castillejo* and other variations, it is a common hill name in Andalucía. Where it appears, we can fairly assume that the hill once featured a castle or fort, possibly a Bronze Age settlement. But this is, as here, often mere speculation. Certainly Iberian and Phœnician settlements were numerous in the hills around Málaga, and the two peoples developed firm trading links.

When the Romans arrived, like an aggressive new board of directors taking over a tired company and sweeping the cobwebs out of the boardroom and the dead wood out of the factory, there were the inevitable sackings and redundancies, and many of the hillside villages disappeared.

The favoured ones were Romanised. When new men take over, there is always the odd promotion to sweeten the bitter pill of change. One Iberian settlement, previously nameless so far as history is concerned, became the Roman town of *Lauro Nova.* Towns are like popular entertainers. Some burn brightly for a short time and are then *passé* and quickly forgotten. Others take hold of the public imagination and go on to be enduring superstars. In between are the solid, unspectacular artists who somehow survive on the club circuit by adapting, like true professionals, to changing times and fashions. A new hairstyle, some fresh songs, a change of name. Alhaurín el Grande is such a place. The nameless Iberian village, bottom of the bill in a summer season revue, not only survived the coming of the Romans, but actually made a name for itself. When the Romans exited stage left and made way for the Moors, it ditched it and re-emerged as *Alhaurín* – 'Garden of Allah'. That's the way to last in this, or any other business – go with the flow, roll with the punches, and always give the public what it wants. Today the town still thrives in its impressively quiet way, with a population of around 18,000. It has a new, not particularly attractive, face, with many modern un-Garden-of-Allah-ish buildings, especially on its outskirts. But like the old trouper it is, it has lots of heart. It knows which songs are the showstoppers, and resolutely keeps them in its act. The old part of town is like a cameo – a medley of old hits set nostalgically among the techno-boogie of the nineties to keep the older fans happy at the back.

The Romans liked what they found. And why not? The valleys were fertile, and the hills were heavy with valuable mineral deposits. The invaders came in droves, and the area around the town today is dotted with rustic Roman villas, as well as statues, carved stones, inscriptions and Roman columns. There is also a small 1st century Roman aqueduct. Marble and jasper are still quarried nearby and the river which feeds the town is fed by mineral springs from the Sierra de Mijas. During the construction of the road to Coín, some Roman tombs were found close to the chalet of Huerta del Niño. A fine and well-preserved stone funeral plaque suggested that the tombs were those of an important, perhaps noble, family.

The Visigothic era was a time of solid, if unspectacular development. To return to the show-biz analogy, Lauro Nova was resting. Things were slow, but it saw no need yet for radical change. That had to wait for the Moors, who burst on the scene shortly after AD 711, with little advance publicity, and took the place by storm. They decided that what the place needed, apart from a new name and a definite change of cuisine, was a castle. They built it on a hill which was ultimately given the name of *Torres de Fahala* (the rio Fahala is the region's chief river). Torres de Fahala was an ideal place for a fort, and had probably been the site of a Phœnician village in what was even then the remote past. Life in and around the newly re-named Alhaurín el Grande was peaceful, by and large, except for the brief period of rebellion led by the restless Omar ben Hafsun in 879. It was probably under the Moors that the present site of the village became fixed. Although Lauro Nova and Alhaurín el Grande can, for all practical purposes, be considered one and the same, the Roman Settlement is thought to have been centred a little to the east towards Coín, in the area known as *Huertas Bajas.* A Moorish gate to 'the garden of Allah' somehow managed to survive the destructive zeal of the Christians when they overran the town and the castle in the fateful year of 1485, and it stands as a lonely reminder of the Arab years to this day.

It goes without saying that the castle was not so lucky. The Moors fought valiantly to defend it and consequently, when it finally fell, the Christians celebrated their hard-won victory by demolishing it stone by stone and putting a church in its place. The systematic obliteration of the Moors' defences and places of worship, and their rapid replacement by imposing symbols of Christianity as the Reconquest firmly took its hold, frequently rolled beyond the boundaries of brutish triumphalism. The Christians were heady with success and anxious to mould a new post-Arab nation. It was not enough that the Moors should be beaten or driven out. They must be stomped into the ground and erased from the earth and history. It is an approach much favoured by tyrants throughout the centuries, and it is sad that the destructive hawks were not balanced by a few more visionary doves who, even at a time of great emotional fervour, understood that a nation is the sum of all its history, and not merely the few elements which are currently in the ascendant. In particular the visible symbols of Moorish religion had to be pulverised, and the souls of the faithful outraged by a deliberate and brazen two-finger salute to them and their Prophet. The philosophy of the time, had it been reduced to a simple nursery rhyme, might have been, 'See a mosque and burn it down – Build a church upon the ground'. In the case of Alhaurín el Grande, the 'church upon the ground' is the now restored 16th century *Iglesia de la Encarnación.*

Some smaller, outlying Moorish villages, like Benamaquis and Fahala, were totally eliminated as new Christian settlers arrived, determined to make a fresh start in what was effectively Year Zero.

When we speak of ancient rural settlements, we necessarily resort to words such as 'village' and 'town', but such terminology can be misleading. It is easy to look at a place like Alhaurín el Grande today and imagine it as a large village of roughly comparable size thronged with Romans, Moors, Christians, or whoever controlled it at various points of its history. It is almost impossible to picture how tiny such settlements once were. Although it had existed in one form or another for centuries, the population of Alhaurín el Grande in 1492 was no more than 350. Not enough to fill the seats of even a modest theatre. A disastrous crowd for a home tie at Halifax Town. It would be another hundred years before they could celebrate the birth of citizen 1000, and even by the middle of the 17th century they still numbered less than 1500. Obviously the expulsion of the Moors must have initially depleted the population, but contrast the pace of expansion with the 20th-century experience of places such as Torremolinos and Fuengirola, which exploded from dots too small for the average map into heavily populated modern cities within a generation.

Another wave of expulsions from the town followed the Morisco uprising in 1570, but the population remained stable thanks to fresh waves of migrants from Extremadura and Galicia. We speak of expulsions and immigration glibly, as though the Moors were simply switched off like lights to vanish from human sight and sensibility, while a new set of actors took the stage and continued the story. The truth is far more complex, as truth always is. Expelled Moors had to go somewhere, and in the days before internal combustion and the jet engine, that was usually not very far. They formed close-knit, wary communities, suspicious of strangers. Stripped of their former power and wealth, the communities tended to be isolated and poor. In time, the descendants of the Moors who stayed would become Spaniards, lost in the mix by intermarriage and osmosis, but it is still possible to find small rural mountain outposts where the people seem a little darker skinned than usual, and where the sight of an unknown face or the arrival of a strange motor car is enough to still conversation in the bars and the squares and to draw a cautious stare.

One thing which drastically affected the growth of Alhaurín el Grande, as it affected almost the entire known world, was the epidemic of plague in 1605. The Black Death, originating in China and Turkestan, first came to Europe in the 14th century. Millions – an estimated third of the continent's entire population – died. Many believed it was the retribution of God for the sins of Mankind and that the world was at an end. In a way it was. It left the world unimaginably changed, and although it never returned with quite the same virulence, it was a recurrent problem for centuries thereafter. In the province of Málaga, the epidemic of 1605 resulted in more than 20,000 deaths. How many died in Alhaurín el Grande is unknown, but the twenty-bed hospital of Santa Catalina was hopelessly inadequate, and the dead were often left in the streets to rot and spread the infection. Since Alhaurín's population at that time was scarcely more than a thousand, it is a miracle that it survived as a community at all. Many less fortunate villages were wiped out.

Seventy-five years later another disaster struck the still recovering town. An earthquake destroyed 122 houses, causing seven deaths and dozens of injuries. If the plague was indeed the wrath of God, the earthquake must have seemed like a short, sharp reminder that it had not been totally appeased. Alhaurín searched its communal conscience and vowed to do better.

War in the twentieth century has been waged on a scale unimaginable to our ancestors, even our closest ones. We have seen cities destroyed by a single bomb sent halfway around the world, and counted in horror the millions of dead. We have proved to Nature that in War we have a self-inflicted pestilence the equal of the plague itself. It was the Great War of 1914–18 which ended forever the romantic notion that inter-tribal, international conflict was in some way the noble pursuit of gallant officers and stalwart men. And it was left to the poets to mark the change.

But war was always misery and tears and the wild futility of unleashed madness. After the earthquake of 1680, Alhaurín el Grande was untouched by disaster until 1810 when, during the War of Independence, French troops arrived to occupy the town and wreak a new brand of havoc. They remained until they were ejected after a battle in 1814. Needless to say, the occupation left its mark. The *Ermita de Santa Vera Cruz* was destroyed by bombardment, during which 108 of the townspeople died. The church has been rebuilt, and the present building bears a plaque commemorating the dead. (See below)

With the French gone, Alhaurín returned slowly to life and its agricultural roots. By 1850 it boasted 30 streets and 1,115 houses. The coming of the railway tied it firmly to Málaga for the first time and opened up new opportunities. But its peaceful development was interrupted, as it was bound to be, by the Civil War of the 1930s. At the outbreak of the war it was firmly in the hands of the Republicans. As elsewhere, they turned their anger on all things clerical (the Church was seen as General Franco's Fifth Column), and few church buildings escaped damage. The Republican domination ended in 1937 when the Nationalists took the town, wreaked their inevitable vengeance, and then left the *pueblo* to carry on.

The Pueblo of Alhaurín el Grande

The main church of Alhaurín el Grande, the *Iglesia de la Encarnación*, is oddly unsatisfying. Until the latter years of our present overly materialistic century, the parish church was at the centre of every community's life. It was a place of joy, celebration and sorrow, and any building which is witness to such a concentration of emotion over many hundreds of years absorbs the feelings until they drip from every crevice and hang in the air like a constant wordless hum on the outer edge of audibility. A tangible miasma which wrings respectful silence from even the most unspiritual. It is that which is inexplicably missing from the *Iglesia de la Encarnación*. The building itself is large and unexceptional, and it now stands among a cluster of bars and shops like a great white warehouse. It has recently undergone a great deal of restoration and repair, but none of this is enough to explain the apparent cold emptiness at its heart. For this church, no less than any other, has seen its share of triumphs and tragedies. Like other churches in Andalucía, it suffered badly during the Civil War. To the right, as you enter, is a statue of the Virgin in a niche in the wall. A sign beneath tells you that it is a replacement for an original destroyed by a mob during the conflict. There are other reminders of such uncontrolled fury here and there.

Yet still the building does not hum. All the churchly attributes are there. The ground on which it is built is hallowed enough. It stands on the site of the sacked Arab mosque, and the base of its tower may well have been the base of the old minaret. It has a fine altar, a brooding confessional, long since blackened by the darkness of its secrets, and the inevitable mechanical votive candles which have everywhere replaced the genuine article. No need for matches now. Simply drop 25 pesetas into the slot as though you were buying a drink from a vending machine, and the next candle in line will light up and automatically deliver your prayer. There is, as yet, no discount for two. Yet in spite of its history and its pedigree, the light, airy *Iglesia de la Encarnación* has the feel of an airport departure lounge where the faithful wait, some with more patience than others, for the boarding call to Heaven.

The original post-Reconquest church was small, but it serviced an area far greater than the immediate municipal district. Over time it was enlarged until, by 1863, it reached the size that we see today.

Close by is a piece of Moorish Alhaurín which inexplicably survived the wilful destruction of the mosque on whose ruins the Christian church was raised. The *Arcos de Cobertizo* is a 12th-century archway which now leads nowhere, but which may once have represented one of the main entrances to the Arab town. On the inner side is a small paved square directly adjacent to the back wall of the church. Foliage and undergrowth now block the arch's exit, but beyond that a steep street leads away down the hillside. There is little doubt that in the distant past this was a track which led travellers to the gateway and into the town.

It is difficult to know exactly when ancient structures acquired the names by which we know them. The word *cobertizo* has two meanings. The first of these is 'pent-roof' – i.e. a roof which slopes on only one side ... This seems a singularly inappropriate name to give to an arch. Its second meaning – 'shed' – is more prosaic still. Again, there seems no reason to believe that the arch was ever connected to anything which could sensibly be described as a shed. Perhaps the name was given to it long after its original purpose had been forgotten, when its only practical use was as a shelter from the heat of summer and the winter rains? The arch has obviously been heavily reconstructed, and a plaque on its inner wall tells us that students from the Escuela Taller Fahala carried out the work during 1997.

From this spot follow the road up to the *Ermita de San Sebastián.* This 17th-century hermitage was built in the wake of the Moriscos' final expulsion, and was intended to ensure that the remaining population stayed devoutly

Catholic. From here it is a short walk to the *Ermita de la Santa Vera Cruz*, Alhaurín el Grande's second church.

This younger sister of La Iglesia de la Encarnación stands in a small plaza, *Plaza del Ayuntamiento*, high on the hill overlooking the splendid valley. It is flanked by the police station and, as the astute will have guessed, the town hall, the *ayuntamiento.* They stand shoulder to shoulder like three sideshow booths at a fairground offering a choice of God, Temporal Justice and Bureaucracy. Roll up, pay your money, and put your faith in whichever takes your fancy. Although the Ermita de la Santa Vera Cruz as it exists today is hardly a century old, it is built on the ashes of the 16th-century building destroyed by French troops during the War of Independence. Traces of its ancient walls are still visible behind and to the right of it. The church was reconstructed and reconsecrated in the 1920s and, like the more venerable Iglesia de la Encarnación, its outer wall bears an inscription carved, rather unhelpfully, in white on white marble. Imagine writing in white ink on white paper, bleaching the result and attempting to read it under a halogen lamp, and you will have some idea of the effect. Staring at the brilliant white slab beneath a blazing Andalucían sun and trying desperately to decipher the secret of its words is to invite sudden blindness, but the diligent researcher snaps his fingers in the face of danger in his constant quest for truth, and of such stern stuff are the present authors made. The commemorative slab was unveiled on the 75th anniversary of the church's reconsecration, and celebrates the event, but it is also dedicated to the memory of the more than one hundred citizens who died defending the town from the French invaders.

Of greater interest than the church are the three Roman pillars which stand on modern brick bases in the adjoining piazza. Discovered locally, at *Fuente del Sol* (see below) and *Mata,* they now stare out across a valley that their builders knew only too well. At night the same stars that lit the sky when they were new and proud and had a purpose still look down, but now they stand before the church, the police station and the *ayuntamiento* like three shivering vagrants wondering what to do when the dawn comes. Oddly, a fourth brick base has been laid nearby, but is empty. Whether this is a spare, optimistically awaiting the discovery of a fourth column, or whether it marks the site of a daring Roman column robbery, is not immediately clear.

After living for a time in the isolated village of Yegen, which was the setting for his famous *South From Granada* (1957), the Malta-born writer and Hispanophile Gerald Brenan lived for many years in Alhaurín el Grande, even though his uncompromising books, including *The Face of Spain* and *The Spanish Labyrinth,* frequently upset General Franco. Today his complete works have pride of place in the local library. When he died in 1987 at the age of 92, his body was taken to Málaga University's Faculty of Medicine for use in medical research, as had been his wish. There it was embalmed and placed in a preserving solution while the grateful doctors decided what to do with it. More than a decade later it was still there, having been used merely to demonstrate the technique of tissue preservation. Interesting, but probably not what Brenan had in mind. The custodians of the remains declared that the body could continue to be used for that purpose for at least another half century. That would sorely test the dead writer's posthumous patience. He had expected students to prod, probe and dissect his mortal remains before they were taken away to be buried beside his American-born wife, the writer Gamel Woosley, in Málaga's English Cemetery. In 1998, residents of Alhaurín el Grande formally petitioned the mayor of the town to arrange for the body to be released for burial. In addition, they wanted his wife's body exhumed, and for both of them to be given a final resting place in a special tomb in their own San Gaudencio cemetery.

One man who is unlikely to have added his voice to the clamour for the return of Alhaurín's adopted son is the owner of the town's most amazing bar – the Bar Costales. After a hot, dry day in the hills and valleys, seek it out. On the wall beside the entrance are painted the words *pequeño museo* – small museum. They are inadequate to describe the astonishing array of disconnected bric-a-brac which fills every corner. Articles of genuine historical interest – posters, old photographs, agricultural implements, a rusting conquistador's helmet – are squeezed together like commuters on a Japanese train with an endless succession of kitsch contemporary ephemera from key rings to crested golf balls and dolls. Each time the eye strays to the display cabinets or the walls, it picks out something new, and often something unashamedly obscene.

Life in the Bar Costales is a continual performance, and the star of the show is undoubtedly the owner and chief barman, Antonio, a man whose sense of humour now resides in the sewer, after many years of squatting in the gutter. Antonio, a victim of throat-cancer, finds it difficult to speak, and uses his lugubrious face to switch effortlessly from Buster Keaton impassiveness to feigned bewilderment at the effect of his increasingly earthy jests on his female clients, and finally to a disarming grin reminiscent of *Carry On* actor, Sid James.

The Bar Costales is not a place in which to sing loudly the praises of Spain's new democracy. Antonio clearly thinks very little of it. The current Prime Minister, José María Aznar, has his head in a birdcage above the bar along with a baby's dummy. From time to time Antonio will spin the cage around and make him whistle. That is the least of his worries. Look around the walls and you will see him constantly lampooned in suggestive and obscene ways along with other contemporary politicians of whom Antonio disapproves, which is to say virtually everybody. Pride of place on his walls goes to flag-bedecked pictures of his political heroes. He appears to stop short of Hitler, although some explorers of the bar's darker corners have reported sightings of Mussolini. Top of the list is Generalíssimo Francisco Franco. The only post-Franco political figure who receives his unqualified respect and admiration is Lieut. Col. Antonio Tejero Molina who, on February 23rd 1981, led a group of armed Civil Guards into the *Cortes* and attempted the world's first prime-time televised coup. His attempt to shoot down Spain's fledgling democracy before it had time to learn to fly failed, but he became a hero to many who would rather have the trains run on time than vote.

If all of this makes the Bar Costales sound like a lewd and reactionary place to which no gentleman would escort a sensitive lady, and from which the politically correct would recoil in horror and dismay, so it is. That it is also a place of warmth and infinite good humour is a reminder that all life is a paradox. There is, after all, sweet irony in Antonio's vicious lampooning of Spain's democratic leaders, and the very concept of democracy itself. A bar which treated General Franco in the same way a few decades ago would have been shut down in minutes and its owner thrown into jail or worse. The Bar Costales is not a condemnation of democracy. In spite of Antonio's best efforts, it is a celebration of it. And the bizarre conjunction of the significant and the trivial, the old and the new, among his museum's exhibits tells a story too. History is not simply weathered stones and unread pages in dusty, yellowing books. It is a million endless stories being written every day. Each of us is the hero or heroine of one, the villain of another, and an insignificant extra in a thousand more. Unless you share Antonio's taste in politics and humour, you will have to leave at least some of your sensibilities at the door of the Bar Costales, like checking in your gun at a wild west saloon. It is worth it. Buy yourself a drink and simply smile and wonder at it all.

Ermita de San Anton

On the eastern side of the new north–south bypass is the *Ermita de San Anton.* Though it once stood in proud isolation, it is now so lost among shabby streets and houses that discovering its entrance delivers the same thrill of achievement felt by those who escape from Hampton Court maze while their friends are still trapped inside and yelling for help. The hermitage is said to have Visigothic origins, and this appears to stem from the fact that when the site was first noted after the Christian reconquest in 1500, a number of tombs were found in its vicinity which contained brooches and crosses strongly indicative of Visigothic burials. This may be misleading, however, since a Christian community seems to have survived on the site even after the Moorish invasion of 711. An inscribed tombstone from the period, measuring 1m x 1.5m, stood at the foot of the altar until the church was looted during the Civil War. It disappeared and was probably smashed to pieces, but it is intriguing to wonder if instead it found its way into some local home where it remains as a doorstop or a table, or perhaps even as an object of veneration.

Eventually the Christian community vanished, though whether by natural wastage or coercion it is difficult to say. Perhaps there was a little of both. Whatever the case, the abandoned hermitage was replaced by a small mosque. When the Christians returned, they naturally wanted to reclaim their sacred site. Out went the mosque and back came the hermitage. The lower structure of the present building dates from the 17th century, and special note should be taken of the bricks in the doorway. However, much of the upper structure was destroyed in the Civil War and rebuilt during the 1940s.

Ermita del Cristo de la Agonia

Places of worship come in all shapes and sizes. Leave the village by the Mijas-Fuengirola road and you will pass, on your right, a shrine which must surely be a candidate for the *Guinness Book of Records.* The tiny *Ermita del Cristo de la Agonia*, standing within sight of the ruins of *Torres de Fahala*, was built in 1783 by Don Francisco Vicente. He felt it was needed because of Alhaurín's rapidly growing population. Since it is too small comfortably to accommodate more than a handful of worshippers, it might be considered something of a token gesture. Nevertheless, it remains popular as a place of private prayer and is much used during the town's annual fiestas.

Baños Hediondos – The Roman Baths

There are few visible and tangible relics of Roman occupation around Alhaurín el Grande, or Lauro Nova, but one excellent and notable one can be found in a valley which appears to have survived the centuries without a durable name. Drive away from the Hurique tower, past a site reserved for the creation of the proposed urbanisation of *Las Delicias*, and you will find a ramblers' track leading down from the hills. If you are riding in a good off-road vehicle the track is perfectly negotiable. If not, you will need to park and walk. If you do drive, however, be wary of hikers, for the path is narrow and winding and you may well encounter walkers going down at a brisk pace or returning somewhat more slowly. On the valley floor is a fast-running stream of crystal-clear water. Along the hills on its far bank there are definite signs of an old trackway, perhaps the remnants of an ancient donkey track or aqueduct. Follow the river a little way upstream and soon you are in a surreal landscape of slippery serpentine rocks which, with a smidgen of imagination, transform themselves into a kind of miniature mountain range over which you are flying like some soaring bird. Try not to disturb the illusion by losing your footing and sliding clownishly into the cold reality of the water. Suddenly and incongruously, you will find yourself staring at the unmistakable remains of a Roman bath. A set of perfectly carved steps leads into a deep, circular pool with a masoned surround. Here, on a hot, Andalucían day, you might be tempted to strip off and soak yourself in its cool luxury. The pool now forms part of the stream itself, but originally it would have been on the bank and fed from the waters by a system of conduits. Who came to bathe in this remote spot? Was this the private domain of some wealthy villa owner whose name and achievements have been swallowed by the years? Or was this place renowned for its water and its beauty and drew visitors in droves to share its benefits, like the sulphur baths at Manilva? Such questions tumble through the mind like leaves caught on a fast-flowing river. Although the local people know of the site, they seem relatively indifferent to it and a request for its name will invariably be met with a shrug and a muttered '*Los baños*'. Since this means simply 'the baths', we need not cry *eureka!* In a sense, this nonchalance is almost refreshing. The valley is inaccessible enough not to have been found and utilised (yet) by the otherwise ubiquitous dumpers of domestic rubbish, and the sparkling waters of the stream cascade across country that is markedly free from the usual human debris of soft-drink cans, bottles and snack-food packets.

Such signs, though, are not far away. On a hill beside the stream stands the shattered skeleton of an old building. Too small to have been a convincing farmhouse, it was probably once used to house workers of some description. Its proximity to the Roman bath suggests at least some tenuous connection, although the building itself would appear to be no more than a century or two old. There are suggestions that it was a kind of dressing, or undressing, room for visitors, and there may have been primitive showers inside, fed by the stream. There is another possibility, to which we shall turn in a moment, but the initial impression on reaching the building is a sad one. Our joy at finding an idyllic spot so free from the polluting tendencies of Man is rudely shattered. Broken bottles, discarded cans, empty food cartons and the remains of a fire are silent witnesses to the fact that this has become a favourite place for revelry. Ramblers are not, on the whole, renowned for their riotous behaviour, and the genuine lover of country walks takes care not to leave such ugly signs of his passing. The nature of the accumulated rubbish suggests that those who deposited, and continue to deposit, it are young – possibly bikers out to test their machines and themselves on the steep slopes and twisting tracks.

Though the people of the area seem unable to give a name to the baths, they do have one. Perhaps the locals are merely reluctant to acknowledge them, for they are known as *los Baños Hediondos* – the 'foul-smelling baths'. This name is shared by *los Baños de la Hedionda* in Manilva, but whereas that more famous spot richly deserves the description (see Manilva), there is here no hint of the sulphurous odour that inspired it. The baths at Alhaurín el Grande are fed by a spring, and they never quite became the attraction that other spas did, chiefly because of their relative inaccessibility and a reputation for inclement weather. Nevertheless, the waters were highly regarded, and if Mahomet was too feeble and infirm to go to the mountain, the mountain had to go to Mahomet, or in this case Paco, Maria and Juan José. Water was taken from the baths to the homes of invalids, even the blind, in the hope of curing their ills.

Within a hundred yards of the ruined building, on either side of a steep gully, are the remains of two primitive lime kilns. This is sandstone country, but there are traces of limestone to be found in the rocks. The kilns would have been used to produce the lime used in the manufacture of bricks and mortar, and also the familiar whitewash which gives the *pueblos blancos* of the Andalucían hills their name and distinctive appearance. But the existence of the kilns in this spot is itself something of a mystery. Although the surrounding rocks are a source of limestone, it is certainly not present in commercial quantities – a fact which may well be largely responsible for the valley's relatively unspoiled survival. It would seem, therefore, that the kilns were used in the construction of the building which now stands beside them in ruins. Both building and kilns are certainly contemporary. However, since the building would appear to have little purpose except to house men working the kilns, we are left in a classic chicken-and-egg situation. Perhaps it was an experiment that failed. The testament to a doomed entrepreneur with dreams of wealth for whom the soil would not give up its meagre riches.

If so, his lesson was not learned, for more than a century later men were still misreading the land and making expensive mistakes. Raise your eyes from the mysterious kilns and look up at the high ridge. There, silhouetted against the sky, you will see the forlorn traces of the next great threat which the valley beat off: The Mighty Alhaurín Dam.

One would imagine that before beginning work on such a project, the precise nature of the geological composition of the land would be thoroughly investigated to ensure that the area was suitable for such a purpose. It would seem, however, that this was not the case, and that work on the dam's construction was started before someone realised that the porous sandstone which forms the local bedrock would allow the resulting reservoir to leak away as though the water was being absorbed by some giant sponge. That all this should have happened within living memory is even more surprising. Once the realisation hit, the project was abandoned and the completed portions of the proposed workings left to stand as mute reminders of Man's enduring folly. Once again, a reliable off-road vehicle will take you to the site. A well-built wall along the ridge leads to a triangular concrete sluice which points like a threatening but unloaded pistol at the valley below. A little higher up, and reachable now only after a rough scramble through leg-lacerating undergrowth, is a solid brick building squatting miserably among the weeds and staring sullenly down at its intended victim with a dimmed but once malevolent eye. It came into the world destined for great, if destructive things only to find itself unwanted and unloved. It is the honours graduate who couldn't get a job. Higher still, and crumbling away, is the dry and useless water tower that was meant to service the workers while the construction of the dam was underway. In the rushing of the stream far below it is possible to hear the mischievous ripple of satisfied laughter.

Torre de Hurique

The most prominent feature of the landscape for the motorist or walker approaching Alhaurín el Grande is a peculiar tower on a hill above the town.

Spotting this from the window of a moving vehicle or from a distant vantage point, the traveller may be forgiven for imagining that he or she has caught a first glimpse of Alhaurín's architectural heritage. Do not be fooled. Closer inspection will reveal that this is in fact a modern creation built in a curious mock-Gothic style that might best be described as '*El Cid*' meets *Psycho*'. In the hills only a few miles from this spot, the BBC filmed their ill-fated Spanish-based soap opera, *Eldorado*. The new Alhaurín tower might easily have been part of a film set too: built as a backdrop to some sweeping romance of star-crossed lovers trapped out of their time. The truth is more prosaic, but no less surprising. This turreted upstart is a water tower, built as the intended centrepiece of that rarest of Costa del Sol phenomena, the Golf Course That Failed.

Disappointment is soon banished. Within sight of the *Tower of the 19th Hole* stands a genuine tower with Moorish and Roman pedigrees. It is to be found in an area known as Hurique. To reach it, follow the signs to *Finca Mota* – a fine, British-owned hostel and restaurant – and drive on as far as the Coín/Mijas/Fuengirola crossroads. Here you need to turn left on to a dirt track and pass by a spring, but from that point the tower will be visible and you can simply home in on it.

The spring is significant. The fincas in the hills around Alhaurín el Grande are still irrigated by natural springs which have been watering the land since before the tower at Hurique was built, and which flow even in the heat of the driest summer. Today the deeds (*escritura*) of each finca include a clause which stipulates the number of hours each month that the waters of the spring will be channelled on to the owner's land. Water is life, and there can be no doubt that until the civilised sharing arrangement was arrived at and agreed, the waters were jealously guarded and fought over. Now the hills are quiet, or at least non-belligerent. The need for a defensive tower such as that at Hurique has long passed, and the worst enemy it has to face is indifference.

For once the enemy seems to have been vanquished. The tower, a sturdy, square edifice of impressive dimensions, is in excellent condition and was given a wash and brush-up in 1987 with a view to opening it to the public either as an attraction in its own right or as a centre for exhibitions. So far this has not happened, but we are nevertheless able to enjoy the fruits of the well-intentioned labour. The tower, though it would appear to have both Roman and Moorish ancestry, dates in its present form from the 14th–15th centuries. It divides itself quite clearly into two sections. The lower, built directly on to the bedrock, is formed from large blocks of stone including, here and there, masoned stones which are undoubtedly of Roman origin. The inescapable conclusion is that a Roman settlement existed nearby, and that the Moors incorporated stones either from an existing structure on the site, or from ruins in the vicinity when they built the tower. This lower section extends to a height of around ten feet and then gives way to an upper section of brick which is much more obviously Moorish.

The well-watered area around the tower is extremely fertile. The terraced hills have undoubtedly been cultivated since at least Roman times, and a discovery of Roman ceramics points to the existence of at least one villa.

We said the hills were quiet, but that is not strictly true. The tower still has its defenders in the shape of several noisy but harmless dogs belonging to the finca that stands in its shadow. Any approaching stranger must be prepared for an enthusiastic and intimidating welcome. Pass around to the back of the tower, and you will find a courtyard now overgrown with weeds which is bounded by the walls of the finca. Interestingly, beneath the whitewash which covers the main wall there is the clear outline of what appears to be a bricked-up Moorish arch. A flight of modern corrugated iron steps leads up to the tower's entrance – a heavy wooden door which is securely locked. Those who have the time to spare and who are so inclined can apply for the keys from the authorities in Alhaurín. Others can simply appreciate a fine and well-preserved structure from the outside.

It is good to note that the preservation of the best of the defensive towers which once peppered the landscape is receiving some official recognition. The same attention is not yet being shown to bakers' ovens. In the long grass to the left of the Hurique tower is a typical brick-built oven which no longer serves its purpose and has been left to crumble. The farmer who built it has presumably decided that it is far easier to buy his bread from the nearest supermarket.

Torres de Fahala

The Moorish fort which once guarded Alhaurín el Grande is long gone, but the two-and-a-half acre hilltop site where it stood can be easily identified from the last remaining substantial section of the wall, which insists to this day upon doing its duty and stands ramrod straight like a proud soldier ready to defend a population which has forgotten him and has ceased to care. A drive to the hilltop will reveal that even he is now tired and ready to surrender. From the Hurique tower, drive back to the *Finca de Mota* and turn on to the dirt track which leads you down into the valley. The remnants of the ruined fort will soon be visible on a flat-topped hill. It is a perfect setting for a Bronze Age hill fort, and is almost certainly the site of the original Iberian settlement. No doubt in its time the fortress was formidable, but when the wheel of history turned in favour of the Christians, it fell like so many others and suffered the inevitable fate.

The defiant section of the wall, which is perhaps twelve feet high, is noticeably narrower at the bottom than the top, giving it the appearance of a rotten tooth which time is finally about to extract. One feels almost afraid of leaning too heavily on it. It is one thing to speak of the inevitability of its collapse, and quite another to be the agent of it.

As for the rest of the fort, little now remains to be seen above the bed of lush grass and clover which has reclaimed the hill. There is a second portion of ruined wall some distance within the perimeter, but the original purpose of the structure of which it was part is no longer apparent. The most notable and eerie feature of the hill today is its forest of fig trees. It is not unusual to find fig trees around Moorish settlements, but curiously, these are all dead. The bare, lifeless branches are like skeletons awaiting the application of flesh. There is no sign of a destructive fire on the hilltop, so the trees have presumably been killed by some catastrophic disease. Perhaps, unlike our brickwork sentinel still warily scanning his beloved valley for the coming Christians, they have simply realised that their war is over and their time is past.

El Molino Morisco de los Corchos (The Moorish Cork Mill)

In ancient times there were many mills in and around Alhaurín el Grande. The historian Madoz listed thirteen, a very apt baker's dozen, although only nine were dedicated solely to the making of flour. Today only one survives, and it is a remarkable place with a remarkable legend attached to it.

According to the story, when the Christians came in 1485, the mill was owned by a Moor named Abderrahman ben Abdal-lah El Mundar. The suffix 'El Mundar' indicates that he came originally from Monda, and for simplicity's sake he was known to all and sundry as 'El Mundari'. El Mundari was, from all accounts, a diligent worker and a kind, generous man who never refused anyone the use of his mill, even though his generosity was frequently taken advantage of and he found himself waiting in vain for his money.

His good character did not save him from the fate of other Moors in the town after the Christians took control. His mill was taken away from him and handed over to one of the incoming Christian families. One might have expected El Mundari to walk away a bitter man with a curse on his lips and hate in his heart, but instead he left with a blessing. He predicted that the mill would never stop working. More than five hundred years later the great horizontal mill wheels still turn beneath the building each day, powered by the waters of the arroyo Sanguino. In times of war and famine, when there was little or no corn to make flour, the mill took instead to grinding cork, which was used to protect grapes as they were carried over bumpy roads to market. It is also said that because the mill works hydraulically and uses no electricity, it was used to provide flour and meal for the black market, since the authorities were unaware of its clandestine operations. This strikes the cynical ear as unlikely. The eye is blind when the hand and the belly are full. In the years after the Civil War, the stretch of railway line between Coín and Alhaurín el Grande was notorious for the smuggling of black market produce under the noses, and almost certainly with the connivance of, the customs guards – the *carabineros.* Different languages seldom employ the same slang phrases and ideas, but are we wrong to detect an echo of disdain in the fact that *carabinero* is also the word for a large prawn? However, before we take a smug and censorious view of all this, we should remember that such petty corruption is the monopoly of no one nation. Consider Kipling's quintessentially English verse, *A Smuggler's Song*, with its memorable lines about brandy for the parson and baccy for the clerk.

The road to the mill is well signposted in the town, and a trip to view it is one of the most rewarding treats that Alhaurín el Grande has to offer. Over the centuries it has ground enough flour, nuts and cork to build a new *sierra* across the landscape, and the latest keeper of El Mundari's promise is small and friendly, and as sweetly Andalucían as the juice of an olive. He is probably in his seventies, but gives the impression that he always was and always will be. He has a son and grandchildren, and whatever happens, the mill wheels will keep turning. In spite of his age, he is boyishly proud of the mill, and is always happy to greet visitors. First he will tell you to walk around, see whatever you want, and stay as long as you like. There are orange groves watered by a maze of irrigation ditches, and you are more than welcome to help yourself to the refreshing fruit in the heat of the day.

When you have seen enough, and rested beneath the fragrant trees, make your way back to the main building, and the old man will invite you in to see the workings of the mill itself. First, though, you must crouch beside the stream which rushes out of the mill and over the two great horizontal wheels set beneath it. By operating a simple lever from inside the building, the miller can set the wheels in motion or stop them as he chooses.

Inside, you will be treated to a non-stop commentary as the old man explains the operation of the grinding wheels and the uses of the various implements which are lying around or hanging on the walls. He speaks only Spanish, but his bright eyes and expressive gestures tell much of his story, and when comprehension fails, the non-Spanish speaking listener can simply wallow in the enveloping poetry of the sound of his words, the feel of the stone, and the age-old smells, and drift into imagination.

Any building which has stood for more than five centuries will have seen much renovation and renewal, but the arch through which your guide will lead you on the next stage of your tour is undoubtedly a Moorish original through which the legendary El Mundari must have walked many times. It leads to a chamber which has two exits. The door to the left leads to a small grassy area where a selection of old grinding stones lean lazily against the wall. This one, says the miller, is for flour, that for almonds, this for cork. The other exit from the chamber is at the top of a flight of steep, uneven steps which take you to the roof, and the point where the water enters the mill and crashes down to drive the wheels below. The channel which delivers the water is divided in two by a heavy triangular stone, so that the wheels can be turned together or individually as the miller chooses.

At the end of your tour he will take you back to the main entrance and pause to show you the photographs which hang on the wall inside the door. It is good to note that they include pictures of schoolchildren being taken around the mill and listening to the miller's tales. They are the future, but this is still a place soaked to its aged skin in the past. He is particularly proud of a large, fading photograph of a young man standing beside a laden donkey on a shining day, lost in the cluttered lumber room of time. It is, he will tell you, his grandfather. And then he will point to the straw sandals his grandfather is wearing, and then to the straw sandals hanging beside the picture on the wall. They are, he says solemnly, one and the same. The sandals on the wall look suspiciously new, but what does it matter? *El Molino de los Corchos* has its own individual contract with time which does not concern us. There is no entry fee to the mill (which has been designated as a national monument), but there is a cork jar hanging from a nail into which contributions for its upkeep can be dropped. Ruined mills are a common sight across Andalucía. It is refreshing, almost amazing, to find one not only in a fine state of repair, but still working, and not transformed into a holiday home for a wealthy expatriate. It would be a churlish visitor indeed who did not find such a unique and rewarding experience worth at least a few hundred pesetas.

Sierra Gorda/Fuente del Sol

High up in the north-west corner of the municipal district lie the ungallantly named *Sierra Gorda*, or Fat Mountains, rising from the valley plain to a height of 330m. Most of the range lies within the district of Coín, but the part with which we are concerned here – a spur which contains a long line of settlements – extends to that of Alhaurín el Grande.

The place we are looking for is known as *Fuente del Sol* (Fountain of the Sun), and we can find it easily enough by taking the Coín-to-Cártama road to point km 12 in the shadow of the mountain. The spring, or fountain, which gives the place its name has been running long enough for the Iberians to have built a settlement here to make use of it as early as 500 BC. It was one of a long chain of indigenous communities, stretched across the land like pearls on a dropped necklace, which traded with the Phœnicians in the Bay of Málaga. As Iberian settlements went, this one was more successful than most, and managed to survive well into the Roman period. More research is needed, but there is little doubt that it will show the original settlement to have been a Bronze Age hill fort built on one of the three tent-shaped peaks of the *Sierra Gorda*.

In 1962, a canal was dug through the area to bring drinking water from the Guadalhorce to the eternally thirsty people of Málaga city. The resulting reservoir is close to Antequera. During the canal's construction, Roman ceramics were uncovered, and this sparked enough interest for an extensive excavation in 1980 which brought to light a particularly rich Roman complex within the boundaries of a present-day privately owned finca. The obvious wealth of the settlement became clearer with each discovery: columns, marble panels, a stone sacrificial altar.

There was even a plunge pool. The wealthy Roman, no less than his modern Spanish, British, Dutch or German counterpart living the good life in the Andalucían sunshine, had to have his pool. This one measured 2.29m x 2.20m, and those who couldn't or wouldn't dive gratefully into its cool water could enter more sedately using the three steps cut into its concrete sides. These had survived in a remarkably good state of preservation. A few scattered coins dated the site to the time of the Emperor Vespasian (AD 69–79). Three of the columns were moved to the *Plaza del Ayuntamiento* in Alhaurín el Grande, where they stand outside the *Ermita de la Santa Vera-Cruz*. (See above.)

We know from the nearby example of Barbi (see Pizarra) that a Visigothic community could conceivably have survived in this area. Certainly the Moors knew it well, and the mountain side here is probably the site of a lost Moorish village known historically as either *Benamaquez* or *Benablaque*. Does this uncertainty mask some long-forgotten tribal rivalry? The two names mean respectively, 'son of Maquez' and 'son of Blaque'. Two big fish in the same small pond invariably spell trouble.

In spite of its undoubted Moorish pedigree, the village was not recorded at all until the area came under Christian domination in 1485. This is doubly surprising because it apparently held a powerful strategic position, dominating the advance into the *Hoya de Málaga* valley. Its location was so formidable that after the fall in 1484 of Alora, 15km to the north, and Setenil, close to Ronda, the Catholic King took discretion to be the better part of valour and put off the inevitable confrontation with Alhaurín until the following year. Eventually he chickened out completely and entered into an alliance with its people instead. The kind of alliance that spiders occasionally make with flies. Displaying the profound lack of understanding of human nature for which tyrants have ever been notorious, he made the fatuous and hopelessly misguided remark: *Yo hare que la pena de estos sea de temor a otros, para que guarden leatád por fuerza, cuando no la guarden de grado.* 'In order to keep the inhabitants loyal we must put fear into each citizen so that their loyalty will be long lasting'.

He began the delicate process of instilling loyalty into his new subjects by hanging 108 of the most prominent men, and selling 110 women and children into slavery. No records have survived of celebratory street parties on the part of the remainder to proclaim loudly their newly-won allegiance amid revelry and song.

The Christians were stung by their ingratitude. Like Hitler several centuries (but not enlightened ones) later, they decided the obstinate place should be completely erased from human memory. It was systematically destroyed. Even the foundations of the settlement, it is said, were auctioned off. But the bidders were clearly pious men. It was, in effect, a charity auction. The proceeds of the plunder and destruction were given to the new church being built a few kilometres away in Coín.

The Nearby District of La Mata

This has been an important agricultural and mineral area for centuries, and the hills are still lined with terraces that have existed since the times of the Romans. There is no doubt that the Romans produced wine here and exported it to other parts of the empire under the name of *Laurin* (from the name under which they knew Alhaurín – *Lauro Nova*).

Chapter Five

Alhaurín de la Torre

Historical Background

'GARDEN OF ALLAH' SEEMED LIKE A GOOD NAME to call yourself after the Moorish invasion, and the two Roman towns of Lauro Nova and Lauro Vetus probably spent a lot of time arguing over who thought of it first. No doubt it was a continuation of the tedious squabble they had when they saw the Romans coming over the hills and both decided to call themselves 'Lauro'. As stubborn as mountain mules, neither would back down and pick another name, so it was necessary to distinguish them by other means. The Romans dubbed the two Lauros 'Nova' and 'Vetus', while the two Alhauríns became respectively 'de la Torre', because it had a tower, and 'el Grande', because it was bigger. Alhaurín de la Torre is still the smaller of the two, with a population some five thousand or so less than its rival, but the gap is rapidly closing and there is little doubt that in time it will outstrip its rival. It has become the most popular dormitory town for those who wish to take the fifteen-minute drive each day to work in Málaga.

Winston Churchill said of Russia that it was a riddle wrapped in a mystery inside an enigma. Alhaurín de la Torre is a pueblo wrapped in a town inside a conurbation. So all-engulfing has the epidemic of construction become, that it squats over the ancient village like a brooding bird, blotting out virtually every trace of its history. By comparison, finding a needle in a haystack is a task too simple to waste one's time on. Of the tower which gave the pueblo its name there is no sign. In the early 1990s, perhaps irritated by the number of visitors asking for it, the *ayuntamiento* built a replica no taller than the average dwarf, on which they inscribed the town's name. It was a sop to its heritage which did nothing to reclaim the lost years.

Parts of the town are pleasant enough. There is a garden which provides a relatively quiet refuge from the burgeoning pizzerias and disco bars, but it is difficult now to equate this Alhaurín with anything that is recognisable as a mountain pueblo. The church, with its plain, undistinguished altar, is wedged among dismal streets like a piece of old furniture left out for the dust cart. Some attempt has been made to make it picturesque by fronting it with a small square containing trees and a water trough which is fed from a small fountain. Unfortunately, the water flows continuously from the mouth of a

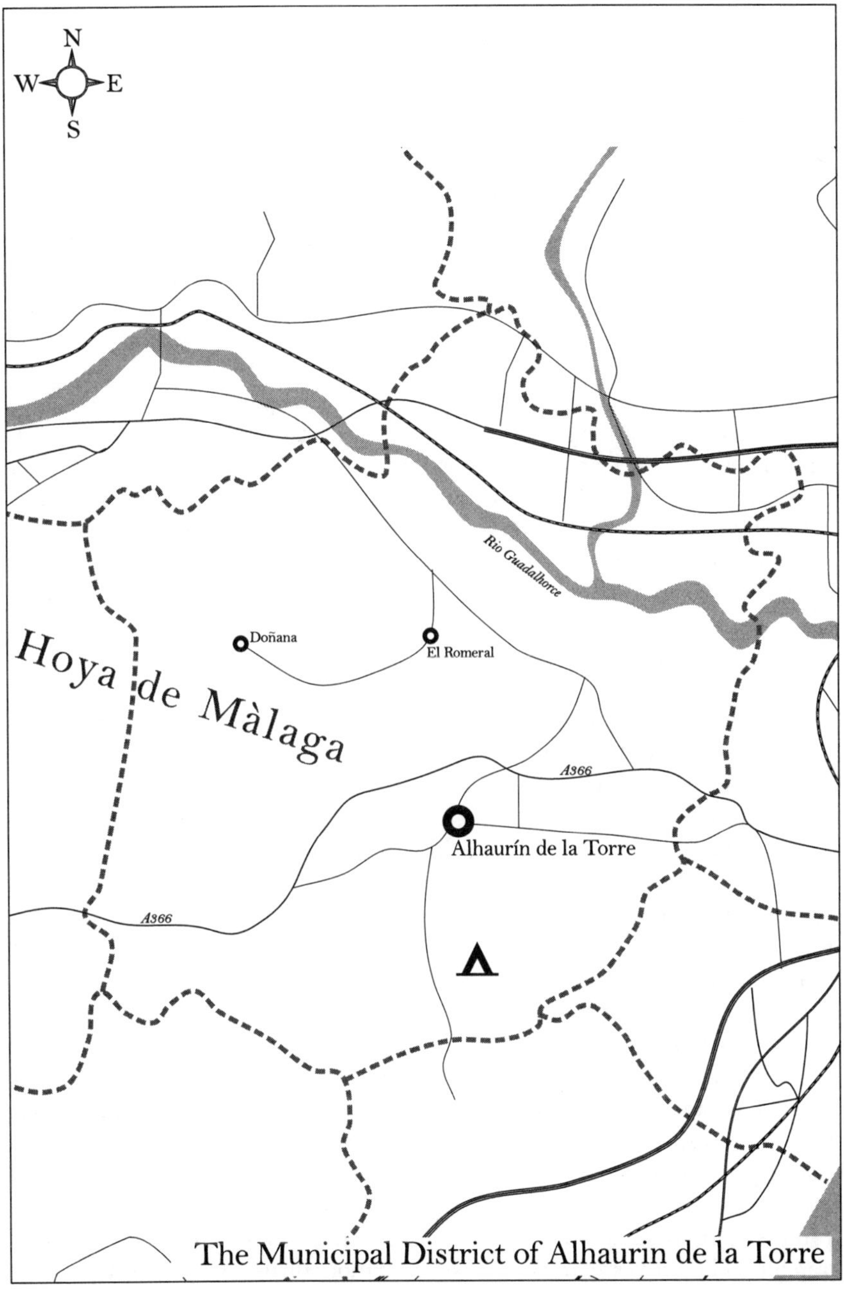
N
W
E
S
Río Guadalhorce
Doñana
El Romeral
Hoya de Màlaga
A366
Alhaurín de la Torre
A366
The Municipal District of Alhaurin de la Torre

stone frog which looks like something bought cheaply from a garden centre which had inconveniently run out of gnomes, and as a fillip to the spirit it fails abominably.

Should you wish to visit Alhaurín de la Torre and carry out your own detective work, it is easily reached. Drive towards Torremolinos from Málaga airport along the main N–340 highway, and look for the C–344 turnoff which takes you towards Churriana. The road winds its way along the Guadalhorce valley and into the Sierra de Mijas and will take you not only to the competing Alhauríns but on to Coín and Tolox and beyond. Alhaurín de la Torre still stands among large plantations of citrus and avocado, but the greedy bulldozers and building trucks are eating into them faster than a school of piranhas chancing on an unwary swimmer.

The fringes of the town, however, particularly the areas of Torrealquería, La Alquería and Cortijo Molina, are well seeded with interesting sites, and in a refreshing move which could profitably be copied elsewhere, the local *ayuntamiento* went a long way to redeeming itself in 1997 by deciding to do something about it. Concerned, as are the present authors, by the traditional lackadaisical attitude to so many important historical and archæological sites, and maybe a little ashamed of their own guilty past, they created the *Carta Arqueológica.* By listing and defining all the known archæological and historic remains in the area, including many which are unprotected and had previously gone unrecorded, they hoped to redress much of the ignorance and apathy which exists in regard to Alhaurín's heritage. It may well prove to be a classic example of too little too late, but it is a bold move which deserves success.

At the exit to the town, near the *hacienda del Cardón,* by the old railway line which once linked Málaga and Coín, is the shrine of a venerated relic which, inevitably, has a rich legend woven around it. The shrine is maintained by the owners of the *Venta del Santo Cristo* and contains what appears to be no more than a piece of wood bearing a painting of Christ. To the sceptical, of course, it *is* no more than a piece of wood bearing a painting of Christ. Like all such relics, it is nothing without the story, so let us take a look at it.

A Christian soldier hiding in the undergrowth from his enemies supposedly discovered it in the fifteenth century. It might, of course, have got there in many ways, but the discovery was considered miraculous enough for it to rate its own shrine, which became a particular source of pilgrimage for young girls who came to light candles (the small ones which float on oil and are known as *mariposas* – butterflies) and ask the image for favours. The cross-shaped piece of wood stood in the shrine for several years until, amid great consternation, it disappeared. It was lost for several months, until a group of workers spotted some doves paying persistent attention to a certain area of bramble. They investigated, and consternation turned to joy as the image was recovered. It was immediately adorned with a pair of doves and carried in triumph back to its shrine. During the political turmoil of the early 1930s the shrine was destroyed, but the Christ survived after being hidden by the faithful in an oven. It seems an unlikely and extraordinarily dangerous choice of sanctuary. Perhaps whoever put it there was simply trying to light the flame? No matter. It survived, and after the fighting and the coming of peace, it was restored once again to the place where it remains.

La Alqueria

To reiterate our previously used showbiz analogy, some places have what it takes and some don't. Alqueria started life as no more than a simple Iberian hill fort sometime around 300 BC, but at a time when a great many such were being abandoned and beginning their long crumble into the dust of history, Alqueria attracted a population and found itself Romanised. It was up and on its way. There seemed to be no reason why it should not run and run, eventually picking itself a catchy Arab name and surviving the upheavals of a millennium and more to become another 20th century refuge for wealthy businessmen and expats. But its act was dull. The Lauro – not yet the Alhaurín – Brothers had learned to tap-dance, sing and juggle. Alqueria was still doing comic monologues and barnyard impressions. By AD 200 the public had seen enough, and began to drift away. But the name at least endured, and the spot that bears it now is a virtual suburb of Alhaurín de la Torre, extending to the boundary with the adjoining municipal district of Alhaurín el Grande. Given the apparently unstoppable expansion of the former, it will almost certainly soon cease to have any real independent existence.

The railway which used to run through it is now a road, beside which the old station house still stands. With the trains gone, the present occupants are reduced to selling olives – *aceitunas* – to residents and passers-by.

To find the station house, follow the route of the defunct railway line out of Alhaurín de la Torre towards Coín. The house is a couple of stops down. Alternatively, take the Alhaurín el Grande road and turn right immediately before you reach the Alora Golf course. Three kilometres down the road you will reach a junction where a stubborn old sign still points you to the *estacion.*

In spite of its apparently imminent swallowing by its voracious neighbour, Alqueria remains even today a solidly rural community, and signs that it was once at the centre of, at the very least, an impressive Roman villa complex are not hard to find. When the roadwork was being done, many Roman foundations were found. At first thought to be the remains of a single villa, it soon became clear that they were too extensive to be simply that. Unfortunately, the needs of the road were too great, and most of what was uncovered soon disappeared again. However, a stroll around the area close to the old station house is very rewarding.

The customers at the combined shop and bar opposite the station are more likely to be interested in football than Alqueria's Roman past, and you will need to walk beyond the premises with their 'new Moorish' extension, and on down the hill.

Easily identifiable stretches of Roman wall have been incorporated into the modern homes, or used to mark their boundaries. If this was indeed no more than the site of a villa, it was clearly of enormous importance. Many of the surviving ruins lie within the boundary of the finca of *Los Montenegros*, and since Iberian as well as Roman ceramics were found there, it is likely that its original settlement came well before the Roman conquest. It was excavated in 1977 and 1981, the digs resulting in the discovery of ceramics, metal objects, mosaics and a large capital.

Though the bulk of the visible ruins now lie on private property, a track from the roadside leading to the finca does offer some rewards. Undoubtedly the most interesting are the remains of a Roman water-tank or bath, now firmly embedded into the embankment, but recognisable enough. At some point in the distant past it seems to have been either repaired or made smaller, but it is still a good and accessible example of typical Roman concrete and masonry.

The whole area is dotted with fig trees, which suggests also a strong Moorish influence. Walk down to the river, and the number and distribution of the Roman traces will be enough to give you some idea of the extent of the site. In the authors' view, it probably never amounted to a town, but it was certainly more than an isolated villa. It has been suggested that this was the site of the Roman town of *Iluro*, but that is far more likely to have been the Roman name for the modern town of Alora. Only a major excavation would provide the necessary evidence, and that is clearly out of the question. As you wander around, please remember that such relics as remain are now on private property, so be discreet and treat them with respect.

Castillejo

This rather common name is, in this instance, given to the second highest peak in the area. It rises some 973 metres above sea level to dominate the coastal sierras behind Torremolinos and Fuengirola. The very ubiquity of the name is a testament to the huge numbers of small forts and look-out posts which once studded the Iberian countryside like peppercorns on a steak.

This particular hill was chosen as the site of a Moorish watchtower, guarding the municipal junction between Benalmádena, Mijas and Torre. Easy access can be gained from Mijas by following the modern track to the top, which now boasts radio masts where the tower once stood. The foothills on the Torre side are slowly disappearing due to predatory quarrying. The hills here contain a number of old lead mines, which, in at least one case, also provided silver. However, it is the insatiable need for cement in a country where new hotels and villas appear on the coast like the offspring of overactive terracotta rabbits that is eating away at the limestone mountain. As a consequence, exploring can be highly dangerous and great caution should be employed.

An easier way to sample what remains of an older industrial age is to follow the Alhaurín el Grande road for about 5 km until you reach *Arroyo de las Minas*. Here, thankfully, the mountain is still intact and well-forested with pines planted during the Franco era. A network of tracks leads to the foothills and an area known as *Llanos de Plata* (Plain of Silver). Many old mines and associated ruins can be explored here in relative safety, but in spite of its name, optimistic prospectors need not apply.

El Retiro

Though the full and official name of these astounding gardens is *El Retiro de Málaga*, they are close enough to Alhaurín de la Torre for us to place them under that heading and help redeem the admittedly bleak picture which we have painted of the modern-day town. Confusingly, they have the same name as the great and better known park in Madrid. For their notes on the history of the gardens, the authors are indebted to the research of Richard Dight, a leading expert on gardens and irrigation systems, who regularly writes and lectures on the subjects throughout Málaga province and beyond.

The original house and gardens were founded by the Bishop of Málaga, Fray Alonso de Santo Tomás (1646–1692). Santo Tomás, whose rise to eminence was not impeded by the fact that he was a bastard son of King Philip IV, retired to the aptly named estate after finally hanging up his mitre. On his death, it was bequeathed to the convent of Santo Domingo.

El Retiro is split into two great sections: the ornithological park and the historical garden. Many of the birds to be found in the park's aviaries are on the world's endangered species' list. The keeping of wild animals in captivity is a controversial subject in our politically sensitive age, but only the most intransigent would prefer extinction. The directors of El Retiro have striven hard to recreate as closely as possible the natural habitats of the hundreds of birds in their care, and you will see carefully reproduced environments matching everything from the savannahs of Africa to tropical forests, semi-deserts and swamps. One zone of the park is designated as a research area. It is used for the study of bird behaviour and the development of confined environment breeding techniques, and visitors are especially requested to treat the spot with respect and not to disturb the birds.

The oldest parts of the garden, dating from the late 17th century, are at its highest point. They comprise a vined trellis walk, tiled octagonal fountain, and a double staircase with a grotto and fountain which leads to a square pond with an island at its centre. Known as the Bishop's Pond, it supplies all the water used in the park by means of a pumped circulatory system. The Bishop's Pond itself is filled by a well which has existed since the park's foundation. Fray Alonso, it is said, spent many hours on the island, meditating and writing.

Close to the pond is a terraced garden, originally used for the growing of vegetables. It now contains fruit trees, a maze, and the Bishop's tomb. He clearly loved El Retiro so much that even in death he could not bear to leave it. A white marble sundial shows the time in all the countries of the known world of the 17th century. Except, of course, on cloudy days and after dark.

In the late 18th century, ownership of the property passed to the Count of Villalcazar de Sirga. He employed the services of the Cuenca-born architect José Martín de Aldehuela, who worked on the house and garden for more than twenty years, from 1778 to 1802. In 1780 he created the square quadripartite garden containing the fountain of the Siren. Made from white marble, and carved in Italy, it portrays a triton and a sea-nymph riding a pair of dolphins. There is a box hedge with marble statues, including a harlequin, satyr and the god Mercury. The trees are a later addition, having been planted in the Romantic period of the mid-19th century.

The Italian Baroque garden was also laid out during Martín de Aldehuela's time, some ten to fifteen years after the garden of the Siren. It contains a cascade divided into three terraces on a steep slope and a square reservoir with a fountain.

The old Manor House has now been restored and looks magnificent among the almost endless natural beauty which surrounds it. As the reader will have gathered from the descriptions given above, El Retiro is more than simply 'a garden'. Each part of it is a self-contained botanical wonder set in sublime surroundings and beautifully maintained. As Dight says, 'the variety of flowers that adorn this beautiful garden in their different seasons is incredible'. This is one part of Málaga or, let us be generous, Alhaurín de la Torre, which no visitor should miss.

Chapter Six

Benahavis

Historical Background

SITUATED 7KM INLAND FROM THE GUADALMINA GOLF COURSE, this pleasant and typical *pueblo blanco* is a favourite destination for tourists drawn not only by its beauty but by its plethora of fine, family-run restaurants. It has also become home to a large number of wealthy foreign residents; so many, in fact, that they now form the majority of the village's 2000 inhabitants. Benahavis is reached by following the rio Guadalmina through a gorge and up into the hills to where it stands, 500m above sea level. Along the entire route there is good access to the river, which at the height of the summer dries to a mere trickle. The riverside offers some good picnic spots, but the road can become busy on Sunday afternoons, particularly in mid-spring, as whole families flood out of San Pedro to set up their day camps on the banks. The valley is situated in the foothills of the Sierra Bermeja, with the 1020m high peak of *Cerro de la Mora* overshadowing the village.

The Benahavis municipal zone of 150 sq kms covers a large slice of the Sierra Bermeja, with numerous peaks standing over 1000 metres. The only road to penetrate this sprawling mountainous region is that which runs between San Pedro and Ronda – a 50km stretch of which passes through the Benahavis district. There is, to be completely accurate, another road to Benahavis and the ruins of Montemayor, but it is a rough track suitable only for those with four-wheel drive vehicles. This runs from the small, but rapidly growing, village of Cancelada in the municipality of Estepona up into the mountains. Cancelada, incidentally, though it is still no more than a small dot on a large map, is not entirely without interest. Each year on the feast day of its patron saint, Isidore, it comes alive for the *romeria*. This is part fiesta, part religious ceremony. After mass in the village church in the early morning, there is a procession to the woodland beside the rio Guadalmansa where music and dancing go on well into the night.

As the name of the village suggests, Benahavis is of Moorish origin, and is the only Moorish settlement in the area to survive. After the Christian re-conquest of Andalucía, Moors were forbidden by the Catholic Monarchs to live within a league of the coast. Because they were further than that from

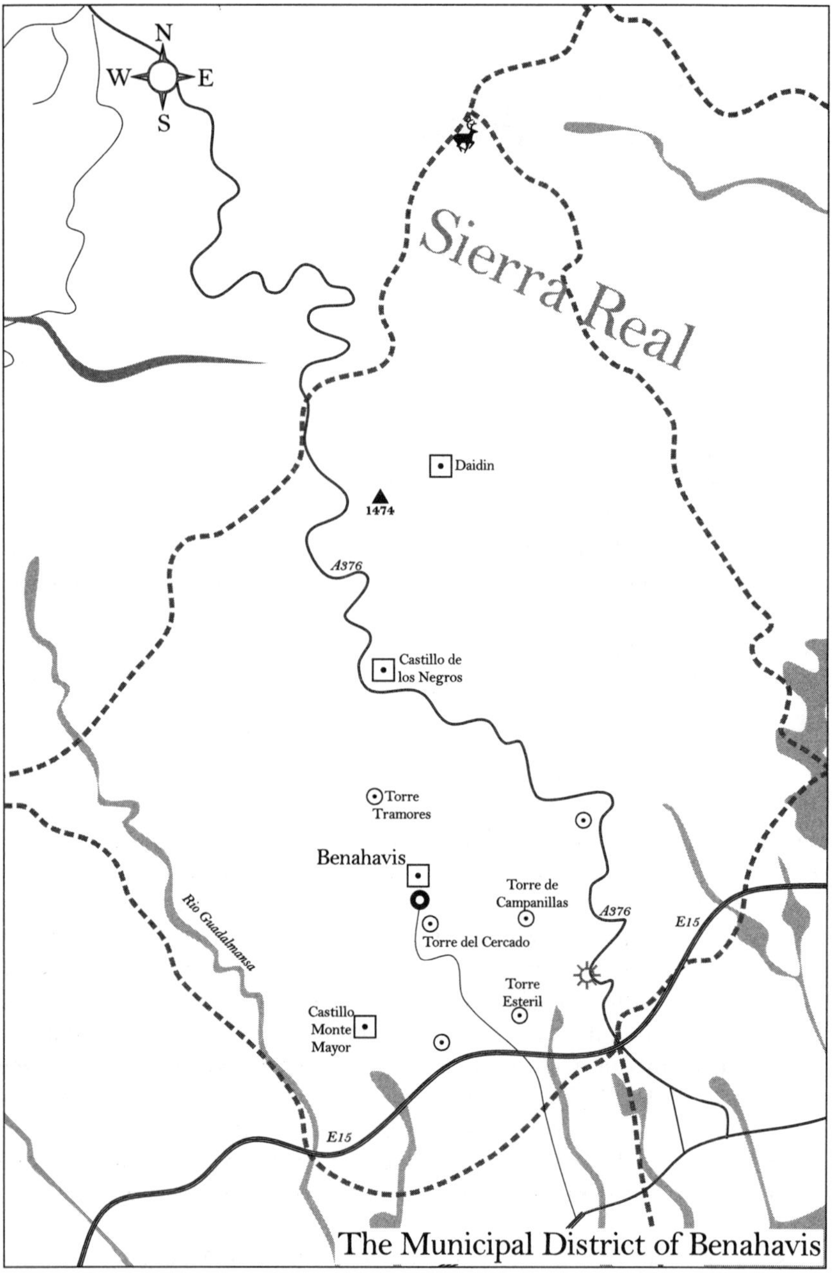
N
W
E
S
Sierra Real
Daidin
1474
A376
Castillo de
los Negros
Torre
Tramores
Benahavis
Torre de
Campanillas
A376
E15
Torre del Cercado
Rio Guadalmansa
Torre
Esteril
Castillo
Monte
Mayor
E15
The Municipal District of Benahavis

the sea, places like Benahavis, Ojén and Istán survived, while many other Moorish settlements were abandoned and finally disappeared.

The castle of Montemayor played a prominent part in an internecine Moorish rebellion towards the end of the 11th century. Muhammad II (al-Mu'tamid) was on the throne of Seville, having succeeded his father in 1069. Mu'tamid was an educated, elegant man who had distinguished himself at the age of 13, when he commanded a successful military expedition against the town of Silves. As a result he was made its Governor.

By the last quarter of the century, Moorish power in the area was already under threat from surrounding Christian princes, and Mu'tamid was forced to pay tribute to Alfonso VI, of Leon and Castille. In 1085, Alfonso took Toledo and invaded Mu'tamid's realm, demanding territorial concessions. In response, the Moorish leader made what was to be a great personal miscalculation. He solicited help from the reigning Almoravid Sultan, Yusuf ibn Tâshufin, who was still revelling in his recent conquest of Morocco and whose forces were formidable. They came to Mu'tamid's aid, crossing the Straits of Gibraltar in 1086, and delivering a crushing defeat to the Christians at Zallaka. Circumstances meant that Yusuf had to return to Morocco before consolidating the victory, but it gave Mu'tamid a breathing space. However, it proved to be short-lived, and when he found himself once more under pressure, he sought Yusuf's aid again, this time travelling personally to do so. It was a mistake. Yusuf stared at his visitor like a stern father who had paid off his son's gambling debts on Monday, only to be asked to settle more on Friday. He sent his army back to Spain in 1090, but this time the *jihad* (holy war) was fought in his own name. He captured Seville and exiled Mu'tamid to prison in Morocco.

Nevertheless, support for Mu'tamid remained strong, especially in view of Yusuf's harsh treatment of captured princes, and inevitably, the discontent eventually turned to rebellion. Yusuf rounded up a great many suspected opponents, especially in Málaga, but a band of rebels in the town, led by a much-respected noble, ibn Khalaf, escaped from prison and seized the castle of Montemayor. They were soon joined by one of Mu'tamid's sons, Abd al-Jabbâr, who was still in Andalucía. He was immediately elected leader, and for a while the rebellion seemed to be going well. A Moroccan warship, stranded near to the castle, became a source of ammunition and provisions, and the towns of Algeciras and Arcos declared themselves for the conspirators. In 1095 Abd al-Jabbâr made Arcos his base for raids which took him almost to the gates of Seville itself. At that point, when victory seemed almost within the rebels' grasp, news came that Mu'tamid had conveniently (for Yusuf) died at the age of 55, still in exile in Morocco. Suspicious though the timing may have been, his death spelled the end of the rebellion. Apparently, so far as the anti-Yusuf alliance was concerned, it was Mu'tamid or no-one. With him gone, they sheathed their swords, shrugged their shoulders, and shuffled home.

For the next four hundred years or so, things were relatively quiet in the Benahavis hills, but beyond them the apparently eternal war was going on, and the Christians were winning it. The Moorish rulers finally capitulated to the all-conquering Christians on June 11th 1485, when all the Arab property in the Marbella area, including Benahavis, was surrendered by Mohammed Abuneza to Ferdinand. Ferdinand placed Benahavis in the custody of Don Pedro Villandrado, Count of Ribadeo, who became the town's first Christian mayor. For the next three hundred years, Benahavis and Marbella squabbled like two cats tied together and tossed into a very small sack. The bickering was only resolved when the sack was opened and the string was finally cut, and Benahavis achieved the status of a totally independent municipality.

A new castle (not to be confused with the hilltop castle of Montemayor) was built on the foundations of the old one in the town, and in time it took on many functions, including that of a prison. Today it has a 19th-century façade and serves as the town hall. However, the 15th-century watchtower, the oldest extant structure in Benahavis, still stands and can be seen simply by walking around to the back of the building. You will also find a restaurant, *Restaurante Cuarto Hondo*, actually housed inside the old stone Arab walls. It is a fascinating and atmospheric place to eat, but the owners have a penchant for cradle-snatching to fill the menu which might upset vegetarians and animal-lovers. The two specialities of the house are suckling pig and roast *lechazo* – tender meat obtained from very young, still milking lambs.

During the Moorish revolt of 1570 the beleaguered Morisco inhabitants of Benahavis got together and agreed to accept the Christian king's terms and surrender. A certain Barcoqui was chosen as their emissary and armed with a safe conduct guarantee from the Duke of Arcos, he set off for Marbella to deliver their letter of submission to the garrison commander. However, there were many on the Christian side who preferred, for their own devious reasons, to see the revolt continue. The Moors were on the ropes and ripe for plunder, and they were greedy for a share in the spoils which they knew would follow a devastating Moorish defeat. All it took was a little ruthless *realpolitik.* Treating the Duke's given word as a flippant ad-lib whispered cheekily in a school play, they brushed aside the emissary's guards and Barcoqui was murdered. As they knew it would, this treachery rekindled the rebellion, which immediately threw up a new leader, El Melque, who established a stronghold close to Istán. His story is told below. (See Istan.)

The Pueblo

The pueblo of Benahavis is surrounded by a chain of now largely ruined towers, like a once well-guarded wealthy child whose parents have finally lost their fear of kidnap. Most of the towers date from the 16th century and the time of the Moorish revolt. However, there are others which could reasonably claim to be much older, and these are discussed in turn.

For centuries the village marked time until the current influx of foreigners began around 1975. These former *'costas'* had tired of the coast and decided to move inland to the mountains and village life. Not too far, though, for Benahavis is only a few minutes drive from the sea. The modern seeker after tranquil isolation generally likes to keep his options open. This influx resulted in a number of new developments, notably that of *La Aldea*, the brainchild of British sculptor David Marshall, who maintains a gallery of his works there. *La Aldea* is virtually a village within a village, and deliberate efforts have been made to give it at least an illusion of old Andalucía, with marble fountains, antiques and old-fashioned doors and grilles. Ironically, the only part which strikes the visitor as being out of place is the gallery itself, but the development of *La Aldea* certainly revitalised Benahavis and is largely responsible for the growth of its population to today's level.

Previous generations had it all wrong. The most effective, unstoppable invading army wears a uniform of Bermuda shorts, t-shirts and sandals. And instead of guns, it comes armed with a deadly arsenal of credit cards. Despite the continuing incrustation of Benahavis by its occupying force of foreign settlers, it is still worth a visit by the seeker after Spain, not least for its celebrated clutch of fine restaurants. Cut your speed and find yourself a parking space well before you enter the pueblo, otherwise you will find yourself out of the other side in the blinking of an eye, and heading up the mountains on a dirt track.

As you walk into the village, the first public building to greet you in its primly polite and formal manner, is the small church. Built as recently as the 1920s, this church has since proved itself too small for its purpose and a larger, more modern replacement is planned for another site.

The central plaza is the main focal point, although the town hall is the only true period building left standing in the village. Walk around the side and to the back and you will see the ancient watchtower which has survived the various re-buildings of the original Arab structure since it was itself raised in the 15th century. It is within the walls beneath the clock tower that you will find the *Restaurante Cuarto Hondo*. If you can resist the temptation to step quickly inside and reach for the menu, cross instead to the new urbanisation, from which you will get a much better overview of the site as a whole.

Almost every step you take in Benahavis, whether along the pavements on either side of the deceivingly wide road which leads you into it, or down any of the innumerable narrow side-streets, will bring you to a restaurant. In an age when a pueblo is a pueblo is a pueblo so far as the increasingly sophisticated tourist goes, a village, to be commercially successful rather than merely stared at appreciatively by hordes of briefly pausing passers-through, needs to find itself a reputation. In Benahavis, they have found it through food. Many visitors return regularly to the town simply to eat lunch or dinner, either at a particular favourite restaurant, or to try each of the restaurants in turn, crossing them off their lists like trainspotters. The competition among the restaurateurs of Benahavis for the discerning clientele which forms their passing trade has led to high qualities of cuisine and service, and it is rare to leave a Benahavis restaurant disappointed.

Though the steep and narrow streets give the place an ancient, timeless feel (if you can turn a temporary blind eye and deaf ear to the ubiquitous presence of sleek modern cars and motorbikes), the majority of the houses in Benahavis are scarcely more than 200 years old. The pattern of the streets themselves, however, does certainly date back to the Moorish period. Indeed, the place was considered typical enough of the time to be used in at least one Hollywood film to represent an 'Arabic village'.

To discover the true mediæval power base of this old Moorish town, you will need either good, reliable four-wheeled drive transport, or a great deal of determination and energy, plus stout feet encased in equally stout walking shoes or boots, and at least a couple of hours to spare. You will need to turn your eyes and feet to the mountains, and your starting place will be the road which branches to the left beside the bus shelter as you drive into the town.

Montemayor

The ruins of the 11th-century castle of Montemayor, despite their proximity to the town of Benahavis, are not easy to reach. A good off-road vehicle can take you reasonably close, but the ruins themselves are ultimately accessible only on foot. The castle once dominated over 100 kilometres of the coastline at a time when invasions and raids by African pirates were still common. Local stories tell of underground passages leading down to the coast which were once used as access routes by the Moorish troops of the Sultan Havis (sometimes rendered as Havib or Avis, depending on how well the chronicler could spell). Havis built a second castle close by for his son and thus *Benahavis* was born. The name means literally 'son of Havis'.

The route from the village to the Montemayor ruins, standing 580 metres above sea level on a commanding hill top, is virtually unsignposted, which, considering the effort needed to reach them, may well be a deliberate policy on behalf of the local *ayuntamiento* to discourage the unprepared and unwary. As you enter the town, the first major turning to the left (there is a bus shelter situated on the corner) leads, as do all roads ultimately, to the cemetery. However, shortly before the cemetery is reached, there is to the left a short stretch of paved road rather like a ramp rising sharply upwards. This marks the start of the path to the castle ruins and except for those travelling in a 4-wheel drive vehicle, it is where the car must be parked and the journey continued on foot.

At the top of the paved stretch of road the way becomes a gravel path leading up the mountain and if on foot, you must be prepared for a walk of about an hour. Eventually you will reach a small clearing with a solitary cork oak tree at its centre – a tree of such an age that it may well have been witness to the castle's fall and destruction. A 4-wheel drive could be taken to this point – about ten minutes walk, climb and scramble from the castle – but from there onwards progress is possible only on foot. But be warned: the footpath becomes progressively steeper and more perilous as the castle is approached, and eventually all but disappears. As the castle walls are neared, the climb almost becomes mountaineering, and there is a very long drop into the valley below. This final part of the climb is not for the unfit or the faint-hearted, and certainly not for anyone with a fear of heights or with slippery shoes. For safety's sake it should be attempted only by those properly prepared, and preferably not alone.

The original entrance to the castle stood, in fact, on the opposite side of the mountain, but there is no modern access road to enable you to approach by that route. You will, so to speak, be coming in by the back door, and there is consequently no obvious natural entrance to the fortress as it is approached. It is necessary to scramble over the first line of defences to reach the outer bailey, which occupies a site of roughly 3,000 square metres. Situated in the centre is the old keep, and a further scramble on to the walls will take you up to the highest point, 580 metres above sea level. This pinnacle is marked by a small stone obelisk on which many of those who have climbed to the ruin have scratched their names, possibly in the sincere belief that they were about to die of exhaustion and wished to leave a last message for their loved ones. Normally we would abhor such thoughtless vandalism, but considering the effort needed to reach the spot, and the sense of triumph when it is done, we can perhaps look upon it just this once with an indulgent eye. At least one of the authors briefly lifted a sharp stone and stared longingly at the obelisk, but ultimately professional decency won the day and he tossed it aside unused.

The first reward for your considerable achievement in getting this far is the staggering view. The phrase, or variations of it, may seem to some overused, but here it is simply the truth. On a clear day, it is possible to see the entire Mediterranean coastline from Gibraltar to the lighthouse at Cabo, near Fuengirola, as well as the North African coast. Any ship crossing the straits or hugging the coast can be plainly seen and this alone explains why the castle, whose construction must have been a daunting enterprise in its day, was built on such an inaccessible rocky mountain peak. As in all such places, there is a curious sense of timeless, melancholy peace and of the slowly turning wheel of history. It is difficult, as you sit, stand or walk among the crumbling stones, not to be reminded of Shelley's great poem Ozymandias: *Look on my works, ye mighty, and despair!* The castle of Montemayor was a symbol of strength, wealth and power. Those who ruled in it, and those who finally took and destroyed it were the greatest, most feared men of their time and place. Today it stands silent and broken on a bare, abandoned hilltop. Long before the Moors swept across the straits and established their eight-hundred-year Iberian empire, Spain was known as the land of rabbits. You may not see them, but there is abundant physical evidence at Montemayor that the rabbits are its masters once again.

Seen from below as you make your trek up the mountainside, the ruins look quite substantive, but once you are standing above the castle by the white, graffiti-covered pillar, you will realise how much of the structure has been destroyed. During the years of the Christian reconquest towards the end of the 15th century, the castle would have presented a formidable obstruction in the path of the Christian troops as they attempted to pacify the local population, but once the area was subdued, it would have been deliberately destroyed to prevent it being re-occupied or used as a rallying point for future rebellious Moriscos.

The original structure of the keep is difficult to define since many of the upper levels have caved in and collapsed into the keep itself. Hidden chambers must still exist, as can be seen from the two northern towers, one of which bears pinkish rendering. From the keep the outer bailey wall can be followed, with towers or bastions at prominent points. Obvious breaches are found, no doubt the work of the marauding Christian conquerors, but the engineering skills involved in taking advantage of the natural rock outcrop have to be admired. From the castle all roads leading into Benahavis can be closely observed, as well as the Ronda-to-San Pedro highway.

The view from the ruins is no longer strategic, but it is astounding. In fact, there are superb views of the mountains and the coast to be had almost every step of the way up the track to Montemayor, and these alone make the walk to the castle worthwhile even for those without the courage or stamina to attempt the final steep scramble into the castle itself.

A second route can be taken to Montemayor, via the golf course of the same name. From the very small pueblo of Cancelada, just off the N–340, follow the signs to 'Montemayor'. It is a long, bumpy and adventurous ride, and if you take it, don't be fooled by the friendly bi-lingual signs which urge you to 'Keep going – *Sigan*', and try to bring you comfort with, 'Nearly there – *Muy cerca*'. These refer to the golf course and not the castle. You will have left the last of them way behind before you are ready to park your vehicle and climb the final hundred feet or so on foot, although the ruins are visible along much of the way, on the right.

On the way down from the castle, heading for Benahavis itself, the ruins of *Torre Tramores* can be seen. (See the Towers of Benahavis)

The Mediæval Towers of Benahavis

If Benahavis was viewed from the sky and, by using a little imagination, considered as a kind of misshapen dartboard painted on the hills, the network of 15th-century watch towers which surround it would look like the wayward missiles of some clumsy thrower. All of them missing the inner and landing way off the bull, but close enough at least to highlight exactly where the bull is. The exception, of course, is the most notable one of all – the one which stands in the central piazza and now forms part of the town hall/*Cuarto Hondo* complex, which we have already discussed in some depth.

These towers were certainly built around this period to act as protection against the *Moriscos*, and as look-out points for the approaches of pirates, both Turks and Moors, who might either seek refuge in the town or simply plunder it. The closest one to the Montemayor track, once you hit the road, is the *Torre de Cercado* (the Enclosed Tower).

Torre de Cercado

This old watchtower still stands on the outskirts of Benahavis, though probably in a much altered state from its original. Take the road marked *Valle de Guadalma*, which is on the right as you enter the village, and you will immediately see it standing in the centre of a large piece of as yet unurbanised land, close to the river. Though its name means, literally, 'the fenced-in tower', there is no sign of such an enclosure today. The visitor can park his car and approach it without hindrance.

The tower was certainly used to guard the gorge which constituted the only entrance to the village from the coast.

The first impression it is likely to give the modern visitor is that of a tiny rustic church, magically transplanted from some quiet English village. To the right is what remains of the tower itself, standing perhaps ten metres high and about six metres square. Attached to this is a long, low structure which may well have served originally as the tower's watertank. There is little doubt that the tower, when built, would have been much higher than it is today. It stood in a guarded valley, in line of sight of the castle of Montemayor; part of the area's defence system. A watchtower not much taller than a man on stilts, as it is today, would have served little purpose.

The site is unprotected, and it is possible to enter both the tower and the subsidiary structure. This strongly bolsters the 'church' impression which is gained during your initial approach, and it seems certain that at some time after the Christian reconquest of the region, the tower was indeed adapted for use as some kind of chapel. To the left of the entrance is a raised area with two niches cut into the wall, which is strongly suggestive of an altar room. In front of this, and to the right as you enter, is the body of the structure which would have been ample for a small congregation. A water trough now stands by the left-hand wall, but this belongs to an even later stage, when the building was used to stable horses.

As Benahavis continues to expand, *Torre de Cercado* is likely to be swallowed by it like a mouse by a snake. Already there is a row of modern houses within a stone's throw of the tower. Whether it will one day be the historic centrepiece of some future urbanisation, or be extracted like a rotten tooth to make way for one, remains to be seen.

Torre Tramores

The ruins of *Torre Tramores* can be seen from the trackway, as you return to the village from Montemayor. However, any attempt to approach it will bring you up against a forest of 'Private' signs which, though probably of doubtful legality, are intimidating enough to make the visit not worthwhile unless the mood for spirited confrontation is upon you. It may be possible simply to walk to the site, following the river bed upstream from the village for a distance of 2.5km, but do remember that the tower was built to guard the northern approaches from the mountains and is today part of a private *finca*, so some form of camouflage, or at the very least a convincingly bewildered foreigner's 'lost and *no comprendo*' grin, is advisable in case of challenge.

Cortijo de Torre Esteril

The name is today misleading. There is no farm, *cortijo*, associated with this tower any more, although the traces of the farm building which was once built on to it are still visible on its walls.

To reach it, you need to head out on the Ronda road from San Pedro and keep an eye out for the golf course 5 kilometres up the mountain. Balls which are badly sliced and roll down the mountain are, of course, considered lost.

The tower, the name of which can mean either 'sterile' or 'futile', is now to be found on the edge of the golf course of *Los Arqueros*. Much farmland in this part of Andalucía has been sacrificed to the all-conquering game. It sometimes seems that courses are being built so close together that players are in grave danger of driving off the tee on Course A and hitting the fairway on Course B, or perhaps an unwary spectator on Course C. The design of Los Arqueros is credited to the Spanish golfer, Severiano Ballesteros. The designer of Torre Esteril is unknown. Time alone will tell which survives the longer. It is intriguing to wonder whether the building of such towers was indeed overseen by a professional, or at least qualified, specialist craftsman, or whether they were built by ad-hoc gangs of soldiers or villagers largely by instinct or inherited folk wisdom, like ant-hills. If we wish to see the designer's hand in the constructions, a comparison can certainly be made between Torre Esteril and the very similar Torre de Sal, which once protected, and now simply overlooks, Bahia Casares. (See Casares)

Torre Esteril is of Moorish origin, and may have originally guarded the Ronda coastal road. However, in time it became just another of the string of towers which once protected the valley. Later still it became an integral part of the farm buildings on the *cortijo* which took its name. Today, it is still in use to stable horses, and the entrance to the tower is barred by an iron gate secured by a shiny new padlock. It is good to see practical use still being made of these ancient structures centuries after their construction and the loss of their original *raison d'être*. So long as they are useful, they will continue to stand, although judging by its current situation, the next practical use for *Torre Esteril* may well be as a look-out point for missing golf ball spotters.

Torre de Campanillas

Although *Torre de Campanillas* (Tower of the Small Bells) is still standing, and easily seen from the roads around the Los Arqueros golf course and

Torre Esteril, it is now within the bounds of a private finca which has taken its name, and thus it can only be reached by permission of the owners. While this may be frustrating for visitors, there is at least the consolation that Torre Esteril is easily accessible, and of broadly similar design to other square towers. Whether monuments such as these should be allowed to fall into private hands, and thereby arbitrarily placed out of bounds to researchers and interested visitors, is a debatable point, but that is the reality and it has to be lived with. The sign *Camino Privado* (Private Road) is becoming more and more commonplace in this part of Spain. The legality of many of the signs may itself be open to doubt – they are more often than not erected by wealthy expatriates who have paid enormous sums for their fincas and feel that entitles them to privacy. One can understand the desire, but there is no doubt that ancient rights of way are being lost, often on no more than the whim of such owners. The natural reaction to such a sign is to shrug, sigh, and turn away, without questioning its authority. Consequently they are proliferating like mushrooms after a storm, and it seems inevitable that sooner or later their legality will be officially challenged by some determined rambler or investigator.

Some idea of the amount of land around Benahavis which is becoming out of bounds for the culturally or historically-minded visitor can be gained by reference to the *Coto la Zagaleta.* This estate, once the property of the famous, many would say notorious, Arab arms dealer, Adnan Khashoggi, has been developed into a paradise retreat for millionaires: anyone who can afford to pay 100 million pesetas for a plot of land. The estate, which covers an astonishing 860 hectares, was originally conceived as an ecological reservation, and it won the Ford Prize for Nature Conservation in 1991. Among the cork oaks, strawberry trees, conifers, gall oaks, and along the banks of the five lakes, deer, sheep, pheasants and goats roam unhindered. No building taller than two storeys is permitted, and only 400 half-hectare plots are reserved for residential use, leaving 660 hectares to nature. It is indeed a paradise, but an exclusive one, and so far as the passing seeker of history is concerned, what lies within its borders is now as remote as the planet Mars.

Other Possible Sites

At least three more possible tower sites exist around Benahavis at former fortified homesteads or centres of law and order. 3.5km to the north-east, at *Casa del Guardia* (grid reference 189465), 2.5km south-east at *Cortijo Torrecilla* (191422), and 3km west at *Casa del Guardia* (143438).

The province of Málaga is well strewn with hunting estates, most of them private, but those who have no taste for celebrating the fineness of a day by snuffing out the life of an animal or two, yet still have an urge for the chase, could do worse than setting out, notebook, binoculars and camera in hand to track down the remains of these and other even more obscure towers. Though it is unlikely ever to rival birdwatching or trainspotting in its popularity, tower-hunting can certainly give those more traditional pursuits a run for their money in terms of both frustration and reward.

As always, note should be taken that the hunt will lead you not only up to and beyond the ubiquitous 'Private' signs, but also into the habitat of other hunters out for more animated game. Do not be mistaken for a rabbit. Similarly, in spite of the questionable authority with which many of the 'Keep Out' signs are erected, think carefully before knocking them aside to move on. The authors of this book have no wish to become the founders of a new rural guerilla movement of sign-burners and trespassers. Despite the undoubted cachet attached to giving a new word to the language (*any* language), the prospect of *Wawnista* becoming a popular Spanish synonym for 'marauding vandal' is not a comforting one.

The canyon carved by the rio Guadalmina which marks the dividing line between the municipal districts of Benahavis and Istán is noted for its natural beauty, but the pools which the river forms as it moves quickly through in its rush to leave the mountain in search of its brother, the sea, can be dangerous. Many of them are of great depth, and the currents and eddies are often treacherous. One particular pool, known locally as *Charca de los Novios* (Lovers' Pool) supposedly got the name one hot August day long ago when two young lovers stopped there to bathe. The girl dived in and was swept away. Desperate to save her, her horrified boyfriend threw himself into the water and was swept away in his turn. The bodies, they say, were never found. Like many legends, this one may have begun life as a mother's dramatic warning to her overly adventurous children, but it would be wise to heed it.

Daidin

Within the Benahavis Municipal District is the reputed site of the lost Moorish settlement of Daidin. We cannot be sure, because Daidin suffered an identical fate to Arboto. (See Istán) It was deliberately erased from the earth and from official record around the same time and for the same reason. Its few Arab survivors were scattered around the hills, taking the memories of their vanished home with them and passing them on to their children, who in turn passed them on down the centuries. Memories fade and oft-told tales become twisted and blurred, but folk memory should never be entirely discounted. It was by paying attention to the folk memories and legends set down by Homer, that Heinrich Schliemann was able to discover the site of the lost Greek city of Troy. Daidin was no Troy, but its suffering was no less real and if it does lie hidden somewhere in the hills of Benahavis, it is to be hoped that its ghosts are finally at peace. A deserted homestead in the north of the district is the alleged site, although the Istán Municipality claims another.

Chapter Seven

Benalmádena

Historical Background

FOOTBALL, EXPERTS INSIST, is a game of two halves. In much the same way, Benalmádena is a town of two halves. The original village bearing the name is a tranquil mountain *pueblo* with quiet cobbled streets which looks down on its wild coastal offspring like an anxious and slightly disapproving mother. Benalmádena-Costa, an unruly adolescent of a resort, has grown rapidly from infancy to sturdy manhood by the sea and has cut its apron strings with a vengeance. The two are still tied together, but by an untidy umbilical knot called Arroyo de la Miel. Although Arroyo de la Miel (*Honey Brook*) has Moorish roots and a long history (its name celebrates the fame and excellence of the honey made there in the 16th century), it has degenerated into an undistinguished urban sprawl, a dormitory town where a large proportion of those employed in the local tourist and leisure industries live. As a claim to fame, it has lost its honey and gained the Tivoli World Amusement Park.

The old village of Benalmádena-Pueblo is situated 2km from the coast and struggles, so far with some success, to remain aloof from its brash coastal love child, which has spread its wings so close to the neighbouring town of Torremolinos that it is now virtually a suburb. It does, however, possess a large and interesting Marina, which is easily the equal of the much-touted Puerto Banus.

Although Benalmádena-Pueblo is still relatively insulated from the brashness below, it is beginning to lose its old Spanish ways due to the inevitable and growing influx of sun-seeking expatriates. Though not yet on the scale of Benahavis or Mijas, Benalmádena-Pueblo does show signs of mutating into that Costa del Sol peculiarity, the Spanish town without Spaniards. Sit at a roadside café and the people around you are as likely to be Dutch, German, British or American as Spanish. Many are tourists, but an increasingly high proportion are residents.

Archæological discoveries in the nearby limestone mountain caves of Los Botijos, el Toro and La Zorrera are evidence that the area has seen human habitation since at least Neolithic times. Certainly the Iberians and Phœnicians knew it well, and left some traces of their passing, as did the Romans, who settled along the municipal coastline. A number of ancient fishing sites have been

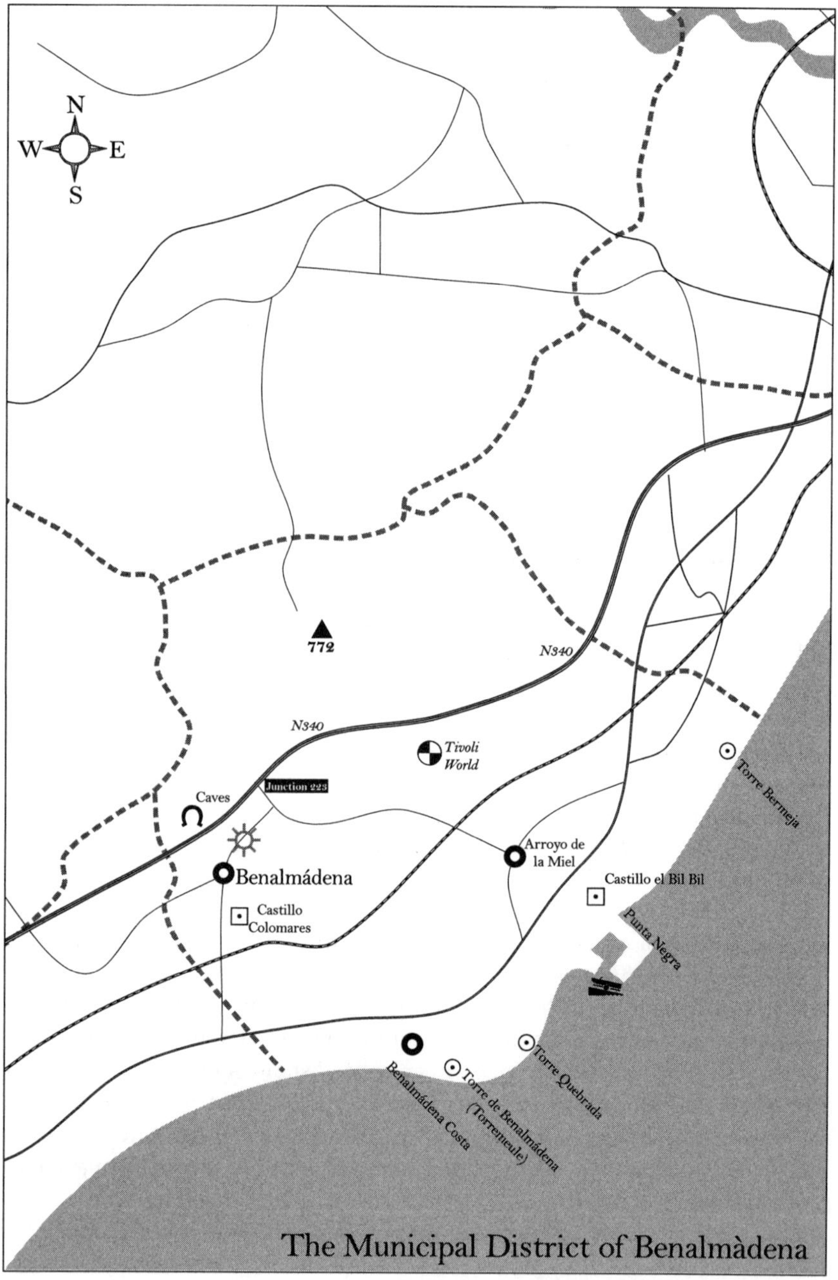
N
W
E
S
772
N340
N340
Tivoli World
Junction 223
Caves
Benalmádena
Castillo Colomares
Arroyo de la Miel
Castillo el Bil Bil
Torre Bermeja
Punta Negra
Torre Quebrada
Torre de Benalmádena (Torreneule)
Benalmádena Costa
The Municipal District of Benalmàdena

discovered and excavated, and the findings are exhibited in the excellent, if small, Archæological Museum which is the pride of Benalmádena-Pueblo. (see below)

Strangely, neither the Phœnicians nor the Romans exploited, to any great extent, the rich mineral wealth of the area. That was left to the Moors, who gave the town its modern name. 'Benalmádena' derives from an Arabic phrase meaning 'son of the mines'. During the Arab era, which stretched on for 774 years, Benalmádena grew into an important source of minerals. The words 'mining town', or 'mining village' will inevitably bring to the minds of British readers images of dour, grey, grime-covered terraced cottages huddling together for warmth beneath black northern skies and lashed by bitter winds. If Benalmádena was ever covered with grime, it has long since been washed off by the rains of a thousand winters. It is clean and clear, and a sign on the wall of the village square commemorates its award of a prize in 1970 for being declared the most beautiful municipality in Málaga province.

The town suffered badly during the Christian reconquest, and was virtually destroyed before being repopulated by Christians from the Guadalquivir valley. In essence it is a familiar story which was repeated all over Andalucía and which will recur with the chilling, if monotonous, frequency of a television commercial throughout this book. Its former Arab inhabitants were either killed or forcibly removed, and their land handed over to Christian 'settlers' – in this case around 150 of them. They rebuilt whatever the soldiers had left half-standing and gradually the town came back to life again. Subsequently it became incorporated into the coastal defensive system. A chain of 15th century towers can be followed along the coastline on the edge of the municipal dividing line with Fuengirola. Torre Muelle, Torre Quebrada and Torre Bermeja are notable, and easily found. At the same time that the towers were being built, a settlement grew up at Los Boliches. The word *boliche* has two meanings, each of them concerned with fun and games. It is the word for the jack used in bowling, and also the name of a child's' ball and cup toy. Consequently, it is intriguing, though no doubt whimsical, to wonder whether it was here that the seeds of the 20th century's pleasure resort-orientated Costa del Sol were sown. The probable truth is dull and prosaic. It is far more likely that the name is connected with the number of small traders, or *bolicheros*, who set up business in the area.

But if we mischievously give way to our whimsical thoughts, and imagine the early inhabitants of the area devoting themselves to the persistent pursuit of frivolous play, we can see the contemporary people of Benalmádena as worthy inheritors of a long tradition. As we approach the close of the twentieth century, ambitious plans are afoot to turn the town into one of the most spectacular tourist attractions in the whole of Spain. Under the overall title, *Proyecto Olimpo* (Project Olympus), plans have been laid to create no less than four impressive theme parks, dedicated in turn to the sea, the earth, nature and the sky. In addition, the main N–340 road will be forced underground as it passes through the town, leaving Benalmádena itself as a model community and, in theory at least, a pedestrians' paradise. The project encompasses all manner of cultural, architectural and structural innovations which will, if implemented, fundamentally transform the town as we see it today.

The Pueblo

Hopefully the brash, ambitious schemes outlined above will affect only the coastal town and leave tranquil Benalmádena-Pueblo as the sleepy witness to a less frenetic past that it currently is. A quiet spot where those who wish to escape the compulsive pursuit of the perpetual fun-filled minute can stop to breathe and feel the joy of escape from the frantic obsessions around them. The best views to be had from the old town are undoubtedly those from *Los Jardines del Muro* – the 'gardens of the wall'. These have as their centrepiece the 17th century *Iglesia de Santo Domingo de Guzmán*, which was heavily restored in 1960. The gardens, which are not particularly large, command superb views of the coast and the surrounding mountains. This is clearly the site of the Arab castle which for centuries dominated the life of the pueblo. The gardens are now home to the parish church of Santo Domingo, and there is little doubt that beneath its foundations lie the ruins of a mosque.

Turn away briefly from the breathtaking seaward views, and look down instead into the village. Those with keen eyes will see, immediately below, the rudimentary remains of two water mills and their aqueducts, crouching among the houses like cats seeking shelter from the sun. This was a very well irrigated area, particularly during the Moorish period, and the hills remain visibly terraced to this day. Benalmádena was built on a fortified spot a little way inland, and like other similar villages, may have been designed to be difficult or impossible to see from the decks of passing ships, leaving the inhabitants in peace from pirates and raiders.

If you take the long flight of steps which leads from the gardens to the parking space below, you will find a true sign of the times awaiting you: one which would have been as alien to Benalmádena's mining and farming ancestors as a probe from the planet Mars. Who are the mystic-minded New Age expatriates, we wonder, who have brought to these timeless hills Merlin's Vegetarian Café Bar?

Archæological Museum

Benalmádena is justly proud of its museum, which is particularly noted for its fine collection of pre-Colombian art. It also offers for sale good quality reproductions. The museum owes its existence to Felipe Orlando, a painter, poet and philosopher who somehow found his way to Benalmádena from his native Mexico and, like many who later followed a similar path, decided to stay. His personal collection provided the museum with its original stock of exhibits. It is well worth a visit, but weekend and early afternoon visitors are going to be disappointed, since it is closed between 2 and 4pm on weekdays, and shut completely on Saturdays and Sundays.

Those arriving at its bolted wooden doors on those days or at those times and turning away with a curse or a sigh will not have their spirits raised by the electronic tourist information machine which has been placed strategically in front of the building as a kind of consolation prize. Like most such well-meant devices, it is invariably out of order. There will, however, be comfort in reflection. So long as slick technological reliability is held at bay, Benalmádena-Pueblo will still be, at heart, however heavily she disguises herself, an Andalucían white mountain village.

Arrive at a decent hour on an ordinary, non-fiesta weekday, however, and you will find the museum doors standing wide and inviting, and carrying the welcome news that entrance is free. Do not expect the V&A. No uniformed attendant will greet you or follow you around, alert for sudden movements and signs that you have come to smash and grab. Indeed, the building's only human inhabitant is likely to be the receptionist/curator – a white-bearded man full of years and slow of speech, who greets visitors with a soft *hola* from the little room to the right of the entrance, where he guards and sells his postcards and his excellent reproductions of many of the pieces to be seen around the museum.

The first room, to the left as you enter, and directly opposite the curator's quiet bazaar, is the only one devoted to non-American or pre-Colombian artefacts. Three of the four walls carry neat, clean glass cases in which you will see pottery and other items found locally and relating largely to the Roman past. A simple map painted on to the wall above one of the cabinets shows the rough locations of most of the finds. There are four: the *Cueva de los Botijos*, the *Cueva la Zorrera*, *Saladero Romano*, and *Torremuelle.*

On the floor are the remains of a small Roman anchor. Two larger anchors can be found outside the room. Printed notices in Spanish, German, English, Dutch and French reveal that these and other items in the collection were discovered by members of a diving club called *Los Delfines* (The Dolphins). The coastline must surely be littered with other similar relics, and energetic, adventurous visitors might like to don their flippers and snorkels and try their luck.

The rest of the small museum (two more rooms upstairs and three more at the bottom of a winding staircase) is devoted to the pre-Colombian collection of Felipe Orlando. Mayan figurines, three-legged pots and cooking vessels from Mexico and Nicaragua and Ecuador, masks, and much more stand here a long way from home in the undisturbed stillness of what was once a grand old house in the Andalucían hills. It is a wordless metaphor for the twisting trails and tricks of fate which wash us all like flotsam across the sea of Life and leave us beached on unexpected shores.

As you leave, the old man at the door will remind you that he has postcards and pottery and books for sale. He will be pleased if you buy, but if you do not, *bueno.* There will be more visitors tomorrow, or next week, or next month, and someone will buy something. Museums such as this have opted out of time, and greet it merely as a slowly passing friend.

Chapel of Nuestra Señora de la Cruz

Nuestra Señora de la Cruz (Our Lady of the Cross) is the patron saint of Benalmádena village. During the latter part of 1997, at a cost of some 16 million pesetas, the old chapel dedicated to her was extensively rebuilt and enlarged. Four new side chapels were constructed, and the vaults were enlarged. These will be used to house and display the treasures of the religious order of *Nuestro Padre Jesús Nazareno y María Santísima de los Dolores del Pueblo*, which had been locked away for many years due to lack of space and a suitable setting. The pride of the village in its patron saint was further displayed by giving the renovated building a facelift and a fresh coat of paint, and improving the entrance and surrounding area to make access easier for wheelchairs. The time and money expended on the renovations did not dull the villagers' desire for more. No sooner was the work on its new side chapels completed, than they became the temporary home for the images usually displayed in the church of Santo Domingo de Guzmán, while that building underwent yet another renaissance.

Neolithic Caves of Benalmádena

The caves were discovered in the 1960s by potholing enthusiasts from Málaga who found cave paintings, human remains, pottery shards and tools from Neolithic and Palæolithic times. Many of the objects are now on show in Benalmádena's museum (see below). Unfortunately, the caves' remoteness was no protection against vandalism and the ubiquitous dumpers of domestic refuse, who seem to have an instinctive ability to seek out sites both of uncommon beauty and historical interest to desecrate. Eventually, in a desperate attempt at preservation, the caves were sealed on the orders of the Department of Culture. In the mid-1990s, teams of archæologists and volunteer potholers set about cleaning them up and properly assessing their condition. The cave of Los Botijos (the jugs) in Sierrezuela was in a particularly bad state, due mainly to the dumping of waste by local construction companies. El Toro, in the Sierra de Mijas, and the site of several wall paintings, had also been ravaged. The work on the restoration and preservation of the caves is continuing at the time of writing, but no final decision has been taken on whether to reopen them to an interested public.

Castillo Monumento Colomares

Easily the most bizarre of the attractions to be found in Benalmádena-Pueblo is this weird construction which is located at the western end of the town, where the exit road turns for the descent to the coast. Travellers coming upon it unexpectedly may be forgiven for feeling that they have stumbled on a misplaced section of Walt Disney's Fantasyland. A mass of rococo towers and ornate stonework, it is the brainchild of Doctor Esteban Martín, who calls it, with some justification, 'A Fantasy in Stone', and has dedicated it to Columbus' discovery of America and the cultures of the Middle Ages.

Construction – perhaps 'creation' would be a better word – began in 1987, and although it has been open to the public since 1994, work still continues on the 'castle' more than a decade later. Entrance to the site will cost you 300 pesetas, plus another 50 pesetas for the small colour brochure, printed in English and Spanish, which will guide you around the various cloisters, fountains, towers and monuments which, in their bewilderingly ornate way, illustrate aspects of the life and historic voyage of Christopher Columbus, as well as other significant points of Spanish history.

The concept is undeniably eccentric, and the visitor is likely to be struck simultaneously by its odd beauty, the certainly impressive quality of the stonework, and the inescapable kitsch incongruity of the place. To add an extra touch of the surreal, the site is connected to a falconry (entrance to which costs extra) where demonstrations of that hunting art are given daily. As you walk among the spiralling towers, wondering quite what to make of them, you may hear, wafted on the breeze, the amplified words of the falconer talking his audience in Spanish and English through the various parts of his demonstration. It is all very strange.

Torremuelle

Visiting coastal towers and other sites in Andalucía can be a dispiriting business. All too often the tower, the villa, the farm, the industrial complex is visible only as a few rotting stones which have been abandoned by the authorities to fight a daily battle against choking weeds and mindless vandals. The stones seldom win.

It is a pleasure, therefore, before setting course away from Benalmádena, to stop off briefly at the tower of Torremuelle and restore one's faith in what can be done with a little effort and imagination. The tower stands on ground immediately above a clifftop restaurant called *El Mirador* (the viewing point). Since virtually every clifftop restaurant in Spain is known as El Mirador, there is a hint that the determination and effort which we noted above have not been matched by innovation and originality, but for that we may be quietly grateful.

Having made your way to El Mirador, there are two simple ways to reach the gleaming white tower above it. Ignore the flight of wooden steps which leads from the roadside to the restaurant's entrance, and take instead either the white stone stairway beside the houses to the left, or walk around to the right-hand car-parking area where, in the left-hand corner, you will find a narrow path leading upwards. Both the white steps and the unpaved pathway will lead you within seconds to a flat area directly above the restaurant, in the centre of which stands a well-preserved, whitewashed tower of clearly Moorish origin.

For once it is not necessary to approach it through acres of thigh-high brambles, nor to peer at the structure through a veneer of coarse graffiti. The builders of *El Mirador* and the dwellings around it decided to make the tower of Torremuelle an integral part of their new vision. It stands proudly and immaculately kept in the centre of its small domain. Around it there is a modern circular stone path, and a patch of beautifully manicured grass. Bougainvillea and other flowers abound, and in the tower's shadow is a small playground designed for children of up to five or six years of age, along with benches so that parents, or anyone simply out for a stroll, can sit and watch, or just enjoy the tranquillity of a beautiful spot.

Torremuelle is a fine example of what can be done with the merest trace of concern and good will. It may have lost its *raison d'être* long ago, but it lives on as a proud tribute to its nameless builders, and a reminder to us of how closely the past, the present and the future are entwined. Three ingredients in the same cake; a cake whose recipe we struggle constantly to get right, but rarely with great success.

Castillo del Bil-Bil

Although the part of the coastline now swallowed up by Benalmádena-Costa was once dominated by Arab watchtowers, the roughly Moorish styled Castillo del Bil-Bil, built beside the beach of the same name, has no historic roots. It dates only from the late 1930s, when the architect Manuel Atencia built it as a private beach house for a wealthy family. Its rather nondescript and plain outer shell, now standing behind a roadside archway entrance which incorporates a restaurant, is in some contrast to its richly decorated interior, which is not without charm. In particular, the central patio, with its Spanish-Moorish-style fountain and transparent dome, is a tranquil place, quite a odds with the touristic bustle outside. The castle came into the possession of the local *ayuntamiento* in 1980, and in the years since it has become not only the headquarters of the justice of the peace and a venue for council meetings, but also a favourite spot for the conducting of civil weddings. A series of fountains around the outside of the castle provide a little coolness on a hot day, and the paintings on exhibition inside may occasionally be of interest, but the visitor in search of Benalmádena's Arab roots will not find them here.

La Era and Benalroma

There was considerable excitement among archæologists and enthusiasts in early 1998 with the discovery of this potentially important site within

Benalmádena's 200,000 square metre *La Paloma* park. As is so often the case, it came about not as the result of painstaking academic research, but as the chance result of construction work. The moment that it was clear that the diggers had stumbled across something exceptional, the work was halted and the investigators moved in. They soon uncovered a section of shell paving about eight metres square, and what appeared to be some kind of oven, along with a considerable amount of pottery.

Indications are that this is an Iberian site pre-dating the coming of the Phœnicians, and its possible importance led to requests from the archæologists in charge to the Junta de Andalucía Culture Department for it to be officially declared an area of archæological and historical importance, thus affording it much-needed protection. It is too early as this book goes to press to be certain of the outcome, but if the protection is granted, construction work will cease and the company involved be granted compensation for its losses. *La Era* may well turn out to be the most important find in the area for many years.

Another less important but interesting site has recently been cleaned up close by at Benalroma, in Benalmádena Costa. It consists of a Roman villa and sauce factory, and lies beside the Avenida de Erasa. Factory is an unfortunate word, inevitably conjuring images of belching smoke, production lines and weary workers clocking off eagerly to the sound of the end of shift whistle. Though we use it accurately enough to describe the manufacturing plant, the proximity of the villa – the owner's house – should remind us that such complexes were far closer to our modern idea of a farm.

Chapter Eight

Cártama

Historical Background

Cártama, now just another *pueblo blanco* visited by the few Ronda-bound tourists who care to wander off the beaten path, has certainly seen better days. Originally a Celtic Iberian/Carthaginian stronghold, it was probably taken by the Romans around 197 BC. The historian T. Livio recorded a battle that year which resulted in the capture of an indigenous settlement which he called *Cetima*. Cetima has not been positively identified, but Livio's description of the town and its defences strongly suggest that Cártama may well have been the place, although others have associated the battle with Munda. (See Monda)

Whatever the case, the Roman town of Cártima (sic) certainly thrived. It was granted the status of *Municipium Civium Latinorum* within the Roman district of *Gaditanus* (Cádiz), and because of its strategic location at the navigable head of the rio Guadalhorce, it flourished as an industrial centre and became fashionable and wealthy. During those years it was known not only for its outstanding baths and villas, but also for its glorious statues of the gods Mars and Venus. The hinterland provided it with a rich supply of raw materials to process and Cártima, along with Suel and Malaca, became one of the three principal sites for the processing of the marble which was quarried in the nearby Sierra Mijas (see Mijas). There was also iron to be mined in the Sierra de Cártima. So far as Cártima was concerned, it was a golden age, and the town was important enough for the Romans to construct a fortress to defend it. The Guadalhorce valley was, in any case, the gateway to Malaca and the promontory at Cártima where the castle was constructed was the perfect spot from which to survey and control the countryside.

With the castle neatly placed to guard it, the valley became popular as an out-of-town (i.e. out of Malaca) residential area for the wealthy, and there is no doubt that many villa sites still remain to be discovered in the area. One which has been found lies close to the present-day *Hacienda de Manguarra y San José*. It is an extensive complex; the bare bones of a luxurious residence which, if it existed today, would undoubtedly be festooned with expensive cars and satellite TV dishes, and bleep incessantly to the sound of mobile telephones.

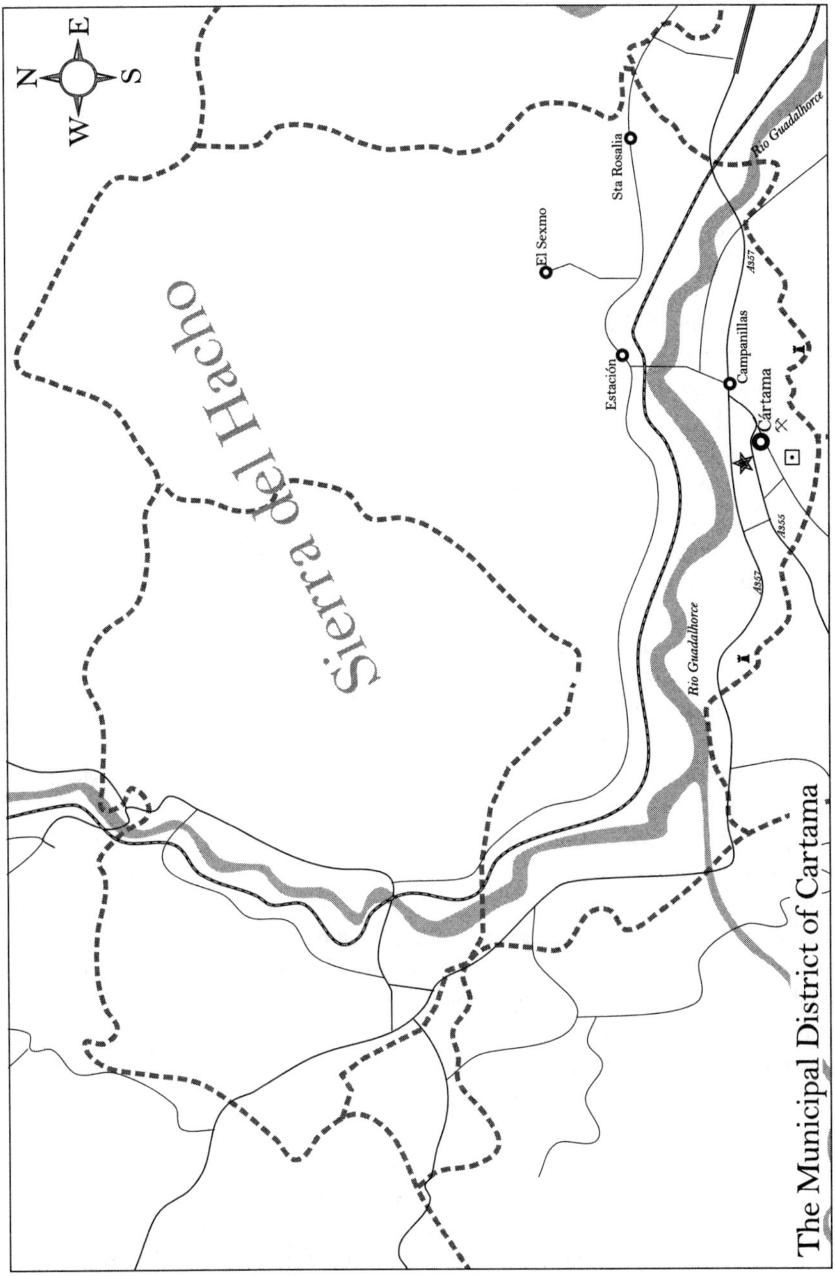
N
E
S
W
Sierra del Hacho
El Sexmo
Sta Rosalia
Estación
Campanillas
Cártama
Río Guadalhorce
Río Guadalhorce
A357
A357
A355
The Municipal District of Cartama

Leonard A. Curchin, in his book, *Local Magistrates of Roman Spain*, has reconstructed from a surviving inscription a rough family tree of a prominent local family of approximately AD 53–54. If they did not own the villa at *Manguarra y San José*, they surely knew the family who did. One part of the inscription records the magistratical office of *decemvir* – one of only three such in the entire Bætican province. The earliest of these is dated around 49 BC and the latest around AD 54, which indicates the survival of a Punic institution in the town almost two hundred years after the Roman conquest.

Cártima's golden age began to wane in the 4th century AD, when Roman control started to fragment. During the years AD 350–353 it suffered badly from raids by North African barbarians and this led to a revival of military activity in the district. Evidence of this has been found on a milestone from the period and a find of late Roman ware has suggested that this was also an early Christian centre.

In addition, there is a small Visigothic necropolis in the town, which suggests the survival of some form of Romanised urban nucleus after AD 500. Only two graves have been found, far fewer than in other Visigothic sites, but this may be the result of the remodelling of Cártama (as it now became known) by the Moors, who used much of the town's existing infrastructure to create their own stronghold. This view is strengthened by the fact that three other Visigothic graves have been found opposite the town in Pizarra.

The Moors valued Cártama as much as the Romans, and rebuilt the old fortifications in their own image during the 10th century. Today, several of their towers still stand. They vary in shape from circular to square, reflecting the fact that the castle has been remodelled numerous times during its history.

In 1485, when the Moorish sun had all but set, the Catholic Monarchs decided to lay siege to Málaga, and decided that the castle at Cártama was the perfect place from which to do it. They needed to take the town first, of course, but that was easy. The people of Cártama had no stomach for a fight. Nearby Benamaquís had resisted the rolling Christian juggernaut and had suffered badly for it. After capturing that town, the Christians had indulged in an orgy of slaughter and destruction which had produced the desired effect of demoralising the remaining Moorish outposts in the area. In any case, it was now clear that the Moorish cause was lost, and there was little to be gained from futile heroics. Like the people of Coín, they gave in to the conquerors without a struggle, and the castle passed bloodlessly into Christian hands. Málaga's Moorish days were numbered, and after its inevitable fall, the Christians appeared to lose interest in Cártama and its castle, which was left to fall into decay. It was more than two hundred years before they realised that, by tradition, they should have razed it to the ground and replaced it with some similarly impressive Christian monument. But by the 18th century such ostentatious behaviour was considered *gauche* and *passé*, and they contented themselves with the erection of a modest shrine to *Nuestra Señora de los Remedios*, which still stands nearby.

An enduring legend from Cártama concerns the Mills and Boon romance of Jarifa and Abindarráez. As with all legends, it is woven around a kernel of historical fact, just as a pearl grows around a grain of sand. It made its first appearance in print in 1565, in a book by Antonio de Villegas, but made its way into later works by writers as renowned as Miguel de Cervantes, Lope de Vega, and Chateaubriand, assuring Cártama of an enduring place in Spanish literature.

Jarifa was the daughter of the Mayor of Cártama. The 15th century was coming to a close, and the Christian reconquest was nearing its triumphal conclusion. Cártama was still in Moorish hands, but much of the surrounding countryside, including nearby Alora, had already fallen. Abindarráez had grown up with Jarifa, and for a long time they believed themselves to be brother and sister, but the truth was far more complicated. He was descended from an African tribe known as the *Aben as-serrach*, which translates literally as 'son of the maker, or seller, of horse chairs'. Unless this refers to a long-lost revolutionary form of transport, we can assume that we are speaking of saddles. In Spain the name became corrupted to *Abencerraje*, and in common with many other members of the tribe, the parents of Abindarráez settled in Granada. There they came into conflict with the powerful Mohamed Osmin al Ahnaf, known as *El Cojo* (the lame). Lame he may have been, but he was more than a match for the *abencerraje*, and the clan was all but wiped out. Only two adult members, according to legend, survived the massacre. They were Abindarráez' father and uncle. Their lives were spared on the understanding that they left Granada forever, and that their offspring too never set foot in the town. They made their way to Cártama, where the Mayor was an old friend of the infant Abindarráez' father. He took them in, and the child was brought up believing that the Mayor's daughter, Jarifa, was his sister. She was encouraged to share the same misconception. When they began to develop feelings for each other which went far beyond sibling affection, they were at first ashamed and alarmed. Eventually they learned the truth, and their story had its first opportunity for a happy ending.

It was not to be. In spite of his long friendship with the father of his foster-child, the Mayor drew the line at a romantic involvement with his daughter, and fought against it every step of the way. The King of Granada became an unlikely ally in his bid to spike the romance when he ordered the Mayor away from Cártama to take charge of Coín. Off he went, taking Jarifa with him.

A weaker man, or a less ardent lover, might have admitted defeat, but Abindarráez was no man of straw. He took to riding into the dangerous countryside, allegedly seeking Christians to fight, but in reality visiting Coín and his beloved Jarifa. On one of his clandestine visits, despite her father's continuing opposition, they agreed to be secretly married. Shortly afterwards, as he was leaving Cártama to put the plan into action, he was surrounded and captured by Christian troops under the command of the Mayor of Alora. Villegas names the Mayor as Rodrigo de Narváez, but this cannot be so.

Narváez certainly existed, but he was Mayor of Antequera seventy years before the time of the legendary lovers.

Realising the hopelessness of his situation, Abindarráez begged his captors to kill him. If he could not have Jarifa, life had no further meaning. The Mayor, whoever he was, listened to his prisoner's story and was moved. He offered Abindarráez a deal. He could travel on to Coín to marry his sweetheart, but only on the proviso that he returned to Alora three days later to surrender himself. The love-smitten *abencerraje* instantly agreed and was sent on his way. No doubt the soft-hearted Mayor assumed it was the last he would see of him, but Abindarráez was either the most stupid man in history, or the most honourable. Immediately after his wedding he revealed his pledge to Jarifa, and, in the face of her objections, insisted that he must return to Alora to keep his word. As soon as she realised that he was not to be swayed, Jarifa vowed to return with him and share his captivity. This was speculative in the extreme. The Mayor of Alora had made no mention whatsoever of conjugal visits.

When, against all his expectations, the Mayor saw Abindarráez return, he was so impressed with the *abencerraje's* courage and probity (or moved to pity by his witlessness), and the obvious intensity of Jarifa's love for him, that he snapped his fingers and freed them both. More than that, he determined to intervene on their behalf not only with Jarifa's father, but also with the King of Granada, to arrange a pardon for their unapproved marriage. After such a courtship, it would be a cruel irony if they did not live happily ever after. Which, of course, they did.

To reach Cártama, watch for the signs on the coast road between Torremolinos and Málaga which direct you to Churriana. Take the indicated road, but bear immediately left as you enter it to begin your journey up the valley of the Guadalhorce. A Roman road once followed this route from Málaga to Alora and onwards to Teba and Ronda, while a second road, opposite the river valley, led to Antequera. Once on the road, you can easily follow the signs to Cártama.

The Pueblo

There is extraordinarily little evidence in the town today that it ever experienced a Golden Age. If the Roman town really did burst at the seams with baths and villas and glorious statues of the gods, they have vanished as completely as playing cards dropped into a conjurer's hat. The solitary tantalising reminder is an impressive Roman column, complete with a carved capital, which marks the entrance to the town at the junction of the *estacion de Cártama* road. There is a small church, *Parroquia de San Pedro,* which bears the date 1502, and may well occupy the site of a former mosque, but other than that the *pueblo* is small and unpretentious, nonchalantly dismissing its previous importance and its often turbulent past with unassuming modesty.

Until, that is, you look towards the sky. The great hill under which Cártama shelters is the boastful blabbermouth that shouts the story the self-effacing village would rather not discuss. On its sides, two or three lines of ancient defence works can still be clearly seen. This was a place worth defending, and worth defending well. And two-thirds of the way up the hill stands the gleaming white *Santuario de Nuestra Señora de los Remedios* – the 18th-century shrine erected to honour Cártama's patron.

The Hermitage Church

To reach the shrine, and the ruined Moorish castle above it, park your car at the entrance to the town, and walk up calle Pilar Alto. The word *pilar* has a number of meanings, one of which is 'the base of a fountain'. Sure enough, at the top of the street a stone water fountain stands beneath a protective arched canopy. The fountain is dated 1872; the canopy 1976. Obviously its importance is undiminished. Unlike fountains in British towns, or even the larger, more sophisticated towns of Spain, fountains in the *pueblos* are seldom merely ornamental or decorative. Despite the near universality of piped domestic water supplies, they are still a functional part of village life and women still come to fill their bottles, their buckets and their jugs. If you are preparing to climb to the shrine and the castle on a particularly hot day, you would do well to take a drink from the Pilar Alto fountain before you begin.

Immediately behind the fountain is the start of a cobbled pathway which zig-zags its way up the hillside towards the shrine. The path is wide but very steep, and when damp, the stones are slippery. On the rocks here and there are daubed rough crosses, which weary cynics might assume mark the spots where pilgrims exhausted by the climb gave up the struggle and died. About half-way up, on a small grassy outcrop beside the path, two stone benches, looking for all the world like a miniature but unfinished model of Stonehenge, have been strategically placed for the benefit of those who are beginning to feel the strain and need to rest before tackling the final few hundred yards. The sanctuary is hidden from view for most of the climb, and when it eventually reveals itself as you turn the last bend, it is a welcome sight. Outside the metal fence which marks its entrance, two more stone benches have been placed. The one on the right bears the inscription, *Viva la santisima Virgen de los Remedios,* and the date 1933. Its counterpart on the left carries the same date, and the name, *Jose Hidalgo Espidora.* Presumably this was the saintly benefactor responsible for providing these restorative aids to those of a certain age and sub-athletic fitness, who wish to cease puffing and panting before respectfully entering the sanctuary itself.

Within the fence, but outside and to the left of the shrine's doorway, is what appears at first to be nothing more than a nondescript brown box, about five feet tall with a rectangular hole cut into it. The effect is of a squat, unadorned Punch and Judy booth. In fact, it is a shelter for the votive candles which the faithful have lit either in prayer, or in gratitude for the answer to a prayer. It is refreshing to note that for once these are real candles, and not the penny-in-the-slot mechanical variety which have become so common.

Nuestra Señora de los Remedios translates as 'Our Lady of the Cures'. It seems ironic that in order to reach her, it is necessary to climb a long, steep and tiring pathway which is only comfortably negotiated by the fit. And woe betide anyone who makes the climb with hope in his or her heart on a Wednesday. It is her day off, and the shrine is closed.

Inside, the 18th century origins of the sanctuary are instantly apparent in the unexpectedly ornate rococo ceiling, the crystal chandelier, and the wall decorations. In contrast, the seven bare wooden benches placed there for the faithful congregation are simple to the point of austerity. A statue of the revered Virgin is the centrepiece of the altar, which stands at the end of the rectangular room, eternally facing the door and the pilgrims who enter. It is a poignant place. On each of the side walls there are four notice boards on to which the devout, the despairing, and the desperate have pinned mementos of loved ones for whom they seek the Virgin's blessing, protection and miracles. Photographs, some recent, others old and faded, ribbons, baby shoes, scribbled names. Faith in the divine power of Our Lady of the Cures is today rarely the initial line of defence for the sick. Most are prepared to give the mumbo-jumbo of modern medicine a crack first. But she is always there. The last and best resort.

Immediately to the right of the altar, there is a small room which is incongruously plain and domestic compared to the flamboyance of the shrine. It contains a simple wooden cupboard, a table, a couple of chairs, a rocking chair. The table is beside a window which looks out on to a beautiful view of Cártama way below. It is a room which might be found in almost any home in the mountains, and it is, strictly speaking, not part of the shrine itself, but part of the living quarters of its keepers, so please treat it with respect.

The statue of the Virgin is far smaller than one is used to seeing in Spanish shrines and churches. It could almost be a child's doll, but it is no less revered for all that, and it is believed to be almost 600 years old. It is said that the image was discovered under a stone by a shepherd boy out on the hills. He thought it was a toy and decided to take it home as a plaything for his sister, but when he got there the doll had vanished from his pouch. When he returned to the hill the following day, he found it back under the same stone. That day the sequence of events was repeated, and the next, and the next. The lad became not only profoundly frustrated, but sorely afraid and went off to tell his story to the parish priest. The cleric gathered the wise men of the village together, and together the sombre posse climbed the hill. To their amazement, they found the image lying beneath the stone, just as the boy had said.

A cynic might have instantly accused the boy of putting it there and chastised him heavily for wasting everyone's time, but cynics were at a premium in Cártama in those days, and miracles were eagerly looked for and frequently found. The image was universally agreed to be *Nuestra Señora de los Remedios* and her determination to lie under stones on the hillside was taken as a sign that she wished a hermitage to be built there to house her. Why she didn't simply hover over the place and point was an issue that was never raised. Having finally got her message across, she allowed herself to be carried to the priest's house, and stood patiently on the altar he constructed for her until her shrine was almost finished. Then one day he found her off the altar and halfway to the door. Whether the shepherd boy had been in the vicinity that morning is unknown.

It was a sign that she was ready to go to her new home, and the entire village marched with her up the hill and placed her in the shrine.

By the 20th century it might be thought that she was a little old for the rigours of world travel, but that is exactly what she embarked on in the 1930s. The Civil War was looming, and anti-clericalism was rife among the Republicans. They believed, with good cause, that the Established Church supported Franco's Nationalists, and church buildings, images and even priests and nuns themselves, were targets for their wrath. Fearing for the safety of their beloved Virgin, the local priest and the poet, José Gonzalez Marín, who lived in the village, hatched a plan. The real Virgin was replaced by a cheap copy, carved quickly by a sympathetic carpenter, and Marín smuggled the real one out of the country and took her to South America. Sure enough, the Republicans broke into the sanctuary, took the false image, and destroyed it. Meanwhile, Marín was touring South America like a travelling showman, drumming up support and financial contributions for the Nationalist rebels by exhibiting the rescued Virgin wherever he went. It was hardly dignified behaviour for a venerated lady of so great an age, but she endured it and returned to Spain and Cártama at the end of the war to even greater veneration.

The Castle

The climb from the shrine to the ruins of the Moorish castle above it is far more difficult, and not for the faint-hearted. You will need to scramble along a difficult, very steep and extremely narrow path, which snakes its way along the mountain rim like a helter-skelter ride without a safety rail.

As we race towards the millennium, it is fashionable to reflect on the uncertainty of our times, and to invest earlier epochs with a golden glow of relatively idyllic peace and security. Climb to the fort at Cártama, or to any other ancient hilltop site, and the illusion is shattered. Those who lived there – Iberians, Romans, Moors – were people who lived their lives in constant fear of destruction and attack. Why else would they place their homes and their defences in such inaccessible, almost impossible spots? Surely not for the views, no matter how awesome. How many lives were lost in the construction of walls on the very edge of high cliffs? How many children, climbing the walls as children always will, fell to their deaths? What of the aged and infirm, no longer able to negotiate the strength-sapping, perilous adventure which leaving and re-entering the defences entailed? What of those who simply couldn't? Did at least one fear – the fear of heights – not exist in these earlier cultures? Acrophobia is among the commoner dreads, and many a modern visitor to Cártama, though physically fit, would find it psychologically impossible to scramble up that path to the summit. Yet people lived here, regardless of the difficulties and dangers. And the reason was fear. They huddled together high above the valley floor, ever alert for approaching enemies; fearful and distrustful of the world outside their comforting walls.

The path begins immediately outside the gate of the shrine. You can take it either to the left or to the right. Of the two routes, the right-hand one is probably the easier. That will lead you into the remains of what was the castle's main keep and bailey. The left-hand track will bring you finally to a deep, arched water tank. The site is large, and many of the old walls have survived. It takes only a little imagination to reconstruct the fortress in the mind's eye. It was unquestionably a formidable place in its time. To say that it dominated the valley that encircles it is a sublime understatement. Now the broken castle walls guard only daisies and buttercups, and the occasional lazy butterfly. Cártama lives quietly in the valley below. Whatever threats it may face in the future are ones well beyond a castle's remedy.

Lovers of the Spanish blood sausage, *morcilla*, will find the home of one of the country's best-known brands in Cártama. It can be bought at No. 8 calle Pilar Alto, as you return from your visit to the shrine and castle. The house is conveniently situated for the carnivorous but historically-minded visitor at the top of the village between the ruins of the castle and the early 16th century parish church.

The Mystery of Cerro Fahala

In the hunt for ancient and often neglected ruins there will be walls, and there will be rumours of walls. The hills around Cártama are dotted with reminders of the area's pre-Roman importance. Two Iberian hill forts once existed three kilometres to the west, in the vicinity of Campina on the southern bank of the rio Grande, and another fortified settlement occupied a small plateau across the river close to Aljeima. All this indicates very strongly that this was a gateway to the Iberian hinterland and probably an important exchange point with the enterprising Phœnicians. Consequently, it comes as no great surprise to learn that a small fortification exists on the summit of the hill known as *Cerro Fahala* (named for the river which runs nearby). In their enthusiasm, the authors climbed a second hill nearby, and stumbled into another ruin and mystery. The mind loves patterns and continuity, and our first instinct was to fit the ruin into the accepted picture and ascribe it to the Iberians, dating its construction to around the 4th century BC. However, anyone visiting the site today is likely to find it baffling and mysterious.It soon became clear that this was too facile.

The imposing limestone hill on which it was built can be climbed with relative ease from its sloping side, while its other edge presents a formidable sheer face, scalable only by those who relish mountaineering. It balloons out of the earth close to the smouldering municipal rubbish tip, as though desperate to rise rapidly above its irritating fumes. If this truly is an Iberian site, it is not the only residual Iberian stronghold in Andalucía which lies in intimate but noxious proximity to burning refuse, but the search for an historical link we leave to other researchers.

On reaching the lush, green summit, the explorer might be forgiven for assuming that there is nothing to see. The vista is breathtaking, the air is filled with the scent of sweet alison, the tall grass blows in the breeze, but there is no immediate sign of any habitation, now or ever. Yet it is there. Make your way to the sheer side. Suddenly, as you approach the edge, you will find a deep, man-made trench which runs around the high rim. It is impossible not to be reminded of the familiar defences associated with the First World War. The trench is about four feet deep and perhaps two wide. Horseshoe shaped, it fits snugly around three sides of the hill like a stone collar. At several points along its route deep cavities have been carved into the rock to give shelter from the elements. Its most prominent feature, however, comes at a point where the ditch forks. One route leads on around the ridge, while the other, much deeper, trench gives access to a cross-shaped lookout position, from which any observer could survey the entire valley. Clearly the remains of a defensive tower, but what did it defend?

At first it all seems perfectly logical, but on deeper reflection a number of stubborn questions begin to niggle. Why does the defensive trench guard the difficult sheer cliff face, while the comparatively mild slope, up which even authors can scramble without too much effort, appears undefended? Why was the ditch dug to defend a hill on which there is no sign of significant habitation? Could it be that we are completely misinterpreting what we see, and that the lookout post is a child of our own century and was intended as a machine gun nest during the Civil War? It is not inconceivable that it was utilised as such, but that is surely not the answer. The ditch is obviously older, and it is tempting to take the easy option, credit it to the Iberians and file it neatly away. Yet there is something unsatisfying about the place. It is like a piece of a jigsaw puzzle which looks the right shape, and bears the right part of the picture, yet stubbornly refuses to fit where you want it to go.

There is another intriguing possibility. During the War of Independence, in the first years of the 19th century, the French occupied this part of the country for two and a half years. Suddenly it is possible to imagine a French gun firmly in place on that dominating lookout spot. From the military point of view, it makes perfect sense. As a solution to the mystery it is far more satisfying than our other suggestions, but a mystery it remains.

The historian and the archæologist frequently have to resort to intuition and speculation. Few sites give up their secrets willingly. This nameless hill clings on to hers with unusual tenacity. Those who built it had a plan and a purpose. Its construction took considerable time and energy. It was *used.* But for what? And by whom? When? As we turn away and retrace our steps down the hillside, the answers are left behind us in the swirling currents of the wind. An eagle catches them beneath its wings and soars into the sky.

Ermita de Casapalma

Why do some churches and shrines survive across centuries, while others are abandoned and left to rot like a carcase in the desert in the comparative blinking of an eye? The *Ermita de Casapalma* was once a place of reverence, but is now shown less respect than a tramp sprawled amid his own filth with a rapidly emptying bottle in his hand.

It is not a venerable building – certainly no more than a century and a half old – yet it has been rejected, stripped naked and left humiliated. For once the puzzle is easily solved, and we have no need to summon Sherlock Holmes. A great new road, passing through the *Casapalma* estate which the shrine once adorned, sliced off the vestry which stood on its left side, and went careering on its way, leaving its stricken victim to die. A classic case of hit and run.

Orange trees are still cultivated almost to the shrine's door, but the last few feet are choked with undergrowth. The remains of the steps down which the congregation once solemnly walked to enter their place of worship are now almost submerged beneath the foliage, but the door stands wide open and inviting. All that is missing is the priest, standing on the steps, checking his watch, and wondering what has happened to his flock.

Well, not quite all. What is also missing is half of the door. It stands open because it can no longer be closed. It was a fine door once, and the remaining half – the right – is still solidly impressive. But someone has taken the left side. Where is it now? Reduced to standing guard at the entrance to some pretentious villa? If so, surely it shudders in shame as it dreams of what it used to be. And how long before someone else returns and takes away its twin into similar slavery?

Inside, the shell of the church is now bare and empty, yet the altar is still in place, although broken, probably deliberately. Stone altars do not spontaneously crumble when left alone. The oddest thing in the skeletal building is the painting which occupies the niche above the altar where the image of the Virgin once stood. It is a garish composition of blue and gold rays emanating from a central spot. It was clearly executed after the shrine had been abandoned, but by whom and why? It reminds the viewer instantly of the all-singing, all-dancing religious cults of 1960s American prime time television, or perhaps the inspirational covers of magazines such as *The Watchtower.* Perhaps some similar sect attempted to take over the *Ermita de Casapalma* and revive it?

But it was too late. Within a few years it will be gone, and probably unremembered.

Cerro de la Horca

The seeker after vestigial signs of ancient inhabitation suffers many disappointments. Armed with a map, a handful of muddied facts, a hotchpotch of legends, educated observation, and his own all-too fallible but sometimes gloriously and rewardingly justified intuition, he scours the country like Don Quixote in search of giants to vanquish. If most of his giants turn out to be windmills, he has at least the satisfaction of the hunt and a well-spent day. One of his chief weapons is the name-place clue. Places are called something for a *reason.* Sometimes the reason is obvious, sometimes not.

It is known that various Phœnician, Iberian and Roman settlements existed in the hills around Pizarra. The likely hills are easy to spot. They may be low or high, but they are flat-topped, self-contained, and easily defensible. One excellent candidate is the hill known as *Cerro de la Horca.* Physically, it fits all of the major requirements. Except for one. It is excessively wet. So wet, indeed, that drainage channels have been built into its sides to take off the surplus water. Its summit is now totally cultivated. Orange trees stand in row upon row. The hill is low, and scrambling to the top takes no more than a minute or two in spite of the damp slipperiness of its lush covering.

If it was indeed home to some ancient Iberian or Phœnician community, the evidence lies tangled in the roots of the trees. But reverting to our place name clue, we get a distant whiff of the sinister. The hill may harbour more secrets than we know. *Horca* can mean nothing more chilling than 'pitchfork' or 'yoke', but it has another more gruesome definition. *Cerro de la Horca* can also be translated as 'Gallow's Hill'.

Gibralgalia

Gibralgalia is a small enclave embedded like a piece of grit between the municipalities of Cártama, Pizarra and Coín. It is an odd place with a brooding atmosphere difficult to describe, but perfectly tangible. A misplaced village which would seem misplaced wherever it was situated. The people seem withdrawn, suspicious, and wary of strangers. Even the name strikes a jarring note. It does not fit. It might almost be in a different language from the places that surround it. *Galia* is the Spanish word for Gaul, and the prefix 'gibral' may well have the same derivation as it does with Gibraltar – i.e. from the Moorish *gebel-al* meaning 'hill of'. If so, the literal meaning of *Gibralgalia* is 'hill of Gaul'. In ancient times, Gaul was a western European region which occupied what is now France and Belgium, plus western Germany and northern Italy. Certainly it never extended to the south of

Spain. The Gauls were a Celtic people who migrated from the Rhine Valley some time before 1500 BC. They disappeared as a recognisable people around the time of the Franks and Visigoths in the 5th century AD.

Could Gibralgalia really be a tiny relic of Gallic influence? Did a handful of Gauls, a long way from home, once jealousy guard their Celtic heritage high in these southern hills? It would certainly explain the inescapable feeling of oddness that the place evokes. Einstein famously declared that the Universe is not only stranger than we imagine – it is stranger than we *can* imagine. How true that also is of history.

Chapter Nine

Casares

Historical Background

To say that Casares is beautiful is a little like calling a press conference and announcing to the world that an apple is a fruit. Of course Casares is beautiful. *All* the white villages, the *pueblos blancos*, of Andalucía are beautiful. Yet there is something special about the sight of Casares as one approaches it which compels the visitor, particularly the visitor encountering it for the first time, to park the car or the bike by the roadside and simply stare. It can be approached from the coast by two routes, the most direct of which is via Manilva. The alternative, however, which is signposted about 9km from Estepona on the N–340, rewards the approaching visitor with a better and more breathtaking view and has the advantage of the Restaurante La Terraza which waits temptingly at the end of the journey, just outside the village at Ctra de Casares km 12. Here you can drink in the magnificent vista along with a cold beer or whatever, as you prepare for your walk around Casares' hilly streets. The village is located on a rocky outcrop 435m above sea level and is dominated by its old fortress and the ruins of a church which was destroyed by fire during the Spanish Civil War (1936–1939).

Its name comes from the Arabic word *caxara*, meaning fortress, although the popular belief is that it is derived from Julius Caesar, who was governor of the area around 61 BC. In fact, there is evidence that the history of the pueblo dates back at least 3,000 years, well before the Roman conquest, although it remained for a long time an insignificant and unremarkable place, hardly deserving even the name of village. If it had a name before the Moors granted it one, it is lost to the ages. When the Romans did come, they left Casares pretty much alone. Its evolution as a significant centre of population had to wait for the later Visigoths and especially the Moors, although the Romans did urbanise another hilltop 4km to the west which they called *Lacipo*.

The hills of the Sierra Bermeja have a long history of human habitation. They are dotted here and there with caves which show signs of occupation during the Neolithic period, so human feet of one kind or another, shod and unshod, have walked the mountains for many thousands of years. As for Casares, recent excavations have dated its first true development as a sizeable community to between 450 and 650 AD, when the site appears to have been

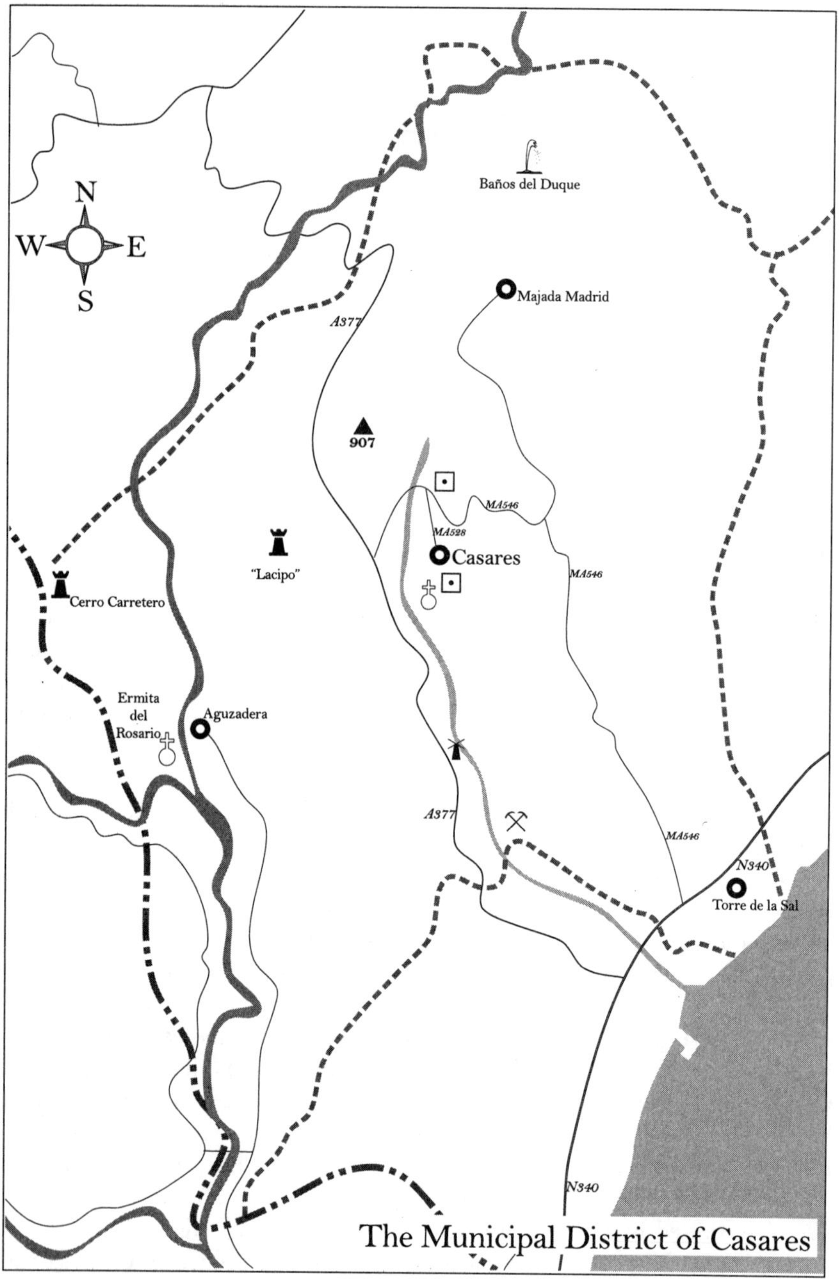
N
W
E
S
Baños del Duque
Majada Madrid
A377
907
MA546
MA528
Casares
"Lacipo"
MA546
Cerro Carretero
Ermita
del
Rosario
Aguzadera
A377
MA546
N340
Torre de la Sal
N340
The Municipal District of Casares

occupied by a Christian monastic community. A settlement developed around this, perhaps initially designed to provide the religious commune with such goods and services as it was unable to provide for itself.

The Moorish invasion of 711 AD was scarcely resisted in Casares. Mountain people lived remote lives – it is difficult in these days of fast transport and modern roads to imagine quite how remote – and the world beyond the hills was at best a distant rumour, and at worst an intrusive trouble-maker. As in many places – Jubrique was another – its existing Hispano-Visigothic population gave a philosophical shrug, threw up their hands, and agreed to pay their new masters 'tributes' in exchange for the right to keep their land and go on leading peaceful, undisrupted lives. It is a concept much admired and imitated by the protection racketeers of our own century and, doubtless, all those that separate it from the era of the Moors. In return for its 'tribute', Casares became a 'protected' area. All in all a shrewd career move as it turned out, for in the wake of the Moorish invasion, the previously anonymous outcrop became an important administration centre. And, of course, it gained itself a fortress and a name. Most of the invaders who came to settle in the village were North African Berbers rather than Arabs, although a mosque would certainly have been a central feature of the growing community. There is little doubt that this would have been situated on the present site of the 17th century church, and that it suffered the predictable fate after the Christian resurgence.

The ruined Alcázar, which dominates the village today, was the major focal point and stronghold of the settlement. It was supplemented by a second fortress built on the mountainside 1km north of the village, where it can still be seen. This smaller castle helped protect the northern approaches and acted as an additional lookout post. Between 1350 and 1484, as the advancing Christians gradually drove the Moors from Spain, Casares was on the border between the two competing cultures. To survive 130 years as a frontier town in such tempestuous times says much for the strength of the community and the tenacity of its inhabitants.

From the middle of the thirteenth century until its final fall to the Christians in 1484, Casares, like most of present-day Andalucía, formed part of the kingdom of the Nasrid dynasty of Granada, the last Muslim dynasty in Spain. The first Nasrid ruler, Muhammad I al-Ghâlib (1232–1273), was a tributary vassal of Ferdinand III of Castile and subsequently of Alfonso X, but after his death the dynasty entered a long period of internal strife, during which its submission to the Castilian rulers fluctuated with dependence on its Moroccan kinsmen. In one such power struggle, in 1361, the Castilian king Pedro I, 'Pedro the Cruel', united with the dethroned Muhammad V in the Pact of Casares, which instigated a campaign to restore the pro-Castilian Moor to power. He had ascended the Nasridian throne on the death of his father, Yusuf I, in 1354 but was deposed by his half-brother Ismail II in 1359. The fierceness of the intra-dynasty rivalry can be gauged from the fact that Ismail in his turn was ejected by his cousin Muhammad VI just a year later. It was then that Muhammad V sought Pedro's help to restore his throne, and this was achieved in 1362 after great slaughter and destruction throughout the Kingdom of Granada. Muhammad VI, knowing that he was beaten, fled to Seville to throw himself upon the mercy of the King of Castile. To beg the merciful indulgence of a man known universally as 'The Cruel' may seem in retrospect naive, and so it turned out to be. Pedro personally killed the usurper with his lance. Tradition holds that as he did so, a dramatic dialogue took place. 'Take that, because of your evil pacts with the king of Aragón!' Pedro allegedly cried, in true Basil Rathbone fashion, and as he fell dead, Muhammad VI, scorning a conventional scream or groan, cried out with some justification, 'O, how little chivalry you display!'

Thirty-seven members of Muhammad's entourage were killed at the same time, though their dying words were apparently too banal to record, and the newly restored Muhammad V of Granada not surprisingly formed a close alliance with Castile.

Pedro's nickname was bestowed upon him, it is said, because of his habit of executing members of his family and other leading nobles who had in one way or another displeased him. This, it is true, did not set him entirely apart from other monarchs of the time, but if we are to believe the contemporary chroniclers, he did take the habit to extremes.

During the reign of Pedro the Cruel old rivalries between the nobility and the crown resurfaced when Pedro's half-brother, Enrique (Henry) of Trastámara, enlisted the support of French mercenaries, led by General Bernard du Guesclin, to overthrow him. For their help the mercenaries were to be paid 300,000 gold florins – 100,000 each by the Pope and the kings of France and Aragón. It is a long and complex story which will take us a little out of our way, but will reward us with a flavour of the time.

Enrique was one of two bastard sons (Fadrique was the other) born to Leonor de Guzmán, the much-flaunted mistress of Pedro's father, Alfonso XI. When Alfonso died of the plague in March 1350, Leonor had hopes that her eldest son, Enrique, might usurp the throne from Pedro, the rightful heir. The hopes were not entirely fanciful, for despite his illegitimacy, Enrique was popular and had almost as strong a following as Pedro himself. Nevertheless, Pedro was duly crowned, and that gave Alfonso's Portuguese widow, Maria, whom the old king had reportedly despised, her chance of revenge. At her insistence, Pedro first imprisoned Leonor de Guzmán, and later had her executed.

Pedro was under contract to marry Blanche de Bourbon, daughter of a French Duke, but his real love was Doña Maria de Padilla. Maria's relations were understandably anxious for Pedro to marry her instead, and he would have been happy to do so, but royal marriages are made in diplomatic bargaining, not in heaven. He was told that that was out of the question. Blanche de Bourbon it would have to be. Blanche, by the way, was all of ten years old. Pedro did his duty and married her, but three days later he left her in the care of his mother and went back to Maria. Casares, no less than the rest of the country, was outraged, and much of the nobility switched allegiance to Enrique. Pedro survived the storm and had many of his opponents executed, including his half-brother Fadrique, whom he ordered to be killed in his presence for the crime of supporting Enrique against him.

Queen Blanche had been brought south to Andalucía for safety during the unrest. Suddenly and mysteriously she died. Although there was no proof whatsoever that Pedro had a hand in her death, or that it was anything more than natural, rumours inevitably spread. They were fanned by the monasteries, for which Pedro had a particular dislike, and seized on by Enrique, who raised an army with his ally, the King of Aragón, and marched on Castile. For a while things went well. Enrique's troops swaggered across the country killing as they went. Jews were their particular target. While they were being persecuted in England under Edward III, the Jews had lived safely in Castile under Pedro. No-one, however, was to dub Edward 'the Cruel'. Neither was Enrique to attract the epithet, yet here he was indulging himself in wanton, gratuitous slaughter. History belongs to the victors, or to be more precise, the victors' authorised biographers.

Ultimately, however, this rebellion too was to fail, and Enrique was forced to seek refuge in France. By 1366 he was ready for another try. It was at this point that he joined forces with Bernard du Guesclin. Pedro hit back by forming his own alliance with Edward, the Black Prince, and the combined English and Castilian forces soundly defeated those of Enrique at Nájera, on the borders of Castile and Navarre, on April 13th 1367. Enrique escaped but many of his troops were captured. Characteristically, Pedro wanted to kill the lot. He had a name to live up to. Edward, partly through chivalry and partly through a desire to obtain ransom for the prisoners' release, objected. The alliance became strained and Edward, who was in any case ill, withdrew with his army to Bordeaux. Without his restraining hand to hold him back, Pedro instantly reverted to type, killing indiscriminately and demanding hostages from the towns in the area to ensure their loyalty. Enrique, meanwhile, brought in reinforcements from France and returned to Castile in September 1367. He was recognised as king by various *cortes*, including those of Córdoba, Jaén and Valladolid, and as Enrique's forces gradually encroached on Toledo, Pedro retreated steadily into Andalucía.

In 1369 he decided on a counter-attack to recover Toledo. He marched north as far as the fortress of Montiel but was easily defeated in battle by du Guesclin's army on March 14th. He fled to temporary security inside the fortress and offered the French general 200,000 gold florins plus the towns of Soria, Almazán and Atienza, among others, to switch sides. It was a tempting offer, but du Guesclin, ever the entrepreneur, reported it to Enrique, who instantly vowed to match it if he would betray Pedro. He agreed, and lured Pedro to Enrique's tent at the dead of night on the pretence of helping him to escape. An inevitable fight ensued and Enrique, a keen student of Pedro's diplomatic style, stabbed his half-brother in the face with a dagger and finished him off as he lay on the ground. Pedro the Cruel was thirty-five years old. On March 23rd 1369, Leonor's eldest son was finally crowned King Enrique II of Castile.

The fortress at Casares was finally seized from the Moors in 1484, and once again the majority of the population took the change in their stride and remained to work the surrounding lands under their new masters.

In 1491 the Catholic Monarchs, Ferdinand of Aragón and Isabella of Castile, whose marriage had united the two royal houses of the Iberian peninsula, ceded the town of Casares to Rodrigo Ponce de León, Duke of Cádiz. The remaining Moors were restricted to the Serranía and a fresh population was drawn in from Jimena, Gibraltar and Tarifa as well as Extremadura and Castilla.

Casares remained a prosperous village until 1570, when, in common with all the pueblos in the Sierra Blanca, its residual Moorish population rose up in revolt. The Duke of Arcos negotiated a surrender with the region's two main Moorish chieftains, El Arabique and Ataifar, who capitulated on the King's terms. It hardly mattered. While other villages fought on to bloody defeat, Casares surrendered, only to be the victim of reprisals when the rebels were thrown from the castle into the ravine below. The subsequent expulsions from the town and the dividing of the spoils between the victors led to a general impoverishment of the region.

This clearly did nothing to quell the rebellious nature of Casares, since its most famous modern native son was the Andalucían Nationalist leader Gil Blas Infante, who was born in the town on July 5th 1885 and executed by Franco's own rebels at the start of the civil war. He is commemorated by a statue which now stands beside the Virgen del Rosario chapel on the Plaza de España.

Casares and its Fortifications

Most people, when they think of Casares, think of a Moorish castle dominating an ancient pueblo. In one sense this is true, but progress over the last 400 years has destroyed virtually all traces of the old Moorish structures.

There are two entrances into the fortifications, and either route heading up out of the town will take you on a circular journey around the ruins. One entrance to the fortifications is an enclosed passageway, while the other resembles some kind of formal gate. The base of the walls is certainly Moorish, but everything above shoulder height almost certainly dates from around AD 1500 and later.

Within the walls of the fortress which sits brooding over Casares like a lazy hen, are the ruined *Iglesia de la Encarnación* and the adjacent remains of the Hermitage of Vera Cruz. Considering the importance of Casares to the Moors, it is surprising that even taking into account the inevitable post-Moor destruction by the Christians, virtually no Moorish influences remain in the fortress, except perhaps in parts of the foundations. The church was built in

1505, when Spain had been free of the Moors for a dozen years. It remained in use until 1845, and the building was badly damaged by Anarchists during the Civil War of 1936–1939. Today it is locked and deserted, with only a printed notice by the door to tell the passing visitor something of its history. These signs are a feature of Casares, but are of limited help to the non-linguist, since they are printed only in Spanish.

The tourist who is used to visiting historic places around Europe and beyond, and finding them neatly segregated from the teeming contemporary life which surrounds them, may sometimes be surprised by the casual interaction between such sites and their surrounding communities in Spain. The ruined fortress above Casares does not stand in proud isolation awaiting the reverent approach of polyglot pilgrims bearing cameras and phrase books. The town clings tenaciously to the hillside like the toughest lichen (many houses and other buildings are built directly into the rock face), and spreads almost to the steps of the ruined church, beside which is the still-used cemetery. The small piazza in front of the church is as likely to be filled with local children on bicycles as it is with tourists staring at the views and the buildings, and scratching their heads as they try to make sense of the Spanish signs.

You should not be surprised, therefore, to see, as you approach the adjacent ruins of the Hermitage of Vera Cruz, lines of washing stretched across them to dry. Resist the temptation to decry this as the disgraceful boorish behaviour of the offensively ignorant. Washing has no doubt been drying here in the mountain breeze for hundreds, if not thousands of years. We shall pass by in an hour – perhaps less – and leave Casares to live on and launder for centuries more.

The most notable feature of the ruined hermitage is a large domed alcove which may have been its altar room. Three of its four walls are still standing, and they are pitted here and there with what seem to be bullet holes. During the savagery of the Civil War, when the church itself was reduced to ruins, it was common for factions to dispose of their enemies by hurling them in time-honoured fashion from the fortress walls into the deep gorge below. For as we have seen, this was by no means a modern idea. It had been used as a way of disposing of enemies and unwanted prisoners for hundreds of years. Certainly many died in this way after the unsuccessful Morisco rising in the 16th century. Could it be that in our own allegedly more enlightened times, the old altar room of the hermitage was used for other, more conventional, but no less horrific executions?

Further evidence of intense Civil War activity in the area can be seen by gazing across from the ruins to the next hill. Close to its summit you will see some curious stone objects which appear at first sight to be chimneys. They are not, however, evidence of present-day troglodytes living in the darkness of underground caves. The spot was used early on in the war by snipers and lookouts. Whoever held the Moorish fortress dominated the ground, and that was no less true in 1936 than it was a thousand years before.

It is not unlikely that many men died there and that the odd memorials were erected in their memory where they fell.

These bizarre structures and protective walls can be reached from the road by winding your way gingerly up a bramble-covered goat track, now home to a large chicken run and an adjoining dilapidated finca. If you choose to make the climb, remember that hills are invariably and mysteriously steeper coming down than going up, and that goat tracks have a habit of hiding in the undergrowth the moment you need to retrace them, so be prepared for a little slithering and scrambling on your descent, and whatever you do, don't slide over the edge.

A walk through Casares – and the only practical way to see Casares *is* to walk – is a continually rewarding experience. It likes to call itself the birthplace of Andalucía and the melting pot of the ages has certainly produced a place that is quintessentially Andalucían and where even the least academic can experience that paradoxical sense of timelessness amid the endless slow passage of time. It is not, however, for the unfit and the infirm. Casares is a hill town and every step you take will be either up or down. The steep walk to the hilltop fortress has as its prize not only the ruins themselves, but magnificent views of the surrounding countryside. But it is tiring, especially in the heat of the Spanish summer, so take it gently and pause along the way. It is certainly worth it. And if you really cannot manage the climb, but still wish to leave Casares having drunk deeply of its history, seek out the *Casa de la Cultura* and the Municipal Library. With admirable Spanish pragmatism, they share their home with a bar.

Roman Town of Lacipo

4km west of the centre of Casares, on the long narrow plateau of *Cerro Pelliscoso*, overlooking the fertile valley of the Genil, lie the isolated ruins of the ancient Iberian and Roman town of Alesipe, or Lacipo, a fortified settlement on a site chosen for its defensible properties. No roads pass through this area and so access is initially via four-wheel drive vehicle and then on foot. The plateau is 100m × 400m in size and although no evidence of Bronze Age occupation has been found, previous occupation from the Ibero-Phœnician period is probable.

Drive west out of Casares, and at the Manilva/Gaucin junction, turn left. After a short drive of 1.5km along the main road you will see a dirt track running into the valley. This was once the main route from Casares to Jimena and San Martin, and those who have no objection to a bumpy drive can still use it. At the start of the track you will pass over a rather ramshackle and dodgy cattle grid, lurking like a lazy predator to grab and hold on to your tyres, but caution will see you safely across. The dirt track leads down to a farmstead and just past this, on the right, a very faded track leads up to a hilltop dominated by a ruined wall. Lacipo stands waiting, and although the track is probably negotiable by four-wheel drive, it is more prudent to park and walk. You will see a simple rustic gate and fence. Pass through and walk up the steep and overgrown path, savouring the sweet smell of the orange trees wafting up from the valley below. Eventually you will enter the Roman part of town.

It was founded by the Romans for the native population in the second century BC, and allowed self-development until a century later when the Romans, perhaps noting its growing prosperity, granted it the status of *civitas stipendiaria.* This allowed the town to remain self-governing and left effective control in the hands of the local population, but made it subject to the regular taxes, exactions and tributes due to Rome on an annual basis. The kind of honour which the people could no doubt happily have done without. A possible obligation may have been to mint Iberian coins during the second and first centuries BC in order to pay the tributes and administration costs of their Roman masters.

The economic strength of Lacipo was based on the production of olive oil, and this may well have formed the original contents of many of the town's water tanks. It undoubtedly attained considerable prominence within Roman Andalucía (*Baetica*), since many written records have survived, providing us with a fascinating insight into the once bustling life of this now barren and deserted hilltop.

A number of native families grew wealthy during this period and were granted, due to their generosity, prominent positions within the community. Today we would no doubt look upon this practice as political sleaze. The Numisii family, originally from Carthago Nova, prospered as a result of their trade in fish sauce with Rome. In the first two centuries AD members of the family held 'magistracies' at Lacipo. Their responsibilities were to ensure that the community obeyed and followed the Roman legal code. When an invader successfully subdues a nation and annexes it to a mighty empire, we tend to forget with the passage of time that, at least in the early years, it is no more than an occupying force. After two thousand years, we can look dispassionately at the actions of families such as the Numisii and perhaps even admire their entrepreneurial skill. Had they existed in Nazi-occupied France or the Channel Islands, we would have considered them collaborators and quislings. Later the title of *flamen* was granted, denoting a more senior magistrate who had judicial authority over the whole of the Lacipo provincial area.

A celebrated *flamen* from the town of Lacipo was *Caius Marcius Cephalonius,* who progressed from the town council to become a *flamen* in the province of *Baetica.* So keen was he for the honour that during his campaign for the post he promised to pay the community 4,000 sesterces if he was appointed, and he must certainly have incurred other expenses besides. What would the early Iberian equivalent of *Private Eye* have made of such an offer?

An inscription from Lacipo has caused some academic confusion as it appears to mention a *quinquivir* – i.e. a commissioner at Rome. If so, this is the only *quinquivir* attested in Spain. However, it is thought that the inscription may contain a mason's error, although if this is the case it is difficult to see why the stone was not simply destroyed and replaced with one that was error free. Chisels and masons were cheap. What is not in dispute is that the inscription dedicates an open-air crypt to Divus Augustus. The dedication is made by Q. Fabius Q. F. Varns-Pontifex (AD 14–37) at his own expense. The tablet now lies alongside other articles from Lacipo in the Archæological Museum in Málaga.

The town was the seat of government for the immediate area; an important centre of administration and wealth. However, the cost of running such a town was considerable and archæological evidence suggests that Lacipo was in decline by the second century AD and may have been abandoned shortly afterwards. It was certainly deserted well before the final years of the Roman Empire. The continual absorption of local aristocratic families into the equestrian and senatorial orders during the first two centuries AD gradually undermined the Roman urban system in Hispania. Towns were no longer required to keep the native population in order and new prominent families found the costs involved in the upkeep of a town at a time of rising inflation to be an expensive luxury.

The area was not completely abandoned, since a principle Roman road (Via XII) ran from the coast along the Rio Genil valley to Ronda, with a secondary paved branch road (Via XIIa) leading from the valley to Lacipo and on to the *Cueva del Baque*. ('Baque' means thump, or thud. Was the place supposedly haunted by things that went bump in the night?) This was undoubtedly a mining community, as the red-earthed mountains contain large iron deposits which were mined from the 3rd century BC onwards. The Cueva del Baque is now in the private hunting estate of Majada Madrid.

In the Visigothic/Byzantine period (6th–7th century AD) the deserted Lacipo site seems to have been used as a burial ground. A total of 25 graves have so far been found in the area of the extinct Roman town. Ten of these are rectangular, thirteen trapezoid (i.e. with unparallel sides) and the remaining two are curved. The curious thing about this cemetery is that unlike other Visigothic grave sites on the Costa del Sol, this one was placed a considerable distance – 3km – from the new capital settlement at Casares. Since there is no evidence that the remains of Lacipo were being lived in at that time, we are left with the mystery of why the dead were carried so far for burial, and why they should have been taken to the ruined symbol of an old enemy.

Today the partially excavated, heavily overgrown remains of Lacipo are not easily defined. The defensive walls seem to have been deliberately destroyed, probably by the Moors and/or the Christians when the area was a frequent battle zone around 1450. Other remains include a stretch of cyclopean wall (i.e. constructed of large, irregular blocks), water cisterns, conduits and pools.

The ruined town today can only be approached from the east, following the highly eroded, zig-zagging Roman trackway up the steep slope on to the flat plateau. The entire site was once enclosed within the now destroyed walls, but it is still possible to follow their foundations throughout their course. At the entrance to the town are two large square bastions flanking the track, marking what must have been the gate. However, the ground is badly eroded at this point and the square keeps, measuring up to fifteen feet in height, have already started on their long slide down to the valley floor.

Lacipo, though, was more than just a Roman town. An Iberian settlement pre-dated it on the hill and it would seem that the Romans merely tacked their town on to what already existed. Today, the remains can be distinctly divided into two halves. The western half represents the original Iberian town, while the Roman zone is to the north. It is the latter which first greets the explorer, though very little of the area has been excavated. Within this zone are to be seen the traces of large public buildings. The excavated sites reveal the administration areas such as the *forum*, with its grain storage pits sunk into the bedrock. Next door there are steps leading upwards to what was probably a Roman temple.

The largest remaining structure, which can be seen facing south, is a section of the otherwise ruined Roman town wall, standing thirty feet high. This particular stretch of wall still stands straight and tall at the top of the hill. It has defied everything that Nature, Moors, Christians, treasure hunters and who knows what have thrown at it for two thousand years. What would its anonymous builders think if they could be suddenly transported into the present era to stand beside us? They would surely feel immense pride that their work should have survived as a monument to their brief lives for millennia. A number of floors had once been incorporated into this structure, suggesting that the wall had a dual purpose, and it was in this area that a monumental marble inscription was found dedicated to the deified Emperor Augustus. This, along with many other finds, can now also be seen in the Archæology Museum in Málaga.

At the western (the Iberian) end of the town, where the native population lived, are the large constructed stone blocks of an irregularly planned set of domestic buildings, surrounded by a much thicker defensive wall. These structures are Turdetanian in style and, unlike those in the Roman zone, are constructed without cement. The stone-worked blocks of which the walls are built are masoned so that they sit firmly upon each other. It is interesting to note that while the later Roman zone used brick, rocks and of course cement, it has not survived or weathered time nearly so well. If our anonymous Roman town wall builders would today stand in justifiable pride at the longevity of their handiwork, how much prouder, perhaps disdainfully so, would be their Iberian predecessors.

Not only the thick, solid walls, but also the stone-covered drainage ditches are still clearly to be seen. Those who can withstand the climb to the hilltop in the searing heat of August will be rewarded with the best view of the remains, since in that month much, if not all, of the vegetation which usually obscures them has withered and burned away under the merciless sun.

The two parts of the town are conveniently, if curiously, divided by a barbed wire fence which is easily crossed. Its purpose is not readily apparent, since the site is unprotected and no excavations are currently underway, but it does serve as a neat demarcation point.

Lacipo's ruins offer today's traveller no great theatres or temples, but the location is tranquil, with stunning views of the mountains and the sweep down the Guadiaro river to Gibraltar. For the historian, this relatively unexplored town is well worth a visit, providing as it does good examples of two types of ancient architecture still standing side by side long after the people who knew them, lived and loved and worked in them, have vanished into the years. But be wary of the idly grazing cows.

Cerro Carretero

The 'oppidum', or provincial non-self governing Roman town of Lacipo, had a much smaller daughter settlement 5km to the west on the other side of the Rio Genil valley. This Ibero-Roman settlement of the 3rd–1st Centuries BC consisted of a small fortified enclosure built in the Turdetanian style, but it was never Romanised. As in the case of Lacipo itself, it was settled by the indigenous population under Roman authority but was abandoned and deserted by the 1st century AD. The fortified settlement dominated the rio Genil valley along with Lacipo and controlled access via the valley into the undeveloped mountain regions, which, though unpopulated, were rich in minerals. The settlement also took full advantage of the well-watered fertile valley and the lowland hills.

There is little to see now, but should you wish to visit the site, follow the dirt track down into the valley and cross over the river as soon as possible. To reach the summit of *Cerro Carretero,* by-pass the old finca and head on up into the hills, right to the top. A map and compass are advisable as this trip needs to be on foot, and there is no immediate help available to the casual hiker. The view from the summit is well worth the walk, as the location of the fort provided a key link between two other important Ibero-Roman settlements: Jimena de la Frontera (Oba), 10km to the west, and Gaucin which was 8km to the north-east. All of the settlements are in line of sight of each other and provided a quick communication-by-beacon system in the early Roman period, when the rest of Spain still remained to be conquered.

Ermita de Rosario

While still in the valley, you might seek out another sign of the area's former habitation. Situated near the *cortijo* (farm) hamlet of Aguzadera, is a small, well-built and recently renovated church. It is on a spur of land between the junction of the rivers Genil and Guadiaro. The area remains deserted for

Benalmádena

The Church of Benalmádena-Pueblo, built on the site of the old mosque.

Castillo del Bil-Bil – Modern building, Moorish style.

'A fantasy in stone' – *Castillo Monumento Colomares* (Benalmádena)

Roman column. Almost nothing now remains of Cártema's golden past.

Cártama

Shrine of *Nuestra Señora de los Remedios* and castle ruins (Cártema).

Casares

Casares, *pueblo blanco*, is beautiful from every angle.

The Roman bridge at Casares.

The Roman town of *Lacipo* once stood close to Casares.

The glory that was Rome – ruins of *Lacipo*.

Coin

Ermita de Fuensanta – beauty and mystery.

Torre de Trinitarios (Coin).

Olive grove, Coín.

Convent of Santa Maria, Coín.

most of the year, but comes noisily alive for one weekend each summer when it is the site of a large religious festival. Thousands of pilgrims converge on the river bank and set up camp, with the church as the focal point of the various services and processions.

The church must surely have appeared in early records, but unfortunately, accurate historical chronicles seem to have by-passed this quiet corner of Casares. What is history in a place where time moves so slowly?

To return eagerly or otherwise to the present century, rejoin the track which leads down to San Martin in the Provincia de Cadiz, or alternatively, retrace your steps back to the Manilva/Gaucin road.

The Valley of the Mills

As you drive away, turning back on to the Casares-Manilva road, you may notice to your left two green-painted mill wheels at the entrance to a winding dirt track. Those who relish adventure hiking might like to park there and walk off down the track into the valley. Those who do not should give it a miss, for you have a long dusty walk down and an even longer, dustier climb back up. The path is steep, and unlike the exploration of a hillside, the hard part comes second. The valley is scattered with mills which, for once, do not lie deserted and unused. The great majority of them have been bought and converted into homes by expatriates of various nationalities. As you walk the path, you may well see signs warning hikers of the presence of vicious guard dogs. Such signs are almost certainly unauthorised, since the path is a public right of way. Nevertheless, heated encounters with irate land owners and hand-to-paw combat with unfriendly Rottweilers are an acquired taste, and unless the visitor is a staunchly committed and courageous advocate of the rambler's right to ramble where he will, it is probably best to heed them.

Majada Madrid and the Baños del Duque

To the rambler or four-wheel drive enthusiast, careering like a free spirit across the countryside as whim dictates, a major barrier is encountered in the area of Majada Madrid. This possible Moorish settlement was turned into a private *coto* (hunting estate) after the Christian reconquest (1484), with many of the former occupants being summarily ejected and sent landless to Casares. It is owned today by an Italian expatriate who keeps the whole area secure with fences and wardens, leaving a vast expanse of cork, oak and pine forest, extending all the way down to the Rio Genil valley, inaccessible to the general public. Though the owner obviously has a right to maintain his privacy, and has paid heavily for the privilege, it is nevertheless a pity, since the estate contains not only especially imported animals for hunting, but also much indigenous wildlife and game. So sensitive is the owner to the possible spread of disease to his animals (heaven forbid they should die before being shot) that all vehicles entering the estate are made to pass through a shallow disinfectant dip. The few humans allowed to enter on foot are exempt.

The name *Majada* is not an unfamiliar one on the local military maps of the area. It means 'corral' or 'animal enclosure', which suggests that this has always been an important grazing and hunting zone within the cork oak forest. A cork factory is still maintained by the *cortijo* today and the cork is harvested from the trees every seven years.

The decision to give the name *Madrid* to this particular corral was probably taken by a previous landlord from that city in order to add an air of authority.

The *cortijo* has been extensively developed by the present owner and now consists of three large villa-type buildings, each one based on three rows of peasant-type cottages connected by cobbled terraces. The ruins of the old settlement have now all but disappeared, due to the construction of garages, stables, a helicopter landing pad, and extensive landscaping that includes a lake for duck shooting.

A Roman road leading up from Lacipo once terminated within the estate close to the *Cueva del Baque*, which was possibly an iron mining area. It also brought bathers to the baths which are known today as *los Baños del Duque*. These lie in the Sierra Bermeja at the northern extremity of the Casares municipal district, but sadly, from the point of view of the Roman enthusiast, well within the boundaries of the Majada Madrid estate.

The baths get their water from a stream known as *Fuente Santa*, flowing from the limestone hills of *Santa de la Gloria*, which rise to 739 metres above sea level. As with the sulphur baths of Hedionda (Manilva), many writers have claimed that Julius Cæsar took the waters here to cure himself of a skin complaint. It is a good story, and probably packed the crowds in once upon a time, but there is in truth little evidence that these baths were used for therapeutic purposes in ancient times. They were first described as late as 1773, when Simón de Zamora of Genalguacil wrote enthusiastically of them to Count Cristóbal de Medina. It may well be that the count suffered badly from that most agonising of afflictions, kidney stones, since Simón tells him that the waters are said to be particularly effective in their treatment.

But by the time that Simón was alerting his friend to this possible cure, the baths had been a fashionable destination for those in search of healing, as well as simple lovers of spas, for almost two decades. In 1757, the Duke of Arcos, after whom the baths are named, built a 36-room hostel for visitors. The land on which the baths were situated was at that time owned by his family, and unlike his modern-day counterpart, he clearly felt it his duty to make them accessible to all who wished or needed to come. Consequently, he included specific accommodation for the poor and for consumptives. In addition, there were separate facilities for those with contagious diseases. The bathing attendants, paid for by the Duke, lived in shacks on the opposite side of the stream. The construction work cost the Duke a little over 22,000 *reales*. Since a *real* was worth 25 *céntimos*, a quarter of a *peseta*, he got the job done for about five and a half thousand pesetas. Today's tourist queuing patiently at the *bureau de change* might think that a remarkable bargain, and it may well have been so. It should be remembered, however, that in the 1920s, almost two hundred years after the Duke of Arcos developed the site of the baths, it would have taken the average rural worker ten years, at 1.75 pesetas a day, to earn as much. In 1757, five and a half thousand pesetas was a considerable investment.

In 1760, the Duke gave the baths to his eldest son. The complex continued to expand. A chapel was built to *Nuestra Señora de los Dolores* (Our Lady of Sorrows), so that those who did not have unbounded confidence in the restorative power of the waters, or who merely wished to hedge their bets, could ask for divine intervention.

The site was further extended in 1798, but disaster struck in February 1810 during the War of Independence. Invading French troops, engaged in a battle with the Spanish led by the Commander of Algeciras, obliterated all the Duke's work. Whether this was accidental – what would today be termed collateral damage – or whether it was deliberate destruction, it is hard to say. A gathering place for the sick and consumptive does not, on the face of it, pose any great military threat. True, the Spanish troops were using it as a base for their horses, but the extent of the destruction still seems severe. Perhaps the French were determined to ensure that their surviving enemies remained ill. Whatever the reasons, the site stayed in ruins for half a century until, in 1856, the Duke of Osuna assumed the mantle of his noble predecessor and rebuilt it, adding a further 36 workers' shacks to house those given the task of caring for a new and even greater influx of visitors. There is evidence that the baths became a convivial meeting place where people went to meet, bathe and socialise, in much the same way as the genteel English would take the waters in fashionable spas such as Bath. New roads were built to facilitate access from Casares and Genalguacil, and because of the difficulty in obtaining abundant and regular supplies of food from outside, the site became largely self-sufficient. A shop was opened where meat (chiefly goat) could be bought, along with milk, cheese and other provisions. The chapel was restored, and there were clinics and a tavern. A 19th-century map of the area, now in the *Biblioteca Nacional*, shows it well populated with farmsteads of 2–4 buildings each.

Which of us has not learnt at our mother's knee that medicine is no good for us unless it tastes awful? This curious notion probably has its origins in the puritan ethic that would have all pleasure a sin, and all pain a positive benefit to both body and soul. Certainly it is a belief dear to those who patronised *los Baños del Duque*, and those who continue cheerfully to drink the waters in similar spas today. Consider the following analysis made shortly before the Duke of Osuna's reconstruction work in the 1850s. The water was said to be clear, with small white globules in suspension, which eventually formed a sediment. The smell was slightly sulphurous, and it had an astringent taste. 'Astringent' indicates that a substance causes the contraction of body tissues. In the case of medicines, this contraction is most readily apparent in the face, as every reader of this book knows. We are back, once more, at our mothers' knees. Its specific gravity was equal to that of distilled water, its temperature 13.5., and 25 lbs (11.5 kg) of the stuff was found to contain:

Muriato calizo	4 grains
Sulfato de magnesia	7 grains
Id. calcáreo	10 grains
Tierra de magnesia	5 grains
Id. de cal	2 grains
Id. de siliza	2 grains

All, our mothers would tell us, highly beneficial, but it will never outsell Coca Cola.

For a while some attempt was made to exploit the waters commercially by, of all things, a cork-production company. Perhaps the plan was to bottle the water and simultaneously boost sales of cork for use as stoppers? One can imagine the marketing men thumping the table with enthusiasm and declaring that the enterprise was a concept of genius and could not fail. In the event, of course, it failed miserably and was quickly abandoned. Today, the baths are owned by the Italian landlord, and there appear to be no plans to re-launch the product on a new-age market. The once thriving complex of hostels, taverns, hospices and shops has been reduced to two roofless buildings beside the baths. There is no doubt that the baths could once again become a favoured spa, but for that to happen, the present owner of the estate would have completely to rethink his attitude to the admittance of strangers on to his land, and this seems unlikely.

The *vaquero* (literally, 'cowboy') streams draining much of this area run throughout the year thanks to the 1449m high Mt Reales which overshadows it, acting like a huge sponge during the winter rains and then slowly releasing the water in a constant flow. Various ruined mills lie beside them high up in the *vaquero* valleys.

Torre de la Sal

This tower, standing on the point near Marina Casares overlooked by Manilva, is actually located in the territorial area of Casares. This reflects Casares' Moorish past, when the castle protected the sea approach to the village and provided a safe haven for friendly vessels, and a spirited welcome for unfriendly ones.

Though most of the coastal towers were built by the Christians between 1470–1550, this particular tower or castle pre-dates this period and is certainly of Moorish origin. It had a particularly long life, and was used as a fortification as late as the 1950s as part of a Guardia Civil Barracks, accommodating approximately fifteen men.

It is unusual also in that it is still more or less structurally intact, allowing the visitor access to its interior. Immediately beyond the entrance is a domed chamber from which a flight of steep, narrow steps leads to a second similar chamber directly above. Care should be taken when ascending, and particularly when descending them. The first high step is especially worn and dangerous, so do be careful not to leave the tower with a twisted ankle or worse. A second flight of steps will then take you on to the roof, where you will be rewarded with excellent views of Bahia Casares and the coast.

There is, however, a very large minus to balance the plusses. Like so many sites in southern Spain, *Torre de la Sal* was once totally unprotected. Access was unrestricted and unsupervised and the results were predictably depressing. The visitor who ventures inside had to be prepared for the pervading stench of urine and faeces, the heaps of abandoned rubbish and the mindless graffiti.

Graffiti inevitably inspire something of a schizophrenic reaction. As we know from the daubings in prehistoric caves the world over, certain members of the human race have always felt an urge to leave their mark on any available wall. Graffiti that are millennia old are looked upon with awe, treated with respect, studied by furrow-browed scholars, reproduced in heavy, expensive books and carefully protected, often by law. Even graffiti which are merely a century or two old are read with indulgent interest and considered among the attractions of an ancient building. But contemporary graffiti fill us invariably with disgust, both for themselves and their usually pornographically inclined creators.

The graffiti which cover the walls of the *Torre de la Sal* are unmistakably contemporary. Recently the Tower has been placed under lock and key. Perhaps, therefore, matters may shortly improve.

Chapter Ten

Coín

Historical Background

IN EARLY 1999 THE COÍN DEPARTMENT OF CULTURE launched a project to decorate the town walls with painted tiles illustrating its history. It was emergency treatment and not a moment too soon, for Coín is a town that has lost its memory. In the tiny one-room tourist office across the street from the Casa de la Cultura (where you can at least see a few interesting photographs of the town as it was in the early years of this century), you will be met by apologies and shrugs if you ask for a map of the town or a brochure detailing a little of its history. Instead the brochures on offer, and they are few, will direct you hither and yon across the length and breadth of the Costa del Sol to places where there are things to do and see and enjoy. But not here, *señores.* Here nothing happens, and never did.

But if nothing happens in Coín it has certainly happened for a long time. It lies in the fertile valley of the rio Grande and a community undoubtedly existed on the site well before the Roman conquest.

The first evidence of an Ibero-Roman settlement is to be found 4km northwest of Coín in the high ground south of *Las Huertas.* This was a large fortified place inhabited by the indigenous population. It was given a name, *Cerro del Aljibe* (Cistern Hill), but did not develop into a town and seems to have been abandoned in favour of the present day site of Coín.

We know the Romans called the place *Lacibis,* but all traces of them have gone. No Roman remains have survived in Coín, although a Roman road did connect the town to Málaga and the coastal road. At Coín the road split; one branch leading to Monda while the other headed towards *Cerro del Aljibe* and the spa settlement of Tolox.

The Roman town acted as a transition market point for the minerals that were quarried in the Sierras Blancas 4–7km to the south. It is known that marble from the quarries was used in the construction of Italica, the Roman town which once stood close to Seville, and which was the birthplace in AD 76 of the Emperor Hadrian. The quarrying of marble and the mining of iron ore, both of which were abundant, continued as late as the 19th century.

For some reason the town was abandoned during the Visigothic period and any lingering traces of the Roman era were obliterated by the Arabs,

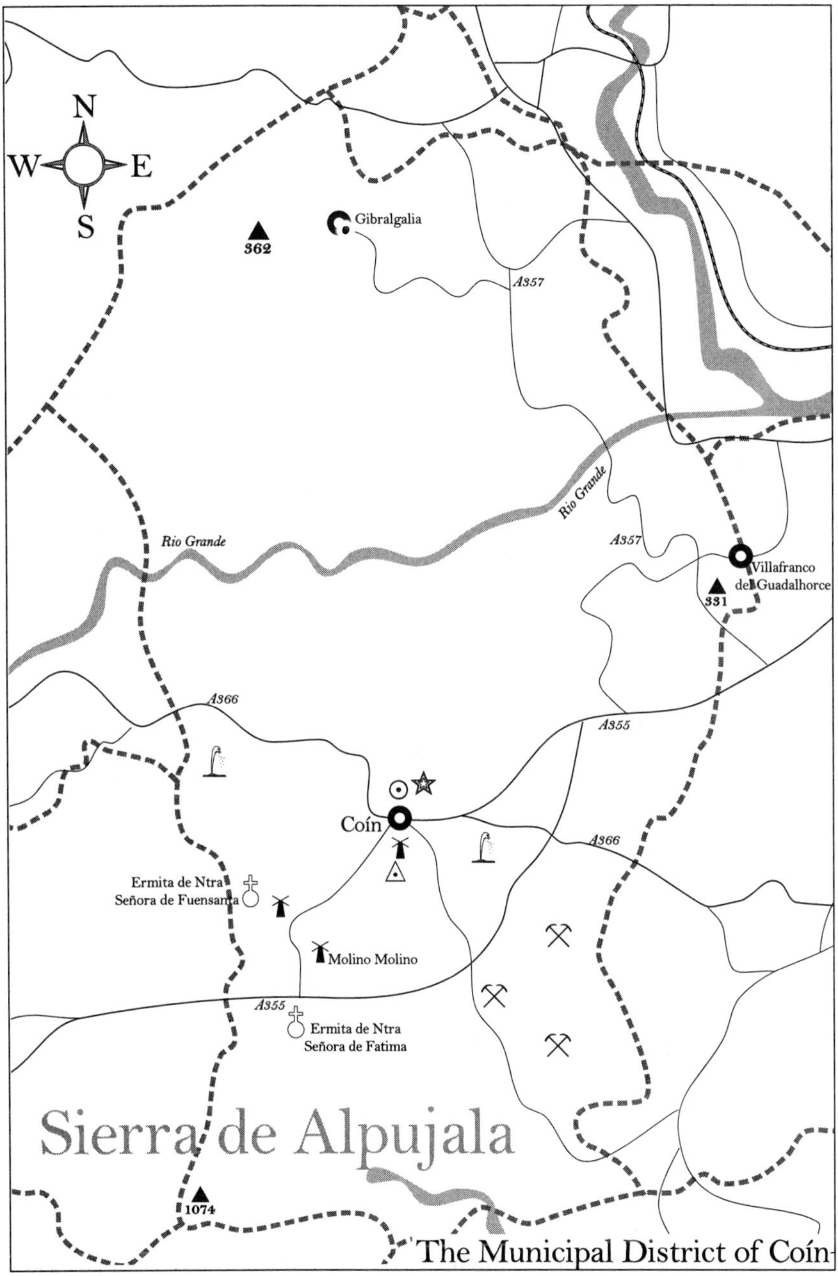
N
W
E
S
Gibralgalia
362
A357
Rio Grande
Rio Grande
A357
Villafranco del Guadalhorce
331
A366
A355
Coín
A366
Ermita de Ntra Señora de Fuensanta
Molino Molino
A355
Ermita de Ntra Señora de Fatima
Sierra de Alpujala
1074
The Municipal District of Coín

who refounded and rebuilt it as *Castro Dazcuan* after their conquest. The date of its resettlement is put at AD 929. However, the echo of its Roman name, *Lacibis,* still haunts the hillsides. As always, the Arab mosque was razed by the incoming Christians and replaced by a church; in this instance the church of *Santa Maria de la Encarnación.* It was Coín's original parish church, built in 1505, with a convent being added in the 18th century. It now stands in the Plaza Bermudez de la Rubia. Coín's main church, the Iglesia de San Juan, with its impressive pillars and arches and its curious crouching silence, was also begun in 1505, but not finished until the middle of the century. It is in the style known as Andalucian Renaissance. A third church, the Iglesia de San Andres y Hospital de la Caridad, was built in 1520 and had an unusual L-shaped floor. Today it dispenses temporal rather than spiritual judgement. It has been turned into Coín's Courthouse.

When the 15th-century Nasrid ruler Muley Hacén churlishly refused to pay the demanded tribute (today we would probably call it protection money) to the Catholic Kings, it sparked a war which was to involve Coín. The town was the scene of a fierce battle between the Christians and a Moorish force led by the valiant Hamet El Zegri. El Zegri came off worst, but for some reason he and his troops were spared the usual celebratory slaughter practised on the losing side in such affairs, and by agreement they were allowed to leave the town chastened, humbled, but alive.

Legend has it that Christopher Columbus was among the Christian troops who laid siege to the town during its final Moorish phase. So tedious did he find the long, dull days that he vowed that as soon as it was over, he would discover America and emigrate. Coín surrendered in 1485, but Columbus had to wait until the final expulsion of the Moors from Spain in 1492 before fulfilling his dream. By that time 'Crazy Chris' was well known on the European court circuit, telling anyone he could successfully corner at a party that if he took a ship and sailed far enough west he would end up in the east. Most of his victims muttered 'jolly good' and instantly spotted a close friend on the far side of the room, but in 1492 the time, the place and the circumstances came together in spectacular fashion. After delivering a final decisive kick to the Moorish rump, Ferdinand and Isabella were understandably on a high. If Spain could really rid itself of the Moors after so many centuries, no scheme seemed too madcap. Word quickly got around that they spent their days dancing and were a soft touch. Columbus seized the moment. To the King and Queen all things were possible in their brave new world. Instead of having the forty-year-old Genoan bore committed to the nearest lunatic asylum, they stuffed his pockets with money and told him to go for it. On August 3rd he sailed from Palos into history. Coín turned over and went back to sleep.

Despite Coín's apparent reluctance to acknowledge that it has a past, like a sometime wanton who has married well, the evidence is there. The ruins of a Moorish *alcazar,* built upon Roman foundations, are still to be found in the town. Captain S. E. Cook, R.N., visited Coín, Cartama and Alhaurin in

1829, and was greatly impressed. 'These villages', he wrote, 'are on rising ground above the river and in beauty of situation and cultivation cannot be excelled. They afford a specimen of the whole country when possessed by the Moors, being surrounded by gardens with orange, lemon and palm trees and abounding in all the fine as well as the more common fruits.' An orange tree still features on Coin's coat of arms.

While in Coín, Captain Cook visited a man (sadly, he does not name him) who had held an important position of state at the time of the Constitution, but who had been reduced to the rôle of superintendent in a nail factory. There is a melancholy irony somewhere inside that transition, wriggling to get out like a worm in an apple. The factory made use of the abundant streams in the hills, and manufactured its nails using iron from the Marbella mountains.

Spain was a troubled state at that time. Isabella II, the eldest daughter of Ferdinand VII, was on the throne and was an unpopular monarch. So unpopular, in fact, that she was ousted by a revolution in 1868 and fled to Paris, where she died in 1904. The years preceding the revolution were restless ones, and Coín saw its share of radical zeal, particularly in 1854, when the local Republicans and workers' organisations demanded the redistribution of the lands of the Dukes of Arcos and Montellano.

Today, Coín is an important market town which serves a varied municipal area of mountain, rich fertile valley and grassy upland. No other true settlements exist except for a hamlet or two lounging on the banks of the rios Seco and Grande.

It was in Coín, incidentally, that the authors received one of those occasional reminders reserved for travellers growing easy with their imagined grasp and usage of everyday Spanish: reminders that they may not be as fluently comprehensible as they believe. Pausing for *tapas* at an unpretentious bar, we confidently ordered for our small party three chicken rolls (*tres montaditos de pollo*) and were served, equally confidently, with two fried crab claws. Spain: a land always waiting to surprise.

The Town of Coín

The drive to Coín is a pleasant one whether you take the mountain route from Marbella or the Ronda road from Málaga. However, parking is difficult in the narrow streets, so once you arrive, it is best to abandon your car on the outskirts and enter on foot. It is hard to imagine now, but in Moorish times the town was walled and had an imposing castle. Its scant remains can be seen from the local bypass, but not from the new Málaga ring road. From the same vantage point, looking across the fertile fields at the town perched on its shallow rocky plateau, it can be seen that it has literally been built into the old walls – growing out of them like some curious stone fungus. Behind these front-line dwellings are two convents and the church of *Santa María de la Encarnación.* The more central of the convents has recently been restored and dates from the 16th century. The other, 17th-century in character, is on the northern outskirts and is visibly in need of attention. At least one other church must once have existed, since a small church tower has been reconstructed and is currently adorning a garden.

In addition, at the exit of Coín at the junction of the main Monda-Ronda road, the eye is drawn to a lone tower standing like a dispirited hitch-hiker who has given up hope of a lift. It is small, and has the appearance of a bell tower, with an arched and pointed top. It may be that the top is a post-Christian Reconquest addition to a redundant Moorish minaret. The authorities have surrounded the tower with a set of small floodlights to illuminate it after dark, but since they have omitted to provide the slightest information regarding its origin or significance, it may be that this is merely to prevent passing traffic from hitting it. Though too small to have pretensions of grandeur, this enigmatic remnant of the past is worth a brief pause before you pass carelessly on your way.

In the town itself, the main thoroughfare zigzags its way through the commercial area, eventually leading you to the southern part of town and the *Torré de Trinitarios.*

Torré de Trinitarios

This unusual triangular tower, which is now an isolated home for brooding pigeons in the playground of the Carazony school, epitomises Coín's ambivalence towards its past. It was built in the early years of the 16th century, originally forming part of the temple of *Santo Cristo de la Veracruz.* In time the temple became a convent for the Trinitarios Order, and it is by this name that the tower is still known. Finally, it was occupied by Franciscan monks. Whether the ladies gave way voluntarily to the gentlemen or were unwillingly ousted is unclear, but eventually the building itself disappeared, leaving only the tower to mark its passing.

In 1993, the Department of Culture promised ten million pesetas to pay for restoration, but it all seemed an awful lot of trouble and at the time of writing, five years later, not a finger has been lifted. Consequently, the tower has continued its steady and largely unlamented deterioration and the combination of heavy winter rains followed by fierce summer sun have rendered it ever more unstable. In 1997, the Mayor, Juan José Rodriguez Osorio, appealed to the Junta de Andalucía to begin the work with the utmost urgency. His concern was less with the salvation of an important part of the town's clouded history, than with the laudable and eminently sensible desire to prevent dislodged stones from falling on to children in the playground. It is to be hoped that the danger will be averted by the restoration of the tower, and not by its removal. In the meantime, to the casual eye at least, the tower appears to have developed an alarmingly distinct list. It may be merely an illusion created by the angles of the hills and the surrounding buildings, but there is a definite sensation of a Pisa-like lean backwards, away from the school and towards the nearby houses. Latest reports say help is on the way, but these may be optimistic rumours inspired by the chance sighting of a mysterious stranger on the mountain road carrying a shovel.

The tower stands at the foot of a steep hill, which leads to a clutch of fine villas. This is clearly the affluent part of town. A curious feature may be seen in the rock face which rises to the left and forms the boundary of the road. A number of window-like holes have been cut into the rock, and are now covered with iron-mesh grilles. Here and there is evidence of entrances which have now been sealed. Gaze through the grilles and you will dimly see an extensive network of caves in which there are some solid, but long abandoned tables and chairs. This odd place was used for worship by a Christian community which survived under Moorish rule (8th–10th century). Are the tables and chairs evidence of some latter-day attempt to revive them for use as a bar, or something of the kind? If so, why did the enterprise fail? Was it simply through lack of business, or was pressure brought to bear? Significantly, on the hilltop directly above the caves stands one of the most impressive villas in the town. (Note: the Tower was finally restored in early 1999.)

Ruined Mill and Aqueduct

Take any of the numerous turnings which lead from Coín's present-day commercial centre and head towards the higher ground – *calle La Bella Jarifa* would be a good choice – and the resulting climb will bring you eventually to the crumbling ruins of a mill. The building itself is of little interest, except to connoisseurs of obscure graffiti, but the irrigation system which once gave the mill its life is not only largely intact, but still in use by the contemporary occupants of a farm which stands a short distance away. There is strong evidence here of Roman technology being brought to bear on the problem of watering the crops, although at the same time, and perhaps a little confusingly, the foundations of the system, and particularly the grand aqueduct itself, suggest a Moorish origin. A large, impressive piece of the main aqueduct stands immediately beside the ruined mill, and the fact that it had obviously gone through repair-work or rebuilding at some point long after its foundation is evidence of just how long this spot has been cultivated. The chief crop on the irregularly terraced hills was, unsurprisingly, grain to feed the mill.

The mill no longer grinds the corn to bake the town's bread, and thereby hangs another poignant mystery of our times. Think back two hundred, even a hundred, years or less. The miller, whiter than a wraith in his habitual coating of flour dust, clasps his hands to the shoulders of his eldest son, and gazing around the rumbling mill and through the window to the fields of swaying corn, says, 'One day, my son, all this will be yours, and in time your son's, and his. No matter what else will happen in the world, people will always need bread, and we shall be here to provide it.'

Yet here stands the mill, cold, eviscerated and abandoned on the hill – just one among hundreds which are scattered throughout Andalucía like a careless frosting of sugar. There is still fresh bread to be bought in Coín, of course – alongside the dreaded, ubiquitous, factory-produced sweet monstrosity *Bimbo* – but the intimate link between the growing of the wheat, the grinding of the corn, the baking of the bread and its distribution in the town has been broken. In the idyllic rural village of the fairy tale and our imagination, in England no less than in Spain, the miller and his mill are essential. They are among the key elements which hold a village together and define its character. Once a village no longer has need of him, it has become a town; living, trading and interacting with other towns. Why make flour on the hill, when it is cheaper to buy it from the factory mill in the next valley? It is a question not of sentiment, but of sound, sensible economics. And one by one the village mills die. Our old miller friend was right: people will always need bread. He could not have been expected to foresee that one day technology and the turning of the years would remove the need for millers.

Ermita de Fuensanta

The shrine of *Nuestra Señora de Fuensanta* is one of Coín's treasures. To find it, drive away from the town towards Marbella for three kilometres, then turn to your right and drive a further kilometre down an easily negotiable track. A beautifully preserved and well-kept chapel with an impressive bell-tower, the shrine is scrupulously clean and almost a caricature of the picturesque. So popular is it with visitors, both local and non-local, that it is provided not only with a large car park, but also has a bar strategically situated beside it. It is located on top of a hill, and the views of the valley below are exceptionally beautiful, providing the peace and opportunity to stand or sit quietly and meditate or simply enjoy the glories of nature. To the left is an old mill complex – *Molino Galiano.* The Spanish have a saying, '*Querer los palacios de Galiano*'. 'To want the palaces of Galiano', whoever he was, means to be unhappy with one's social position. '*Querer el molino de Galiano*' might be adopted as a sister phrase meaning to long, if only for the time it takes to stand and stare, for the tranquil, uncomplicated existence of the man who presumably gave his name to the mill and whose life was ruled not by urban clamour and the constant bleeping of the telephone, but by the seasons and the running of the stream. It is a hopelessly idyllic vision of a life which was probably hard and unyielding, but the view from the *Ermita de Fuensanta* is peculiarly conducive to such romantic daydreams.

Odd, then, that it should be famous for a much more sinister reason. In a field beside the shrine stands a simple whitewashed house with cracked walls and a large hole in the roof. It is empty now, except for its ghosts, and if any house deserves to have ghosts it is this one. It is the *Casa del Ermitaño* (hermit's house), and on January 7th 1893 it was the scene of a particularly despicable murder. Juan García Collet, the priest who lived there, had a protégé named Juan Porras Villalobos. At Christmas, 1892, his father, Juan Porras Sánchez, an esparto grass craftsman, paid a visit to the shrine to wish the priest the compliments of the season. Unfortunately, he had been celebrating rather too well before going there and turned up at the house drunk. The priest thanked him for his good wishes, but noting his visitor's condition, asked his servant, Antonio Barea, to help him get home. Barea was feeling disgruntled. On the way he grumbled about his master, and told of a cache of money which he said the priest had hidden away for distribution to charity after his death. Whether the story was true or not, the two men decided that charity was all very well, but that it should most certainly begin, and end, at home.

Between them, it was later alleged, they planned his murder. If true, neither of them seems to have had the courage to do the deed himself. Instead it was left to Juan's two sons, Juan Porras Villalobos and his brother Manolito, and one of their friends, Juan Bernal Palma, known as *el Guareño* because he came from Guaro. On January 7th 1893, the three youths broke into the house as the priest was praying, tied him up, and demanded to know the whereabouts of the cash. Finally one of the three took a gun and shot him in the mouth.

All three were arrested, and along with Juan Porras Sánchez and the servant, Barea, they were tried and convicted of murder at Málaga Provincial Court in October 1893. Juan Bernal was given a life sentence, while the other four were condemned to hang in Coín's main square.

There then came a curious twist. Public executions were, as they had been in England until not too long before, popular spectacles. There was nothing like a hanging to draw a large and noisily enthusiastic crowd. Here was a chance to see retribution handed down for a senselessly brutal killing of a defenceless priest by three youths. We may deplore it, but all looked set for an impromptu fiesta. Yet the people of Coín rallied together to prevent the executions. Their petition reached the *ayuntamiento*, who, on June 13th 1894, asked the Queen Regent to grant each of the murderers a Royal Pardon. The Provincial Government took up the cry, and the pardons were granted.

The reason for the villagers' action, as given in Bartolomé Abelenda's book, *The Coín Crime*, was continuing grief at the death of their priest, and a feeling that they had seen enough blood shed. Abelenda, who wrote his book in 1945, was an ex-mayor of Coín and presumably knew what he was talking about. Nevertheless, the idea that the people of late 19th century Coín were pioneers in the fight for the abolition of capital punishment and that the authorities pardoned four callous murderers simply to spare them the trauma of a hanging does not ring true. Mobs then, as now, were notoriously bloodthirsty, and legal authorities have never been noted for their willingness to bend to public emotion. There is certainly more to the death of Juan García Collet than was revealed in Abelenda's book. Was he as well loved as we are led to believe? Was the guilt of the accused really proven? The secrets lie behind the walls of the crumbling house beside the beautiful shrine of *Fuensanta*, forever out of reach.

As you look down from the hermitage into the beautiful valley of the rio Pergilas, you will see several mills and also a mediæval pack horse bridge which can be approached from a dirt track. The valley must have been known to the Romans, since two kilometres downstream, in an area known as *San Román*, is a house called *Casa de Baños* with an associated water basin which strongly suggests the former existence of a Roman bath.

If you wish a closer encounter with the mills – *Molinos Galiano, Moreno* and *Pergila* – these can be approached either from the hermitage or via the old road.

Ermita Nuestra Señora de Fátima and Castillejos

At KM3 on the Marbella-Monda road (and incidentally on a very bad corner), a dirt track leads south for three kilometres to a hermitage devoted to Our Lady of Fátima. The world is a stranger place than we can ever hope to know. Those who scorn the idea of meaningless coincidence and look for omens and the hand of the divine in every corner can usually find them. For several months during 1917, in the Portuguese village of Fátima, three peasant children claimed they saw visions of the Virgin Mary. It became one of the most famous such incidents of modern times, and Fátima is now among the world's most revered places of Christian pilgrimage. Odd then – or is it? – that Our Lady should have chosen to reveal herself at a spot which bears a name sacred to many Muslims, particularly Shi'ites. Fátima, or Fátimah, was the youngest daughter of the prophet Muhammad, founder of Islam, and the only one of the prophet's children to produce a long line of heirs. Was the Virgin demonstrating her power over Islam, or calling for mutual respect and toleration? Or does it mean nothing at all? The authors, diplomats to the core, leave the reader to decide.

A further three kilometres south of the hermitage is a 1,073m high mountain top straddling the junction of the municipal districts of Coín, Monda and Ojén. *Castillejos* is a name common enough to make García seem rare, but it does suggest that this was once the site of a Moorish lookout tower with views to the sea and across to Álora, 25km to the north. This particular *Castillejos* can best be reached by road from Puerto de Ojén. Head for the hilltop radio antennae.

El Dorado and Fuente de Nacimiento

El Dorado, or Eldorado, is one of the most evocative terms in any language. Now almost synonymous with Utopia, it instantly conjures images and dreams of a golden place of wonders, wealth and lazy, sun-blessed luxury. But the original El Dorado, or Golden One, was not a place but a man. He was supposedly the ruler of a town close to Bogotá in Colombia, who had the odd and decidedly erotic habit of covering his naked body in gold dust at fiesta time and then leaping into the waters of Lake Guatavita to wash it off when he sobered up. The legend was current at the time of the Spanish conquistador invasion of South America, and one accomplished raconteur used to hold his colleagues spellbound by his tales of meeting El Dorado in the town of Omagua. What the Golden One was doing there, and whether he was strutting around naked covered in gold is unclear, though if he was not, it begs the question of how he otherwise verified his identity.

The stories fired the conquistadors' collective imagination, and on the assumption that any place which had enough gold lying around for it to be spectacularly squandered in this way must be practically made of the stuff, they set off from Peru to find the Golden One and relieve him of his body paint. They were not alone. The Germans, not yet content merely to be first to the sunbeds, began a similar quest from their base in Venezuela. Since Venezuelans and Colombians do not today speak German, it is superfluous to say which team was ultimately the more successful. But neither ever found El Dorado. The gold-covered king remained elusive, but as the search, and the resulting Spanish Empire, spread through the valleys of the Orinoco and the Amazon, the name Eldorado gradually became attached to a legendary country bursting at the seams with so much gold that, if it had ever been discovered, the precious metal would have become practically worthless overnight.

When the BBC decided to set a soap opera among English ex-patriates living on the Costa del Sol, *Eldorado*, seemed a perfect choice of title. They built a set a little way out of Coín, to the east along the Alhaurín el Grande road, filled it with lots of stock soap-opera characters and situations, and set the cameras rolling. How could it fail? Miserably, as it turned out. *Eldorado* became the most derided and short-lived soap opera in British television history. The audience, it seemed, wanted to see gritty, down-to-earth types living out their drama-drenched lives in Manchester, Liverpool, or the east end of London. They were not interested in idle traitors who had left the old country to soak up the Spanish sun.

So the set was soon abandoned. For a while it became a kind of kitsch tourist attraction, and there were rumours that it was going to be used for the making of pornographic films, but gradually it was forgotten, like the series itself. To reach the spot, drive out of Coín into the *Reserva de Castro-Ducan.* This now contains a well-equipped chalet complex for visitors, and the reserve is an excellent spot for hiking, riding and other healthy pursuits.

At the turn-off to the reserve, next door to the now abandoned *Venta El Dorado,* whose fate was too closely linked to the ill-fated programme, is the source of the *rio del Nacimiento,* which supplies the drinking water for Coín. The river is well-named, since *nacimiento* means 'birth'. The source is a natural spring bubbling from a great crack in the rocks. This is now enclosed within a sturdy Victorian-style building which is usually locked, though it is possible to see the spring clearly through the iron gates. Two flights of steps lead down into the water, showing that it has also been used as a natural bath. There is a lengthy carved inscription on the wall, telling the story of the spring, but this is so weathered that it is frustratingly unreadable, at least from outside the complex. There are also mechanical pumps to help the water on its way.

In the courtyard surrounding the building which houses the spring, benches have been set beneath the trees. There is a drinking fountain, and on a pedestal at its centre there is a bust of a worker. Sadly, no explanation is given of whether this represents an individual, or workers collectively. On his shoulder he carries a pick, but in the absence of an explanatory inscription, its significance is difficult to determine. This is a fascinating and pleasant place, and a more than adequate compensation for the loss of Eldorado. An obvious Roman site, it is now being landscaped and civilisation is returning.

Las Huertas

Las Huertas – 'the orchards' – lies four kilometres northwest of Coín in an area called *Loma de Cuenca*, or 'low ridge (or hill) of the river basin'. With such names it is clear from maps alone that this is a favoured, fertile spot. Habitation here extends back to at least 800 BC, when it was the site of an Iberian hill fort. Evidence suggests that it was in use for over five hundred years, and was finally abandoned around the time of the establishment of the Carthaginian Empire.

Another Iberian fortified town was founded at about the same time as the fort at *Las Huertas*, but managed to survive the coming of the invaders to become Romanised, living on until around AD 200. It can be found in the *Sierra Gorda*, at KM 12 on the Coín-Cartama road. (See Alhaurín el Grande)

Chapter Eleven

Estepona

Historical Background

THE PRECISE LOCATION OF THE ROMAN FISHING and agricultural settlements of Salduba and Silniana is uncertain. Silniana has been linked to Estepona, but more likely occupied a spot close to what is now San Pedro de Alcántara. It was destroyed by a seaquake in the 4th century AD. As for Salduba, some commentators put it firmly on the site of modern Marbella, while others suggest that it corresponded to the old part of Estepona. It is not important, and we shall never know for sure. If either Roman town, or another whose name is forgotten, did once exist around the site of Estepona's castle, it all but vanished beneath the feet of the Moors and Christians. The town's modern name is probably derived from the Moorish *Astabbuna.* Because of the massive redevelopment, there are no substantive Roman remains to be seen in the town today, although a few foundations and ceramics have been found. Estepona is in many ways the poor relation of its more celebrated neighbour Marbella, although the gap is narrowing due to its increasing popularity as a tourist resort and its fine harbour for luxury yachts. *Puerto de Estepona* may not yet fully rival its neighbour, *Puerto Banus,* in this respect, but there are signs that it may one day do so.

If Estepona was not Salduba or Silniana, we have no record of its name before the arrival of the Moors. In spite of its undoubted antiquity, it is totally absent from written historical records until the Caliphate era. Towards its end, the town had already seen better days, since Aben al Jhatib, writing in the 14th century, tells us that it was in a state of decadence, that its monuments had largely disappeared, and that it was living entirely on its reputation as a source of delicacies – presumably fishy ones. Since monuments need to be erected before they can enjoy the sophisticated luxury of falling down, Estepona must surely have been a place of some importance before the Arabs came, or during the earlier part of the Moorish era. The fact that previous writers chose to ignore its existence is therefore something of an historical mystery. (It is possible, of course, that records disappeared with the seaquake.)

Its shy anonymity did not spare it from the turmoil of its times. Like the red-faced schoolboy at the back of the class who tries to remain invisible, it was bound to be picked on by the teacher. At the end of the 13th century,

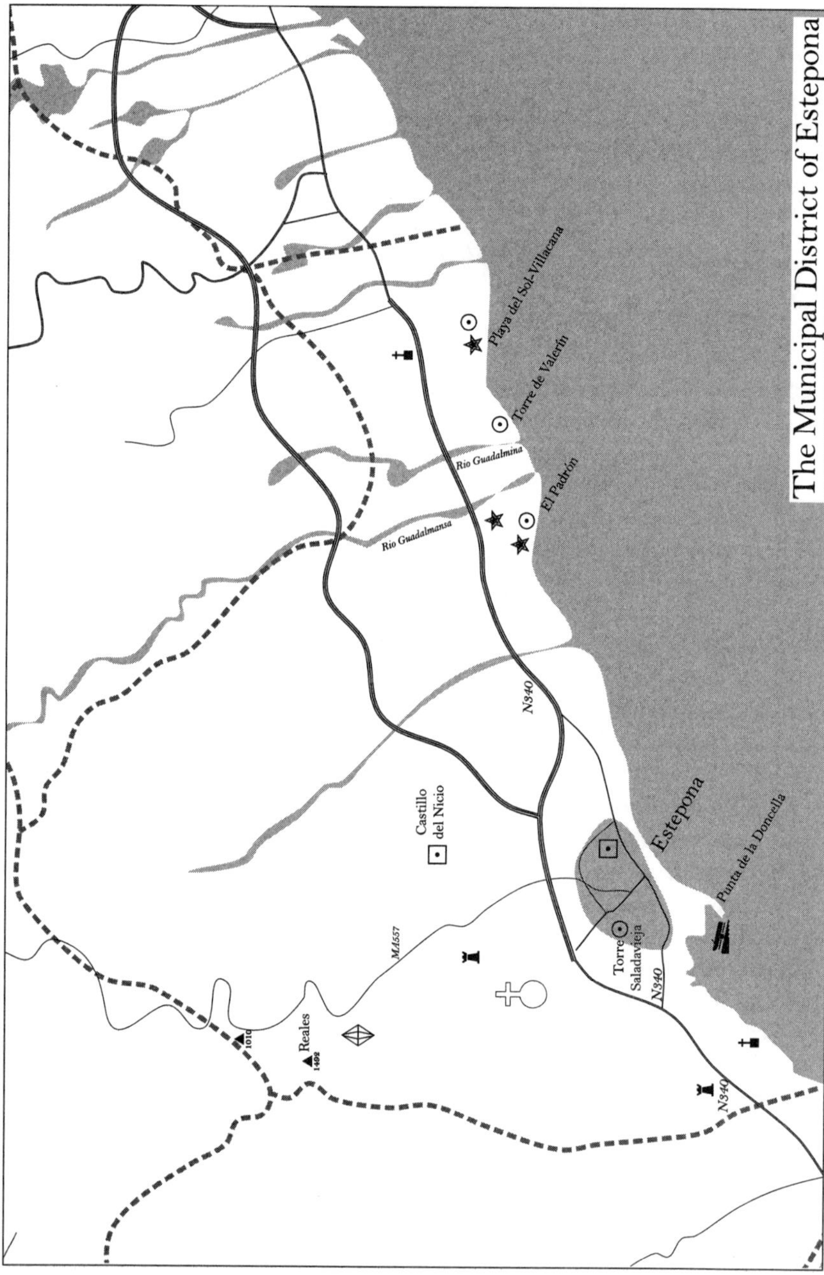
The Municipal District of Estepona
Playa del Sol-Villacana
Torre de Valerín
Rio Guadalmina
El Padrón
Rio Guadalmansa
N340
Castillo del Nicio
Estepona
Punta de la Doncella
Torre Saladavieja
N340
MA557
Reales
1492
1010
N340

the King of Castile was Alfonso X, known as The Wise. His son, Sancho IV, rebelled against him, as headstrong sons of even the wisest fathers are prone to do, and sought an alliance with the Nasrid King of Granada, Muhammad II. By this alliance, Muhammad gained Sancho's support in his own struggle with the Moorish Sultan, ibn Yusuf. Yusuf, at that time, controlled not only Estepona, but Ronda, Algeciras and Tarifa. Tarifa became a target, and together the forces of Muhammad and Sancho laid siege to the town, which fell to them in 1292. The alliance collapsed when Sancho immediately reneged on his promise to hand the town over to Muhammad in exchange for other territories. Good gamblers never waste time weeping about the turn of a card. They simply reshuffle the pack and deal again. Muhammad called Sancho a few well-deserved unprintable names and looked around for a new ally. His choice was inspired. If Sancho did not get on with his father, perhaps Yusuf also had a rebellious, disgruntled heir? He did. Muhammad found what he wanted in Yusuf's son, ibn Ya'qub, from whom he eventually obtained the ceding of Estepona, along with Algeciras and Ronda.

Tarifa then faced another siege when 5,000 Moroccan troops crossed the straits in the spring of 1294 at Muhammad's behest. If Sancho had believed that Muhammad would cheerfully accept his treachery and send him a congratulatory postcard, he was mistaken. The town was valiantly defended for the Christians by Alonso Pérez de Guzmán, 'Guzmán the Good', but after a bloody and bitter struggle, Tarifa was back in Moorish hands before the year was out. As the 13th century came to its close, therefore, the forces of the King of Granada were concentrated in the area of the Sierra Bermeja, around Estepona, which found itself unwillingly in the front line of the Christian/Arab struggle. The Christians attacked with ferocious regularity, burning and looting wherever they went.

Sancho died in April 1295, but the Christian onslaught continued under his son, Fernando IV. They took Gibraltar in 1309, once again with troops commanded by Guzmán, and kept it for 25 years before the Moors regained it. Guzmán must have been a formidable general. Whenever there was a difficult job to do, it seems that Guzmán was sent for. However, in spite of his occasional successes against the Moors, he never succeeded in taking Estepona.

By 1313, the Nasrid ruler was Nasr, who clearly had a penchant for the snappy abbreviation. No doubt his friends called him 'Naz'. He had replaced his brother, Muhammad III, and was a declared vassal of the Castilian monarch, which basically meant that he paid him to leave him alone. But his rule was fashionably insecure and there was strong opposition from his nephew, Isma'il. It was time for another alliance, and Nasr solicited help from his Christian friend, the Infante Don Pedro, uncle of Alfonso XI, who had succeeded his father to the throne. Together they defeated Isma'il's forces at Alicún.

But alliances were as permanent as ice sculptures in a furnace in those stormy days, and the wheel of history was spinning like a windmill in a hurricane. Despite his setbacks, Isma'il was ruler of Granada by 1318, and it should come as no surprise that before long he, in his turn, was signing a pact with Don Pedro. We can imagine them, almost before the ink was dry, embracing each other like long-lost friends, calling for a flagon of wine and making the rafters ring with chorus after chorus of *Dear Old Pals, Jolly Old Pals* and *Let Bygones Be Bygones.* By this treaty, Ismai'l ceded Estepona to the Catholic monarch. For the first time in its history, it was now a fully integrated part of the Castilian Kingdom. At least it was given a welcome rest from burning and looting.

Since there was little of value in Estepona apart from its delicious fish, its chief attraction had to be its strategic proximity to the Straits of Gibraltar. Despite the treaty, the Christians held on to the town for less than twenty years. In 1325, in a story straight out of the Arabian Nights, Isma'il met his death at the hands of an Arab noble from whom, it is said, he had stolen a beautiful captive. He was succeeded by his son, Muhammad IV, who did not, so far as we know, steal any beautiful captives, but still managed to get himself assassinated only eight years later while returning from a foray to help the Moors of Gibraltar, who were under siege yet again by the forces of Alfonso XI. He was killed by a couple of sons of a tribal chief named Otsmen. If it was not an unfortunate case of mistaken identity, or a prank that went horribly wrong, they presumably had a very good reason.

The demise of Muhammad IV brought Yusuf to the Nasrid throne. The old pact between the Christians and the rulers of Granada fell by the wayside, and after the ensuing brawl, Estepona was once again under Moorish occupation. The inhabitants of the town must have felt like tennis balls in a Wimbledon final.

All of this interminable fighting over a decadent fish port was put suddenly and cruelly into perspective in 1349 when Estepona and much of the coast suffered a burden far greater and more deadly than the seemingly endless war. It was the year of the plague. Many towns lost as many citizens in flight to the countryside as they did to the Black Death, and plague was no respecter of nobility. In March 1350, as he was on yet another march to his favourite battleground of Gibraltar, Alfonso XI was struck down and died.

This merciless demonstration of the power of Nature, and their equal helplessness in the face of it, did not stop the two sides from fighting. Estepona was fought over for another century and more, but in 1457 it was finally game, set and match to the Christians. It was captured from the Moors by Enrique IV of Castile. The town as seen today owes most to the redevelopment which followed the final Christian invasion. For in spite of the tenaciousness with which both sides had battled for and held it, Estepona was then little more than a village. A year after it was taken for the last time, king Enrique ordered the building of a church on the site of the inevitably destroyed mosque. When the burning and looting started, it was always the mosque that got it first. The Christians were always great burners of mosques, Moslems, heretics and witches. It is a curious notion – the belief that a God who loves Mankind should revel in the stench of burning human flesh.

It was around the church that the community began to grow. On the same site today stands the school of Simón Fernández, and all that survives of the church is the clock tower. Work on the building of the Castle of San Luis began around the turn of the century. It was intended as a defence against possible further attacks by North African Berber pirates. With the history of the past few hundred years still fresh in their minds, we can forgive the new inhabitants of Estepona a little paranoia. Finally, under a charter of 1502, when the infant town housed no more than twenty-five families, the land was divided among the victorious new colonists from northern Spain, and as a result, many of the side streets around the castle and the church were built between 1507 and 1600.

Until 1729, Estepona was merely an administrative district of Marbella, but by then it had grown from a child into a strapping youth. It was in that year that it was finally granted its own independent identity by a charter of Felipe V.

The southern stretch of the Costa del Sol has long been a favourite target for smugglers. In the 1990s, cannabis, tobacco and other drugs are the chief cargoes, but this is by no means a recent phenomenon. Tobacco has been surprisingly high on the list for at least a couple of centuries. The Hon. R. Dundas Murray noted in 1849 that an estimated 80,000 people were actively involved in one way or another in the illicit trade. Indeed, he was personally convinced that the entire peasant population of Andalucía was implicated in it. Shortly before he arrived in the area, an astonishing 700 mule-loads of tobacco had been illegally landed in one operation at Estepona. It is unlikely that this took a few clandestine seconds. Murray wryly concluded that a certain amount of connivance on the part of the authorities was indicated. Officially, strenuous efforts were being made to stamp out the trade, and a special anti-smuggling fleet had been formed, but Murray's scepticism was undoubtedly well founded.

Estepona entered the 20th century as a village of 9,000 farmers and fishermen. Though the farming land was fertile and the crops plentiful and varied, they had suffered considerably from disease over the years. With the new century, the diseases were gradually conquered, but the ancient way's days were already numbered. In 1900, 50,000 goats and sows grazed on the hills. Seventy years later the number had shrunk to 6,000, and the decline goes on, although the Los Reales goat's cheese factory remains an important part of local industry.

A census of 1940 is interesting. Still little more than a village, Estepona boasted eight weavers, five rice manufacturers, two tailors, two blacksmiths, a gunsmith, a printer, a lawyer, two vets, a couple of cabinet makers, three dressmakers, two customs agents, two midwives, and no less than five doctors. There was a hardware store, shoe shop, pharmacy, a bank, a college, a sawmill and a cinema. Since this is Spain, two cake shops were considered the necessary minimum. There were three inns, seven taverns, one restaurant, one refreshment stall, a bodega and a single hotel. The site of the hotel is now occupied by the Cafeteria Real – formerly known with prophetic irony as the Bar Manicomio – the lunatic asylum.

The constant redevelopment of the town throughout the centuries is indicative not only of its strategic significance, but of the continuing importance of its agriculture and fishing. Its present renaissance as a leisure centre appears to ensure Estepona a prosperous future, and in recent years it has achieved a measure of fame or notoriety, depending on your point of view, as the approximate site (it is a mere 4km away) of *Costa Natura*, Spain's first purpose-built nudist village, where those who wish to acquire an all-over tan, display their superb physiques, or who merely lack judgement, can go to flaunt convention and slash their laundry bills. Medical concerns about the effects of prolonged exposure to the sun may have dented Naturism's claim to be the healthiest of lifestyles in recent years, but there is much to be said for it as a breaker of social barriers and taboos. Our inhibitions about the human body would have been considered bizarre by the Phœnicians, Romans or Greeks. That those who wished to go naked should have to do so within their own ghettoes or risk punishment by the law would have seemed incomprehensible. Centuries of religious exhortation have equated nudity so closely with sin and sex that to the modern mind they are almost synonymous. We take our clothes off, at least in our imaginations, for nothing else. It is this sense of shame and guilt about our bodies which is at the root of much modern sexual paranoia, and by removing it, Naturism can certainly still lay claim at least to being a psychologically healthy way of life. Yet to most of us still living in the shadows of the Victorians and the pulpit, being caught naked in the street remains a nightmare we can live without.

Entrance to *Costa Natura* (and we must ask you to excuse the expression) is for members only, but temporary membership is available to touring naturists and the uninhibited curious. However, anyone going along in the hope of ogling hordes of naked Arnold Schwarzeneggers and Claudia Schiffers is destined for disappointment.

The Town Centre of Estepona

The sea front at Estepona belies the true identity of the town, which still manages to maintain some of its mediæval character. Be brave, and head into the low-rise urban sprawl around the Banco Atlantico, and you will find yourself in an orange square very similar in style to the more famous one in Marbella. To get right to the roots of the town, make for the lone church tower which today marks the site of the college of *Simón Fernández*. This raised area was the location of the old castle, and marks the beginning of the town's development in the 16th century.

The Castle Quarter of San Luis and Torre del Reloj

There is little left to see of the great castle which once stood at the heart of Estepona, and what remains is not now readily apparent, but it is possible to trace the ruins around the high ground. Its construction followed the seizing of the town in 1457 by Enrique IV. He also built new defensive towers along the coast, since, although they had been expelled from Estepona and their domination of the Peninsula was effectively over, the Arabs – mainly Berbers – were still perceived as a problem. Pirate raids were not uncommon and if not wildly destructive, at least a great irritant.

From the college, head for the indoor market and the *Plaza Casa Cañada*, where a small garden has been laid out beneath the walls for visitors to rest among the flowers. The centrepiece of the garden is a rusting old cannon, which was once part of the castle's defences. The existing walls probably date from the 16th century, though they may incorporate some earlier stonework, possibly Moorish.

To see more of the castle, walk around the actual *calle Castille*, where the wall meets the road. What is left is either hidden by 19th-century town houses, or has been blasted away to facilitate the construction of a block of flats. From the flats, a path winds back to the plaza and garden behind the market.

It is interesting to note that the castle area still includes a high proportion of public buildings. Among the various plazas, one of which houses a bandstand, you will find not only the college and church tower, but also the market and the town hall.

The church was completed around 1473. It is the oldest Christian-built ecclesiastical building on the Costa del Sol, but today only the clock tower survives – a favourite meeting place and reference point. Inevitably, since the site is now a school, the square is usually noisy, and seems to be a popular choice for the playing of football – Spain's fastest growing religion.

Plaza de Las Flores and Parish Church of Nuestra Señora de los Remedios

The previously mentioned orange square has had a number of names over the years. Beginning as *Plaza Real*, it became in turn *Plaza de la Constitución*, *Plaza de José Antonio* and finally (at least for now), *Plaza de las Flores*. They were great times for the makers of street signs. Somewhere along the way it was also known briefly as *Plaza de Abastos* (Provisions Square), where the markets alternated with bullfights. Confusing, and downright dangerous if you turned up on the wrong day to buy potatoes. In the square you will find the Casa de la Cultura, which is itself worth a visit, and contains a good library. Until forty years or so ago, the building was a hospital – the *Hospital de la Caridad de las Madres Carmelitas Terciarias*.

When the square was being renovated in the 1980s, fragments of Roman and Moorish pottery were uncovered, confirming that the original town had not been limited to the site of the later castle alone. It became so after the Moorish defeat, and the site around *Plaza de las Flores* was not inhabited again until the end of the 18th century, when the town began to grow once more, breaking out of the castle walls to spill down the hillside like a slow stream of lava.

The church of *Nuestra Señora de Los Remedios* is close by in the *Plaza San Francisco.* It was built in the 18th century of local sandstone, which is rich in iron ore. As you walk around the outside walls, you will see many pieces of iron ore still embedded in the stone blocks. These have made the building a magnet for tourists. (The authors apologise profusely for the inclusion of that joke but, regrettably, cannot consider refunds.) For more than forty years during the middle of the 18th century, it was a Franciscan monastery – the hermitage of Vera Cruz. Later it became for a time the hospice of *La Purisma.* The main door of the church, indeed the church as a whole, is an odd mixture of American colonial architecture and rococo, and in the entrance archway stands a statue of the Virgin Mary with a relief showing the sun, moon and stars. The effect is curious and not entirely satisfying, although this is undoubtedly an impressive building in many ways. Sadly, the relentless urban development of the past half-century means that it does not dominate the village skyline as it once did, and was intended to do.

Torre de Saladavieja

This unusual tower is signposted on the southern extremity of Estepona. Turn off the main road at *Punta Doncella* and drive up the incline into the urbanisation. The tower has been incorporated into the development as a natural traffic roundabout. The curious thing about the *Torre de Saladavieja* (The Old Salt Tower) is that although it is round, it is built on a square base. It is conceivable that the base is the remains of a Moorish tower, possibly destroyed by the Christians, who later replaced it with their own round tower, using the existing foundations. This must, however, remain speculation. *Torre de Saladavieja* is just another of the many tantalising historical puzzles which Andalucía contains.

Estepona – East

Aqueduct of Salduba

Here comes that name again. East of Estepona, just past the Continente supermarket on the beach side of the N–340, you will find a small aqueduct, generally known by the name of the disputed Roman town. Escalating development in the area makes it difficult to park close by, but the Continente car park offers a convenient spot to leave your vehicle and walk. Niggling feelings of guilt may be assuaged by popping briefly into the supermarket to make a small purchase.

The site of the aqueduct is easily located, since it is opposite the impressive *Palacio de Exposiciones y Congresos,* outside which fly the flags of all nations, or at least a great number. As you approach the site, you will pass a fountain, which incorporates two statues. These represent a fisherman and a farmer – a tribute to the two foundations of Estepona's wealth before they were superseded by tourism.

Looking incongruous surrounded by hypermarkets, exhibition halls, and yet another of the ubiquitous urbanisations, is a shoreside patch of ground still given over to private smallholdings. Walk past and around the compact white building at its edge, and you will see the stretch of aqueduct standing out of sight of the road among the unkempt vegetation. Well over a thousand years old, it was used to carry water from a well to irrigate the small fertile valley. Though the arches are Moorish, the pillars are almost certainly built on Roman and Visigothic foundations.

The large water tank which fed the irrigation channels can still be seen, and if you follow the aqueduct from there you will come to the well from which the water was, and is, drawn. This is most impressive – fifteen or twenty feet deep with a fine arch two-thirds of the way down on the right-hand side. Originally, the water would have been drawn up and fed into the aqueduct by a donkey operating a wheel-and-pulley system. Today an electric pump is used. Unemployment among Andalucían donkeys owes much to Thomas Edison.

Around the aqueduct there are uncultivated fig, orange and banana trees, which suggests that the well and aqueduct have been in more or less continual use since their construction more than ten centuries ago. It remains to be seen how much longer either can survive. The relentless spread of the urbanisation is already threatening this anachronistic patch of ground, and may well roll over it like a concrete fog before too long.

Just a two-minute drive further along the coast, the urbanisation of Hacienda Beach hides another well-aqueduct-water tank complex. Simply drive in and the tank is instantly visible to your left. It is very large, with a paved floor. The aqueduct itself is not particularly long, perhaps thirty or forty yards, and unfortunately, the area corresponding to the well from which it drew its water is fenced off.

The diligence with which modern man strives to obscure the past is illustrated by the fact that the arches of the aqueduct have been deliberately hidden by the strategic planting of bougainvillea vines. As beautiful as bougainvillea is, it seems a pity to use it to hide what ought to be a fine and unusual asset to the urbanisation. It is like hiding an embarrassing old relative in the cellar when the neighbours come.

El Padrón

A recurrent theme in this book is the indifference with which the Spanish authorities have consistently treated many archæological sites. After excavation, they are often left abandoned to the ravages of time and vandals.

Evidence that a new, more enlightened approach might just be creeping in came during the preparation of this book, but hopes were soon dashed.

The events centred on work being carried out close to the mediæval tower at El Padrón. The name has an interesting selection of meanings. It can mean nothing more than an inscribed or commemorative column, and may simply be a prosaic description of the tower. It can also be used to refer to a list of inhabitants or an electoral roll, and, intriguingly, to an over-indulgent father. In other contexts it might even denote a mark of shame, a stallion or a breeding bull. Those who seek to illuminate the past through the study of place names are free to light the blue touch papers of their imaginations and retire.

A good lookout point is a good lookout point, and it is not surprising that Christian towers from the 16th century frequently stand on the site of earlier Moorish ones, which in turn mark the site of even older Roman settlements, and so on. The tradition continues, since it is far from unusual to find modern Guardia Civil barracks in the same areas. Just such is the case at El Padrón.

Cursory excavations close to the tower in 1989 uncovered what were obviously Roman remains, but their existence was largely ignored until 1997, when the site was chosen for the building of that most urgent of Costa del Sol necessities – another luxury hotel. At that point, new excavations were undertaken, ostensibly to establish whether the remains were of notable importance. On the face of it, that was good, encouraging news. If they turned out to be particularly fine, the building of the hotel would not be allowed to proceed. If there were only one or two points of interest, they would be incorporated into the structure of the hotel in much the same way as the old Roman bridge is incorporated into the Hotel Puente Romano (see Marbella). It was, or seemed to be, at least a decent half-step in the right direction. However, there was more than a suggestion from the outset that the digs were little more than a PR exercise designed to demonstrate the poor quality and unimportance of the remains in order to facilitate their obliteration by the new hotel.

Many of the remains had, in fact, already been destroyed by the building of the modern highway which runs beside the site. They had simply been sliced away, and Roman tiles and other bric-a-brac can still be found jutting from the resulting embankment.

The authors visited the excavation site in the early part of 1997. It was deserted, and apparently guarded by a fence and a padlocked gate, which swung nonchalantly open with a lazy, yawning squeak, at the mere touch of a finger. (Honest.) Beside it was the abandoned Guardia Civil barracks. Its windows had been smashed, probably by children anxious for the sound of breaking glass rather than as a defiant act of rebellion. The barracks had been built on to the old tower itself, using it to form one of the main corners of the building. A ladder was still in place leading from the barracks to the tower's high opening, showing that it must have served its purpose as a lookout spot right till the end. An abandoned television aerial pointed uselessly towards the sky – one application of the tower that its builders could only have foreseen in Nostradamus-like dreams.

The only guards left to watch and object to our approach were the geese which flapped and squawked in the smallholding beside the barracks, but their raucous warning brought forth no defenders to beat off our low-key assault. It was as though the land had already accepted its fate and had meekly surrendered.

The site seems once again to have centred on a fish paste and oil factory. Did the Romans ever eat anything else? The houses were not impressive. They appeared to have been of such poor quality that they generated a sense of indecent haste and carelessness in their construction. It may seem a fanciful notion, but might they not have been thrown together quickly to house refugees from towns inundated by the great 4th-century seaquake which devastated so much of the coast? Only one of the visible remains was recognisably the foundation of a building. For the most part what was left looked like no more than scattered rubble.

Unfortunately, the area seems to have been used by subsequent generations for agriculture, and a great deal of the Roman structures were destroyed by the terracing of the hill. The later use of the site as a Guardia Civil barracks also contributed to its decline. Consequently, as noted above, much of what was discovered in the 1997 excavations was of little interest and of poor quality. Even as we stared at it, it seemed to us unlikely that any of it would survive, except beneath the earth awaiting the hotel's own abandonment and the attentions of another generation of archæologists whose grandfathers are as yet unborn. Every settled place on Earth is more than the skin of its latest incarnation. It is a seed which brings forth different flowers at different times, but is forever embedded in the soil. An eternal flame that is never truly extinguished.

Our misgivings were soon realised. On a later visit, less than two months later, we were greeted by a depressing tableau. All but one tiny corner of the site had already succumbed to the bulldozer. Where the rough remains had lain, there was now a great crater. Whether the investigatory excavations had indeed been merely a pretext or not, the hotel builders had got their way. Defiantly, one corner remained. Perhaps, we thought, the intention was to leave at least that scrap as some small reminder of what had been. But the unmanned bulldozer was standing close by. And it looked hungry. Within a year it was all over. The hotel was built, the ruins and the barracks were gone.

Roman Rustic Settlement of Arroboyero

The existence of this important site in the hills behind Urbanisation Dominion Beach came to light due to a casual remark by a farmer who told of unearthing large numbers of pottery fragments and ceramics as he tilled his land. Intrigued archæologists went out to take a look and instantly realised that the place was of major importance. The ground was literally strewn with fragments of Roman pottery of all sizes and there were also large pieces of stone.

The researchers began their excavations almost immediately and within days the immense value of the site was confirmed. In its centre are two wide parallel walls over five feet in height and about ten metres long which disappear towards the summit of the hill. Although the existence of the site was inexplicably unknown to the professionals, it was known to many of the locals and over the years large blocks of stone had been removed and taken to Estepona to be used in building work.

To the sound of bolting horses followed by the slamming of stable doors, it was decided to restrict news of the find and details of its exact location so that the archæologists could proceed with their excavations and investigations without the distraction of inquisitive visitors and writers of impudent books.

It soon became clear that this had been more than a mere farmhouse. The sheer volume of pottery which was found suggested a manufacturing centre, and this was confirmed when a potter's seal was uncovered which bore the initials LSRLA. Half of a Roman lamp was discovered, weights from a loom, a filing stone, fragments of white marble, jug handles, amphorae bases, floor bricks, nails, candlesticks, and two coins – a sesterce bearing the crowned head of the Emperor Hadrian and another featuring the uncrowned head of Trajan. Hadrian lived from AD 76 to AD 138, and Trajan from AD 53 to AD 117, so unless the owner of the site was an enthusiastic collector of old coins, we can date it with reasonable accuracy to the latter part of the first century and the early part of the second.

There are no traces of post-Roman inhabitation of the Arroboyero site and it is possible that it was destroyed in the seaquake which struck the Mediterranean coast on 21 July AD 365. A move to El Padrón was quite feasible for the survivors.

Castillo del Nicio

Situated on a hill top called *Cerro del Castor*, between the deep valleys of the Rios Padrón & Castor, are extensive ruins dating mainly from the late Moorish and Christian periods. They have been called the least visited, least studied, and least known of the major archæological sites in the province of Málaga. The recorded history of the site is limited and so theories as to its true origins are largely speculation, but the discovery of Roman, Arabic and Christian items suggest that it may have begun as a settlement sometime in the late Bronze Age and survived for a considerable time. The name *Nicio* appears only in the 19th century and is not the original one, which is lost in antiquity. The ruins are badly decayed and this has been accelerated over the last hundred years by the continuing activities of treasure hunters.

To reach the site, first drive into the Forest Hills Urbanisation, pass the less than picturesque cement works, and then rejoin the road and follow the Forest Hills signs. This development never quite took off and as you drive through, you will see many abandoned or half-finished buildings. Easily the most grotesque is a huge slab-work monstrosity which was intended for use as an old folks' home. No old folk need feel saddened by its pre-nascent demise.

Here you will lose the tarmacked road, and although a conventional car could continue the journey if the driver and passengers have a cavalier attitude to the health of its suspension and are confident of the solidity of their own teeth, a four-wheel drive is preferable. The rough road is very steep, but mercifully free of potholes. There eventually comes a point, however, where even the most optimistic conventional vehicle driver must show the white flag and move forward on foot.

The hill on which *Castillo del Nicio* stands is in direct line of view to the one which is the site of the impressive castle of Montemayor. As you walk up the slope towards and through the gap in the ruined walls which marks the castle's entrance, your attention will be drawn to the immense amount of rubble with which the hillside is strewn. It is as though the castle was struck by a mighty hammer-blow from some cosmic giant, which shattered it to shards in an instant. We are used to the idea of Moorish structures being deliberately destroyed by the conquering Christians of the 15th century, but it is difficult to stand or walk amid the silent ruins of *Castillo del Nicio* and not feel that something peculiarly cataclysmic happened there.

To the right of the entrance are the remains of a wall whose survival, even in such a dilapidated state, is remarkable in view of the total devastation that surrounds it. Follow the line of the old walls up the hill to the summit, and you will find the ruins of the central hall, or keep. Much of it has been demolished or has toppled drunkenly under the weight of the weather and the years. Ceramics and roof tiles litter the site, suggesting that houses were built within the confines of the walls. In addition, beads and other household effects have been unearthed. They are of widely differing styles and dates, from which we may conclude that although the site has been occupied many times over the centuries, the occupation has not been continuous. Leading from the summit there is a spur of land surrounded by a curtain wall, and it is probably here that the population sheltered with their livestock in time of refuge. There is also a large defensive tower at the eastern extremity of the site, which would have prevented any secret approach from this side.

The reader who follows the trail to at least some of the places described in this book will be rewarded with many stunning views, but it is doubtful whether any will match that from this spot. From the ruins of the one remaining tower, the sight of the distant hills and the valley below is truly awe-inspiring. Even in the inferno of high Andalucían summer the gentle sound of running water floats up from the valley and mingles with the buzzing of insects and the occasional cry of a bird or the bark of a distant dog. It is difficult to imagine the castle churning with life as it once did, and even more difficult to imagine the apparent violence of its destruction. It is a haven of undisturbed tranquillity under the mid-day sun, but who knows what ghosts haunt its dark corners at midnight?

Since the history of *Castillo del Nicio* is largely unrecorded, we find ourselves in a maze of speculation. There is, for example, no conclusive evidence of occupation during the Bronze Age, but its position and layout does at least suggest that it may have originally been built as a hill fort.

Roman occupation is more certain. The discovery of coins dating from the reign of Emperor Honorio (393–423) indicate that it was used during the latter days of the Roman Empire, and this may have been as a result of the disintegration of the empire and the quest for any available defence. Others have suggested that the Roman population moved inland after the 4th-century sea-quake which destroyed their town near San Pedro.

In 1485 the area around Estepona was invaded by Christian forces, and fleeing Moors are said to have moved to the site and re-fortified it. This idea is supported by the discovery of four Moorish coins from that period, as well as 13th and 14th century pottery. This attempt to stem the tide of the Christian advance was unsuccessful and the site was quickly taken. The received wisdom is that the Christians subsequently 'built' the structure which (barely) survives today. Written records exist which detail the castle's 'reconstruction'. If true, its virtual obliteration becomes even more puzzling. The most careless or indifferent treasure hunter or stone looter could not wreak havoc on such a scale, and Nature reclaims her own in a much more gentle manner. *Castillo del Nicio* has not been left to crumble quietly down the years – it has been smashed to pieces. Its true story lies in its scattered stones, but we have long since forgotten how to read it.

That the site truly is ignored and seldom visited can be seen in the relative scarcity of that universal human calling card, discarded rubbish. Rusting Coca-Cola cans and broken beer bottles are nowhere to be seen. Whether this represents the absence of civilisation or the presence of it, we leave the reader to judge.

Torre Guadalmansa and the Roman settlement of Las Torres

It is easy to fall into the trap of bewailing the plethora of modern tourist and expatriate urbanisations along the Costa del Sol as so many irritating blots upon the landscape. The present authors are no less guilty than others. But these contemporary human bee-hives are merely the latest chapter in a story which has been writing itself into the fabric of the coastline for thousands of years. Wave upon wave of invaders have come and gone, and each invasion has left its mark for those who wish to see it. In time the present invasion too will pass, leaving its own elusive record in the sand.

It is no coincidence that so many of the sites to which we refer are to be found close to flourishing urbanisations. Once a good, solid site for a town is found and established, only a disastrous change of climate, a severe geographical upheaval, a pitiless plague or a devastating war is likely to see it totally abandoned. It is far more likely that each succeeding set of invaders will take over and remould what is already there.

The urbanisation of Guadalmansa takes its name from the tower which stands beside it on the seashore. The tower in turn is named for the

Guadalmansa river which runs close by. In common with the majority of such towers, its one entrance is high up on its side, and the only method of entrance and exit would have been by ladder or rope. Most of the towers along the coast are mediæval and post-date the Christian reconquest. This may be true of *Torre de Guadalmansa*, but it is unusual in that it is square rather than round, which suggests that it may be Moorish. Easily visible from the spot, just a little way inland, and lending weight to the assumption, is the commanding Montemayor, on top of which still stand the impressive ruins of a Moorish castle.

Immediately beside the tower, excavations in 1915–16 and in 1929 revealed an extensive Roman villa complex. The first excavation uncovered the remains of a large building and several pools, which led the leader of the dig, José Martinez Oppelt, to conclude that it had been a *termas*, or bath house.

The building had been richly ornamented with geometrical mosaics and marble columns. Five excellent mosaics were found and recorded at the time. Other items discovered included the shaft of a marble spiral column and adjoining building materials, as well as pottery and a small bronze bust of a woman.

Approximately 18 buildings were ultimately discovered, three of which had underground water depositories. The site was certainly wealthy, as coins, anchors, bronze and iron keys, clay vessels and brass needles were also unearthed.

Archæologists should be eternally grateful for our age-old propensity to lose our money. Many a site has received its first tentative dating from the loose change left lying around by those who had clumsy fingers or holes in their purses and pockets. On this particular site, which became known as *Las Torres*, the coins uncovered ranged from the era of the Emperor Vespasian (69–79) to that of Maximus (235–238).

Initially, the mosaics were left in situ, but by the time that Pérez de Barradas came to carry out the second set of excavations in 1929, he found the site in a pitiful state. Little, it seems, changes. Shocked by what he saw, he ordered their removal to prevent their inevitable destruction by thieves and vandals. The astonishing thing is that no-one in authority appears to have noticed this wholesale looting of a valuable archæological site in the intervening thirteen years. Clearly, with so many pieces of the past littering the Andalucían landscape, it would be impractical, even undesirable, to attempt to preserve and protect every one. The past must give way to the present if we are not to stagnate. Living space is not infinite. Nevertheless, it seems astounding that sites as rich and important as *Las Torres* should simply be abandoned after excavation and left to the mercies of nature and the unscrupulous.

Peréz de Barradas unearthed a great many more items of interest: yellow and black ceramic pots, pieces of glass and crystal, more coins, a lamp, and intriguingly, a large bronze bust of Gordian II. Since Gordian II was Emperor for only three weeks in 238, and even then only jointly with his father, Gordian I, the making of the piece can be dated with some confidence to that year. If it took more than 21 days to make, it is doubtful that the sculptor got his fee. If he was a freelancing entrepreneur he probably cursed his luck, shouted a few obscenities about the fickleness of politics, and sought out a new career.

The extent and variety of Pérez de Barradas' finds revised the original opinion that the site was merely a *termas*. Barradas concluded that it was an extensive complex, perhaps even a small town, dedicated to, or certainly made wealthy by, the manufacture of *garum*, the much prized and ever-popular fish paste. Since this was made from the intestines of fish macerated in vinegar, we may wonder today at its universal popularity in all parts of the Roman Empire, and its apparent ability to make millionaires of its most skilled manufacturers. But that is what it was, and that is what it did. Had MacDonald's existed in Roman times, its success would have been founded on the Double Whopper Quarter-Pounder Garumburger.

Since Pérez de Barradas removed the mosaics to the safety of a museum, only the tower of Guadalmansa remains to be seen today, and a wide shallow pit is all that is left to mark the site of the excavations. The visitor can, however, find a poignant reminder of the previous richness of the site simply by taking a walk along the adjacent shoreline. An examination of the cliff face is almost certain to yield a few fragments of pottery, if nothing else.

El Torréon

Connected with and to the site at *Las Torres*, is the funeral vault built within the hillside of *El Torréon* on the banks of the rio Guadalmansa. The hill, with its commanding view of the coast, was a natural site for early settlers to choose, and the whole terrain is littered with fragments of ceramics from different eras. There are also traces of ancient walls, but they are very badly preserved.

During his work at *Las Torres* in 1915–16, Oppelt also investigated the tunnel situated in the vertical wall of the river bank and found a gallery containing a glass amphora, a glass funeral urn, and a quantity of mortar and stone items which led him to conclude that it was the site of a Roman sepulchre.

Again, his later excavations in 1929 led him to revise at least part of that perception. He discovered more funeral urns, and a great deal of typically Iberian pottery. It seems clear that the tunnel at least existed in Iberian times, and may have been utilised by the Romans later. About 18 metres from the entrance it splits in two, and many of the pottery finds were made at or near that point.

Barradas became convinced that this was a crematorium. The funeral chambers had been linked to the outside by a corridor and a chamber which had subsequently collapsed. He found a tortuous corridor around 1.80 metres in height, with an average width of 55 centimetres. A little less than twenty metres from the entrance, this opened on to a rectangular chamber 11 metres deep, 4.30 metres long, and just over 3 metres wide.

Estepona

ıe Marina,
ɛtepona.

urch of *Nuestra*
ĩora de los
nedios.

Little now remains of Estepona's castle.

One of the many watchtowers on the cost, Estepona.

Castillo del Nicio – obliterated.

A hermitage church sheltering beneath Sierra Bermeja.

Fuengirola

Fuengirola still has its quiet corners.

Castillo Sohail, Fuengirola.

econstructed Roman temple façade
los Boliches, Fuengirola.

estored aqueduct beside the
oman settlement close to the
metery.

Istán

A Moorish echo in the shadow of the *Sierra Blanca.*

Guaro – Málaga's smallest municipal district.

Guaro

There was some evidence that a wooden ceiling had once covered this vault. The chamber was entered by way of a six-step staircase which led to a landing 1.55 metres long, 30 centimetres high, and almost a metre wide.

Later, Barradas discovered yet another chamber hidden behind dense brambles. It was very similar to the vault described above, even though it appeared to date from the time of the site's final abandonment. He was of the opinion that the hillside probably held many more such vaults, but no more have been found.

At *El Torréon*, new discoveries continue to turn up from time to time. A new gallery was uncovered on the left of the tunnel in 1980, about 25 metres from the entrance. The floor of the chamber was once again littered with pottery fragments, many of them painted in the typical Iberian style. Later still, two polished stone axe-heads were found.

Although the entrance to the tunnel and vaults is still visible, the stretch of wall in which it is found is now part of an industrial site which is fenced off and guarded by a large green metal gate. If the visitor is unlucky enough to arrive on a day or at a time when the site is deserted and the gate locked, he or she is reduced to peering at it through a hedge.

Estepona – Hinterland

From the centre of town, head out to the by-pass and on to the *Parque Municipal San Isidro Labrador*, below Monte Reales. Look for a turn-off to the right which leads to that favourite Mecca of the independently-minded tourist, the municipal rubbish dump. If you reach the hermitage, which is set in a picnic area, you have driven too far and should turn around and retrace your steps. Keep your eyes open and think rubbish.

Los Castillejos and the funeral vault of the Amargosa mine

Little is known of the original purpose of either of these Bronze Age sites, which are just 500 metres apart, but they must have been historically linked and it is generally agreed that the site is the oldest in the Estepona area, dating from around 900 BC. There is a degree of sophistication about the structures which suggests Celtic influence.

Unfortunately, the hill on which the small fort of *Los Castillejos* stands is immediately adjacent to the eternally smouldering municipal rubbish tip mentioned above. A sign enigmatically prohibits passage to both people and animals. Figures for the numbers of literate animals in the area scholastically equipped to read this are currently unavailable. The 250-metre climb to the hilltop is steep and demanding, and on a bad day, when the wind is in the wrong direction and the smoke from the tip swirls around it like a pungent fog, it is also a choking one. Those fit and eager enough, however, could reach the summit in around 15–20 minutes. The defences are in ruins, but the north walls are well-defined and built of large blocks of masoned stone. Red clay was used to fill any cracks and this is still visible today.

The site is small, covering only one hectare, and it is therefore unlikely that it was used as a permanent settlement. The tough climb to the site indicates that it was more probably a place of refuge during war – a secure place overlooking a fertile valley leading down to the sea. It is still possible to find shards of pottery at the top, but these do not date from the Celtic period.

Within the walls of the fort there is a small cave four metres deep, which may once have led to a larger chamber. Local tales tell of buried treasure and one particular legend has it that a Moorish lord hid his worldly wealth on the site and that his spirit protects it to this day by hurling stones at anyone who approaches by night. Consequently, protective helmets and tactical evasions should not be necessary during the daytime. On the other hand, considering the pungency of the smoke from the rubbish tip, oxygen masks might be a useful accessory. Close to the foot of the hill lie thousands of worn out and discarded motor car tyres. At the time of writing these are, mercifully, not burning.

300 metres before the rubbish dump, on the approach road to *Cerro de los Castillejos,* a sulphur spring can be seen flowing out of the mountainside. It is here that the funeral vault of Amargosa is situated. It should be said that the purpose of the vault is much disputed and it may have originally been a mine following the sulphur spring into the mountain. Certainly a sulphur spring seems to be a peculiarly inappropriate and impractical choice for a cemetery.

The tunnel is presently 10 metres long, 1.25m high and 80cm wide. A funeral altar is thought by those who champion the burial site theory to have been located 3m inside, and the mine was probably abandoned because of the abundance of water and the lack of raw materials such as copper or tin to be found in the surrounding mountains.

In the summer, the spring is dammed, and the resulting pool of deep water is bright blue due to the high sulphur content. Sadly, the tunnel is now on private land and the visitor is left to gaze forlornly at the spring outlet from the side of the road.

Sierra Bermeja

Nature is never beaten. If we pollute the planet beyond its capacity to keep our own species alive, Nature will shrug and continue without us. While the primary purpose of this book is to direct the reader to visible reminders of Spain's human history, we should not forget that the land, the wildlife and the vegetation tell stories of their own.

Estepona has grown rapidly from an inhabited pinpoint too small for any but the largest map, to a sprawling urban machine. It would seem to be a perfect example of how human beings conspire, when they congregate in sufficient numbers, to strangle the life out of the natural world. Yet barely beyond its boundaries is a virtually unspoiled wilderness in which it is still possible to wander for hours and not see another human face. To reach it, which will take you no time at all, leave the Estepona ring road at the sign for *Peñas Blancas.*

It is as simple as that. Once on the road you will soon be lost among the mountains of the Sierra Bermeja. The foothills are strewn with small fincas, many of which are built on Roman foundations, and the area was much developed for agricultural purposes during the Moorish era. Be careful on the narrow, winding mountain roads. The bends are sharp and you can never be sure what is around the next one, be it a rare vehicle coming in the opposite direction, or a herd of lazily ambling goats. Keep one ear open for car horns and bells.

The Sierra Bermeja forms part of the foothills of the Serranía de Ronda. *Peñas Blancas* is 1,000 metres above sea level, and gets its name from the colour of the dolomitic marble which forms much of the terrain. *Alto Los Reales,* little more than 4 kilometres further along the road, is 500 metres higher. At *Peñas Blancas* you will see a sign pointing you in the direction of the *Refugio de Los Reales,* 4.5 kilometres away. The road is narrow and often in a bad state due to the frequent winter rains. Nevertheless, it is usually possible to negotiate it with caution in an ordinary (i.e. non 4-wheel drive) vehicle. Two kilometres along the road you will find a marker indicating the best place to begin your walk, should that be your aim. Enter the forest, and a kilometre or so along the path you will cross a wooden bridge and find yourself in a sheltered nook where a ceramic mural has been erected, giving visitors information about the trees.

The pines, which are as abundant here as quills on a porcupine, are of a species unique to the Serranía de Ronda, and known to compulsive nature-labellers with tongues considerably more flexible than their pencils, as *abies pinsapo boiss.* The offending anorak here would appear to be Edmundo Boissier, a Swiss botanist who came to the area in 1836 looking for something to name after himself. He would have settled for a humble roadside weed, but the Lord, in benevolent mood, delivered him a tree. The tradition of giving each atom of the natural world an incomprehensible Latin name owes much to the pioneering work of Carl von Linné (1707–1778), who liked the idea so much that he picked one for himself and became Carolus Linnaeus. Since he was Swedish, things might have been worse. Naturalists ever since have dreamed of discovering some plant or animal which does not yet feature in the *Observer's Book of Nature,* and earning some kind of academic immortality by giving their name to it. The trick, of course, is to pick something which is not on the verge of becoming extinct.

During the 1940s the pines sheltered bands of anti-Franco guerilla fighters who lived as outlaws in the hills. These beautiful trees, which can be as much as 30 metres tall where the Sierra's special climate is at its most favourable, have one close relative across the water in North Africa: the *abies moroccana trabut* (Boissier presumably never crossed the straits). In the tertiary period, which began 65,000.000 years ago and continued for more than 60,000,000 years, great geological changes were occurring on the Earth. The Spanish fir tree was even then part of the great coniferous forests which covered the land. As continental drift drew Africa and Europe apart, many families – animal and plant alike – were broken up like twins being separated at birth and brought up by loving but different aunts. Several million years on, the Spanish and Moroccan fir trees are still recognisably cousins, but they have diverged enough to become distinct species. The history of the world in a pine cone and a falling leaf.

One point of which travellers in the area should be aware is the existence of a military radio installation close to the summit, with an access road which may only be used by authorised personnel engaged in its operation and maintenance. The presence of the installation is controversial, not only because of the impact of the road on the area, but because some people believe that the transmissions have a strong negative effect on the environment. This suspicion is currently heightened by the fact that many of the trees are suffering from a bizarre and so far undiagnosed disease. In addition, extensive forest fires, particularly in 1966 and 1976, caused them great damage.

The pine has been a part of Estepona's history since its earliest days. It provides perfect wood not only for the building of houses and furniture, but even more importantly, of boats. Any town which aspires to establish itself as a trader in fish must first have the means to catch them. In its wisdom, Nature made pinewood a poor burner, and placed it high enough in the mountains to make it uneconomical to decimate the forests for firewood. All of these factors combined to ensure that the trees would be respected and their wood used for more noble purposes. Its closeness to the heart of rural and coastal Spanish life – the home, the ship in peril on the sea – is no doubt the reason for its widespread association with, and use in, religious ceremonies.

There are two of the villages in this part of the mountains which are well worth a visit. The first is Genalguacil, birthplace of Simón de Zamora, who alerted his friend Count Cristóbal de Medina to the restorative powers of *Los Baños del Duque* in 1773. (see Casares) It has a pleasing church in the *Plaza de la Constitución*, and two very welcome drinking fountains situated respectively in calles *Alta* and *Baja*. Beyond that there is almost nothing – not even a pension at which to spend the night, or pavements on which to walk. Genalguacil is as much an historical monument as any ruined castle. By all the laws of logic, places like Genalguacil should not exist in a Europe standing on the threshold of the 21st century. That they do is a kind of miracle. Tiny specks of mountain life as tenacious as lichen. From the inevitable *mirador* it is possible to look out across the rio Genal and see two similar specks hanging precariously onto the slopes: Algatocín and Benarrabá.

The other village on this side of the river is Jubrique. This should not be confused with Ubrique, home of the celebrated matador, Jesulín. Jubrique, like Genalguacil, is a tiny, anachronistic spot with a permanent population of around 1000 people. On its outskirts is a moon-shaped cemetery with a simple but fine 16th century church. Unlike its neighbour, Jubrique does at least have one small pension where, with luck, a room may be had in the high season.

Tourists are more common on the banks of the Genal river than in the mountains. Having descended from Los Reales or Jubrique, you may wish to have a bite to eat and a cooling drink at the riverside inn before moving back into the mountains on the other side. It specialises in fresh-caught rabbit, but if you wish to sample it be sure you have an appetite. The landlord has no time for picky eaters. Here, it's the whole rabbit or none at all. The opposite pathway will lead you to Benarrabá – even smaller than Genalguacil and Jubrique, with only 700 inhabitants. In spite of this, it is the site of the ruined castle of *Monte Porón.* Visitors are rare enough here, as well as in Algatocín and the other two villages, to rate inquisitive stares. Walking their impossibly narrow streets is as near as we are ever likely to get to time travel. We should be wary, though, of thinking of these places as idyllic paradises. To the visitor, pummelled and choked each day by the traffic and the sheer pace of life in the city he or she has temporarily left behind, they certainly are. But a few days refuge in the peace of the mountains is a far cry from living there 24 hours a day, 365 days a year for a lifetime. Within living memory, the outside world was remote enough to be an irrelevant rumour. People lived and died in the villages, working on the land and knowing nothing else. A man might live to be ninety and never stray more than a few miles. But in an age of television and the internet, nowhere is truly remote any more. The young look into their magic boxes and see a world that stretches their imaginations far beyond their tiny towns. And increasingly they leave, perhaps dreaming of returning one day wealthy and full of years and experiences, ready to sit quietly once more in the mountains and dream. But will their towns be there to come back to, or will the microchip and Bill Gates finally polish them off? The authors' guess is that they will not. As the future wraps its tentacles ever faster and more tightly around us, there will be an even greater psychological and physical need for such islands of a tranquil, if illusory past. The continued existence of each particular Genalguacil or Benarrabá cannot be guaranteed, but places like them will survive, as they always have. They must. They are part of us and we, even those of us who never sit beneath their trees and breathe their sweet, unsullied air, are part of them.

Estepona – West

Arroyo Vaquero

On the beach side of the main N–340, behind the urbanisation of *Arroyo Vaquero*, lie more than a dozen graves, at least two of which are definitely Roman. They have suffered badly over the years from the attentions of grave robbers and rubbish dumpers. The site was excavated in the 1980s, but has since been allowed to deteriorate and is now neglected and overgrown.

The urbanisation is a short drive north along the coastal road from the castle at Duquesa. When you reach it, pull off and park where the identifying sign stands beside an iron gate. A brief walk up the bank to the left of the sign, and along an indistinct footpath through long grass, will take you to the site of the graves.

In Roman times, this high ground was a peninsula surrounded by two small estuaries, and it was this isolation which prompted its use as a cemetery. The precise location of the community which it served has not been identified, but it may possibly have been in the area of the mediæval tower across the river, in what is now the urbanisation Bahia Dorada.

On the corner of the site are traces of the ruins of what may have been an early 4th-century church, but recent road works have destroyed any positive evidence which might have proved the point. Large stone slabs which would have covered the rock-lined graves scatter the area, and other graves, as yet undisturbed, can be seen in the small embankment. The site survived the Romans, and was probably used well into the Visigothic period, but was deserted by the 7th century.

The graveyard is now on the very edge of the coastal highway, and its long-term survival is doubtful. Like so many such sites throughout Andalucía, it is a tiny tear in the fabric of time which 'progress' and neglect will mend seamlessly sooner or later. Nevertheless, there is almost certainly much still lying beneath the earth awaiting proper excavation, and the freshly dug holes with which the site is littered are strong indications that even now it is still being pillaged by enthusiastic or commercially-minded amateurs.

From the graveyard behind Urbanisation Bahia Dorada, you will be able to see a self-contained hilltop connected by a spur to the high ground. This was the site of yet another Bronze Age hill fort, but little research has been done on the location. The alert may also spot an incongruous railway tunnel. The railway it was meant to serve was never built.

Heading inland from this spot towards the Estepona Golf Club, a brief detour will lead you to the remains of a tower. Take the track on the right of the river in preference to the conventional road. The remains are to be found approximately 3 kilometres along the track, after the Golf Club turn off. They form part of a small finca surrounded by orange groves.

Chapter Twelve

Fuengirola

Historical Background

INVASIONS, LIKE TUMOURS, CAN BE EITHER MALIGNANT OR BENIGN. Or at least relatively so. Like many towns on the Costa del Sol, Fuengirola has changed out of all recognition since the advent of mass foreign tourism in the early 1960s. It was then the quietest of fishing villages; a place whose unhurried life revolved around the harvest of the sea as it had done for thousands of years. Today high-rise blocks, built largely to accommodate summer tourists and resident expatriates, stand together like unbrushed teeth in the mouth of a rudely awakened ogre. Young men who might once have spent their lives casting nets or tilling fields find work in the service industries which have developed to cater for the new colonists. Some idea of the size of the foreign community in Fuengirola can be gained from the fact that by late 1997 there were no less than 5000 non-Spanish residents on the town's official census, of which almost 1500 were English. It can be reasonably assumed that for every expatriate who obtains his Spanish *residencia* and properly registers, there are at least three who do not, and since the official population of the town remains under 50,000 it can be seen just how overwhelming and financially important the foreign influx has become.

There has been settled human habitation of the land around Fuengirola for at least two and a half thousand years. The Phœnicians are thought to have had a settlement here called *Suel*, and the town was still known by that name in Roman times, though the Moors later amended it to *Sujayl* (*Sohail*).

The Romans granted it the status of a municipality as long ago as AD 53, and their chosen name of *Suel*, possibly inherited from the Phœnicians, was said to have been inspired by a star which was visible from the castle. As with so many such legends, the story should be treated with caution. All too often they are passed on uncritically and achieve a dubious but unchallenged reality. Any star visible from the castle would have been equally visible in essentially the same spot over a great distance. The idea that one particular star out of the millions which fill the night sky became so closely associated with a particular castle or tiny town that it adopted its name is essentially absurd, but the story is there, and you will hear it recited by scholars with the utmost seriousness.

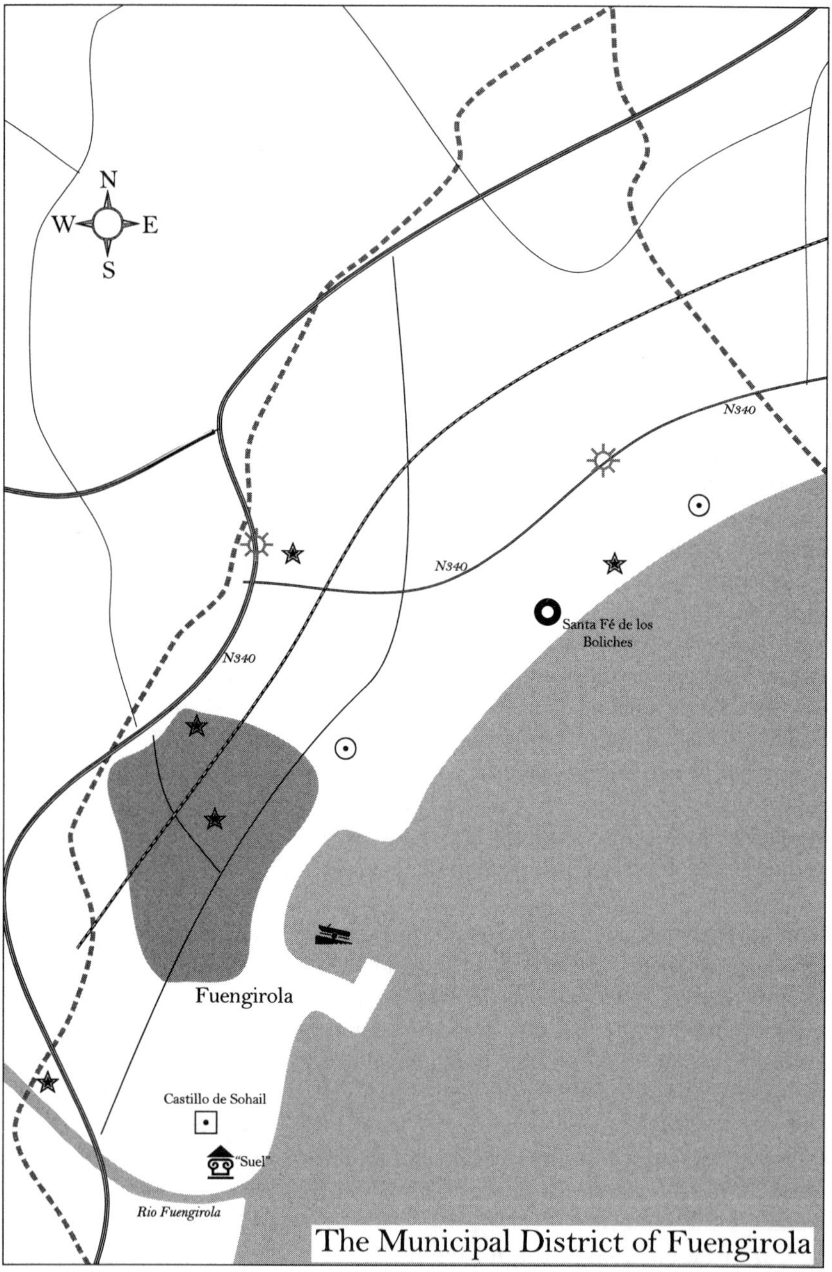
N
W
E
S
N340
N340
N340
Santa Fé de los Boliches
Fuengirola
Castillo de Sohail
"Suel"
Rio Fuengirola
The Municipal District of Fuengirola

Fuengirola

The name 'Fuengirola' seems to have appeared in the 18th century. The town had long since lost any lustre it had in Roman and Moorish times, but had managed to achieve some new importance as a provisioning centre for Genoese ships on their way to the Straits of Gibraltar. The suffix 'girola' is said to refer to this Genoese connection. If there is truth in this assumption, we are left to wonder why the town is not called 'Fuengenoa'. Alternatively, the name 'Fuengirola' could be pedantically and literally translated as 'movable fountain', which is equally mysterious but slightly more convincing.

The present day town and beachside development has grown up on salt marsh silt deposited in a long-lost estuary. Habitation during the Roman period was centred on the site of what was later to become the castle of Sohail, and also, at the other end of the town, in the area of high ground behind Los Boliches.

Though the Moors had a reasonable fortress here, the main seat of power in the region was Mijas, which sits majestically in the mountains behind Fuengirola, looking disdainfully down.

Mijas remained the administrative centre until this century, when Fuengirola finally carved out its small coastal strip of a municipal area. (See 'Centre of Fuengirola')

Centre of Fuengirola

Difficult though it may occasionally be to believe, Fuengirola does possess an old quarter hidden among the high-rise buildings and the garish, quivering streets. It is concealed like the images in one of those infuriating magic-eye paintings which, if you stare long enough at them, suddenly leap out at you and take you by surprise. The old quarter is based around the main square and church, and leads down to the sea front. There is a definite historical feel to the old streets, but it is immediately apparent that it is far less strong than the equivalent sector of Marbella, with its various towers and sandstone facades on important buildings. Remember that until only fifty years ago, this was no more than a fishing village of approximately 150 houses, with a similar village a little further up the coast at Los Boliches.

A walk around the old town is pleasant, especially after a meal or before going out for the evening. There is, of course, a bewildering choice of bars and noisy discos, but for a quieter alternative why not try the theatre, which hosts regular local amateur productions of surprising quality?

The true heritage of Fuengirola, however, lies abandoned on the outskirts of the town.

The Castle of Sohail and the Roman Town of Suel

The 10th-century Moorish castle of Sohail, rebuilt in the 18th century but today once again in comparative ruin, stands on high ground around which the Roman town of Suel is thought to have once been situated. It was built in the year 956 during the reign of the Caliph Abderramán III, and somehow managed to survive the wholesale destruction of Arab monuments and strongholds after the 15th-century Christian re-conquest in reasonably good condition. Indeed, by the 18th century, when much reconstruction work took place, it was in full use and played an important rôle in the government's efforts to control the age-old problem of smuggling. During 1997 it underwent yet another renovation at the apparent snail's pace that simultaneously drives visitors to Spain frothy at the mouth with frustration, while investing the country with much of its unhurried charm.

Certainly there is much evidence of Roman occupation of the area on and around the castle hill, including the discovery of cremation pots behind the El Castillo apartment complex. Modern road development and the construction of the adjacent El Castillo flats have, however, destroyed and obscured much of the Roman past.

Below the castle, on a hillside rolling gently towards the beach, is a living link with the Moorish past in the form of a small orchard of fig trees. No doubt this has always been a favoured spot for lovers to meet in the moonlight and make love. Some traditions survive more easily and with more vigour than others. Anyone pausing to pick the fruit may be forgiven for concluding that these are curious hybrid trees, which bear a second, far more contemporary crop. The ground around each one is liberally strewn with discarded condoms.

In Roman and Moorish times the plateau was much larger than it is today and stretched across the modern deep road-cutting. The *calzada Romana*, the old Roman coastal road that ran from Málaga to Cádiz, lay in this area, but no excavations have taken place to confirm its course.

Evidence for the existence of the Roman town comes from two recycled pieces of Roman stone which were used in the building of the castle. One of these, a column pedestal, records the name of Suel and the town's granting of municipal status in AD 53. In the second century AD the townsmen were given Roman citizenship and to celebrate the federation with the Empire, a statue dedicated to Neptune, the Roman god of the sea, was raised in a special sanctuary in the town.

During this period a further federation was developed with Malaca (Málaga). This gave the citizens of both the Roman towns equal status and the treaty covered economic, religious and military matters.

Records of the inscription on the statue survive, but no other substantive evidence remains today of the Roman settlement. It is probable that the site was partially abandoned by the end of the 2nd century AD and that the new population growth was centred on the numerous villa complexes in the area.

The last time that shots were fired in anger at the castle would appear to have been during the Peninsular War, when, in 1808, it was occupied for a time by invading French troops. They did their own share of restoration and filling up of holes, and the result was more or less the building we see today

– an odd mixture of Moorish, 17th century and Napoleonic influences. The original outer wall of the castle has survived in very much stunted form a few yards in front of what is now the main entrance. Its chief purpose now seems to be to provide a place where visitors can sit, eat, drink, and then leave their inevitable litter.

The castle site is very much worth a visit even though some of what remains to be seen dates only from the early 19th century. Most of the Roman masonry would have been used in the foundations of the castle and further excavations may yet reveal much of interest below the inner bailey. The cutting of the N–340 road destroyed a great deal of evidence and the only area of the town which is still untouched by 20th century progress is in the vicinity of the 19th-century blockhouse.

A landscaped path takes you up the mount to the entrance, which was positioned with some thought. Any invading army would have had to enter an enclosed ramp, which was heavily defended. An attack by this route would have been difficult and costly, and the only other option would have been to breach the walls in another place, which would have been even more difficult and hazardous.

Inside the castle complex, only about half of the curtain wall remains from the Moorish period. It seems that the western half of the castle disappeared, but was rebuilt and re-defended by the occupying French troops during the Napoleonic Wars. The 19th-century additions are easily identifiable because of their rifle slits. A modern reconstruction of some of the walls has recently been undertaken in, of all materials, concrete. It gives the visitor a greater understanding of the complex, while simultaneously robbing it of its authenticity. But what, ultimately, is 'authenticity'? Any building which has stood in one form or another for hundreds or thousands of years and undergone innumerable repairs, renovations and 'improvements' is as 'authentic' in parts as the curate's egg is good. Given enough time, each succeeding addition or refurbishment attains its own venerable claim to a kind of 'authenticity', just as the most radical young political firebrand inevitably becomes, should he live long enough to lose his fire, a respected 'elder statesman'. Nevertheless, the most recent repairs are certainly the most slapdash. Gaps have simply been filled with plain concrete with no attempt having been made at disguise. Invisible mending this is not.

While the latest renovation work was underway, only hard-hatted members of the work team were allowed to pass through the castle's entrance, and when the team was not on site – at the weekend, after hours, on public holidays, etc. – a great corrugated steel door was left locked and impenetrable except to a recklessly determined and well-equipped gang. Whether by design or not, a small gap between the left side of the door and the castle wall allowed disappointed visitors to crouch and peer through. Anyone doing so was rewarded by the riveting sight of an abandoned wheelbarrow or tool awaiting the return of its phantom operator.

The very tall were able to stand on a convenient rock and, by stretching, look through the windows which are cut into the wall, but most weekend arrivals who came expecting to wander within the complex were left instead to wander disconsolately outside it, looking forlornly at the cacti and the neatly-kept lawns which surround it on three sides. On any given Saturday or Sunday, you might have found a handful of sad-faced, camera-clutching tourists standing before the locked gate as though they were desperately seeking the magic word which would send it swinging open.

Happily, as 1997 drew to a close, such disappointment became a thing of the past. In November, the castle was once again thrown open to the public. Inside, the authorities have set aside a room as a museum in which visitors can see some of the pieces – twenty-six in all – which have been recovered during excavations, and which span most of the historical periods through which the castle has existed. One particularly impressive item is the 17th-century tombstone of Leonor Osorio, the mother of the castle's keeper at that time. This came to light in 1989 while the preliminary work for the proposed renovation of the ruins was being undertaken, and was discovered by pupils of the workshop school.

Along with the archæological finds, there are photographs and drawings covering the castle's long history, and a diorama illustrating life inside its walls during its last great heyday in the 18th century. Sixty percent of the 1,800,000 pesetas needed to restore the room and make it fit to house the museum came from the Andalucían Government, with the rest being provided by the Fuengirola *ayuntamiento* (town hall). It is to be hoped that more such collaborations will happen in the future.

The only parts of the complex not reopened to the public in November 1997 were the two ancient Moorish towers. Before the renovations began, and hopefully again very soon, it was, and will be, possible to climb these and appreciate from the top the defensible properties of the site.

There are still sardine-canning factories in Fuengirola today, maintaining a link that extends back to Phoenician times. One of the most important products of the former town of Suel in the Roman period was fish sauce. This came in various varieties with names like *garum*, *liquamen* and *muria*, and at the southern foot of the castle hill there are the remains of an important Roman factory dedicated to its production. The site is immediately adjacent to the beach and separated from it by a Roman wall of stone, behind which are to be seen a number of concrete-lined tanks about 2m square and 1.5m deep. At its height, the complex would probably have extended over a wide area and well inland, with domestic areas for the workers, but only its southern edge has been properly excavated.

The modern visitor should welcome the fact that the production of fish sauce has long since ceased, since the method of production involved filling the tanks with fish directly from the shore and allowing them to rot. Local residents might have been forgiven for campaigning to have the complex shut down and replaced by a glue factory. Smelly the process may have been, but the end product was greatly prized among the people of the empire and exported far and wide in the characteristic jars, or *amphorae*, which turn up in Roman sites in many regions.

The Girón Property

Immediately below the castle, on the seafront, stands a large villa set in its own grounds. During the Franco era, this was the home of José Antonio Girón. Girón was one of the dictator's chief ministers, and clearly amassed a considerable fortune. There have long been plans for the Fuengirola authorities to buy the estate from Girón's family and turn it into a tourist-pulling theme park. Fuengirola clearly does not believe it can have too many tourists.

Since the property lies immediately in front of the 'Castillo Sohail', many visitors will undoubtedly assume that the castle has been newly constructed as a park attraction à la Disneyland. If the plan goes ahead, it will, however, retain something of its dignity by being used for what the *ayuntamiento* calls 'official cultural purposes'. Exactly what these will include remains to be seen. 'Culture' is a chameleon among words, capable of changing not only its colour, but also its shape.

It is intended that the scheme will be financed largely by private investment. In return for their money, investors will be granted concessions in the running both of the park and of a revitalised castle. It is easy to see that under such circumstances 'culture' would adopt new and ever more amorphous meanings with bewildering speed.

Cemetery and Sewage Farm

A visit to a cemetery and a sewage farm may rank low on the list of priorities for the average tourist, but those made of sterner stuff will find a detour to this particular complex unexpectedly rewarding. Take the modern road which leads up the mountainside from the castle, along the bank of the river. The municipal cemetery is, not surprisingly, a quiet place today, but in Roman times the area in which it is situated was a bustling centre of population which could be reached only by boat, since it was located in an estuary which has long-since silted up. Leave your car in the car park, and take a walk around. To be accurate, the location actually lies within the municipal boundaries of Mijas, but in Roman times it functioned very much as part of *Suel*.

The British visitor who is used to the idea of cemeteries invariably being found in churchyards, and changing their aspect from sombre and contemplative during the daytime to downright spooky at night, may initially find their Spanish counterparts puzzling. Though they may be placed close to a church, this is not always the case. The Spanish, whenever possible, bury their dead above ground in vaults. These are set out in neat rows, and are usually fronted with glass-covered alcoves in which may be placed a religious icon, or a photograph of the person or persons who lie within. There is an abundance of flowers, but the overall atmosphere, though melancholy, is seldom overbearing. The cemetery at Fuengirola is just such a place. Come upon it by chance, and if you failed to read the sign over the entrance, you could be forgiven for imagining that you had stumbled on a small park or low-key industrial complex, with its immaculate lawns, its simple, unadorned buildings, and its lack of overt outward religiosity.

During the construction of the cemetery and sewage farm complex (which is, it has to be said, a curious combination), numerous excavations were carried out. These uncovered evidence that the site may once have been the location of a Roman water works. As well as a hypocaust and water channels, diggers found settling tanks and beds, and a large tank lined with concrete (*opus signinum*). A little further away, up the hill, was a shallow concrete basin of considerable size, which probably collected water from a network of underground channels (drains). These were lined with tiles. Assuming that this was a water works, it almost certainly existed to service the public baths in the town of Suel, which stood at the bottom of the hill. The only likely alternatives are that it was part of a farm, the private bath-house of a wealthy villa, or just possibly that it served an industrial olive-processing plant. A great deal of this site is still unexcavated, which leaves us much room for speculation.

The two sites are still hidden around the buildings which make up the modern cemetery complex, but they are hidden in different ways. The shallow basin is concealed with the cunning skill of the master illusionist who knows that the best way to render something invisible is to place it fairly and squarely in full view of his public. Pull into the car park outside the cemetery walls, and as you do so you will pass a slightly sunken circle of white, stone ground, in the centre of which now stands a controlled explosion of rose bushes, like a floral arrangement decorating a circular table in a vicarage drawing room. Close to the rim at one side is a small sunken section which may once have been part of a short flight of steps. The water collected in the basin in Roman times might have been used for many things, but it is a pleasant whimsy on a hot day to imagine the workers perhaps washing away the sweat of their labours by bathing and swimming in the pool.

Of greater interest is the second site, which is to be found a few yards away. There was a time, and not so long ago, when the mighty steamroller of Progress would simply have flattened everything in its path, and the new would have risen on the crushed bones of the old, leaving nothing behind but their ghosts. Not so here, although the way in which the site has been protected is to say the least curious. One might have imagined that, having found a site of historical interest which demanded preservation, the builders of the new complex would have stopped short of it, or moved their building a few feet to the left or right, like the driver of a truck swerving to avoid a child in the road. Instead of this, the construction covers the site, but that part of it which stands above what is known as 'Cortijo Alebedo' is raised on columns. It is as though, in their rush to get the work done, the builders had suddenly found themselves trampling through a prim spinster's parlour, and had run the last few feet on tiptoe, pirouetting perilously close to the china cabinet. This is where you will find the remains of the hypocaust, channels and tanks mentioned above. The hypocaust, which was a feature of wealthy Roman homes as well as public baths and buildings, was a sophisticated central heating system which distributed hot air from a central furnace through a network of shafts and flues.

A locked gate bars access to the site itself. The keys are available on request from the relevant authorities, but the casual visitor who cannot spare the time can see much simply by peering through and over the surrounding walls. The *ayuntamiento* has placed an informative sign among the ruins, but this is far enough back from the gate to be readily legible only to those with perfect vision. Others should consider carrying binoculars. It is a pity also that, having avoided smashing the china in the spinster's parlour, money enough could not have been found to pay a man to come around once a week to keep it clean and tidy. The sign and the stones stand, as so many do, sadly neglected among lounging clumps of silently jeering weeds: the lager louts of the floral kingdom.

Carvanjal (Torreblanca del Sol)

To the north-east of modern-day Fuengirola, on the mountain side of the N–340 shortly before it reaches the Torreblanca flyover, are the ruins of a first-century Roman villa. A side road at KM219.8 provides ample parking space and access can be made along the pavement of the old by-pass. The entrance to the site is protected by a gate, but if this is closed, it can be circumvented by climbing the 3m bank and stepping through the broken-down fence. The site was discovered in 1961 and although it has been excavated, it has, like so many others, been allowed to decay and is now badly overgrown and strewn with rubbish.

Only the remains of the bath-house (*termas*) area have been discovered, and it is probable that the main living quarters were a little way inland. The various hexangular tubs have been excavated and can be seen on the northern side of the boiler room. There are fragments of mosaic flooring among the water channels and traces of walls, but an excellent set of moulded ceramic tiles which was unearthed during the excavation was removed and is now on show in the library at Los Boliches. We may feel regret at such treasures being taken away, but we are consoled by the certain knowledge of the fate that awaited them had they not been.

The layout is somewhat confusing and this may be explained by the conversion of the baths into fish-salting tanks for the production of *garum* in the 4th century, when extra channels would have been dug and a second set of tubs or vats built over the originals. If this assumption is correct, it would have been a very late development of the trade since the fish sauce industry in Spain had greatly declined by the end of the 3rd century AD.

Two hundred years later, in the 6th century, the site was appropriated by Visigothic settlers who used the area of the bath house as a burial ground.

Thirty-two tombs were found beneath the villa floor during the 1961 excavations, but all had been plundered at some point in the distant past. A few can still be seen at the southern edge of the complex, though in a much neglected state.

Also discovered was the headless white marble statue of a man, possibly a god, dating from the 2nd century AD. The torso, 80cm in height, has a robe across the lower regions. Along with the statue found at Finca del Secretario (see below) this is now on view at the archæological museum in Málaga.

A visit to Carvanjal today produces many of the emotions so commonly provoked by other similar places throughout the province. Its ruins have survived, but barely, and by the skin of their teeth. A long channel, perhaps the remains of a Roman swimming pool, ends abruptly where it was cut viciously by the building of the modern highway. The fence which surrounds the site, and the gate which provides access, are rusty and ill-kept. The ruins are choked with weeds, and the interested summertime visitor must hack a path through brambles, nettles and high grass, cursing his or her decision to wear sandals and shorts.

Beyond the gate, the modern world rushes by oblivious, uncaring and intent on transient pleasure. Land is precious on the Costa del Sol. The plot which does not support a bar, a restaurant, or an hotel is an idle brother not pulling his weight. In places such as Carvanjal, the overwhelming feeling is one of rejection. Someone, somewhere, has decreed that this place is of particular historical interest and must be preserved, and preserved it shall be, but grudgingly and with more than a hint of petulance. It can stay, but so far as those who have been given custody are concerned, it can continue to rot. What they would really like to see on this prime site beside the N–340 is another hotel, another block of flats, or maybe another restaurant. They would be respectful. They would call it the *Casa Carvanjal*, and in honour of its vanished past, they would serve excellent fish (though not *garum*) and dress the waitresses as Roman slave girls. Stones are merely stones, but Culture must not die.

Finca del Secretario (Santa Fe de los Boliches)

During the construction of the Fuengirola by-pass in 1978 workers unearthed a headless statue which has become known as the 'Fuengirola Venus'. The marble Venus stands 144cm high and only the bare-breasted torso with a brief loin-cloth around the lower regions has survived. Several similar statues from the 1st century AD are known and they are thought to be copies of a Roman original which has been lost. Those writers who hold this view presumably believe that home-grown sculptors had never seen a woman and lacked imagination. At the same time a fragment of a second statue and six stone steps were found, but it was not until ten years later, while more construction work was being done to the south of the by-pass, that the true importance of this site was realised.

The stone steps led down to an elaborate bath-house complex which contained a heated circular pool (*caldarium*), a cold plunge bath (*frigidarium*) and a marble sweating or changing room (*tepidarium* or *apodyterium*). The luxuriousness of the bath-house, with its marble wall panels and intricate hypocaust system for the circulation of hot air below the floors of the heated areas, indicates that this was part of a very rich villa, although the site of the villa itself has yet to be discovered.

Close by the bath-house, to the west, was an industrial area where large pottery kilns were located, of which five have so far been discovered. Pottery vessels of various kinds, notably *amphorae* of the kind used for fish-sauce, were made here. Still further west, another flight of steps led upwards to a rectangular stone building of considerable size, in the northern half of which were twelve large, square, concrete-lined *garum* tanks. It would seem that this was a self-contained industrial complex making not only the *garum* itself, but the containers used to export it. Clearly the owner was a man of considerable wealth and the bath-house may have been not only for his own use but also for that of his workers. The site survived in productive use from the 1st century AD until the decline of the Spanish fish-sauce trade two hundred years later.

It is currently under development as an official tourist site, with fencing and descriptive information boards.

Los Boliches – Roman Temple

A recently reconstructed Roman temple is to be found one kilometre north of the marina of Fuengirola on the main *Paseo Maritimo* of Los Boliches. Only the entrance gateway remains of the original, but a modern metal skeleton has been erected to give an idea of the size and outline of the building.

The gateway blocks came from the hills near Mijas, and it would seem that the stone was quarried and masoned here and intended for export. For reasons which remain obscure, the exportation never took place and the temple facade is now more prosaically an attraction for tourists. However, it is unlikely that many of them know it for what it is, and the majority probably pass it by without thought or glance. Sculpture of various kinds is common along the *Paseos Maritimo* of Costa del Sol towns, and casual visitors passing steadily between beach and bar, and less steadily in the opposite direction, may well imagine that this is a modern embellishment, instead of a unique echo of a glorious and distant industrial past.

Torreblanca

On a hilltop overlooking Los Boliches is a white lookout tower which, after months of thought and discussion by committee after committee, was given the name 'Torreblanca'. This was built to replace an earlier tower which can be found along the coast, half a kilometre to the north. A wide estuary once existed between this point and the castle. Romans would have been able to swim and drown in it, and no doubt did both. By 1500 it had become sandbanks and marshland. Today it is covered by apartment blocks. Tomorrow will no doubt take care of itself.

In recent years, Torreblanca has been famous chiefly as the site of Fuengirola's festering rubbish tip. In late 1998, after years of complaints from the residents of the housing estate which bears the tower's name, the authorities decided to clear the tip and carry the rubbish to Málaga. In Málaga, street musicians led the celebrations.

As soon as the last margarine carton, cardboard box and fly-blown remnant of *chorizo* is safely on its way, the former tip will be transformed into a green zone. And at its heart will be a golf school. There is a profound irony here, but try as we may, it remains tantalisingly outside our grasp.

Chapter Thirteen

Guaro

Historical Background

SECRETS OF A WRITER'S NOTEBOOK. The authors first visited Villa de Guaro, the smallest of the municipal districts of Málaga province at around 30 sq km, on a sweltering Sunday afternoon in September, and took away the impression of a wet Wednesday morning in Grimethorpe. A few scribbled words in a notepad tell it all: 'Went in, came out, nothing. Passed a few nuts on the way.'

But just as likening the houses which have swallowed up the castle at Tolox to a blob from outer space, this initial impression is both misleading and unfair. Guaro is a small island of mountain life carved out of the greater municipal district of Monda, and it is simultaneously dying as a living, working community, while showing some primitive signs of possible revival as a new target for Spain's wealthy foreign invaders. It is far too early to say whether this will prove to be its salvation. For now, Guaro is a village with a missing generation, or to be more accurate, a missing *male* generation. So many of its young men have drifted away in search of work elsewhere, that groups of girls are left to linger idly on doorsteps and street corners waiting for a boy to pass by as a birdwatcher might wait patiently for an elusive species of hawk.

The place clearly has pretensions towards tourism. A sign at its entrance proudly declares it to be the *Paraiso Natural de las Almendras* (Natural Paradise of Almonds) – hence the authors' flippant and unflattering reference to nuts in their brief notes. It even boasts a College of Almonds – *Colegio de las Almendras.* To what does this refer? Is it simply the name of the school, as it might be 'Smith's College', with no relevance beyond that? Or is it a place dedicated solemnly to the teaching of the art and science of the growing and harvesting of nuts?

Guaro, small as it is, does have a place in history, if only a very minor one. It was a small and Moorish settlement, and during the Moorish revolt of the late sixteenth century it was chosen by the Duke of Arcos as a place to garrison his troops, who had been chosen to watch over the area. Troops need barracks, and a place large enough to house his men, possibly a castle of some kind, must surely have existed in the area at the time. The military

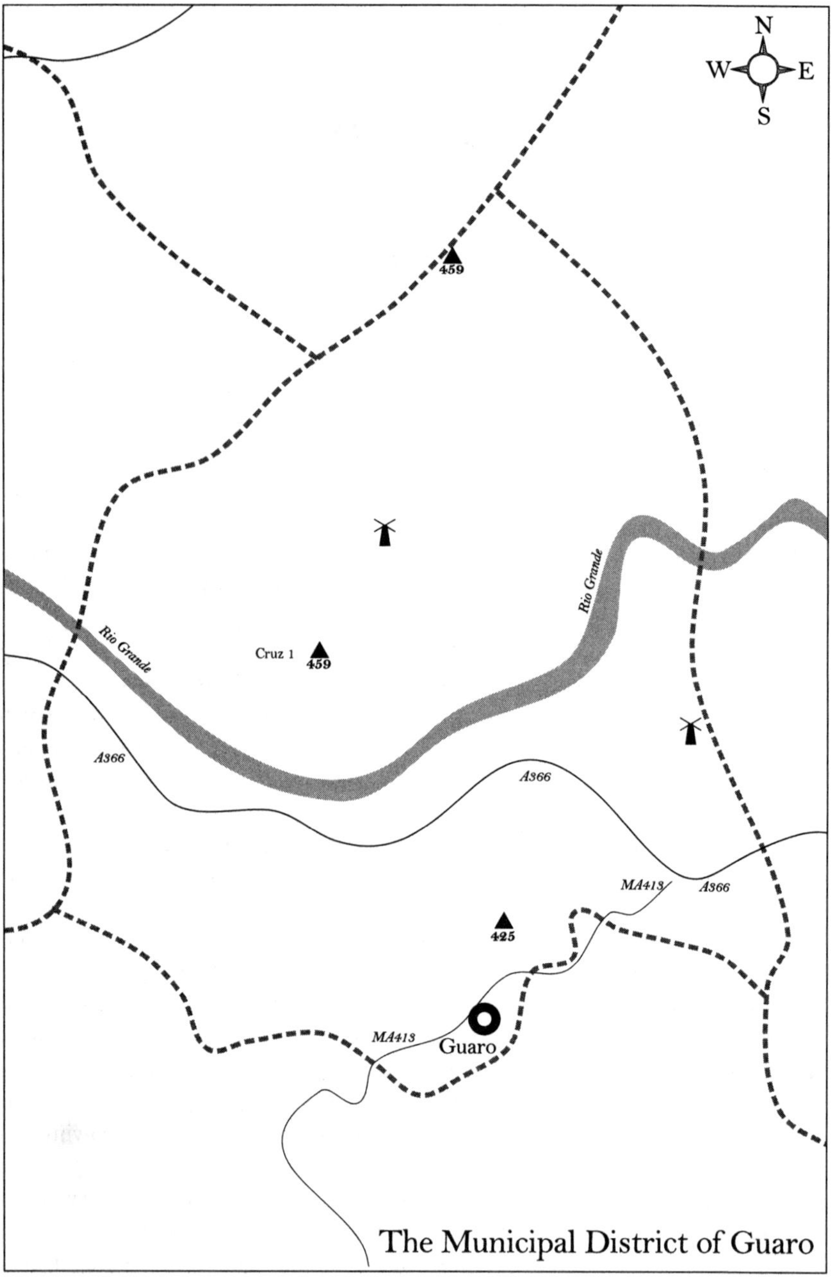

The Municipal District of Guaro

tradition lingered. In the heart of the old quarter until the 1940s stood a barracks used by the once hated Guardia Civil. It is likely that it occupied the space once reserved for the Moor-repressing men of the Duke of Arcos. During the Civil War it was a feared place, where torture and brutality were as common as a breakfast of *churros* and coffee.

It survived for a few years after the end of the war, and then the guards moved to a newer building which still exists. Nevertheless, to the villagers the old building was irrevocably 'the barracks'. For decades it was left to moulder quietly in the sunshine – owned by the local *ayuntamiento* but used, if it was used at all, merely for storage. That all changed in 1993 when, with an eye to the hoped-for future golden age of tourism, it was decided to renovate it and turn it into a small hotel. The year before, with a grant of 40 million pesetas from the Employment Authorities, a training centre for bricklaying, electricity, plumbing and smithery had been established. It wasn't enough, and more money had to be provided by the Rural Employment Plan to see the project to fruition. Nevertheless, it led directly to the plan to refurbish the decaying barracks. Four of the school's pupils got together to form a co-operative to see the plan through, and by the late summer of 1997 the eight-room hotel, the *Hostal Villa de Guaro*, was a reality. Guaro may be on the ropes, but it is fighting back.

The Pueblo

Guaro gives to the casual visitor the impression of being a modern creation, but this is misleading. The village is old, and at its heart are the characteristic narrow mediæval streets. To appreciate them to the full, park your car close to the Almond Institute and do your exploring on foot. There is, in truth, very little of architectural or historical interest to see, but the atmosphere of an old mountain village is intact, and the walk is pleasantly satisfying.

Church of San Miguel Arcángel

Although the church is dedicated to Saint Michael – *San Miguel* – the patron saints of Guaro are San Sebastián and the Virgen Inmaculada, whose images are to be found inside. For a village so small to lay claim to two patron saints may seem a little presumptuous, but it may be nothing more than an echo of indecisiveness and eventual compromise on the part of the community's founders.

The church was built in the 15th century, but was renovated as early as 1605, indicating that the quality of its original building work was extraordinarily low. It struggled on for more than three centuries, becoming steadily more dilapidated, and was eventually subjected to much badly needed remedial attention at the end of the Spanish Civil War. Like many another church in Andalucía, it may well have suffered wilful damage during the conflict.

It is a cross-plan church with one main aisle. A fine arch stands on Tuscan pillars and there is also a rectangular balcony of black wrought iron and a shrine holding the image of San Miguel. On the right, the square church tower is in three sections. The centre one is arched, and the third houses the church bells.

Santuario de la Cruz del Puerto

This 18th-century sanctuary can be found 500 metres beyond the cemetery along the Cañada road from Guaro to Rio Grande. It is a small chapel set beside four cypress trees, and on May 3rd each year – a day known as the Day of the Cross – a procession makes its way to the shrine.

For some reason, the *Santuario de la Cruz del Puerto* was for a long time a favoured meeting place for people who had left Guaro to move to other towns and provinces (a tradition which, as we have seen, still continues). It is one of those pieces of information which inevitably begs more questions than it answers. Why did people who had left Guaro feel the need to meet discreetly beyond the town's boundaries should they return? Was leaving Guaro considered a betrayal? A sin which merited instant excommunication? And did these people meet there by arrangement, letters having been smuggled in and out of Guaro to arrange the tryst? Or did they simply come as near as they dared to their home town and linger close to the sanctuary, hoping by chance to see an old friend? Guaro, as noted above, has lost many of its present generation of young men in the quest for work, and one wonders whether the cypress trees of the *Santuario de la Cruz del Puerto* still bear witness to their misty-eyed midnight revisitings.

Ermita San Isidro

A small chapel on the banks of the rio Seco at KM54 along the C–344. The area is a popular camping site, and the chapel is notable mainly for the pilgrimage of which it is the goal, and which takes place annually on May 15th. The procession is followed by an exhibition of local crafts and folklore.

The old school, which provided the childhood memories, good and bad, of generations of the rural population, is also still in existence. It is a sad sight now. As in so much of Spain, the rural community has withered as more and more families have migrated to the towns. Now only a few smallholders are left, and the school stands empty and silent.

A kilometre down the road, at KM53, is an old mill fed by the waters of the *Arroyo Santo*, just before they join the rio Seco.

About Guaro there is little more to say. Perhaps the only other point of note in Málaga's smallest municipal district is the hilltop *Cruz*, 423 metres above sea level. But it is of only passing interest. Although the Iberians settled many hilltops along the Grande River system, this does not appear to have been among them. Guaro, it seems, has always been neglected.

Chapter Fourteen

Istán

Historical Background

ISTÁN IS ANOTHER SETTLEMENT OF ARAB ORIGIN, tucked away beneath the Sierra Blanca at the head of the valley of the rio Verde. The mountains rise to 4000 feet, while the village itself is 1000 feet above sea level and situated 15km from the coast on the edge of the grandly named *Reserva Biosfera* and the Serrania de Ronda hunting reserve. The rio Verde winds past and goes on its way, cutting through the hills where small and steep arable fields are serviced by a network of rough tracks which make them accessible only to donkeys, determined hikers and four-wheel drive vehicles. In 1972 a dam was completed between the village and the sea and many of the views on the road to Istán are dominated by the huge reservoir which has built up behind the barrier. A road does lead down to the dam, which is known as *Presa de la Concepción*, but this is closed to the public. The existence of the reservoir has given the area its own distinctive micro-climate, making the summers more humid than they were, but keeping the chill off the winters. From here, drinking water is supplied to towns all along the coast.

The area was noted for the quality of its drinking water long before the dam was built, and the pure mountain water that runs continuously from its streams is even more prized in these health-conscious days. Food faddists, spurred on by eager advertising copy-writers, have made 'natural' and 'good' virtually synonymous. They should try eating a toadstool. But the water is good here, and as you approach Istán you will invariably see motorists stopping to fill containers at the spots where the precious fluid cascades freely from roadside fountains.

The turn off for Istán is 5km from Marbella along the N–340 just beyond the Hotel Puente Romano, and it is ironic that as you begin your journey to this echo of the defeat and expulsion of the Moors, you will pass not only a fine new mosque – the first to be built in Spain for five centuries – but also the sumptuous palace of the King of Saudi Arabia. The Arabs have returned to Marbella, but this time in peace and with riches undreamed of even by the kings of Granada.

The rio Verde valley undoubtedly saw some Roman agricultural activity. The remains of an impressively large villa have been uncovered at the mouth

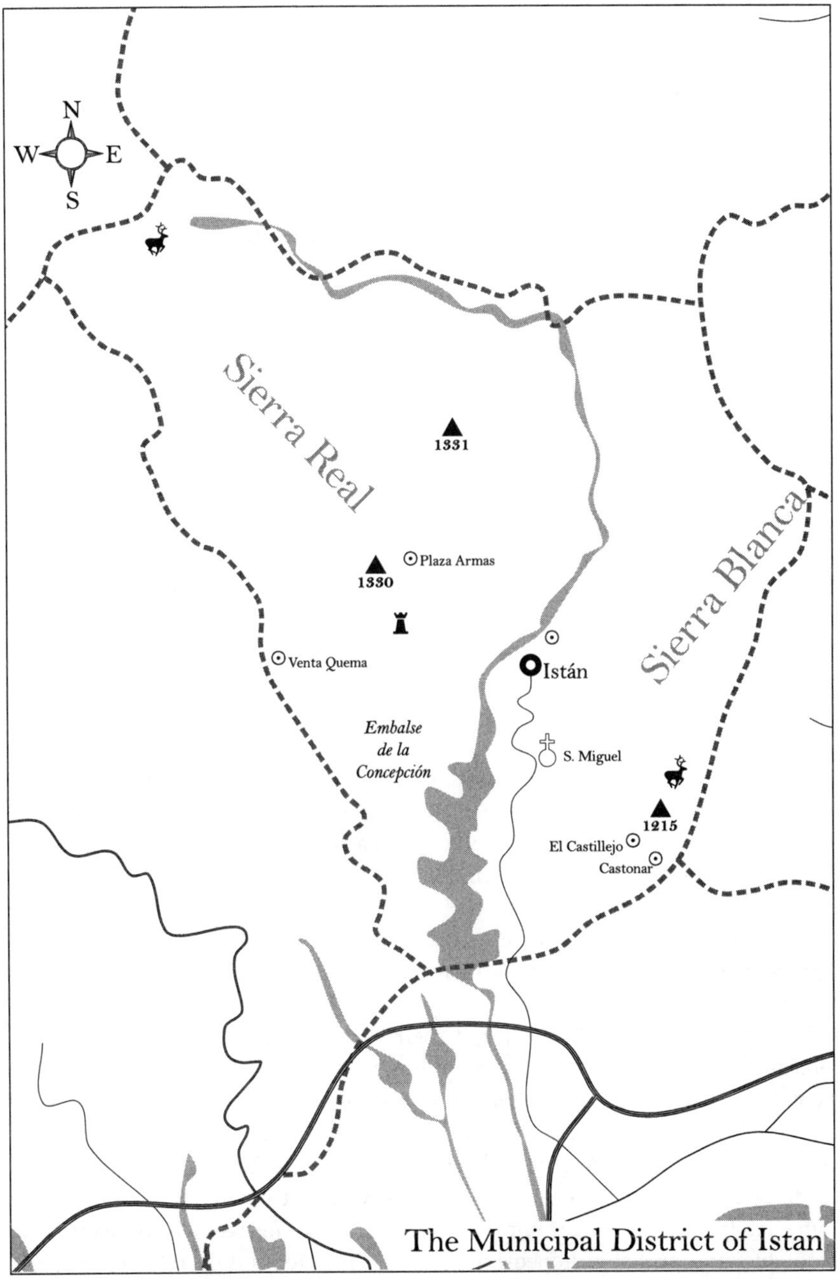
N
W
E
S
Sierra Real
1331
Plaza Armas
1330
Venta Quema
Istán
Sierra Blanca
Embalse
de la
Concepción
S. Miguel
1215
El Castillejo
Castonar
The Municipal District of Istan

of the river (see Marbella), but any others which may have existed in the area are now lost beneath the waters of the reservoir. The Romans undoubtedly exploited the rich mineral resources in these mountains, especially lead, but centuries of further mining after their demise have obliterated all traces of their work.

The Moorish settlement of Istán was certainly in existence by the 9th century and in time it grew into an important stronghold, protected by the fort and settlement of Arboto, which became the seat of Omar ben Hafsun. Some time around the year 980, he briefly rattled the chains of history by attempting to carve himself an independent kingdom from the mighty Caliph of Córdoba, but with limited success.

Istán was not alone in those days. The entire valley developed into a thriving and complex society under the Moors. Besides Istán, there were two other solidly established villages and three associated fortifications. Of the three villages – Istán, Arboto and Daidin – only Istán was destined to survive, and even the precise location of the other two has been forgotten. Man makes his mark on the mountains for a time, but ultimately the mountains brush his works carelessly away, though in the case of Arboto and Daidin, nature had some vigorous human help, as we shall see. In their heyday, a well-used road system linked the villages and ran from Istán up the river valleys to Ronda, Tolox and Monda. Today the roads are no more than lanes and tracks in the forest, used only by adventurous hikers and nature lovers.

Istán slumbered peacefully in the Sargasso Sea of history until 1448, when a Christian army led by Juan de Saavedra Urdiales, out to bloody a few Moorish noses, ventured forth from the frontier lands of Jimena and Castellar and moved boldly across the countryside and down the coast as far as Estepona, which they captured. Drunk with success, Juan became even more ambitious and set his sights on Marbella. However, the Moors of the rio Verde valley and Marbella were not yet ready for relegation to the history books. They mustered a large army of their own and defeated the Christians in a battle close to the mouth of the river. The exact site of the battle is not known, but the fighting was fierce enough, and the Christian losses so great that the event took on the glow of legend and was marked by a commemorative poem.

The Christians sulked and licked their wounds until 1485, when in more determined mood they crossed the mountains from Ronda intent on avenging their defeat and claiming the valley once and for all. This time the Moors took the beating. Marbella surrendered to the Castilian king on June 11th, along with Istán and Arboto. There was an uneasy calm until 1499, when Cardinal Cisneros ordered everyone in the village to convert to Christianity immediately. It was an attempt at evangelism by decree which reaped the inevitable, and probably hoped-for reward. The Moors duly rebelled, though they waited until 1501 to do it, and that gave the Christian authorities the excuse they needed to instigate Plan B. They did it with such severity that the village of Arboto was virtually wiped out. By such gentle means was the conversion to the religion of peace, love and universal brotherhood achieved. The parish church set the seal on the triumph when it was dedicated in 1505.

Ironically, the Arab population of Istán increased a year later when all Moriscos living within one league of the sea were forcibly moved inland to prevent them communicating with their North African kinsmen. A census taken in 1561 lists 131 heads of family. Allowing for an average of four people to each house, that would give Istán a population of around 520–530. It is interesting to note that many of the names included in the census are Castilian corruptions of Arabic names, such as Juan de Algarbe and Luis Almazari.

It might be thought from this that the Moors were by then thoroughly subdued and assimilated, but they had one more flash of fire inside them. In 1569, stung by continued repression, the Moorish populations of the pueblos of the Sierra Bermeja, the inland ghettos behind the Marbella coastline to which they had been confined, rose up in what began as a peasants' revolt and ended as a full-blown civil war. Istán was not to be left out.

After the betrayal and murder of Barcoqui, the peace-seeking emissary from Benahavis (see above), a Morisco outlaw named El Melque took up the fight. He held a strong natural fortress close to Istán above the rio Verde, where he had 3000 men and 2000 arquebusiers. (The arquebus, a heavy but just about portable matchlock gun, had been invented around the middle of the 15th century and was then a formidable weapon.) In spite of these apparent advantages, his position proved vulnerable. First, the Duke of Arcos tried to lure him from his lair with a sworn but dubious guarantee of fair play. El Melque wisely ignored this, so the Duke brought a large force from Ronda and laid siege. The Christians attempted to deploy their men in silence but the premature discharge of a firearm by a soldier from Sentil gave them away. No doubt *sentilero* enjoyed a brief vogue as a synonym for 'clumsy oaf'. As a result of this anonymous but immortal *sentilero* shooting himself, perhaps literally, in the foot, the assault almost miscarried, but in spite of its inauspicious beginning it was eventually successful and El Melque was killed. His surviving followers scattered into the sierras in small, ineffective groups and the victorious Duke of Arcos withdrew, leaving a small garrison in Istán to fight off any further armed raids.

The area was by now rebel free but economically bankrupt, and in an attempt to rebuild the valley's infrastructure and prosperity, the Christians encouraged an influx of people from Castile and Murcia. To this day, the local name for the inhabitants of Istán is *panochos*, from the fact that many of the settlers who came in response to the Christian initiative were from a Murcian village called *El Cristo de Panocho.*

Even as the *panochos* were making their way to Istán, the villages of Arboto and Daidin were already deserted. Four years after the Moors' final abortive rising Istán had a population of 238 loyal Christians. When a new census was taken in 1576, this had risen to 251 – still less than half of what it had been in 1561. It is, in retrospect, a minor miracle that Istán survived at all. Perhaps due to famine or the sheer ruggedness of life in the remote hills, the population slumped to a mere 150 by 1587. It seemed as though the village was destined to disappear like its two vanished neighbours. But somehow it pulled itself together and slowly began to grow. It took a long time, but by 1719, when the church was enlarged to accommodate the swelling congregation, the inhabitants once again numbered over 500. Then the plague struck. Take any century from the twelfth to the eighteenth, look upon it as a play, and the plague is always the black-coated villain skulking in the wings, ready to swoop on stage whenever the pace slacks to terrify the audience. Less than a dozen years after the renovation of the church, the population was back at 200. Those who were left might have been forgiven for considering the place cursed and moving on to greener pastures, hoping to find somewhere better blessed by the Lord and the gods of Nature. But they would not let go. Istán might be cursed, but it was home. They stayed, determined to keep it alive. The measure of their success can be seen in the fact that only twenty years later the village was teeming with more than a thousand inhabitants. The population reached its peak in 1887, when it almost matched the year at 1,879. The twentieth century has been less kind. Only 1,343 people were recorded as living there in the census of 1991. By then the pull of the coast and the promise of work in the booming tourist centres had become irresistible magnets to many, as is the case in so many mountain villages.

Today the weekends here echo not to the sounds of battle and prematurely exploding arquebuses, but to the rattle and buzz of energetically wielded hammers and saws. There is much rebuilding and many houses are now as much as three or four storeys high. Nevertheless, in spite of the encroachments of the 20th century and the fact that most of its buildings are scarcely a hundred years old, Istán has managed to retain a remarkably unaffected *pueblo blanco* character. The most obvious reason for this is the very narrowness of its streets, which has effectively kept at bay the 20th-century's champion polluter, the motor car. Istán today serves mainly as a dormitory town for the coast and only a few families are still engaged in farming. It seems likely that even they will abandon the old ways before long. In 1990 the 20th century came belatedly lurching into the village when a new transmitter brought a clear TV signal to it for the first time. Can it be mere coincidence that the following year, by popular demand, it built itself that other essential – a new football pitch?

The Pueblo

At the entrance to the village a sign warns visitors of the narrowness of its streets and asks them to park their vehicles and explore on foot. This is no mere helpful suggestion, but a virtual necessity. However, that is not to say that Istán is a pedestrian's paradise where the threat of being flattened by a car can be forgotten. Despite its compactness, there are inevitably a few who simply cannot face the journey from A to B, or even A+, without mechanical assistance, so do remain alert. You will find no fancy restaurants as you wander around (though excellent *tapas* and *raciones* are available at the bars) and it was not until January 1998 that the village acquired its first hotel.

The building of an hotel is a significant moment for a village. An isolated, close-knit, self-sufficient *pueblo* has no need of such frippery. Any well-intentioned stranger needing food and a bed for the night will be found them before he passes on his way. The village may be aware of the world, but it sees no need to acknowledge it. An hotel changes all that. The village suddenly ceases to be a place that travellers merely encounter along the way, and becomes a destination in its own right. The stranger on the road is no longer passing by, but arriving. He is a visitor – a tourist – and he must be properly welcomed. It is a farewell to innocence; a rite of passage hardly noticed at the time, but ultimately of great significance.

Wherever you walk in Istán, you will hear the characteristic sound of running water. A complete set of fountains was restored to the village in 1952 and these provide an endless stream of pure mountain water to refresh inhabitants and visitors alike on hot summer days. That, at least, is the theory, and although it is probably safe to slake your thirst from the roadside springs of Istán, it should be noted that in neighbouring Coín an investigating team in 1998 declared the water from at least half of that village's similar fountains unfit to drink.

The opening of Istán's first official hotel came hot on the heels of the inauguration of its first tourist office in late 1997. The office is sited in *calle Marbella.* 'Office' is perhaps too grand a word. The information centre is located in a kiosk of the kind you would normally visit to buy ice cream or your daily ONCE lottery ticket. Curiously, almost as if it constituted some form of penance or punishment, it was manned by two conscientious objectors who opted to do community work as an alternative to military service. On the day that the authors visited it, only one of the two-man team was present. He spoke no English and could offer only a small booklet on the Costa del Sol, and an uninformative leaflet about Istán. However, the kiosk does have a computerised multi-lingual information screen on which the visitor can tap up details of what there is to see and do not only in Istán, but also in Coín, Tolox and other towns in the area. The office is open from 10am to 2pm, and then from 5pm to 8pm, but since the screen is far and away its most useful asset, and is located on the outside, this is largely irrelevant.

In spite of its shortcomings, the tourist information kiosk is the best place to start your tour. Spend a few minutes checking the screen, and then walk down *calle Marbella* into the old town. The first building of interest is *la Casa Parroquial*, the Parish House. Built around 1828, it spent some time as a restaurant before assuming its present rôle. This in itself is a refreshing reversal of the norm in tourist-oriented Andalucía, where buildings so often give up their respectable 9–5 jobs to become restaurants. Continue along the road and you will quickly reach a small square containing the parish church of St Michael – *San Miguel.*

San Miguel is not merely the Patron Saint of Spanish beer drinkers, but also of Istán. Saint Michael the Archangel, to whom we owe Michaelmas Day (September 29th), is a popular saint throughout the Christian world and has given his patronage, and occasionally his name, to many towns and cities far larger and more significant than this one. Nevertheless, as in all such places, the inhabitants consider him to be one of their own and hold him very dear.

Parish Church of San Miguel

The church is so simple and unpretentious that it suggests the congregation are a little embarrassed at interrupting the Lord with their prayers while He's busy, and do not want to make too much fuss about it. It was built in 1505 at the instigation of the Archbishop of Seville, though why the idea of building a church should not have occurred independently to the people of Istán remains unclear. Maybe it was simply another example of their shy modesty and unwillingness to harry the Almighty. Incidentally, a great many other churches in the mountain villages of this area also date from 1505. It would appear that the twentieth anniversary of the Christian reconquest of the mountains was celebrated far and wide with a building boom probably unmatched until the present century.

The church received its first major renovation in 1719, and was again renovated in 1960. There is a single aisle and an altar so minimalist in style that it might almost be called a table. The sole rectangular nave is 230 metres long and there is a modern wooden roof. The bell tower appears to be solidly square, but is in fact only two-sided. Perhaps the only part of the building which has any pretensions to flamboyance is the baroque belfry. On the walls are statues not only of San Miguel, but also of the ubiquitous and ever popular San Antonio and also of the Virgen del Carmen. And that, really, is that. A good, solid country church, where the hard business of life and death can be carried on with quiet dignity under the watchful eye of the director of it all.

Torre de Escalante

To see *la Torre de Escalante,* move on to the recently refurbished town hall, which has an interesting mural telling the history of the village. It is also where you must go to obtain the key which will give you full access to this last surviving remnant of the Moorish towers built during Arab rule. It used to be hidden behind a green door at the end of a side street off *calle San Miguel,* and though it is not dazzlingly impressive, it is probably the most interesting architectural feature to be seen in the village. The Nazari-style tower was built in the 15th century on the highest point of what is today *calle San Miguel.* The Christians allowed it to remain standing after the reconquest, and added a number of alterations. It is square, with arches and vaults, and still has the remains of a vaulted roof. There is also a patio which was at one time used as a stable. The tower takes its name from its last resident inhabitant, Don Pedro Escalante. Today it is owned by the *ayuntamiento*, who set the permitted visiting hours.

The green door has now gone and has been replaced by a wire mesh fence through which the tower is clearly visible. Maybe the *ayuntamiento* grew tired of handing out the key, or of hearing disappointed visitors return it with complaints that it wasn't worth the effort. For although the fence is padlocked, and approach must still be made to the town hall for the means to open it, the ruined tower is so close and, to be frank, so unimpressive, that few will feel the need to do so. It was obviously once an imposing structure, but all that now remains is an arch and a stretch of crumbling wall lost among weeds and hemmed in by houses. It is the dust which the years have swept under the carpet but which has escaped the sanitising vacuum cleaner of houseproud progress, and for that at least we should be grateful.

This scruffy ruin, squatting in a backstreet like a dissolute tramp, is all that has survived of what was probably the castle which overlooked the village at its highest point in the mediæval period. The walls, though they are now only half a step from being officially classified as rubble, do give some idea of the structure's former size. The horse-shoe arch remains attractive in its own dilapidated way, and is easily the best feature of what remains. Without it the ruin would undoubtedly have been cannibalised to build new houses long ago.

Los Coscojas – Islamic Necropolis

In the eastern part of the village, on the trackway of *del Tajo Banderias* is an area known as *Los Coscojas*, taking its name from the abundant kermes oak trees. This is the site of one of two Islamic cemeteries found in the municipal district which are of historic interest. Though it clearly suffered tremendous, and probably deliberately inflicted, damage after the final Morisco rising, tombs have been found and excavated inside the rock. The tombs contained both adults and children and many were from the same mediæval period, suggesting that they may have been victims of the plague which had such a devastating effect on this and other villages.

Fuente del Perro

Just 500 metres along the valley north east of Istán lie a group of mills known collectively as *Fuente del Perro*. The buildings date from the 18th century, but are certainly modifications of Islamic technology. Exactly why they acquired the name of 'Dog Fountain' is unclear, but a wise man would be wary of drinking the water.

Ermita San Miguel

This curious little shrine in honour of Istán's patron is on a hillside a short distance from the village, and the spot has become a favourite one for picnics and barbecues. Indeed, the *ayuntamiento* has thoughtfully provided not only seats, but also a brick-built barbecue grill specifically for the purpose. The shrine is in a small cave a little way up the hill. It is tiny, and consists of nothing more than a statue of the saint behind a locked glass and wrought iron door. Outside are the remains of votive candles and a rubbish bin. Despite this, the path to the shrine is inevitably littered with discarded cans and bottles. It is difficult to know whether these have been tossed aside on the way up, before the bin was spotted, or on the way down after it was ignored. It is odd that so many seem devout enough to pay their saint a visit, but so disrespectful as to choke the pathway to his home with garbage.

The saint is not imprisoned here all year round. On his feast day – September 29th – he is given temporary freedom. The townspeople meet *en masse* and walk in procession to the shrine. In the afternoon, after much eating and drinking at the picnic site, the saint is carried shoulder high from his grotto and paraded through the streets of Istán before being returned to his cell. This may be as much to ensure that he does not forget the place as for the faithful to pay their homage and respects. His progress is followed by the crowd who then celebrate with another mass picnic. The annual *Feria de San Miguel* is held over the weekend which falls nearest to September 29th.

Arboto-Armas

This now depopulated area was the site of a mountain fortress and Moorish settlement. It is situated 5km north of Istán on a spur of land between two rivers. To reach it, follow the old Istán–Ronda road to *Puerto de la Trocha* (trail pass) and then walk on towards *Plaza de Armas.* Do not undertake the walk lightly, however. It is no afternoon stroll for the dilettante. Serious walkers only need apply, and a full round trip could take as much as twelve hours. There is, to be candid, no solid archæological evidence to prove that Plaza de Armas was the site of the lost Arboto fort, but a persistent oral tradition that this was so has survived for countless generations.

During the various skirmishes, squabbles and uprisings which filled the years immediately after the Christian reconquest, Arboto was the undoubted centre of Moorish resistance. Determined once and for all to rid themselves of this troublesome thorn in their side, the Christians finally took it by the scruff of the neck and destroyed it at some point in the 15th or 16th century. It is chilling to realise how easily we can write and read such words at a distance of five hundred years without experiencing the horror that they should inspire. In 1942, Richard Heydrich, Hitler's representative in what had become, under Nazi occupation, the Protectorate of Bohemia and Moravia, was assassinated. The Fuehrer's response was characteristically brutal. He selected a village at random (his unfortunate choice was a mining settlement called Lidice) and on June 10th of that year his troops 'liquidated' it while he stood grinning on the sidelines and watched. All of the 200 men in the population of 450 were shot. The women were deported to concentration camps, and any children young enough to be indoctrinated into the Nazi culture were dispersed to German institutions. The entire village was then bulldozed and every trace of it coldly eradicated. That, in essence, is what had happened to Arboto five centuries before. The destruction of Lidice is within living memory, and was even captured on film by the Nazis as an example to others and a proud tribute to their unchecked ruthlessness: the God-given privilege of the Master Race. As a result, the enormity of its evil overwhelms us. But we should not allow the sea mists of time to blind ourselves to the fact that the people of Arboto were no less real and their suffering no less acute.

Lidice was luckier than Arboto. In 1947 a new village was founded nearby, and the site of the original was marked by a memorial rose garden. The obliteration of Arboto, both on the ground and in records, was so total that its precise location has been a source of controversy ever since. The few Moors who miraculously survived the onslaught scattered and fled to wander the mountains until settling dispirited and impotent elsewhere.

A clue which suggests strongly that Plaza de Armas was indeed the site of Arboto is the existence of an Islamic necropolis, now heavily overgrown and eaten away by erosion. More speculatively, the presence of a spring bringing ample supplies of water to the area makes it an ideal spot for such a community and fortress to have been sited.

Venta Quema

In the 19th century, a post house which stood on the old Ronda road was believed to mark the site of a lost Moorish fortification. Its name, *Venta Quema*, is interesting, since the word *quema* means 'burning'. Names are seldom picked casually out of thin air, and if this one was not simply the name of the man who built it, we can assume that it had some significance. Did it celebrate some previous conflagration at the inn, or was it inspired by an earlier burning – that of the Moorish fort and village which preceded it? For the Venta Quema was certainly in a strategic location, and local opinion holds that it stood on the site of another of the valley's lost Moorish settlements.

The ruins of the Venta Quema lie beside the forest road which once led to Ronda. Its strategic position is obvious. Not only did it dominate the road and lines of communication, it also guarded the valley of the rio Bote. The surviving wall is almost two metres high and stretches for approximately a hundred metres, suggesting that in ancient times this was indeed more than a simple fortification and may even have been, as some insist, the site of Daidin.

Access to the rio Bote valley and the ruins can only be gained by going into the village of Istán and then out along the old Ronda road that turns south-west towards the reservoir. Follow the reservoir south for a kilometre and a half along a new forestry trackway until you reach an inlet. This is the rio Bote. From here a much older trackway leads on up the valley. Three and a half kilometres along the path, you will find some terraced land and a group of farm buildings. Walk on and begin your climb out of the valley close to the Istán/Benahavis border in an area known as *Caseron de la Venta del Bote.* There, in a spot which clearly dominated the surroundings, the castle/settlement was situated.

El Castillejo and Lastonar

These two fortifications were mutually supportive and guarded the rio Verde valley from any planned attack from the direction of Marbella. The actual fortification of *el Castillejo* can be identified from the road, 5 kilometres south of Istán. Shortly before you reach the entrance to *Cortijo Castillejo,* glance to the left, and high above you will see a small, flat hilltop backed by a small peak. You may need binoculars to see it clearly, but the hilltop is crossed by a substantive wall which marks the boundary of what was once the fortress's bailey. The keep was situated on the peak, but is now in ruins.

The peak is 539 metres above sea level and the fit and active can reach it by taking a 1000-foot climb along a stream bed. As always, anyone adventurous enough to do so will be rewarded with stunning views of Gibraltar, Montemayor and the coastline.

Park the car at KM4.2 and ignore the gate and 'Private' signs, since these lead steeply to a number of plots which are currently (1998) being developed into a small rustic urbanisation. Follow the stream bed as far as you can and then start your hard half-hour scramble to the top – a climb of 600 feet. Be warned. This is not easy. It is exhausting, and only for the genuinely fit. In addition, the mountain is criss-crossed by goat tracks which can easily lead you astray. It is better to ignore them and to keep your eyes fixed firmly on the summit, approaching it as far as is possible in a perfectly straight line. At the top is a terraced platform, but there is no sign of a tower. The site is littered with tiles and fragments of pottery. It was obviously a superb defensive spot, surrounded on three sides by sheer cliff faces. The views confirm the line-of-sight theory, with Montemayor peeping over the mountains, and a good view of the rio Bote valley and the ruins of *Venta Quema.*

In close proximity to the castle ruins is a wall and a Moorish cistern, used for collecting and storing water. Some way south of the spot there are lead mines, which would certainly have been exploited by the Moors.

A kilometre and a half south of *el Castillejo* is another Moorish defensive fortification on the boundary which divides the Istán and Marbella municipal districts. The purpose of the fort was to guard the approaches from Marbella and Sierra Blanca. We live in an age where nations are on the whole homogeneous and civil wars are mercifully rare. The existence of innumerable fortifications and defences across the face of Spain reminds us that there was a time when the land was populated by self-contained isolated groups, always wary of their neighbours and living in daily fear of attack from the next valley. Each generation longs for the golden peace of the last, and each is longing for an illusion.

Lastonar was very much a tower built for look-out purposes only, and very little remains to be seen today. For this reason only the most determined should attempt to seek it out. The location is hard to find, and the approach along the rocky terrain is both difficult and dangerous.

Chapter Fifteen

Manilva

Historical Background

MANILVA DID NOT ACHIEVE THE STATUS OF *villa* (municipality) until 1796, a year after it was carved out of the greater municipality of Casares. It is a quiet place for eleven months of the year, but comes alive in the first week of September, when the population of 4,500 is swollen many times by the visitors who come to share in its annual wine festival. It has long been justifiably famous for the succulence of its grapes, which are delicious when eaten fresh, but fulfil their true destiny only when fermented. The Romans may have used the area's soil for vineyards, but if so the practice died out during the Moorish occupation and had to wait long after their departure to be revived.

There are traces of Bronze Age inhabitation in the area (see Cerro del Castillo below), but it did not achieve any real prominence until the time of the Romans. The Moors favoured it less, and gradually the town faded away like an old photograph left lying in the sun. By the 16th century it was deserted. This caused concern to the people of Málaga, Marbella and Ronda, who felt that the coastline to the south of them was unprotected. Because of this, a conscious decision was made to create a new town and repopulate the area. Poorer peasants from the north of Spain were offered land if they agreed to settle in the vacant Moorish holdings. The shrewder ones paused briefly and stroked their chins. There had to be a catch, and indeed there was. The area was still subject to raids by sullen, resentful Moors, and even Turkish pirates dashed ashore occasionally to do a little plundering. Anyone taking up the offer of a free house and some free land would have his work cut out to keep it. The project called for courage and the pioneer spirit, and both were in good supply. To give the new arrivals a fighting chance of avoiding the pirates' attention, the village was sited 3km from the sea on a semi-defensible hill. After that they were on their own. Things were not easy, but Manilva took root and began to grow. By 1600, it already had a stable population.

In its quiet way, Manilva encapsulates Andalucía's historical progress. The original Bronze Age hill fort shows traces of later Punic contact, and the Romans were very active here. The main Roman road (Via I) that ran from

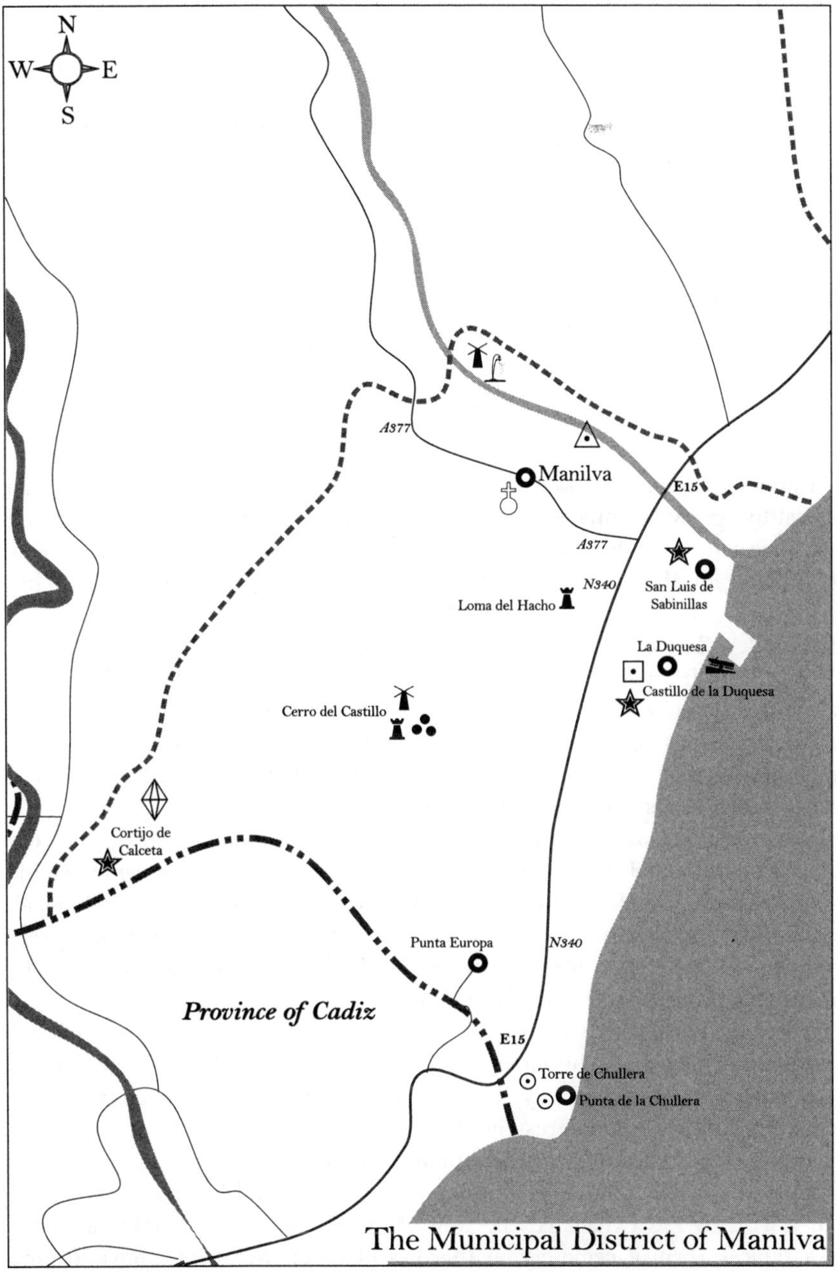
N
W
E
S
A377
Manilva
E15
A377
N340
San Luis de
Sabinillas
Loma del Hacho
La Duquesa
Castillo de la Duquesa
Cerro del Castillo
Cortijo de
Calceta
Punta Europa
N340
Province of Cadiz
E15
Torre de Chullera
Punta de la Chullera
The Municipal District of Manilva

Cádiz to Rome passed through their settlement at Duquesa, where a paved secondary branch road (Via Ia) followed the rio de Manilva valley to the sulphur baths. (See Roman Baths of Hedionda)

The Moors abandoned it, but left their mark too. Moorish influence can be seen in one of the towers at Punta de la Chullera, the deserted settlements at Cortijo de Calceta and Martagina, and, in the valley below, Manilva.

Later Christian activity was centred on Castillo de la Duquesa and Manilva itself. It was not the scene of any notable battle, nor did it feature in any great, significant historical event. Like most of us, it knew someone who had a brother who knew a man whose cousin had a sister whose friend had an uncle who knew somebody famous, but Manilva was very much a spectator in the stalls, watching the pantomime while stubbornly resisting the bow-tied compère's efforts to involve it in audience participation.

The Pueblo

Because it is simple and unpretentious, Manilva is often overlooked. Although a healthy, growing village, tourists tend to give it a miss because they are not directed to it by guidebooks or signs. Those foreigners, *extranjeros*, who come for the wine festival each September are generally locally-living expatriates who learn of it by word of mouth, or hear the singing from the next valley. There is a wealth of written material on the likes of Casares and Gaucin, which frequently swamps the interested visitor with information, while this quiet settlement does not even get a second glance. However, for anyone who has time to spare, a brief stopover is a rewarding experience, and offers a good excuse, September or not, to sample the excellent local red wine, which keeps badly and is best drunk when new.

Leave the car at the entrance to the town and walk in along the old through-road, which has now been heavily pedestrianised. The centre of the village is well provided with bars, which give it an air of genuine old Spanish authenticity. It is hard to imagine that the settlement is scarcely 500 years old. Try not to look like a marauding Turkish pirate and you will be guaranteed a warm and friendly welcome.

The most conspicuous feature of the village is the church and its adjoining cemetery. The parish church of Santa Ana is old, but not ancient, having been built in the 18th century. There is nothing particularly distinctive about it, and it has little of interest in the way of adornment or decoration. It is simply a good, solid place of communal worship, functional without being flamboyant. It has three naves separated by arches, and having said that, all but a Tolstoy has exhausted the well of description. Immediately alongside is a typical Spanish cemetery, with rows of clean, well-kept, above-ground tombs. Even the oldest is comparatively recent – dating only from 1877 – and apart from a couple more from the 1890s, they seem to be exclusively from the 20th century. What attracts the attention of the foreign visitor, however, is the comparative abundance of English names from the late 1980s and the 1990s. Nothing so readily illustrates the solid establishment of the British community in the area. Burial under a foreign sky is a declaration; a silent way of saying, 'I was born far from here, but this was my home'. It is the final ineradicable mark of the settler.

A great deal of building is going on in the outskirts of the town, and although the centre itself still has the air of a village, it is clear that if construction continues at the same rate, it will become an urban sprawl within a few years. But the wine will still be good.

Cerro del Castillo

The Bronze Age hill fort of Cerro del Castillo has long been designated an historical site, but ironically, it was only after a grass fire swept through the area in 1993 that it became distinct enough to be properly seen and appreciated. Nature soon began covering its traces once again, but with only a little imagination, it is still possible to stand among the ruins and feel the weight of the years around you.

To reach it, turn inland opposite the seashore urbanisation of Aldea Beach, and drive past its sister development, Aldea Hills. To proceed further along the dirt road you will need a 4-wheel drive vehicle, or should be prepared for a walk of around half an hour.

To the left, beyond Aldea Hills, you will see the gaunt ruins of an abandoned farm. It is a poignant reminder of the immense changes which the tourist-led upheaval in the traditional economy of the Costa del Sol has wrought. The farm is wedged like a stubborn stain between the expatriate honeycomb of Aldea Hills, and a rash of large villas, home to other expats of greater wealth. Exactly when the farmer washed the soil of the fields from his hands for the last time and bowed to the inevitable we cannot say, but it is intriguing to wonder whether he was a broken, bankrupted victim of the change, weeping for the lost inheritance of his unborn sons, or whether he sold his land at an enormous profit and drove away laughing in a Porsche.

Despite the plague of such urbanisations, which has spread like uncontrolled acne across the face of the coastal land over the last few decades, not all of them are a success. As you leave the luxury villas behind, you will see on the right the skeleton of an urbanisation which was never completed, and which now stands like some eerie concrete ghost town through which shrieking birds fly and the hill winds howl. Perhaps they are duetting on some age-old gypsy lament. The reason for this nameless development's failure is a mystery. Perhaps the money ran out; perhaps the developer ran off. Maybe it is just a little too far from the beach. Beyond comfortable walking distance for the British, and too far accurately to throw sunbed-reserving towels for the Germans. Whatever the case, it has been abandoned to the birds and Nature.

A little further on the path forks. The right hand track leads into the valley, which has attractions of its own, but to reach Cerro del Castillo, take the left turning and drive or walk on to the plateau. Along the ridge you will see stones among the undergrowth like crouching warriors warily watching your approach. These are all that is left of the fort's once impressive walls. Pass through a natural breach in the hill and you will find a large open space with the walls behind and around you, and an escarpment in front which leads down to an extremely fertile valley. In a land where the unforgiving summer heat regularly reduces rivers to stretches of baked mud, the attraction of this valley for the fort's builders is clear to see. Through it courses a river which miraculously continues to run even in the infernos of July and August. There the agriculture which provided the fort with food would have been carried on. It is interesting to note how the walls of the fort follow the contours of the hills, except along the ridge of the escarpment. This was clearly considered defence enough in itself. The views of the valley and the coast down to Estepona are excellent. To us they are merely beautiful. To the inhabitants of the fort in its heyday, they were vital.

Cerro del Castillo, which simply translates as 'Castle Hill', was a large settlement dating from the 8th century BC, and it was very much a thriving part of the Bronze Age seaboard Iberian culture, trading successfully with the Phoenician colonies. It covered an area of approximately 8 hectares on the escarpment ridge and down to the spring, 1km to the south, where the Romans subsequently established their own outpost around Cortijo de Calceta (see below).

The major surviving feature of the site is the defensive walls, which can be traced from the top of the escarpment all the way down to the spring. As noted, the steep sides of the ridge did not require defensive banks, but some form of wooden paling was probably erected. Supporting the defences, there are large mounds which would have been primitive bastions from which missiles could be thrown on to anyone attempting to breach the walls. This was a bad time to be an itinerant seller of trifles.

At the highest point of the fort there is a terrace which may well have been the inner sanctum. Some type of communal buildings could have been constructed in this area, with the bulk of the habitation being in circular family huts made of stone, with rush roofs.

The site did not develop after its original construction and no purpose-built walls of masoned stone were used. This suggests that the site pre-dated the Celtic influence and was either abandoned around 900 BC, or no longer played an important role in the locality. Why this should have been so is puzzling. It was easily defended, it was perfectly placed to benefit from the proximity of the fertile valley, and surely even our pragmatically-minded ancestors were not totally blind to the beauty of its setting. All we can say is that in spite of its obvious attractions, the people ultimately lost interest in the place and left. However, Punic pottery has been found which does indicate that a settlement of some kind survived almost to the dawn of the Roman era. Exactly how and why living, thriving communities wither and die is one of history's great conundrums. Cataclysmic events, either natural or man-made sometimes provide the answer, but where these are not apparent, as at Cerro del Castillo, we are bound to sit among the stones and wonder why the people eventually tired of their home and drifted away.

Much damage is currently being done to the site by treasure seekers, and even a landscape gardener, who is quarrying rock from the bastions for use in ornamental gardens. The Spanish authorities have been slow to respond to this destruction, even though there are tough laws against such plunder. There is also a strict embargo on the use of metal detectors, and when caught, offenders are dealt with severely. Unfortunately, in the wildness of the hills, all too many go unapprehended. It would be too much to expect the formation of crack snatch squads to keep such sites under constant surveillance, ready to swoop in on wrongdoers like vengeful eagles from the sky; but abuse of the law as blatant as that by the gardener and others could surely be stopped by the application of a little will, and the occasional injunction.

Cortijo de Calceta (Stocking Farm) and the Pine Woods

As you leave the fort behind you, the dirt track forks again. The road to the left leads ultimately to Sotogrande, in the province of Cádiz. Since the historical heritage of Cádiz is beyond the scope of the present volume, we shall not be driving (or walking) that far. However, the stretch between the fort and the Málaga/Cádiz border is not without interest. Across the valley is a terraced hillside with the remains of what appears to have been a Moorish settlement, probably abandoned unwillingly after the Christian reconquest, when Moors were forbidden to live within a league of the sea. The village, it should be noted, is situated so that it would have been completely invisible from the shore, and therefore, hopefully, immune from the unwelcome attentions of scavenging pirates meandering opportunistically up and down the coast in search of loot.

Access is possible only on foot, and it is necessary to ford a well-watered stream which runs throughout the summer. The ruins are officially described as those of a rustic Roman villa, but the most visible remains today are the Moorish terraces and the foundations of a farming community. One or two ruined buildings can be seen, but these most certainly date from the later Christian period.

Double back along the track to the hill fort junction, and head further inland, taking the track that leads up and along the rise, and you will pass through an area of scrubland, *Llanos de Tábanos* (Horsefly Plain), which was once covered with pine forest. Sadly, the pine forest was devastated during the 19th century by the depredations of charcoal burners, and now only a small patch of forest survives, close to the border between the provinces of Málaga and Cádiz. Within this, as a silent witness to the destruction, a stone lime kiln can still be seen.

During the winter months, a walk around the forest is a rewarding experience, with lush green views down to Gibraltar and up the coast to Marbella. However, we should add a word of caution. Although this is largely public land, it is widely used for hunting during the season. The hunters are apt to become irritated by the presence of noisy vehicles and chattering people who disrupt their silent stalkings. If there are signs of hunters in the area (for example, the track into the valley may be deliberately blocked by a hunter's car), proceed with cautious discretion. Under no circumstances act like a rabbit.

Martagina

Turning back from the remnants of the forest, return to the track junction. Beside the hill fort, the deserted village of Martagina can be reached in one of two ways. Either head back to the modern-day ghost town, and take the track to the left into the valley or, if you prefer and have an afternoon to spare, descend into the valley from the junction itself. This is probably best done on foot, for although it is navigable by 4-wheel drive, it is very steep, and as you approach Manilva, it is necessary to ford two rivers. At the first river crossing, a goat track on the left-hand side leads you to a more substantial donkey trail that eventually leads down to the sea. This makes an excellent walk in fine weather and probably marks the old route to the coast. The gorge has now been dammed, creating a pleasant lake. Within the valley, on a small plateau, are the remains of a water mill, barns and other buildings, marking the site of yet another lost community.

This settlement was probably once part of the community of Martagina, which as late as the 1920s was still home to more than a hundred people. Today only one house remains inhabited, with a smallholding of well-cultivated vegetables on a patch of land leading down to the gorge.

To reach the lost village, cross over the dam and climb out of the gorge towards the ruins around the spring which fed the fertile valley beneath the Bronze Age fort. Only the spring now remains, having watered without favour Iberian, Roman, Moor and Christian, as the millennia fell slowly upon each other like autumn leaves in a gentle breeze. The site was occupied as late as the 18th century, but is now deserted.

The mill is of great interest. The water from the spring entered a stone-lined reservoir, and was then funnelled down a vertical shoot, turning the millstones. The water was then used to irrigate the side of the valley, and even today characteristic Moorish crops such as fig and banana trees flourish in this oasis.

This was very much an agricultural settlement, with animals reared in the uplands around the fort.

Roman Sulphur Baths of Hedionda and Aqueduct of the Manilva Valley

Sulphur, the ninth most abundant element in the universe, is one of nature's great jokes on the human race. Known to the ancients as *brimstone*, it is one of the elements essential to life as a constituent of various biologically active compounds, and it has many industrial uses in processes ranging from the bleaching of dried fruits and the vulcanisation of rubber, to the manufacture of matches, fertilisers, insecticides, fungicides and fumigants. Pure sulphur is odourless, but fun-loving nature frequently combines it with hydrogen to produce hydrogen sulphide – a compound present in natural gases which, to put not too fine a point on it, stinks. It produces the characteristic odour of rotten eggs.

Nevertheless, sulphur has long been renowned for its medicinal properties, perhaps in the belief that anything that smells *that* bad *must* be good for you. Bathing in sulphur springs to maintain or improve the condition of the skin or to cure some epidermal complaint has been common since antiquity.

In the valley below Manilva, close, but mercifully not too close, to the popular 'Roman Oasis' restaurant, are the Roman sulphur baths of Hedionda. (To be absolutely accurate, they lie within the municipal district of Casares, but can only be approached from Manilva.) Our ancestors were blunt, no-nonsense people. The baths take their name from the stream, which feeds them, and the name means 'stinking'. They are signposted 1KM from Manilva on the Gaucin road. The high sulphur content of the waters is due to a sulphur spring, which flows from the limestone outcrop above the valley, and they attracted the attention of the Romans 2000 years ago. How could they not? An arched bathing complex was created of which four chambers still exist, although other adjacent water channels can be seen, which suggest that the complex was once much larger. During his period as governor of southern Spain between 63 and 60 BC, no less a person than Julius Caesar is said to have cured himself of a skin infection by bathing here, though it was probably several days before he was able to get close enough to his friends to tell them.

Sadly, in an artless attempt at preservation, a modern concrete canopy has been erected over what survives of the original Roman structure, although this can still be seen from the entrance by those not willing to take the plunge. A small first chamber leads, via an archway and tunnel, to a much larger inner chamber. Hardy types not put off by the all-pervading stench of rotten eggs still come to immerse themselves in the cool, murky, health-giving waters and to take away (although there are signs telling them not to do so) samples of the alluvial mud for use as face packs and poultices.

Even more sadly, the site is ill-maintained and terribly neglected, with both the canopy and the surrounding wall heavily daubed with graffiti. But things may be about to change dramatically.

As this book was being readied for publication, ambitious plans were announced to restore the baths and to create an entirely new infrastructure for the area. The scheme envisages the construction of a clinic to provide beauty and slimming treatments, geriatric care and seawater therapy. The clinic is intended to be the centrepiece of a large hotel complex, which will incorporate a private spa. The existing spa is to receive a long-overdue renovation and to be surrounded by what the authorities have called an 'archæological garden'. A second new spa, for public use, is also to be created within a rural accommodation complex, and the entire site is to be made more accessible by the building of new roads and parking areas. Finally, it is proposed that security guards be employed to prevent the kind of abuses we have noted above. The plans originate with a private company, Balneario Casares, S.A., but much will depend on the attitude of the relevant authorities, who must grant the necessary legal permission. If the project is allowed to proceed, the Roman baths of Hedionda could well become the major attraction that they deserve to be. However, visitors to the proposed hotel would be well advised to check the direction of the wind before opening their windows.

Across the river from the baths there are the ruins of 18th-century farm buildings which re-used Roman masonry. It is clear from this that some kind of service settlement did evolve around the complex. To find these, follow the river downstream for approximately 75 metres until you come to an old, but recently restored, single-arch aqueduct. This was used to help irrigate the fertile valley further down and its course can be traced for much of the way. This irrigation system is certainly Roman in origin, but much of the infrastructure was rebuilt during the Moorish period.

On the bank across the river, the ruins of buildings can be seen. As noted, the structures themselves are not Roman but did utilise existing Roman masonry.

2km upstream towards Casares, there are some interesting mills and irrigation channels. Access is easily gained by following the stream bed and this makes a pleasant walk as the river valley closes in. Once again, the ruins are reputed to have been Roman in origin, but so extensively altered by the Moors that they are really far more indicative of that period. Nevertheless there is a satisfying series of dams and watercourses to discover.

This valley is made for the adventurous hiker. It ultimately connects with the mills of Casares, but it is an all-day walk and scramble. (See Mill Valley, Casares) Access is via a youth centre, but do not be intimidated by the surrounding fences. Adopting a sprightly step and an 'I know where I'm going' air, keep to the river valley and follow the footpath through the complex.

Aqueduct

The less adventurous can follow the modern road down to the coast, where, about half-way along on the right, they will find the 100-metre-long surviving stretch of an aqueduct also reputed to be of Roman origin. This did not span the whole valley, but was used to drive a large water wheel as part of a mill complex. A rustic cottage now stands on the foundations of the Roman/Moorish mill house, but Roman brick can be seen throughout the structure.

Water to power this mill was almost certainly channelled off by aqueducts at the Roman baths, which kept the water above the valley bottom until it reached the mill complex.

San Luis de Sabinillas

The present-day fishing and tourist village bearing this name is very much a new settlement, having developed only within the last hundred years. Before then it was no more than a deserted beach dotted here and there with small fishing huts. The site, however, was not always so barren. During the Roman period it was an industrial settlement, a satellite of the large Roman community at Castillo de la Duquesa.

Excavations have shown that the ceramics and fish processing plants were enlarged in the 4th century AD. The finds were particularly rich in North African ceramics. Despite the obvious activity in the ceramics industry, however, it is clear that the community was primarily concerned with the production of salted fish and garum paste – a fish paté of which the Romans apparently could not get enough, and which was exported to all corners of the Empire.

A hoard of coins dating from the first decade of the 5th century AD suggests strongly that the community was already suffering from the effects of the shattered commercial infrastructure of the declining Roman Empire and from Barbarian incursions. For whatever reasons, Sabinillas did not survive as a community into the Visigothic period, and virtually disappeared from the map until its modern revival. Today the village specialises in good fish restaurants, none of which appear to serve garum paste, and the only point of historical note is the modern church and square, although these are still far too contemporary to excite the visitor in search of Spain's heritage.

Roman fishing village of Castillo de la Duquesa

The 18th-century fortress of Castillo de la Duquesa stands on the coast in the middle of what was once a large Roman fishing village. It has been suggested that the village may have been called Saltum in classical times, but no definite Latin name has survived. However, for ease of reference, this is the name that we shall use. Excavations in 1989 uncovered much of the village's infrastructure, making it one of the most extensive and impressive archæological sites in this part of Andalucía. Then the curious Spanish attitude to such treasures intervened. The exceptional bath house site, to the south of the castle (see below), was preserved, while the rest was simply covered up again and the site allowed to return to the unsightly wasteland it had been before. A favourite spot for the dumping of domestic rubbish when it was not being used to stage the annual fair. Saltum, if such was its name, had reappeared briefly like Brigadoon, and was gone. Knowledge of what lay beneath the surface meant that the site was, in theory at least, protected by law, but that did not prevent an ambitious developer from setting his eyes on it. At least the bath house seemed safe. Although it was unfenced and unprotected, it was kept free of weeds and as 'Plaza de Baños' it became a fine adornment to the present-day village, as well as a tangible part of its heritage. Then, in 1997, they decided it was time that Saltum saw the light of day again. By the spring of 1998 a sprawling complex had been uncovered of great richness and variety. The vastness of the complex indicates that this was a large and important working community established for the production of salted fish.

The bath house, the only part preserved after the earlier excavations, and easily the most impressive of the ruins, is to be found south of the castle on the outskirts of the village, which also bears the name of Castillo de la Duquesa. It consists of two large chambers and a hot house, or boiler room, whose oven and underfloor heating system (*hypocausts*) leading to the other chambers can be clearly seen. These two chambers were probably the *tepidarium* and *calidarium*. The white mosaic floors have survived and these areas would have been used for changing and meeting or simply sitting around in to pass the time of day. But once again, the often incomprehensible official attitude to sites such as this has to be commented upon. At the very time that the rest of Saltum was being unearthed again in 1997/98, the bath house site suddenly became neglected. A mesh fence was erected around it, which suggested that it was about to receive improved protection and attention, but it was then left to rot like a mediæval prisoner tossed into a dungeon and forgotten. As teams of enthusiastic volunteers toiled in the sun to reveal the hidden delights of the remainder of Saltum, the new weeds around the bath house grew higher and higher and the mosaics became increasingly lost in the undergrowth. In addition, since the protective fence was permanently unlocked, it did nothing to prevent the entry of those who simply wished to use the site as a place to eat and drink and leave their rubbish. This curiously schizophrenic attitude to the two sites – in effect two parts of the same site – is, to say the least, perplexing.

The main part of the excavated village lies to the west of the bath house, between the castle and the main road. Here there once stood a Roman villa. Today no walls remain above three feet in height and the few mosaics which have survived are of only one colour – red. Even before the 1997/98 excavations it was possible to follow the outline of the building and its various rooms, but this was obviously made immeasurably easier as a result of the dig. It would be nice to think that on this occasion the uncovered site might be genuinely and permanently preserved. A site of this size and impressiveness, in such an unusually accessible spot, would surely become an attraction for visitors if it was properly treated. But such things cost money, and prime land on the Costa del Sol is solid gold to developers. Previous experience, and the current neglect of the small and comparatively easy-to-maintain bath house area, inevitably lead to pessimism. If *Saltum* really is to be compared to Brigadoon, then the 1998 revival may well turn out to be its last.

To the north of the castle, a vast heap of rubble currently marks the site of the former Guardia Civil barracks, which were demolished in 1996. The barracks were built on what was once the 'industrial' area of the Roman site. Fish-paste tanks have been excavated here which were used for the production of *garum*. The remains of water conduits and salt pans can be clearly seen and it is certain that much more lies waiting to be discovered below the barracks. This area is also included in the 1997/98 dig, and at the time of writing, the rubble is being removed and the earth is beginning to give up its secrets. Hopefully government funds will continue to be made available in the future for the necessary excavations to be completed.

In the meantime, what has been allowed to happen amounts almost to official vandalism. Nowhere is this more apparent than in the area a little north of the barracks, towards the modern urbanisation. This was the site of the Roman *necropolis*, or graveyard. Though it yielded more than thirty skeletons, only ten scattered graves in poor and plundered condition were found. Sadly, even this gravesite has been all but destroyed by the indiscriminate dumping of rubbish. The settlement also possessed a stone mill and a well, although these are now hard to locate on the ground.

The castle itself was built in 1767 by Francisco Paulino of Seville. As a reward for his industry and his services to castle builders, who found work hard to come by at that time, the Spanish King Carlos III granted Paulino the command of a company of cavalry. What he did with them is a matter of conjecture. The old rhyme about the Grand Old Duke of York springs unbidden, and perhaps unfairly, to mind. Today his castle is used as a school for carpentry and other skills, and although a sign on the entrance prohibits entry except to those engaged in the work, a well-behaved and unobtrusive visitor is unlikely to be challenged and ejected. The first room to the left as you enter is currently used as the project director's office and most of the rooms which are not ringing to the sounds of hammers and saws or the screams of the electrocuted (trainee electricians are among those receiving tuition) are being used to store tools and protective clothing, all of which makes it difficult really to see and appreciate the structure beneath. Nevertheless, it is infinitely preferable for the building to continue as a living, working entity than to be allowed to fall into the ruinous neglect which is the fate of so many others.

Duquesa Golf Club (Loma del Hacho – 'Beacon Ridge')

There was golf in Roman times, but to paraphrase Star Trek's Mr Spock's observation about Life, it was not golf as we know it. Romans who wished to keep fit and have a little innocent fun at the same time took part in an activity called *paganica*, which involved strolling around the countryside whacking a feather-stuffed leather ball with a bent stick. The name *paganica*, by the way, was not intended to imply that the activity was un-Christian. It was derived, as indeed is our own word *pagan*, from the Roman name for a countryman or rustic – *paganus*. No-one has yet traced the family tree of Severiano Ballesteros back to some early *paganica* open champion, nor have archæologists unearthed at this site the remains of oft-hit leather balls, suspiciously shaped sticks, or crudely altered score cards. Nevertheless, the central hill around which this 18-hole golf course is built did see a brief period of Roman occupation and is officially scheduled as a Roman site. Its probable use was actually for defence and as a beacon hill until the fall of the Empire. Fragments of Roman pottery and masonry have been discovered, but no serious excavation has taken place. Eighteen holes in the ground seem to be enough so far as the present owners and players are concerned. Earlier occupation from the Bronze Age is also probable, though if our Bronze Age ancestors found time for similarly frivolous pursuits, they have gone unrecorded, along with their scores.

As pure speculation, the authors offer the suggestion that this may have been the original Romanic settlement in the area at the time of the Roman invasion, but that it was deserted when a trading post was established below in Castillo de la Duquesa.

Torre de Chullera

On the main road to the southern edge of the Province of Málaga, at Punta Chullera, you will find the intriguing remains of the Torre de Chullera. Lurking defiantly behind the inevitable urbanisation, which has crept closer than most armies managed, it offers a magnificent view of the coast to Estepona in one direction and Gibraltar in the other. The square base of the tower survives, with one proud column still standing on it, challenging the worst efforts of gravity, weather, tourists and time to bring it down. It is as though its makers are still pointing a defiant finger heavenward, summoning the help of their god – whoever it was. Only the sand and the sea know for sure.

Down on the rock point close by, stands a second tower from the 16th century. This one is more conventional, being round and of the same style as those to be found over the provincial border in Sotogrande. Though once merely a ruin, the top half has been restored.

Chapter Sixteen

Marbella and San Pedro

Historical Background

MARBELLA, 'Beautiful Sea', is a haunt of the rich, the famous and the unashamedly notorious. Luxury yachts bob quietly on the waters of Puerto Banús like corks tossed into a pool of flat champagne and the suburbs are filled with fine villas where conspicuous consumption is the order of the day. The town's controversial mayor, Jesús Gil y Gil, whose hobbies include owning the Atlético Madrid football team, has set himself the task of cleaning up Marbella and making it the number one destination not only for the rich, but for the tourist of more modest means on the Costa del Sol. He has vowed to rid the streets of beggars, and in doing so he may well be reflecting on Marbella's past reputation as a beautiful place to see from a distance, but not to visit. Travellers in the eighteenth and nineteenth centuries were advised to give it a wide berth if they wanted to hang on to their clothes and possessions, and the warning even became a kind of risqué proverb, *Marbella es bella, pero no entrar en ella* (Marbella is beautiful, but don't go into her). This surly, inhospitable attitude was said by some to derive from the fact that a large percentage of the population was of Moorish ancestry, intent on avenging, in some small way, the final defeat and maltreatment of their forebears. Then, as now, there were always those who blamed the parents.

Perhaps, when the Moors inherited the town, they attributed Marbellan petulance to a lingering Roman strain, while the Romans spoke unflatteringly of the Phœnician side of their character. For although it may be convenient to file Marbella neatly away as a product of Spain's Roman and Moorish past, its roots go far deeper. Excavations at the mouth of the rio Real during 1998 uncovered traces of Phœnician habitation from the early part of the 7th century BC. It was an important find, since it represented the only tangible archæological evidence of the existence of a town on the spot at this period. The leader of the dig, Pedro Sánchez, rightly referred to the stones, the Bronze Age utensils and pottery which his team collected as Marbella's 'missing link'. Older sites have been found along the coast, but there were signs, even in the earliest weeks of the Sánchez excavation, that the settlement at rio Real may have been among the most important of its time. It came to light, almost inevitably, during the moving of earth in preparation for the building of yet another

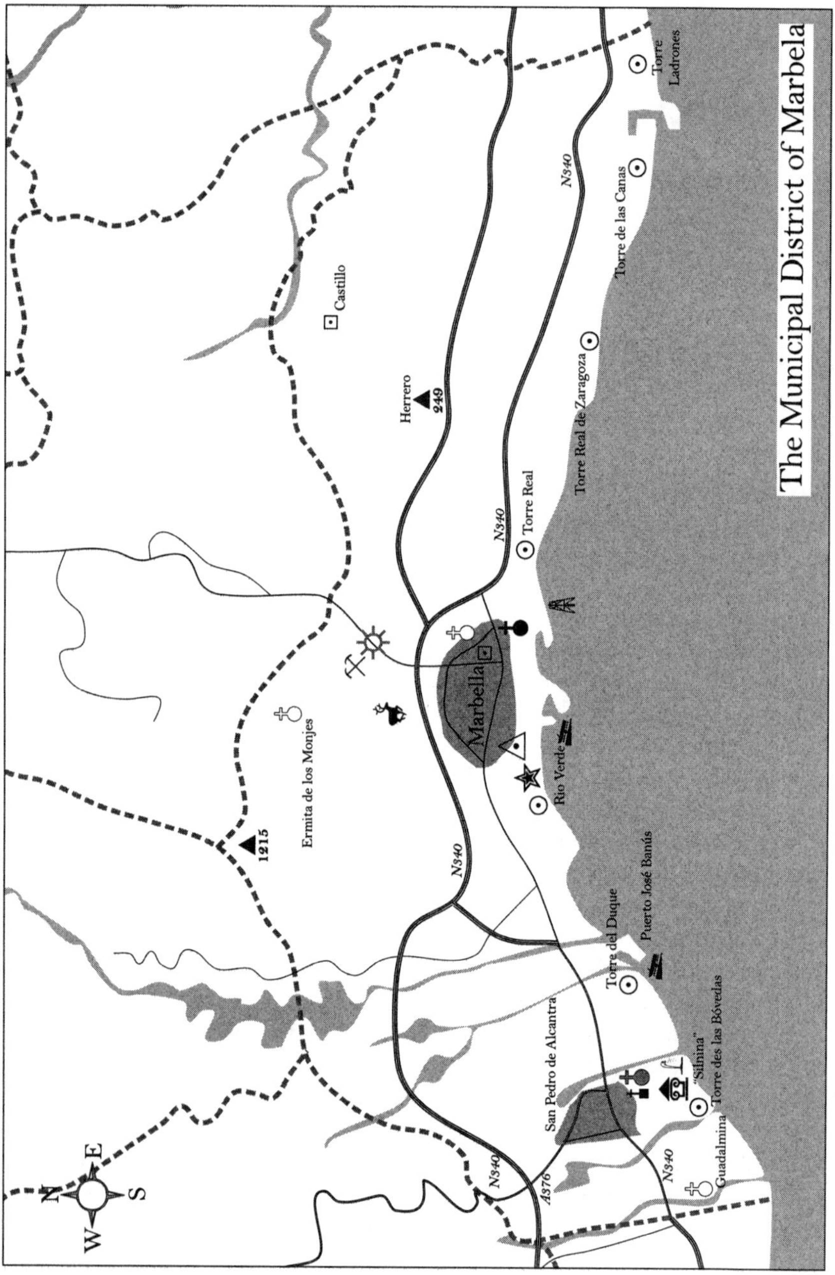
The Municipal District of Marbela
Torre Ladrones
Torre de las Canas
N340
Castillo
Herrero
249
Torre Real de Zaragoza
Torre Real
N340
Marbella
Rio Verde
1215
Ermita de los Monjes
N340
Puerto José Banús
Torre del Duque
San Pedro de Alcantra
"Silnina"
Torre des las Bóvedas
Guadalmina
N340
A376
N340
N
E
S
W

residential complex. Sadly, but not surprisingly, the great earth-crunching machines, stomping and raging like unleashed bulls, destroyed much of the site before the importance of what they were crushing was realised and they were belatedly subdued. It took a formal complaint to the authorities by the Marbella Association for the Defence of the Historical-Artistic Heritage, usually known less pompously as 'Cilniana', to do it. When the dust settled, it was not easy to assess the amount or extent of the damage, but what remained was tantalising. It was not, for instance, a single-level site. There was evidence of no less than six successive but quite distinct settlements. The Andalucían Department of Culture came to an agreement with the developer in April 1998 which not only allowed the excavation to commence, but called upon the developer to pay for it. That may sound eminently sensible, but one cannot but harbour a lingering doubt about the clear conflict of interest involved. Property developers are not noted for their noble devotion to the preservation of important historical sites, and nowhere is this truer than on the Costa del Sol. Pedro Sánchez observed wryly that the only limits to the excavations were monetary ones, and that he supposed 'the developer would prefer it if we found fewer remains'. Just so. Without being too cynical, we can imagine the developer pacing impatiently up and down, puffing anxiously on his cigar and wishing that those interfering academics would go away and let his bulldozers get on with the job. At the culmination of the dig, a report will be sent to the Heritage Commission, and the future of the site will rest in their hands. If they consider it of major importance, they have the power to order its preservation. If not, the development will be allowed to go ahead. In such circumstances, is it not legitimate to raise a quizzical eyebrow at the knowledge that the excavation's purse strings are in the hands of those who, quite naturally, would wish to see it fail?

In the final years of the twentieth century, due to its success in attracting the patronage of the cosmopolitan rich, Marbella has reputedly become the wealthiest community in Spain. Nevertheless, many of the Moorish walls and narrow streets of the old town remain to be seen and the town hall, dating from the 16th century and standing on the Plaza de los Naranjos, is still a focus of activity. Beneath the Plaza de los Naranjos, and in the immediate vicinity, there are masonry foundations thought to mark the site of the main Roman constructions, including baths.

Though important both in trade and coastal defence, the ancient city seems to have had little backbone for a fight. It was sacked by African pirates in AD 170 (admittedly along with Málaga and other Bætican coastal settlements), and the Moors took it almost without breaking into a sweat, when they swarmed out of Africa early in the eighth century to begin their eight-hundred-year occupation of the Peninsula.

The Romans had an important centre here which was known as Silniana (or Cilniana). The site of the Roman town is thought to have coincided roughly with what is now 'San Pedro de Alcántara' (see below) but to have been destroyed by the devastating seaquake which struck the coast in the 4th century. The eastern part of Marbella was called 'Barbésula' by the Romans, and this name became changed, during the Arab occupation, to 'Barbella'. Alcántara, incidentally, was a name given by the Moors to a number of places, and indicated the site of a Roman bridge. Just to make the whole thing even more confusing, it is thought by some that the Romans called Marbella itself 'Salduba'.

During the Moorish era the land around Marbella and extending into the Sierra Bermeja mountains was a more or less homogeneous unit within which the town thrived. Marbella was part of the Kingdom of Granada, and remained so until the Christians took the town away from the fast-fading Moors in 1485. With the Christian conquest, the harmony was destroyed. The mountain villages were still inhabited by resentful, rebellious Moors, many exiled from Marbella itself, while a more settled Christian community took root on the coast. This dichotomy lasted until the final expulsion of the Moors, when the pattern of land ownership altered rapidly.

The adjoining community of 'San Pedro Alcántara', despite its Roman roots, remained arable land until the last century, and is in reality a new town. We shall return to San Pedro later.

Marbella

Parking is not a problem in Marbella itself, but rather than head for the beach and its glossy attractions, cross over the main thoroughfare to the compact low-rise old quarter, dominated by its church towers. A good starting point is the Plaza de los Naranjos and the old Moorish fortress. The Plaza de los Naranjos (Orange Square) has been a focus of Marbella life since at least 1485, when the town was taken from the Moors by the Catholic Kings. It sits at the centre of a network of narrow streets packed tight with shops and restaurants of all kinds, and is an excellent place to pause before beginning your exploration.

In the square itself, you will find the town hall (*ayuntamiento*), which was built in 1568, and bears a stone inscription celebrating the fall of the town to the Christians 83 years before. The building next door is almost as old. It was built in 1602 and was at one time reserved for the Chief Justice, but Marbella proved that it had its priorities just about right when it kicked him out and turned the place into the tourist office. But the fountain which faces them on the other side of the square easily pre-dates both buildings. It was erected by the town's first Christian mayor, and has been standing in the spot since 1504.

Alcázar

There are two main theories about the Moorish Alcázar (fortress) in the old city of Marbella. The first is that it was originally a Roman building, which was re-built and re-inhabited by the Moors. Much of the evidence was destroyed during the mediæval reconstruction work, but the foundations of the northern wall do indicate a Roman origin.

Alternatively, the castle may have been built entirely by the Moors, but with material that was plundered from nearby Roman ruins. Incorporated into the walls in the area of the modern c*alle Trinidad* are several worn limestone *ashlars* (straight-edged hewn stone blocks) which are thought to have come from a Roman temple, while on the eastern side of Plaza de los Naranjos the foundations of various buildings from the Roman era have been found.

The castle, which forms a rectangle 90m × 160m, is in two distinct parts. The castle itself, including its arms courtyard, is to the north, while the citadel or garrison is situated to the south.

In the north-east corner is a beacon tower overlooking the stream of La Represa, and this would have been used for the lighting of warning fires. Several other towers remain, but some have certainly disappeared over the years, as has the barbican, the wall which once extended from the castle to La Represa stream. Indeed, the stream was once known as 'La Barbicana'. The wall, or at least the outline of it, was still visible into the second quarter of the present century but has now entirely vanished, leaving only its ghost in a few fading old photographs.

Given the importance of this site, it has been very badly served by successive local governments. Apparently unrestricted construction of unsuitable buildings, including houses and schools, has been allowed around the walls, and spurious 'battlements' with absolutely no historical justification were added in 1955. Schools occupy the interior precincts and use them free of charge. Consequently, in the view of many, not least the noted Málaga archæologist Juan Temboury, 'the most beautiful and unusual feature of the town has been irretrievably damaged for all time'.

He may have been unnecessarily pessimistic. Once again, Jesús Gil has taken firm and characteristically controversial control. His first act has been to order the demolition of the unauthorised houses. This will be followed by the demolition of the schools (presumably during half-term), and also the homes of the teachers employed there. Finally, the interior of the castle will be excavated and cleared. His ultimate aim is to restore the walls as closely as possible to their original state and turn the castle once again into an important historical monument.

The Holy Trinity Convent

High on Gil's list of priorities is the resurrection of the Holy Trinity Convent, the Santìsima Trinidad, which once stood between the Plaza de la Iglesia, calle Viento, calle Salinas and calle Trinidad.

The convent was founded after the Christian capture of the town in 1485. Despite its name, it was actually a monastery. The Trinitarian monks who lived there ran the Bazán Hospital, and were instrumental in the rescue of many slaves. Miguel de Cervantes, the celebrated author of *Don Quixote*, sheltered there briefly in 1580. He had been held captive as a slave in Algiers for five years, after a ship on which he had been sailing from Naples to Spain was attacked by Turkish corsairs off Marseilles. Several attempts were made to secure his release by payment of a ransom, and the monks played an integral part in the final successful one. They carried the ransom money, raised by Cervantes' mother, to Algiers in May 1580, but it fell short of the 500 gold ducats being demanded. Christian traders operating in the town raised the difference and Cervantes sailed back to Spain in October, taking refuge at the Santísima Trinidad before going on to Madrid.

By 1814 the place was rapidly crumbling, and the authorities were asked to carry out urgent repair work. They took a look, made sympathetic noises, and then shrugged their bureaucratic shoulders. There was no money, they said. They could not afford it. If it fell down, it fell down, and that was that.

It did not physically fall down, but it certainly slipped well down the social scale. In the latter part of the nineteenth century it became Marbella's cemetery, which was at least in keeping with its pious past. But what would the monks have made of the primitive cinema which it became in the early years of the twentieth?

The 1950s were bad years for the convent. As the outside world went wild to the sounds of rock 'n' roll, most of the building was systematically destroyed to build a school and a home for the elderly. There is a poignant irony there. Two projects to serve the people at either end of their lives. The juxtaposition of the two institutions became a constant reminder to some of what was to come, and to others of what once had been. And between the two, a few yards of stone. So deep a chasm, so short a journey.

Only the cloister was left, and that became almost invisible as it crouched shamefully between childish laughter and old men's dreams.

In 1997, the current owners of the convent, knowing how keen Gil was to see his ideas become reality, demanded 40 million pesetas (more than £165,000) for it from the *ayuntamiento.* They considered the price outrageously high and not at all in the finest charitable traditions of the convent's founders. They promptly refused to pay, saying instead that they would take out a compulsory purchase order and set what they considered to be a fair price. Though Jesús Gil is, and will no doubt remain, a controversial figure in Marbella, gratitude will certainly be due to him if his plan bears fruit. 'Let no one be in any doubt', he has said, 'that the Holy Trinity Convent will be restored by the Town Hall, giving due respect to its history.'

A Walk Through the Town

Before Gil began his crusade of restoration, it was difficult not to agree with Temboury, but at the same time a walk through what remained and remains of the old town of Marbella is rewarding, if only to experience the relative tranquillity which exists only a few yards from the brash, bustling contemporary streets. The church is particularly fine, with an ornate, impressive altar, yet even here the realities of the new Costa del Sol impinge. A sign at the door offers confessions not only in Spanish but also in English, French, Portuguese, Italian and German. By the time that this book appears, there can be little doubt that Russian will have been added.

Behind the church, on 'calle Hospital Bazán', you will find the 'Museo del Grabado Español Contemporáneo' (Museum of Contemporary Spanish Engraving). The museum is housed in the old Hospital Bazán itself – a 16th-century building restored by the Junta de Andalucia for its present purpose. Those without a taste for the modernistic engravings of avant-garde artists such as Rafaci Cahogar may find the actual building of greater interest than the exhibits on its walls, but there is also a good reference library, where students may research in undisturbed silence. Entrance to the museum currently costs 300 pesetas.

There are plans to expand this museum to incorporate an adjacent historic building, which will also be restored. This will be used for offices and functional rooms, leaving extra space in the old hospital building for the ever growing number of exhibits. Compulsive engraving continues even as the city sleeps.

Until the present century, the social centre of Marbella was undoubtedly the Plaza de Los Naranjos. It is still a popular place for people to meet, eat, drink and talk in the sunshine. But towards the end of the 1930s, the focus began to shift more and more to Alameda Park, the great green splash in the southern part of town.

It had been in existence by then for at least a couple of centuries and had once covered a far greater area. Back in the 18th century it had covered 20,000 square metres and stretched from the town walls in the north to the southern seafront, and from Avenida Puerta del Mar in the east to Avenida Miguel Cano in the west. There were no high-rise apartment blocks and hotels then to spoil the superb view of the sea and the mountains. Consider that at that time the entire town covered only 90,000 square metres, and you will begin to see the relative size and importance of the park.

It is curious that the park should achieve its greatest popularity as a social gathering place during a period of comparative decline. Towards the end of the 19th century, the English-owned Marbella Iron Ore Company, which was operating the local mines and was responsible for the construction of the iron quay, wanted land on which to deposit the mineral ore. Its eye fell on the part of the Alameda corresponding to today's Avenida del Mar. The town found itself in a classic no-win situation, which was cynically exploited by the company. Surrender the land, they said, or lose two hundred jobs at the mine. In those poorer days before the tourists, it was a blow the town would not have been able to survive, and the park was sacrificed. It was not until 1942, long after the Marbella Iron Ore Company had rusted its way into history, that the land was reclaimed and reconstituted as the Avenida del Mar.

The park today cannot be compared in size or grandeur to its glory days of the 1700s, but it serves nevertheless as the social and festive centre of

Marbella, and visitors who wish to feel the pulse of the town will inevitably be drawn to it.

Marbella – West

Hotel Puente Romano

Head out of town along the N–340 road, and situated in the plush and very up-market Marina Puente Romana development you will find the appropriately named and very elegant Hotel Puente Romana. The name is no mere idle whim, for tucked away behind the hotel is a well-preserved Roman bridge which has been incorporated into the complex. Though technically on private land, access can be gained via the back entrance of the hotel restaurant or from the gardens of the hotel apartments without the necessity of booking yourself a room. Simply stroll in nonchalantly, and try not to look like a scavenging tramp.

The deep natural gully has been adapted into an artificial waterway for the gardens and is well stocked with fish, and even swans, which makes wandering around a delightful experience, though care should be taken to observe and abide by the many 'Private – Keep out' signs. The bridge itself is still used by the hotel guests for its original purpose. The masoned sandstone and brick structure would have carried the Roman coast road, the Augustus Way, over the stream, but all visible traces of the ancient causeway have now disappeared. Nevertheless, in its time it was of considerable importance, leading from Cádiz all the way to Rome. But then, of course, all roads did.

The bridge as we see it today has, admittedly, been renovated from time to time over the centuries, but the basic frame remains and is certainly Roman in origin.

Rio Verde Roman Villa

Continuing along the N–340, a little before you reach the new by-pass and the road bridge over the rio Verde, you will see the remains of a Roman villa on the beach side of the road. Its presence is indicated by a small sign which will direct you down a side road that is hardly better than a track, but the short journey is well worth making.

This country residence would have been owned by a wealthy out-of-towner, a prominent citizen of the Roman town of Silniana (see San Pedro). Today its remains are to be found just beyond the modern bridge of the rio Verde as you travel away from San Pedro, and are set within a beach-side urbanisation. They are protected, like the ruins of Las Bóvedas and the church of Vega del Mar, by a fence and a locked gate. It was once possible to obtain access to all three sites merely by asking for the keys at the San Pedro tourist office, but this is currently no longer the case. Whether the practice was stopped because visitors abused the privilege is not clear. For many years the office was housed within the San Pedro arch, which marks the entry to the town, but in late 1997 it was moved to new premises at 71 Avenida Marqués del Duero, the town's main street. The office is open from 9am until 8pm, and tours of the premier archæological sites can be arranged. At the time of writing, there is no tour on Mondays or at weekends. On Tuesdays and Thursdays the tour is scheduled for twelve noon, while on Wednesdays and Fridays it takes place at seven in the evening. However, the situation is constantly changing, and readers are advised to check the current arrangements. It can also do no harm to ask for the keys. It is not necessary to book these tours, but should you wish to do so or require further information, telephone the office on 952 781360. However, it should be noted that the sites are fairly open, and even from beyond their fences they can be viewed quite well. Each is equipped with easily read explanatory signs, though these are only in Spanish.

In the remains of the peristyle courtyard of the Rio Verde villa, built around AD 100, is an astonishing mosaic, unique in Hispania. The courtyard is in the centre of the building and is surrounded on three sides by a terrace measuring 16m x 7m. Its borders are decorated with a spectacular and well-preserved black and white geometric strip 16m long by 0.6m wide. The mosaics upon it depict an extraordinary variety of household objects, kitchen implements and food in black and white *tesserae.* Among the illustrated items are a pair of boots, a kitchen table covered with ribs of pork, a rabbit, a headless chicken, a fish, clams, a meat knife, an array of drinking cups, fish sauce amphorae and a portable stove. As Koppel states (1985, pp 63–66), 'Dinner guests passing from the peristyle to the two Triclinia would thus have a foretaste of the culinary delights to come.'

The courtyard itself would once have been surrounded by slender marble columns, but these have long since been carried away to adorn some more modern villa and only their supports remain.

The terraces lead to more rooms decorated with mosaics, one of which depicts the head of a mythical man, indicating that the room in which it appears may have been the villa's shrine to a Roman god. In giving this opinion, the authors differ from the conventional view that the head is that of Medusa, queen of the Gorgons. The Romans adopted Medusa and the Gorgons, and much else, from earlier Greek myth. It is said that they associated her with good luck. Since a mere glimpse of her was enough to turn a man to stone, the idea seems bizarre. One trembles at the thought of what the Romans considered a stroke of ill fortune.

Alternatively, she represented protection. That, at least, makes sense. A picture of Medusa on the wall to tell all and sundry that the house was firmly under her guardianship. Let would-be burglars shiver in their sandals while their muscles could still twitch. The Greeks certainly used pictures of Medusa as warning signs to keep the ill-intentioned and impudently inquisitive at bay, but to perform that function, the images had to be clearly visible to those they wished to deter. Medusa could not perform her trick simply by having her name invoked, in the way that a saint or benevolent god might sprinkle his miraculous blessings into a home if he was asked nicely enough. To turn people to stone, both she and the victim had to be physically present. That, it is true, made her the perfect watchdog, but since gazing upon her humanly carved or painted image did not have the same dramatic effect, and even the people of 2000 years ago knew that, its function as a protective emblem on buildings had to be merely a symbolic one. It was there to warn would-be burglars that the building was protected and that should they be foolish enough to enter, it would be the worse for them. The Roman equivalent of the conspicuous burglar alarms, some of which actually work, which we see today clinging to the walls of the new villas which stand where the old once did. Yet this mosaic was not set in a prominent position on the villa's outer wall, but on the floor of one of its inner rooms, where its deterrent effect on potential intruders was nil. Finally, Medusa turned men to stone because she was petrifyingly ugly. Glaring eyes, huge protruding teeth, a snake's tongue and most of all a nest of serpents on her head instead of hair. The serpents it was who did the actual damage. If the mosaic on the floor of the Rio Verde villa truly is meant to represent Medusa, then the artist can be counted among the worst in history. The terrifying image described above has been rendered in a way which would not frighten a nervous granny alone in the city at midnight. It is a face entirely without menace – almost that of a benevolent uncle about to tell one of his favourite stories. We say 'uncle' deliberately, because anyone seeing the mosaic for the first time would have to make a great effort of will to see the face as that of a woman – even a woman as ugly as Medusa. The mosaic also incorporates pictures of ducks, birds and cups, none of which have any apparent relevance to the Medusa story.

To the villa's northern end there is a bath room with its own plunge pool. Many of the rooms are small, but only further excavations will reveal the true wealth and size of the house.

Numerous objects have been recovered from the site and are on exhibition in the Archæology Museum in Málaga. Among the most interesting finds is a fragment of a small white marble statue, which would have once been a feature of the villa's shrine. Three marble skirting-board panels have been restored and can also be seen hanging in the museum. Other items include a perfectly preserved earthen wine jug and an ornate cup.

Evidence that the villa may have been either partially or totally destroyed by fire comes from a block of a dozen coins from the time of the Emperors Nero, Vespasian and Adrian (AD 54–138), which was found among the ruins. These were fused firmly together due to the oxidisation of the copper from which they were struck.

Though no part of the remaining structure stands more than four feet high, the villa's outline can be clearly followed and the mosaics alone make a trip to this site worthwhile.

San Pedro Alcántara

Inextricably linked to Marbella, but rapidly gaining its own identity since it was granted a large degree of autonomy in 1984, is the neighbouring town of San Pedro Alcántara. In its modern form it owes its existence to General Manuel Gutiérrez de la Concha, the first Marquis del Duero, who created a farming colony on the spot in the early 1860s, naming it in honour both of his favourite saint and his mother, Petra de Alcántara Irigoyen. The project attracted tenant farmers from all over Spain and the Marquis' enlightened approach, involving professional training and the importation of state-of-the-art techniques and machinery from abroad, notably America and the United Kingdom, should have assured the colony of success. Gutiérrez had a Utopian vision which encompassed the building of an observatory, a library, mills, factories, a fish farm, in fact an entire new town. He embarked on the project with massive promises of state aid, both practical and financial, but, as is so often the case, the deeds fell far short of the encouraging words. He was left to support his farm out of his own pocket and by 1865 he was a ruined and bitter man.

But General Gutiérrez was not the first person to see the potential of this spot on the fertile plain. Close to the Guadalmina Hotel are the remains of the earlier Roman town of Silniana. Until the end of the last century the only access to this part of the coast was via the old Roman road, but today San Pedro can be reached by taking the N–340, the new dual-carriage highway, which follows roughly the same course. The stretch of coast between Marbella and Estepona was celebrated in Greek and Roman times for the excellence of its fish, particularly tuna. The tunny industry declined with the coming of the Visigoths and the Moors, but the name of one Moorish *atunero* has passed into legend due to his uncanny – some said magical – ability to predict exactly where the best fish and the biggest catches could be found. Abdul el Bekar, 'el Tun'ni', would sit by the sea on a clear night studying the reflection of the moonlight on the surface, and carefully noting the shifting of the rays and ripples. Next day, he would tell the fishermen where they would find the biggest shoals of fish. He may have been the equivalent of the amateur village weatherman whom the villagers swear by, and whose hopelessly wrong predictions are forgotten, while his good ones are multiplied by a thousand and spoken of in awed whispers. Whether his talent was real or illusory, it was unique, and the secret died with him.

After the failure of General Gutiérrez' great 19th-century dream, the town decayed once more and began its long, and largely unlamented, return to the dust. In the nineteen-forties one writer described it as 'a half-ruined hamlet'. It was to remain so for several years more until, like its illustrious neighbour, it began its tourist-fuelled renaissance.

Today, along with its new assertiveness, the town has found a certain pride in its short past. Fifty million pesetas was raised by public subscription to renovate the parish church, built in 1866 as part of General Gutierrez' already dying vision. To match the parishioners' generosity, the *ayuntamiento* chipped in to provide the building with a new floor. Very important, floors, especially in places where people might wish to kneel and pray. Although it is still well under 150 years old, this is the second time that the church has been radically renovated and transformed, and on this occasion special attention has been paid to restoring the main altar, which features a tableau of the town's eponymous patron saint, San Pedro Alcántara.

In spite of the wholesale reshaping of the land by General Gutiérrez, and the relentless tramp of today's tourists, there are still some fine echoes of the Roman past to be seen in the vicinity of the town.

Hot Bath House (*Termas*)

The spectacular remains of the *termas,* or hot bath house, can be found among the trees of a small eucalyptus wood beside the mediæval torre de las Bóvedas (Tower of the Domes) to the south of the hotel apartments. The area is pitted with trial excavations which expose various foundations of the old town. This is all that remains above ground of the Roman town of Silniana, which would have been built on the high ground near the present day tower. Some of the town may have been lost to the sea in the earthquake of AD 365, while other parts have succumbed to development and the wheel of progress.

The baths were completed in the early part of the 3rd century AD, and were built using sand and stones from the beach. These were mixed with lime to produce a compound known as *opus caementicium.* It reacted with air to form a material of intense hardness which has weathered the centuries extraordinarily well. The arches and door lintels were made of brick. Macarios Fariñas del Corral, writing in 1663, referred to the ruins by their present-day name, and also mentioned underground aqueducts more than a league in length which fed the baths in their heyday. If these once existed, they are now long gone. The surviving structure is the central octagonal bath room, which has a small plunge pool, also octagonal, sunk into the floor. This domed room was probably the *tepidarium,* or temperate room, and would have been the focal point of the complex. Four sides of the chamber served as entrances, and each of the others contained an apse housing a statue. Beneath the domed roof with its skylight is an interior gallery giving access to a number of cubicles. The exact purpose of these is not clear. Above this upper part was a terrace. A visit to the baths was not merely a chance to wash away the dust of the day and scrub well behind the ears. It was a social occasion. A chance to meet friends, to linger and to talk.

Four exits led from the central chamber to seven smaller octagonal rooms, all of which were inter-communicating with the exception of two, whose access was directly from the central complex. How many business dealings, we wonder, were settled in these rooms by the shake of a damp hand? How many plans hatched? How many hatchets buried?

The chamber nearest to the sea contained a second plunge pool, and this was probably the *caldarium*, or hot house. Further excavation will, however, be necessary to establish the true depth and dimensions of the pool. The other minor chambers contained the *frigidarium* (cold plunge pool) as well as massage and dressing rooms, but most of the vaulted ceilings have collapsed, thus denying archæologists an easy identification of the true nature of each one.

Only an estimated 50% of the site has been excavated, but already a vast network of heating vents and water tunnels has been exposed. The probable location of the boiler house can be found to the east of the complex, though this interpretation is open to challenge due to the lack of conclusive masonry evidence. At least one Spanish historian has suggested that the site was merely a spa at the end of an aqueduct, while others consider the building to have been a reservoir, but these views are not widely shared, and all the available evidence points strongly to the conventional theory that this was indeed a public bath house.

During the 1960s a villa and a spa were incorporated into the structure, but thankfully, archæologists are slowly removing the blue paint, modern decor and electrical wiring from the ancient building.

Until 1990, a eucalyptus forest could be seen to the north of the site, and foundations which may well have been part of the vanished Roman town could be followed. However, a modern complex of town houses now covers them, and details of what, if anything, was discovered or destroyed during the construction do not appear to have been published. Once again we are left in the realm of the wistful guess and playful speculation.

In the 1990s, the architect Tristán Martínez carried out emergency repair work to prevent further deterioration, and the site is today fenced off so that visitors can view the remains safely without trespassing on the semi-excavated areas.

Byzantine Early Christian Church of Vega del Mar

Cross the Arroyo de Chop, 400 metres north of the Roman bath house, and in the modern urbanisation of Linda Vista to the south of El Ingenio you will find the ruins of this early church. Like the ruins of the bath house, they are located in a small wood and, though not particularly spectacular or visually stimulating, they nevertheless represent an important Byzantine and Christian site.

The Byzantines, the people of the Eastern Roman Empire, attempted, under their emperor Justinian (AD 527–565), to re-establish Roman rule over many of the lands which formerly belonged to the Western Roman Empire and which had fallen to new Germanic masters. They were not entirely without success. Although they would never have an empire on the scale or with the grandeur of the good old days, they scored a few hits and enjoyed a few years of hope. Thus, in AD 552, Southern Carthaginensis and Baeticia were annexed to form the Byzantine province of Spain. This illusory new dawn lasted a lifetime in human terms – the blink of an eye in historical ones. The Visigoths ended the sixty-nine-year occupation when they succeeded in reconquering all the old Roman territories by AD 621. During the Byzantine tenure of the Peninsula, in the year 572, Bishop Andrea of Iria Flavia established a church just outside the boundaries of Silniana, and it is the ruins of this and its associated buildings which we see today.

Though Roman, Silniana must have already been in decline, if not close to complete abandonment, although some residual habitation must have been in existence to justify the building of the church close to the town boundary. Perhaps the hope was that a new church would bring new life and new people to the place. This was certainly a new building. There is, for once, no evidence that the church was built on the site of an earlier construction or ruin. It was a fresh start for Silniana, but the decline of the town was too far gone to be halted.

The site was discovered accidentally in the early years of the 20th century when workers from the agricultural colony at San Pedro Alcántara set out to plant the eucalyptus trees which now surround it. Initially it was called 'The Moors' Cemetery' due to the tombs which were found. Permission to excavate the site was sought by the community's administrator, José Martínez-Oppelt, and this was granted in 1916. No official report of the subsequent diggings was ever published and all significant finds were despatched to Madrid, first to the community's headquarters and ultimately to the National Museum of Archæology, where they remain. Unfortunately, in the confusion which followed the initial discoveries by the eucalyptus tree planters, many items simply vanished, and perhaps lie gathering dust on their descendants' shelves to this day.

The walls of the church were exposed during more thorough excavations in 1930. This time they were led by a professional archæologist, José Pérez de Barradas, who also uncovered the burial ground described below. The church is unusual in having two apses, one at each end of the nave. The eastern apse, which faced towards the Holy Land, was the chancel and contained the altar. The western apse would also have housed some kind of altar or shrine but its purpose is unknown.

The church is rectangular, with a central nave and an aisle on either side. It also contained a sacristy and baptistry, with a cross-shaped font set into the ground. This was large enough for the total immersion of a mature adult, as was the custom in the early years of the Christian era. In fact, in Visigothic times, baptism was an impressively elaborate affair. Acceptance into the Christian church was seen quite literally as an escape from the clutches of the Devil, and so the baptism ceremony began with the candidate undergoing an exorcism to drive the demons out. This occurred immediately after the entrance into the baptistry from the eastern atrium and was followed by prayers rejecting Satan while all present faced westward. When these prayers were completed, they turned to the east and made professions of faith while being anointed with oil, after which they entered the font one at a time, walking solemnly down the steps cut into the sides, and were immersed three times in the holy water as the Christian Trinity was invoked. Finally, as the Devil fled shame-faced, outnumbered and defeated, another anointing took place with *chrism* – a mixture of olive oil and balsam – and the newly liberated and saved Christian would dress in a white tunic to take communion.

The church is surrounded by a cemetery including some two hundred tombs of various sizes made from bricks or tile slabs set into the ground. Excavations have recovered a number of skeletons with their personal possessions, such as clay vases, earrings, coins and fragments of buckles. Several engraved tombstones have also been found, one of which is dedicated to a girl called Firmiana. There is also a marble slab bearing a carving of an eagle and a rabbit. Many of the finds are now in the provincial museum in Málaga or the smaller display at the town hall in Marbella.

In the wake of the 1930 excavations attempts were made to preserve the site, but these were abandoned during the Civil War and apart from the font, little remains of the building today beyond the foundations and floors. In its heyday the roof would have been supported by wooden beams and covered in clay tiles.

Interestingly, the Spanish refer to the complex as a *basilica*, the Roman word for a town hall. The early Christians modelled their churches on the *basilica* and it is this form which we find throughout the Christian world today. Although strictly outside the scope of the present volume, it is worth noting that the oldest *basilica* yet discovered in Spain is to be found at Carranque in Toledo. Dating back to the close of the 4th century, and built as a final resting place for Maternio Cinegio, uncle of the last Spanish-born Roman emperor, Teodosio, the Carranque *basilica* is 80 metres long and includes the remains of a dozen domes, which would once have been 12 metres high. The fact that it was richly ornamented with expensive materials brought from the east proves that, although now virtually forgotten, Teodosio and his family were wealthy, powerful and important in their day. The site continues to give up its secrets to a team under the guidance of Dimas Fernández-Galiano, who besides being a noted and respected archæologist, is also the President of the Spanish Mosaic Association.

Guadalmina

On the southern outskirts of San Pedro, centred on the Guadalmina Valley, there is a modern urbanisation, which has taken the valley's name. Before the developers moved in and built the almost compulsory golf course during the 1960s, this was a large agricultural estate, which at its height earlier this century was a sugar cane plantation.

Just off the beach side entrance to the urbanisation, there is a small chapel. It is often described as ancient, and looks almost Byzantine in style. However, it is in fact scarcely more than 250 years old, and belonged to the estate until its recent donation to the Diocese of Málaga. It is not open for general viewing, but is still used as a functional place of worship, and is a particularly popular choice for weddings.

Marbella – East

To reach the sites described in this section, head east out of Marbella, drive past the Torre Real, and take the first turning at the new Marbella hospital.

Castillo de Calderón

There are two famous Calderóns in Spanish 17th-century history. The first, Rodrigo Calderón, conde de Oliva and marqués de Siete Iglesias was born not in Spain, but in Antwerp around 1576. During the reign of Philip III, he was shrewd enough to attach himself firmly to the king's favourite and chief minister, the duque de Lerma. It was, in modern parlance, a good career move, and he profited well from it. Unfortunately, Lerma had as many enemies as friends, and when he fell from power in October 1618, Calderón went with him. He was arrested, tortured, and thrown into prison after being implicated in the murder of one Francisco Xuara. He stayed there for two years and then, on the eve of his release, his luck was out again. Philip III died and was replaced by Philip IV. The new chief minister, Gaspar de Guzmán decided it was time to start afresh and make a complete break with the previous regime. Unfortunately for Calderón, this apparently could not be achieved without his execution. He died bravely. So bravely, in fact, that his demeanour on the day (October 21st, 1621 in Madrid) gave the Spanish language a new expression: *Tener más orgullo que don Rodrigo en la horca* ('To be haughtier than Don Rodrigo on the scaffold').

Almost his contemporary, although he outlived him by sixty years by picking better friends, was the less flamboyantly named Pedro Calderón de la Barca. Born in Madrid in 1600, this Calderón went on to become one of Spain's greatest poets and playwrights.

There is no evidence that either of these celebrated Calderóns had any connection with the castle which once stood in the hills above Marbella and which bore their name, but there is little doubt that it was standing in their lifetime. Today it is marked on larger maps as *ruinas castillas*, but in truth there is very little left for the modern visitor to see. It has been superseded on the same site by a modern villa, also called Castillo de Calderón. It is possible to see on the hillside, below the level of the villa, the remnants of an ancient wall and the stump of a tower. They are surrounded by a mesh fence, perhaps to prevent loose stones from rolling down on to the Marbella Golf Club which it overlooks. It is not possible to reach the wall, but those who wish to drive into the hills, which can be reached by turning off the coastal highway at the Marbella Hospital just beyond Torre Real, will be rewarded with beautiful views of the valley below and the coastline down to Gibraltar and the Straits.

Torre Ladrones and Torre de las Canas

Torre Ladrones, standing beside the modern Puerto Cabopino, is undoubtedly one of the most unusual of the ruined towers to be found along this stretch

Manilva

The Roman sulphur baths af Hedionda.

Castillo de la Duquesa – impressive Roman site.

Cerro del Castillo – the fort is now almost lost to the undergrowth.

Opposite: The Alcazar, Marbel

Marbella and San Pedro

Old Marbella.

The world's least terrifying Medusa? Rio Verde Villa, Marbella.

The mosiac floors of the Rio Verde villa, Marbella.

The Hot Bath House (*Termas*)

The early Byzantine church of Vega del Mar, Marbella.

Not the Caribbean, a Marbella beach scene.

Moorish sunset – the mosque at Marbella.

ijas. Note the square bull ring.

cently restored Moorish fortress, Mijas.

Torre de la Cala (Mijas-Costa).

Ermita Del Calvario (Mijas).

Old mill complex and aqueduct (Mijas-Costa).

of the coast. Its solid square base is clearly Moorish and built of grey stone, but above this is what must surely be a later Christian addition of red brick. The immediate impression is of pieces discarded from some monstrous Lego kit and put together by the bored child of a giant. The stone base has weathered the centuries well, but the brick portion is cracked and crumbling. Can we doubt that even five hundred years ago some venerable critic stared at the newly completed hybrid and mumbled, 'They just don't make towers like they used to'?

The tower stands at Punta Ladrones on the Playa de Cabopino at the very edge of Marbella. *Ladrón*, it should be noted, is the Spanish word for a thief. We have seen that in former times the whole of the population of Marbella was tarred with this brush, but whether the name was bestowed by outsiders as a warning to travellers, or whether the inhabitants of this particular spot were notorious even by Marbellan standards, we shall never know.

This stretch of shoreline is notable for the number of pine trees which border it. It may well be that Punta Ladrones was once the site of an oceanside Moorish village, perhaps compulsorily evacuated after the Christian reconquest, when Moors were forbidden to live close to the sea. At the same time Moorish monuments such as the tower would have been destroyed and replaced, perhaps with careless haste, by Christian constructions. This could explain the noticeable difference in quality between the brick half of the tower and its stone base.

In the shadow of a tower stands a deserted and indescribably filthy hut, probably once used by the Guardia Civil, and now abused by unfastidious travellers and tramps. We have noted elsewhere that Guardia Civil barracks are often found close to the old watchtowers, since a good lookout spot is always useful, but it is a pity that, once redundant, they are not removed. Left to stand, they inevitably inspire the worst elements of the human spirit and rapidly decline into festering and foul-smelling rubbish heaps. Of course, a wholesale change in human nature would be preferable, but at the time of going to press that seems unlikely.

A kilometre and a half back towards Marbella is the Torre de las Canas. *Cana* can mean grey hair, and anyone searching for clues in ancient names in a foreign tongue will rapidly develop it. An alternative meaning is prison, or prison cell, so it may be that the tower once had a more sombre use than simply watching for pirates. (There is an obvious connection here with the English slang term for being in prison – 'in the can'.) In age and design it corresponds to the tower at Cala del Moral (see Mijas), but though it is still standing, it is in a very poor state of repair.

Chapter Seventeen

Mijas

Historical Background

MIJAS HAS COME A LONG WAY. If Marbella is truly the wealthiest community in Spain, then Mijas cannot be far behind. It is a now familiar story. For the greater part of the present century Mijas was a poor, virtually destitute, agricultural community clinging to life like an asthmatic old man who, against all the odds and in the face of medical logic, somehow continues to draw his daily breath. Built on the small outcrop which is now the site of the present day church, the tiny village was approachable only by a single road – no more than a ramp – which, to use modern-day reference points, led from the Plaza de la Constitución to the bull ring. It hardly existed at all. Then came the tourists. They liked what they saw and some of them, generally the wealthier ones, decided to stay. The floodgates were open, and there was no shutting them. Today almost 90% of the property in Mijas is foreign-owned and more than sixty nationalities are represented among its present population of around 75,000, although only a small percentage live in the old village. The rest are spread across a municipal district covering 148 square kilometres, which includes Las Lagunas (The Lagoons), an area of workers' homes close to Fuengirola, and the beach at La Cala (The Cove). Urbanisations have sprouted like mushrooms after the rain and at the last count they numbered almost 180. Spaniards are outnumbered by at least two to one, and if the expatriates have their way, Mijas will sooner rather than later become the first Spanish town to elect a foreign mayor. It is a miracle, therefore, that in spite of it all, Mijas has somehow managed to remain picturesque, while becoming a virtual caricature of the kind of 'Spanish village' which most tourists wandering the mountains want and expect to see.

It is situated on the steep slopes of the Sierra de Mijas, behind and above Fuengirola, 1300 feet above sea level. To reach it, simply follow the signs on the N–340 Fuengirola by-pass. These will direct you to a winding road which, after a journey of around 8 kilometres, will deposit you on Mijas' doorstep. The town is a honey-pot for tourists, so parking can sometimes be a problem. Your best chance will probably be in front of the town hall in the main square.

The North European culture of the predominant expatriates is very evident

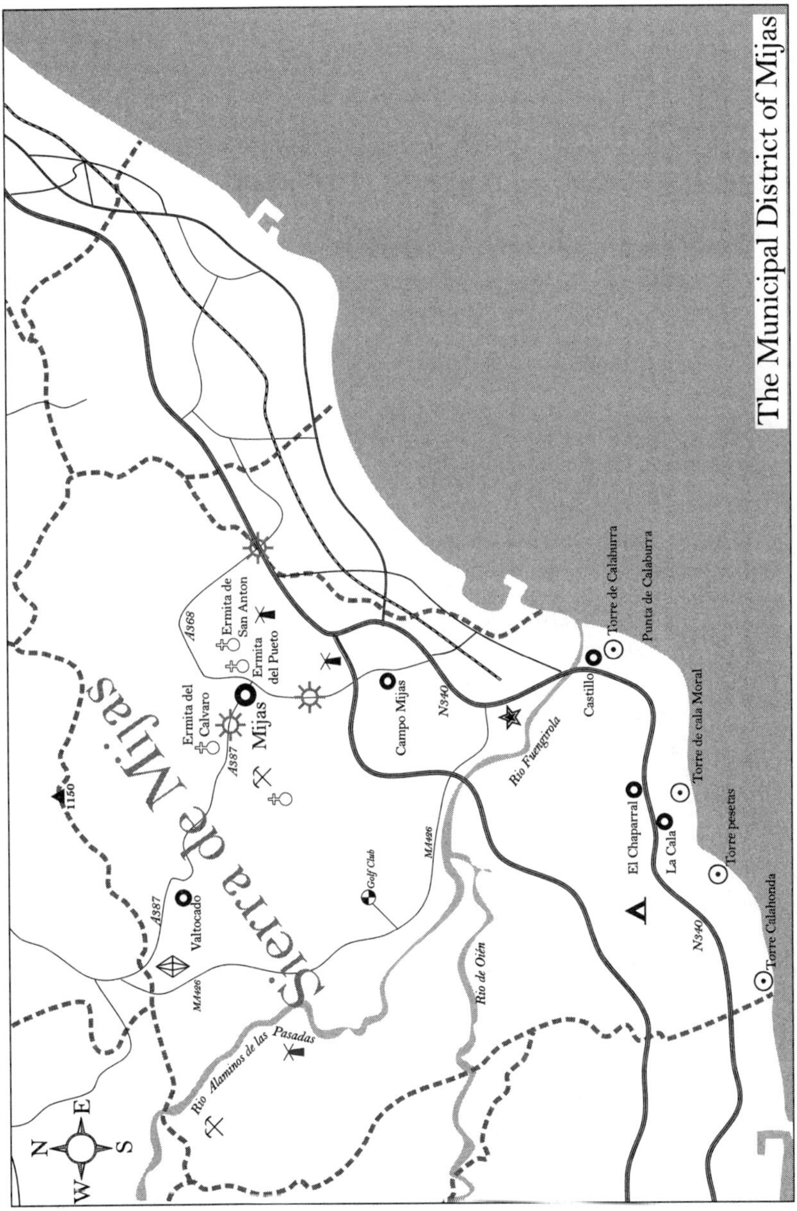
The Municipal District of Mijas
Sierra de Mijas
Mijas
Ermita del Calvaro
Ermita del Pueto
Ermita de San Anton
A368
A387
1150
Valtocado
A387
MA426
Golf Club
MA426
Campo Mijas
N340
Rio Fuengirola
Castillo
Torre de Calaburra
Punta de Calaburra
Torre de cala Moral
El Chaparral
La Cala
Torre pesetas
Torre Calahonda
N340
Rio de Ojén
Rio Alaminos de las Pasadas
N
E
S
W

in Mijas. Souvenir shops ring the main square like lounging lions waiting for their prey to stroll up and beg to be eaten. Yet oddly, despite its intensive commercialism, Mijas is still a pleasant place to visit, being famous not only for its wonderful views of the coastline and its lingering Arabic traces, but also for its *burros*, or donkey taxis. These are unlikely to feature in a future action movie chase. It is difficult to imagine the hero leaping aboard one and screaming to its handler, 'Follow that burro!' It is even more difficult to imagine the donkey co-operating. How long they can continue at all in the brave new world of animal liberation and political correctness remains to be seen, but for the time being such considerations have passed the town by and those who fancy a gentle jog around the streets on a sleepy donkey have only to pay the price.

Mijas has been wealthy before. The Romans called it Tarnisa, and used it as a base to exploit the large deposits of iron ore in the Sierra de Mijas to the south of the *pueblo*, and the marble they quarried in the heart of the mountain range.

It fell to the Moors very quickly, as any town which uses donkeys as taxis was always likely to do. By the year 714 it was in the hands of Abdalaziz, son of Muza, who made a pact with the local population. They probably shrugged their shoulders behind the upstart Arab's back and returned to tilling their land. In the 9th century the Christian convert, Omar ben Hafsun, rebelled against the Caliphs of Córdoba and established his own kingdom with Mijas as one of his strongholds, although his chief base was at Bobastro, near Antequera. During the rebellion, Mijas was held at various times by both sides. One can imagine the inhabitants getting thoroughly fed up with the whole business. After Omar's death in AD 917, Mijas regained its stability, rejoining the Islamic fold and remaining in unconverted Moorish hands until the fall of Málaga in 1487, when, predictably, the Arabs were disinherited and evicted. Their lands and possessions were given instead to nine Christian families. It was the nearest that mediæval Spain came to the concept of the National Lottery. The local mosque suffered the usual fate and was destroyed to make way for the church which now occupies the site. There is a tiny touch of defiance in the fact that the final scrap of the old Moorish defensive wall still stands close to the church, like a cheeky urchin sticking out his tongue at the town's new masters, and ready to run.

A surprising number of religious hermitages were established in the area. The Ermita de Nuestra Señora de la Pena, which is built on the foundations of the Moorish defences, can be found at the end of Alarcon Square, while the Ermita del Puerto is outside the village and offers superb views. The Virgen de la Pena is the town's patron saint, and there is a wooden statue of her at her shrine which is said to date back to the year AD 850. Each year during Holy Week there is a pilgrimage to the shrine of the Ermita del Calvario, built on a hilltop above the village by Carmelite monks in 1710. Exactly why so many hermitages were established in so small a community is open to question, and it may be that the village proved particularly difficult to convert to Christianity after the fall of the Moors. On the other hand, the existence of a statue of the Virgin carved at the height of Moorish regional power might argue the reverse. Maybe, like many mountain people used to fighting the elements, the people of Mijas were just plain stubborn or, given its frequent change of masters during Omar ben Hafsun's rebellion, merely confused.

In the 17th and 18th centuries, it was very much a working village – the equivalent, perhaps, of a mining village in the Welsh valleys. The hills around Mijas contained many quarries producing agate and marble, and many of the workers made their homes there. The stone they produced was used in building projects throughout Andalucía, including the construction of the never-to-be-completed Málaga Cathedral, and the Alcazaba in Seville.

Another minor point of interest is the town's bullring, which is unique in being square, albeit with rounded corners. Whether this confuses the bulls more than the matadors or vice versa has no doubt been the source of much debate in the town's bars since it was built in 1900, but like the question of life on Mars, it remains unresolved.

Away from the cluster of souvenir shops in the main square, you will soon find yourself walking steep, narrow streets typical of a Moorish settlement. The centre of village life is the Plaza de la Constitución.

Undoubtedly the oddest recent story from Mijas became the basis of the book *In Hiding*, written by the English author Ronald Fraser, who lived in the town. It concerns Manuel Cortés Quero, a left-wing Republican who became the town's Mayor shortly before the outbreak of the Civil War. In 1937, as the nationalists advanced, Cortés made his escape, and the war's end in 1939 found him fighting in Valencia. He returned to Mijas shortly afterwards with the intention of surrendering to the authorities. This, however, would have meant a certain prison term and quite possibly execution. And so, embracing the principle that discretion is the better part of valour, he decided instead to lie low for a while. A few months should do the trick. As things turned out, he stayed hidden in his house for more than thirty years, his existence known only to his faithful wife, Juliana Moreno López. The secret was kept even from their daughter, Maria, who had been eighteen months old at the time of her father's 'disappearance'. She learned the truth only on the eve of her wedding, which Cortés secretly attended. Maria had two daughters of her own from whom the secret had to be kept in case they spoke indiscreetly to their friends. They were told that their grandfather was absent-minded (*ausente*) and couldn't remember his name. This was eventually to give him one of the two nicknames by which he became known: *el abuelo ausente de Mijas* – the absent-minded grandfather of Mijas. He was also more puzzlingly known as *el topo*, a word generally applied to someone clumsy and half-blind, like the cartoon character Mr Magoo.

Cortés finally decided to come out of hiding in 1969. Accompanied by his wife and the current Mayor of Mijas, Miguel González Berral, he gave himself up to the Guardia Civil in Málaga. He was by then 74 years old. Times had changed. Franco was still firmly in power, but the Spanish tourist boom was well underway, and there was little to be gained by imprisoning, still less shooting, a man who had in any case imprisoned himself for thirty years. He was granted a pardon, and lived on into his nineties. He died on 16th March 1991. His wife Juliana, who had supported them through his lost years by working at home and by walking to Málaga to sell eggs, had died in 1985. In 1939, Cortés had turned his back on an isolated, poverty-stricken community clinging like withered moss to the mountainside and he emerged into the blinding sunlight of a virtual suburb of Fuengirola ringing to the jingle of its new prosperity. He must have stared at the exhibits in the brash new tourist-orientated museum and wondered whether the years away had made him one of them. But bizarre as his story is, it is not unique. After Franco's death in 1975, many similar tales emerged throughout Spain.

The Pueblo

First time visitors to the pueblo of Mijas could do worse than to head for the centre and make their first port of call the museum. It is less than perfect, but it does give some insight into the fascinating background of this once rural outpost.

A reminder of its mining past survives in the old iron ore mine track which runs south-west from the village and once led workers to the many mines in the vicinity. Two kilometres along this route, close to an old mill, a cross marks a junction which takes the traveller finally into the vast Mijas hinterland. Nearby is 'Cortijo de los Castellanos' – 'Farm of the Castilians'. How long it has borne this name it is difficult to say, but it does suggest a triumphant yell to heaven as the last Moor was driven away.

Museum and Art Gallery (Casa Cultural)

The combined municipal museum and art gallery in Mijas is a perplexing place. It is housed in what was formerly the town hall; a rabbit warren of a building directly opposite the late 18th century Iglesia de San Sebastián, close to the main square on a street otherwise unashamedly given over to commercialism. Entrance is free, and although there is much of interest to see, the visitor is likely to emerge ultimately unsatisfied by it all. A wander around its rooms, devoted alternately to rural history, mineral exhibits and exhibitions of mainly contemporary paintings, is a little like listening distractedly to the rambling monologue of a loquacious acquaintance who cannot quite make up his mind what to talk about.

The tour begins well enough, with a long room filled with farming tools and the essential accoutrements of rural Spanish life. We are guided through the exhibits by a series of framed excerpts from autobiographical writings describing life in the hills circa 1920. These, helpfully, are in both Spanish and English. They are clearly intended to be graphic and poignant, and it is perhaps unfortunate that they occasionally capture instead some of the 'when I were a lad' black humour of the celebrated 'Monty Python' sketch in which a group of Northern English working-class stereotypes vie with each other to produce ever more exaggerated and grotesque descriptions of the harshness of their childhoods. With the currency exchange rate currently (1998) hovering around 240 pesetas to the pound, it is worth noting that the average wage of a rural labourer in 1920 was 1.75 pesetas a day.

There is a model of a lime kiln, and much else of interest, but at the core of the exhibition something is wrong. It is difficult to *feel* the years in the way that it is, for instance, in the rural museum at Pizarra. There is a sterility here, almost as if the exhibits were newly made replicas with no real story to tell. The first room leads to a courtyard and a series of rooms intended to reproduce life on a typical early 20th-century farm or mill, but here again the sterility intrudes. The mill wheel is smooth and white and unmarked by a single day's labour, the living room is clean and tidy, the bed neatly made. We are looking not at the vibrant heart of Spanish working-class life, but at life-size 3-dimensional postcards, the big brothers of the kind that can be bought at any of a dozen shops outside on the street.

Another problem is that the moment we leave the first room, our loquacious acquaintance forgets how to speak English, reduces the volume of his voice by at least a dozen decibels, and proceeds to mumble at us quietly in Spanish. There are interesting notices on the walls telling of the town's history, and of the five mills of the vanished village of Osunilla (see below), but they are in dim corners, difficult to read and, to non-linguists, unintelligible.

Then, suddenly, he's off again, brightening up to show us a cabinet glistening with minerals gathered from the Mijas hills, each one bearing the name of the mine from which it comes: La Trinidad, Cerro Torrón, Jarapalos, Peñoncilla, Cruz de Juanar. These are headstrong hills, each one with a mine of its own. But though excited, our friend has still not regained his grasp of English. He tells us that the Sierra de Mijas was formed in the Triassic period approximately two hundred million years ago and that it consists chiefly of marble (*marmoles*), dolomite (*dolomitas*) and so on, but only in his native tongue. It may seem churlish to complain. We are, after all, in Spain, and we should not baulk at being asked to make an effort. But in a town so firmly in the grip of a dominant immigrant community, and a building ringing to the babble of tourists, we feel an unworthy passing irritation, especially after the false promise of its bilingual welcome.

Encouraged by this journey back to the prehistory of Mijas, we look around for relics of its chronicled past: the gulf between Triassic minerals and the human deprivations of 1920. Where are its Roman roots? Its Moorish heritage? The story of its Christian reconquest? On these matters our talkative friend is uncharacteristically silent. Instead he is asking us to look at his collection of paintings and sculptures, mostly contemporary, of varying quality, and with no identifying theme. Bewildered, we wander back to the street, feeling a little like an audience leaving a cinema after seeing a film whose plot escaped us somewhere between the first and final reels.

The museum is open every day. During the week you can visit it between 10:00 am and 2:00 pm, or 5:00 pm and 7:00 pm. On Saturdays and Sundays, the evening hours are from 4:00 pm until 8:00.

There is another museum of sorts in Mijas. In truth, it is closer to a fairground freak show: a collection of miniatures housed in a converted bus. You will see a shrunken head, clothed fleas, and scripts and paintings executed on grains of rice and the head of a pin. If you are fascinated by such things, it is easy to find and worth a brief visit, but the entrance fee, at 500 pesetas (300 for children), is a little high. Special rates are not available to midgets.

The Bullring, Auditorium and the Parish Church of the Immaculate Conception

Mijas may have acquired a cosmopolitan coating, but it is still at heart a mountain village, and you would expect spectacular views. These are abundant, and there are few better than those available from the gardens which surround the town's church and the adjacent bullring and auditorium.

The church, built in the *mudéjar* style, replaced the former 9th-century Arab mosque early in the 16th century. In 1510 a bell house was added, as much to warn of the danger of attack as to call the faithful to prayer. It is a pleasing building, though its interior is unusually dark. Two aisles border the nave, separated by pointed arches which bear not carvings but paintings of saints. The interior walls were heavily whitewashed in the course of the 18th century during an epidemic of the plague. Cleanliness is next to godliness and, it was hoped, good health. On one of the church's outer walls it is still possible to see the whitewashed outlines of an original 16th-century doorway which at some time, for reasons which are unclear, was bricked up.

Though the Christian edifice virtually obliterated its Moorish predecessor, a few traces of the ruined fortress remain, and there are Arab echoes in the surrounding gardens, which are rich in fig trees. There are also pines which are home to the curious 'processional' caterpillars which you may see crawling down the bark, or around the base as they descend from the trees to pupate. They move slowly, nose to tail, like a child's train on an invisible track. Treat them with caution. When touched, they produce a painful and unpleasant rash. The Israeli army, to give one example, is sensibly prohibited from camping beneath pine trees to avoid the possibility of these furry nuisances falling on to the soldiers' heads.

Sharing this self-contained and easily defensible hilltop with the church and the gardens, are a modern auditorium where concerts and theatrical events are held, and the unique square bullring with its own small museum and souvenir shop.

It is difficult to imagine, as one agonises over whether to purchase castanets, pencil cases or plastic models of the saint, that this plateau outcrop was once the site of a vast castle complex. Save for a few small and tantalising traces, it is gone like last year's olive crop. But at least some attempt is being made to preserve the little that is left. Walk back down the ramp and *calle Castillo*, and you will find an old arch-covered roadway. This is all that now remains of the former Moorish gateway into the town. Take a few seconds to stand and let your mind wander back to a time and a town that had not heard of souvenirs and postcards. And then turn away, for you are a visitor, a tourist. You are the thief that came not in the night but in the glorious blaze of day, to steal the very thing you wanted the village to keep. It is a paradox, as so much of life is a paradox, and it is too hot for paradoxes. Suddenly an English voice behind you breaks into your reverie. 'Oh, Ida – I could murder a cup of tea.'

Santuario de la Señora de la Pena

Nuestra Señora de la Pena (Our Lady of Sorrow) has been the official patron of Mijas since being declared so by the village council on September 8th 1682. Each year since then a festival in her honour has been held on that date. It is easily the most important fiesta in the town's calendar and is now spread over five days, from September 7th to 11th.

As you would expect in these legend-haunted hills, the revered image of the Virgin, which has sheltered for centuries in this natural rock sanctuary, has a colourful tale attached to it. They say she was carved over a thousand years ago, but when the Moors came she went into hiding and stayed hidden for eight centuries. A long time for mortal men, but the blinking of an eye to a saint. In 1586 she decided that the coast was clear and sent a vision of a white dove to lead two young shepherds, Juan and Asunción, to her. They followed the dove, and their father followed them and, sure enough, the hidden effigy was found. Similar stories of the miraculous discovery of such images abound in Spain. By obscuring their generally mundane origins at the hands of the village carpenter, they bring to the statues an awesome mystery which draws reverence from the faithful as blotting paper soaks up ink. The image *becomes* the Virgin, and assumes all her powers. Hence the chaotic attempts of the crowds to touch the images during their annual Holy Week parades through their adopted towns and villages.

What happened to the rediscovered Virgin for the next seventy years is not clear, but in 1656 a Carmelite monk, Diego de Jesús María y San Pablo (Diego believed in hedging his bets), began the creation of her shrine. It was apparently slow work, for the Virgin had to wait more than another fifty years, until 1710, before she could finally move in. In the meantime, as we have seen, the townspeople soothed her impatience by declaring her their patron saint.

La Virgen de la Peña has remained there ever since, except for a brief period during the Civil War. Like many another religious icon, the effigy was in great danger from anti-clerical loyalists, and the parish sacristan took it away and hid it at home. We can forgive the Virgin for heaving a weary sigh and thinking, 'here we go again'. But this time her concealment lasted only until the day of Franco's victory.

Diego de Jesús María y San Pablo created the shrine, but not the cave. The existence of the grotto now dedicated to the revered Virgin pre-dates her formal adoption as patron saint, and was cut into the mountain rock around 1520 on what are clearly Moorish defensive foundations. Above it there are the remains of a Moorish tower. Frustratingly, the path to the tower has been blocked and it is not possible to climb up to it. We say 'frustratingly', because a determined and agile person could easily scramble the few yards up the rock face to where it stands, but this is not an isolated and deserted spot in the mountains, and any such display of bravado and initiative would undoubtedly be frowned upon and quickly dealt with by the authorities.

The shrine is split into two rooms. The first contains the altar and the statue of the Virgin, while to the right is a second chamber in which gold-embossed robes are displayed in glass cases. The effect is of moving instantaneously from a place of worship into the side room of a museum. As in all such shrines, there is a section of wall on which the faithful hang mementos of loved ones, often children, so that they may receive the holy blessing. Those who have seen such shrines around Spain will know that more often than not, the mementos consist of photographs and written petitions to the Virgin. Oddly, these are prohibited here. Instead, locks of hair have been hung from the wall, and the resulting cluster of tresses, dangling from the rock like the scalps in a Red Indian's trophy cabinet, has a distant but distinct whiff of the gruesome.

It is impossible to escape fully from the clutches of banal commercialism in Mijas. Even the shrine to Our Lady of Sorrow shares its rock with a souvenir shop where you can buy such devout reminders of your visit as castanets, purses and pencil cases. Our Lady has much to be sorrowful about.

In front of the sanctuary are several ornamental water tanks containing dark, dank water. Quite unnecessarily, the public are warned that this is *agua no potable* – not for drinking. If it were, there is little doubt that it would be swiftly bottled and on sale in the shop.

Ermita del Calvario

The early 18th-century shrine which was bequeathed to Mijas by Carmelite monks can be clearly seen from the village. The Carmelites never believed in making things easy for themselves. The order was founded around the middle of the twelfth century when a group of rudderless pilgrims and ex-crusaders gathered on Mount Carmel in Palestine, close to what they believed to be the fountain of Elijah, the Old Testament prophet. These first Carmelites were dour hermits who took vows of poverty and spent their lives in work, begging and prayer. They met at appointed hours to pray, and then scattered to their individual cells to sit in silent contemplation. There is no authenticated case of a Carmelite monk laughing.

Like many of those drawn to the uncompromisingly religious life, they clearly believed that the harder and more austere they made their earthly existence, the closer they came spiritually to God. There is more than an echo of that philosophy in the very setting of their Mijas shrine. The route to it from the village is now bisected by the modern and very busy bypass, which provides the opportunity for cheats and the less agile to park at the *mirador* (look-out point) beside the Venta Sierra Mijas (where you can add to your growing collection of postcards and souvenirs) and begin the walk to the hermitage half way.

Beside the busy road you will see a short section of wall topped by a path leading upward at a sharp angle. A small cross, bearing the number 3, has been placed on top of a cairn of stones. Along the journey to the hermitage, which is made each year by the faithful during Holy Week, there are thirteen Stations of the Cross, but the first two are below the level of the bypass, on the road from the village. The stony, uneven path, twists and turns among the pine trees like a restless snake which has eaten a bad mongoose. In good weather, unburdened by heavy religious images, and in sensible footwear, the walk is not unduly strenuous, and might almost be described as pleasant. However, it must be remembered that during the Holy Week processions, many penitents will choose to follow the Cross barefoot or even shackled. In such circumstances the path, with its thousands of sharp stones and its tangled undergrowth, becomes a nightmare. Faith in the soul-cleansing power of physical suffering is still a powerful and mysterious emotion.

The shrine itself, as befits an austere brotherhood, is small and bare and unpretentious. There is an altar, a statue of the Virgin, a Crucifix or two, but no seating. There are, however, a few benches placed at strategic spots along the mountain path for those who need to rest on the journey. At least one of these has had its seat removed, either by vandals or Carmelite purists, leaving only the sharp metal legs to mock the weary. The spirit of the Carmelites lives on. If anyone is going to sit and rest here, by golly, they certainly aren't going to be allowed to enjoy it. The Carmelites may have felt the need for self-abasement and suffering, but they certainly appreciated a good view. The vista from the patch of ground in front of the shrine is broad and bright and breathtakingly beautiful.

Ermita del Puerto

Today, every spare patch of ground in Andalucía, particularly coastal Andalucía, is snatched up by someone who wants to build a restaurant or an hotel. There are places, and Mijas is certainly one, where the unavoidable impression is that in former times the same was true of people who wished to build churches and shrines. No matter how small the village, there was always room for another monument to a favoured saint, or an alternative place of worship. The Ermita del Puerto is a late-comer. It was built in the mid-19th century, and the fact that it bears no particular saint's name is a fair indication that by then all the good names had been taken. *Puerto,* as well as 'port', can also mean refuge, or shelter. The area around the hermitage is also known as *El Puerto,* and the shrine was strategically sited at the junction of the Benalmádena/Fuengirola/Mijas road, so that worshippers and refugees from all three places could find convenient sanctuary. The road which runs north from the hermitage leads to a weighbridge and on to a commercially operating marble quarry, which marks the mountainside like a bald patch on an otherwise abundantly hairy head.

Ermita San Antón and Abandoned Marble Quarry

The ubiquitous popularity of Saint Anthony – *San Antón* – in this small corner of Spain is something of a mystery. His name jumps out at every turn; not only from the numerous shrines and hermitages dedicated to him, but from street signs and even the chosen names of commercial businesses. Clearly his assistance is frequently called upon and his reputation for delivering the goods extremely high. Yet he has no particular connection with this region. He was born in Lisbon in 1195, and in 1220, after a spell as an Augustinian monk, he switched allegiance and became a Franciscan. He was a tireless evangelist and, according to legend, when people would not listen to him, he preached instead to fish. In this way many a sole was saved, and in time he became the patron saint of the lower animals. His ambition, they say, was to be martyred while preaching to the Saracens. It was an ambition he never achieved. Instead of being burnt at a Saracen stake, or squashed flat between two Saracen stones, he had to settle for dreaming of such glory as he taught theology in colleges in Italy and the south of France. He was on his way to Padua in June 1231 when he succumbed to a bout of dropsy and died. He is buried in the town. Since dropsy is frequently, though not exclusively, related to over-indulgence in alcohol, it is tempting to wonder whether, thwarted of his macabre ambition, the prospective saint sought solace in the overflowing cup. There is, after all, more than one way of getting stoned.

At some point in his relatively short life, Anthony (or Ferdinand, to give him his baptismal name) acquired the reputation of a miracle worker and whatever he did, it must have been good, since after his death it took less than a year for Pope Gregory IX to declare him a saint. He was canonized on May 30 1232. Both the town of Padua, and his home nation of Portugal claimed him as their Patron.

It is, as saints' lives go, an unremarkable tale. No banishing of snakes, no great crusades, no spectacular, yearned-for martyrdom, and finally an undistinguished death from dropsy. Yet his example, the stories of his miracles, and above all a reputation for absolute goodness quickly spread beyond the walls of the colleges where he taught, and they took a strong hold in Andalucía, and indeed throughout the Catholic world. His body lies today in a stone tomb behind the altar of the great Basilica of Padua, and countless pilgrims still shuffle by it each year and rest their hands briefly upon it as though saying goodbye to a recently departed relative. It is this peculiarly close bond of comfort between the long-dead teacher and millions who never knew him which makes his name so potent even now.

This particular shrine erected in his name stands on a stark hilltop a little way outside Mijas, two kilometres along the Benalmádena road, on the site of the vanished village of Osunilla (not to be confused with the old town of Osuna, which still survives in the province of Seville). To say that it is a curious place is to risk losing its oddity in understatement. At first sight it appears ordinary enough. Just another well-kept hillside hermitage set aside for St Anthony to work his miracles. But almost immediately there is a sense of something incongruous. The gardens in front of the little church are dotted with small statues which, though of a religious character, seem somehow out of place. Each of them has a hand-written notice in front of it containing either a quote from the scriptures or, as in the case of the statue of the *Virgen Niña de Jerusalen* (the Virgin Maiden of Jerusalem), a plea for her to pray for us.

Walk around the hermitage to the right, and the oddity is suddenly compounded. In spite of the statuary and the notices, the undergrowth is surprisingly rough and untidy. There, bizarrely, is a carved stone kennel bearing the picture of a dog and two paeans in honour of Man's most trusted four-legged friend: *A la fidelidad del perro* and *La oracion del perro.* It is not immediately apparent whether this is the tomb of a particular dog, or a monument erected to the glory of dogs in general, but a cluster of similar though smaller statues strongly suggest the presence of a pet cemetery.

A little beyond the stone kennel is a half-scale reproduction of Michelangelo's David, and finally a large wooden cross erected at the high point of the hill, overlooking the valley. Walking among the numerous incongruous statues it is difficult to dismiss the impression that you have stumbled into a miniature religious theme park which never quite succeeded. The impression is greatly magnified when you turn left instead of right in front of the shrine and walk around to the back of the building, passing more 'pet cemetery' statues and memorials on the way. Suddenly, astoundingly, the unsuspecting visitor is confronted by a large, deep cave containing so many crosses and statues of the Blessed Virgin that it might almost be a sculptor's studio or a mason's warehouse. This, common sense tells us, must surely be a place of great religious significance and pilgrimage. And so it may be, but a handwritten sign at the mouth of the grotto tells the story of St Bernadette and her vision at Lourdes in February 1858. Instantly it becomes a tableau celebrating an event far away and long ago in another country. Is this cave genuinely holy in its own right, or are its statues the equivalent of the nativity scenes erected in supermarkets and high streets across the world at Christmas?

The front wall of the shrine bears a plaque telling something of its history and the history of the area. When the troops of King Ferdinand swept through the hills in 1483, knocking over Moorish villages like so many skittles in a bowling alley, there were three settlements here. Besides Mijas, there were the villages of Osunilla and Oznar. The latter two did not survive, though the name of Osunilla does live on to some extent. Saint Anthony's hermitage was erected in the 18th century, allegedly at the request of a group of sailors saved from a violent storm on the stretch of coast below the hills. Why this miraculous rescue should be instantly logged in the miracle book of the non-seafaring dropsical Lisbon theologian is not clear, but he it was who got the credit.

Long before Anthony's time, there was a Moorish fort here, and a stretch of wall remains, screening the private villa which, along with the shrine, now occupies the site. The fort encircled a large settlement on the plateau but, as previously noted, the village was deserted after the reconquest.

Having seen the 'pet cemetery', the 'Lourdes grotto' and Michelangelo's David standing proudly naked in the grass, we may be forgiven for assuming that this place has exhausted its wonders, and that it is time to move on. But like a good magician, it has saved its best trick till last. Take the path in front of the shrine, which leads, down and around the hillside. There, hidden from view, you will find several large caves which have obviously been inhabited until very recent times, and perhaps shelter the occasional gypsy or traveller even now. The first of these contains, alongside the inevitable accumulation of rubbish, the vestiges of two stone huts which have the look and feel of Mexican adobes, and its roof is blackened by the smoke from numberless fires.

There are drainage channels cut into the ground around the caves, to collect water for whoever lived there. The 'adobes' are clearly contemporary, or very nearly so, but the inhabitation of the caves must extend over many centuries. The surrounding hills have long-established terraces and are well cultivated. The stone water channels are strongly suggestive of a Roman origin, but Romans were not noted as cave dwellers. It is a mystery until you turn and cast your eyes on to the slopes of the hill. The landscape is a mass of marble rocks, with here and there obviously man-made pools. Many of the rocks bear the unmistakable signs of Man's attention. Grooves and cuts and chiselling. The Ermita San Antón is built on the site of an abandoned marble quarry.

We know that the Romans quarried these hills for marble. The stone was highly prized and carried far and wide for use in temples and fine villas. A proper analysis of the stone here might perhaps prove a link between the quarry and, for example, the temple facade which stands on the seafront at Fuengirola, having never been exported as intended. (See Fuengirola)

Visiting the Ermita San Antón is like spending an hour in the attic searching through the contents of a long unopened trunk filled with disconnected bric-a-brac. Treasures and trifles thrown together in the same dust, and all of it fascinating.

Finca Los Osunillas

It is never easy to pinpoint the exact location of long-lost communities. Although the Ermita San Antón is identified with the site of the vanished village of Osunilla, the fact that a finca bearing the name is located on another nearby hilly outcrop raises an element of doubt. The finca is on private land, so access is restricted. There are iron mines behind it, and it is possible to see a few 19th-century mining houses from the roadside. Each June a *romería* is held in the area – that eminently practical Spanish invention which neatly combines a pilgrimage to a holy shrine with a highly enjoyable picnic. If the finca now stands where the people of Osunilla once walked and gossipped in the sunshine, the echoes of their ghostly words are well beyond our hearing.

Close to this spot is a road junction which leads you to the 973 metre high Castillejo, no longer alive with sentries watching for signs of approaching enemies, but capped instead by a set of television repeater towers. (See Alhaurin de la Torre)

Torre de la Cala

This defensive tower, the 'tower of the cove', dating from 1540, is down on the coast in Mijas Costa. La Cala, which grew up around the tower as a small fishing village, has become one of the most important centres of population around Mijas-Costa, containing as many as 149 urbanisations of varying sizes, and at least three camping sites in La Debla, Calazul and Los Jarales. The tower once stood in proud isolation – its occupants scanning the horizon for signs of approaching hostile ships. Now it finds itself under siege from a species of invader they could never have imagined. A mighty conquering force that came armed not with swords, but with the far more deadly weapon of foreign money.

In earlier times, the tower, which stands 18 metres high, was known as the Torre Vieja de la Cala del Moral, a possible reference to the admirable rectitude of its inhabitants, but more likely, in this instance, to refer to the secondary meaning of *moral* – 'mulberry tree'. There are four holes from which its defenders could shoot, and two smaller towers on top of the main one. Ironically, these are decorated with Moorish tiles, since Torre de la Cala is one of four towers built in the years after the expulsion of the Moors to warn of possible attacks from vengeful Moorish pirates. The fact that it was built half a century after they had gone shows either that the threat persisted, or that the new Christian population was paranoid. It appears to have worked largely on the 'no news is good news' principle. If the pirates came in the daytime, smoke signals would warn the people to run, hide or fight. If they came sneakily at night, the job would be done by beacons. In the absence of both, the happy villagers would walk with a jaunty devil-may-care spring in their step and greet each other with the comforting words, '*No hay moros en la Costa*' – 'There are no Moors on the coast'. It is a phrase which has curiously survived to this day in spite of the ubiquitous presence of African street traders offering leather goods, watches and sparkling trinkets.

Inside, the tower is split into two rooms – the upper one containing the large fireplace which was used to create the signals.

In February 1996, it was handed over to students of the Mijas workshop school, who set about its restoration with energetic skill. Within a year it had been returned to its former splendour and began a new life not only as a tourist attraction, but also as a centre for artistic exhibitions. As is common in Spain, its opening hours tend to be erratic. At the time that the authors visited it, it was open only during the hours of 7pm to 9pm, and on weekdays only. Weekend visitors, and those passing by during the day had to content themselves with looking at it from the outside only. If this strikes the reader as odd, it strikes the authors as no less so. These times will almost certainly vary according to the time of year, and the possible attractions of an exhibition, so interested readers are advised to check. And at least it survives in fine condition, thanks to the patient skill of the workshop students, forming the centrepiece of a complex of bars and souvenir shops beside the beach in the Parroquia de Santa Teresa de Jesus.

Its three sister towers are the Torre Calahonda, Torre Pescas and Torre de Calaburra, which stands next to the Punta de Calaburra lighthouse. *Calahonda* translates literally as Catapult Cove, so ships came close at their peril. The meaning of *Calaburra* is less clear, for though *burra* is the name given to a she-donkey, it is also applied to an overworked woman. What we would today call a household drudge. Maybe here we have yet another instance of sly Spanish irony.

Chapter Eighteen

Monda

Historical Background

TRAVELLING INTO THE SIERRAS along the C–337 beyond Ojén, you will find, crouched in a valley like a sleeping cat too full of milk to stir, the small town of Monda. The town stands at an altitude of 1,200ft and has a population of less than two thousand. Its remoteness made it, until recently, a favourite drop-out spot for hippies, but a new road from Marbella and a rash of real-estate developments outside the village have woken it up to the 20th century just in time, perhaps, for it to be left behind by the 21st.

The old Moorish castle around which the town developed was built on the foundations of an Ibero-Roman fortified enclosure established in the 3rd–1st centuries BC by the Romans for the use of the indigenous Iberian population. Beyond this the Romans had little interest in its development and its probable main purpose was simply to protect the Roman town of Coín from invasion via the mountain approaches. Nevertheless, the mountains, such as the Sierra de Ojén, were an adequate source of lead and also contained small deposits of silver. Access to the outside world was only possible via the paved Roman branch road leading to Coín, since there was no equivalent route over the mountains to Marbella.

Apart from its curious modern day castle (see below), Monda is an undistinguished dot on the map, saved from total anonymity by one highly questionable claim to fame. The locals will tell you that this is the site of the Battle of Munda (45 BC), which brought an end to the Roman civil war between the forces of Pompey the Great and Julius Caesar.

The war had its roots in the 1st-century BC revolt of Quintus Sertorius, a military commander who had organised the indigenous Iberian populations along Roman lines and wanted to turn Spain into an independent state. He had some success against the armies of Metellus and Pompey, but the war was a long drawn-out affair in which Sertorius was compelled to seek many dubious allies. In 72 BC, one of these, M. Perperna, led a conspiracy in which Sertorius was murdered. As a result, the final victory went to Pompey.

Pompey, in turn, lost control of Spain to Julius Caesar, a one-time ally whose daughter he had married. Caesar had been one third of a powerful triumvirate alongside Pompey and the millionaire Crassus. As a young holder

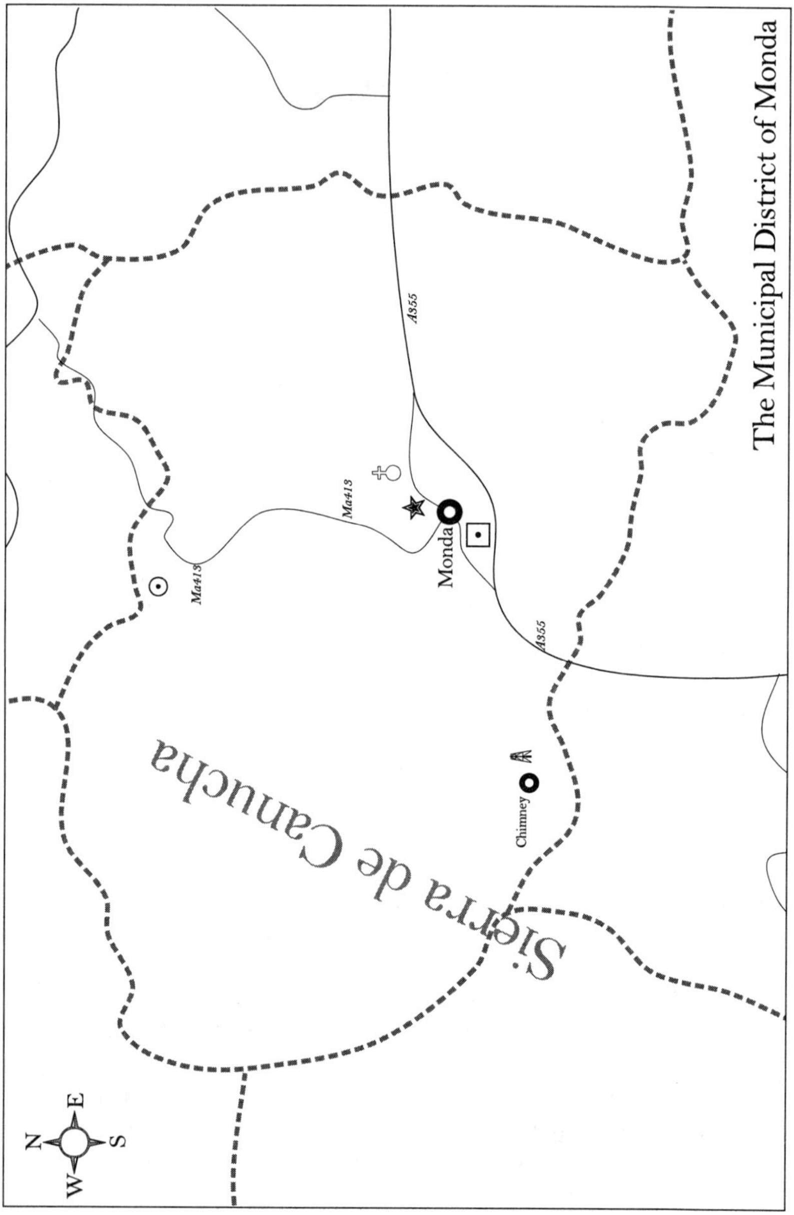
The Municipal District of Monda
Sierra de Canucha
Monda
A355
A355
Ma413
Ma413
Chimney
N
E
S
W

of minor posts with a shrewd eye on the main chance, Julius had supported Pompey, the successful military commander, and Crassus, the man with the money. Power and wealth – the classic combination. It served him well, and resulted in the first major coup of his career when he was elected Chief Priest in 63 BC. Three years later, snubbed by the Senate after his governorship of Spain, he established virtually autocratic rule along with his two powerful allies. This was the informal First Triumvirate, and it led to Caesar's first consulship, during which he ruthlessly repressed opposition.

They were an unbeatable team, but as historians of rock 'n' roll will tell you, great bands always fall out and fall apart sooner or later. By 56 BC internal jealousies – the almost inevitable companion of shared success – were already weakening the bonds between them. The alliance finally collapsed after the death of Julius Caesar's daughter (Pompey's wife) in 54 BC, and Crassus' death in battle the following year. The rumblings exploded into full-scale civil war in 49 BC, when a decisive battle at Ilerda (Lérida) delivered Spain into Caesar's hands. A year later Pompey was dead.

It was not quite the end of the Pompey cause, however. His sons Gnaeus and Sextus fought on and after a defeat in 46 BC at Thapsus, they took refuge in Baetica, the last stronghold of their cause, and seized Córdoba. Julius Caesar came personally with his army to crush the revolt even, it is said, fighting with the 10th legion. After many withdrawals, the Pompeian forces took up positions on high ground at Munda, close to Urso (now Osuna), east of Seville. Unwisely they came down again to engage Caesar's troops in combat and during the battle, in response to a cavalry attack, Gnaeus ordered a tactical shift which the rest of his panicking army readily, and perhaps gratefully, interpreted as the beginning of a retreat. As a result his forces scattered in complete disorder and were easily beaten. Gnaeus was killed while attempting to flee, but Sextus succeeded in escaping from Spain. A little resistance dragged on through the spring and summer, but the war was effectively over.

It will be seen from this that the claim of Monda to have been the site of this momentous battle is, if not deliberately spurious, at least the result of some highly wishful thinking. The real fighting took place a long way to the north, possibly close to Ronda, though the actual site is today generally recognised as the town of Montilla. Nevertheless, it is a good story and the people of Monda will no doubt dine out on it for many years to come.

Prosper Mérimée, the author of *Carmen*, was not only a skilled writer but a renowned archæologist and a keen student of Roman history. Shortly before writing what was to become his most famous work, thanks largely to the composer Bizet, Mérimée visited Andalucía to carry out research into the site of the Battle of Munda. His findings were published in the *Revue Archéologique* in June 1844, but he also used his experience as a backdrop for *Carmen* itself. The narrator of the story is an archæologist engaged in precisely the same task.

Almost nothing now remains in Monda of the Roman occupation, save for a single small and hard-to-find bridge on its outskirts.

The construction of the Moorish castle may have begun as early as the 8th century AD and its original name is thought to have been 'Castillo de Al Mundat'. It must have been destroyed or have fallen into grave disrepair, because Omar ben Hafsun felt the need to rebuild it even before the 9th century was out. However, like their Christian adversaries, the Moslems spent an awful lot of time fighting among themselves, and in 990 Saib Ibn Al Mundir came along and destroyed it again. It lay dormant until the 11th century when the Hammudies decided to have another go and put it back together once more. On this occasion it lasted much longer and in time became an important garrison.

Its prominence lasted until the spring of 1485, when invading Christians under the command of Capitán Hurtado de Luna overran it and confined the Moslems to the village built inside the castle walls.

From this period comes an enduring legend. In 1485 de Luna became Monda's first Christian mayor, and moved into the castle, which bore the name of 'El Mundat' in honour of one of his Moslem predecessors. Colloquially, however, it was always known as 'la Villeta'. In 1508, the lordship of Monda passed to the Duke of Escalona, who confirmed de Luna in his post.

Hurtado de Luna had a daughter of exceptional beauty whose name was Beatriz. The people of Monda were crazy for nicknames, and on her too one was bestowed. They called her *la buena Villeta.* Passions were about to stir. Over in nearby Tolox the Mayor, Sancho de Angulo, conveniently had a son. The son's name was Arturo, and since he appears not to have achieved the honour of an enduring nickname, we can assume that he was not of exceptional beauty. He was handsome enough, however, to win the love of la buena Villeta, and he and Beatriz used to meet at the shrine of the Virgen del Almendro, though it is unlikely that they went there to eat nuts.

One day he came bearing sad news. He had to leave for America with his father. The lovers said a tearful farewell and vowed eternal love, pledging to wait for each other until the end of time. Arturo, as a somewhat odd token of his devotion, took an almond flower and offered it to the Virgin of the shrine. Then, like a fleeting glance, he was gone.

For a long time the flower remained miraculously fresh. Beatriz took this as a sign that Arturo was well, and that their love was still intact. Then suddenly one day it withered and died. As it did so, drops of blood fell from it and the rest of the flowers around the shrine. Beatriz, a strong believer in omens, and a pretty morbid one at that, instantly decided that Arturo must be dead. She did not give the alternatives – a broken leg, a severe case of gastro-enteritis, a new love – a chance. 'A new love' and 'dead' were in any case synonymous so far as she was concerned.

Always a melodramatic girl, la buena Villeta received this supernatural newsflash badly. With Arturo gone, life held nothing more for her and she fell at the feet of the Virgin and promptly died of grief. Since that day, the almond flower has had a reddish tone and, not surprisingly, the ghost of Beatriz is said to walk the castle. If it still does, her views on the changes it has undergone since its extraordinary resurrection would make interesting reading.

After 1485, the indigenous population was left more or less in peace for the next decade and a half but a subsequent unsuccessful Moslem uprising resulted in a decree in 1501 that they should either convert to Christianity immediately or leave Spain. The validity and sincerity of such enforced conversions may be open to grave doubt, but it satisfied the belligerent authorities, who ticked off the names of those Arabs who learned to say the rosary, and kicked out those who either couldn't or wouldn't. Those who stayed, the *Mudéjares*, became subject to the Marquis of Villena who took control of Monda and Tolox in 1508.

A further revolt in 1570 stretched the Christians' brittle patience too far and the castle was destroyed and all of its inhabitants expelled by Arévalo de Zuazo, who petulantly gave their lands and possessions to eighty Christians brought in from the north. This kind of story is so common that one must seriously begin to doubt the tales of continual 'Arab uprisings' which resulted in the sad necessity of dispossessing the unruly Moslems and giving all they owned to Christian 'settlers'. For centuries after the arrival of the Pilgrim Fathers in the New World, the natives were subjected to genocidal attacks, often masked by false 'treaties', from the invading Europeans, who wanted their land and were determined to take it. Popular history and Hollywood converted this very successfully into a tale of brave and hardy peace-loving pioneers battling against vicious, bloodthirsty savages who couldn't be trusted. The only good injun, went the popular slogan, was a dead injun. One detects a similar slant in the stories of 16th-century Arab 'uprisings'. When it comes to conflict, history is written by the side that won. After eight hundred years, the Arab hold on the Iberian Peninsula was broken. The populations of the mountain Arab villages may not have liked it, and the Christians may well have considered them a continuing threat. Peace is not a synonym for tolerance and understanding. The Christians were not interested in leaving Arab communities intact. They wanted them fragmented, or better still, eradicated. They wanted the Arabs out. What finer excuse for their righteous wrath than an 'uprising'?

Whatever the truth of the story, the Arévalo Eighty eagerly arrived to take over the land. They were forbidden to live within the ruins of the castle and settled instead at the foot of the hill, where their descendants still remain. The castle was ignored and uninhabited for almost five centuries until it attracted the eye, and the ultimately frustrated imagination, of a German nobleman.

Undoubtedly the most popular man in Monda during the first half of the twentieth century was José Lomeña Bernal. Originally from Guaro, Pepe Lomeña, as he was universally known, lived in an old oil mill and achieved an immense and widespread reputation for wisdom and generosity. Today many such mills – those which have been lucky enough to survive – have become home to wealthy expatriates, many of whom profess a self-conscious devotion to what have become confusingly known as 'alternative lifestyles'. Alternative, we wonder, to what? In Pepe Lomeña we have found their spiritual grandfather, although he would probably have been unable to say exactly what a 'lifestyle' was. He simply lived. He was entirely self-educated, but built up a vast store of knowledge on all manner of subjects. His Solomon-like judgement was frequently sought in disputes whose solution baffled the efforts of lesser men. He was an expert botanist and practised natural herbal medicine, but his restlessly inquiring mind led him to experiment with other fringe treatments. He was the eccentric smarty-pants you just couldn't help liking. A friend to all and a good companion.

There is little doubt that were he alive today, Pepe Lomeña would have been the first man in Monda, possibly in Spain, to install a computer and joyously surf the internet. His love of nature and the rural life did not prevent him from developing an equal interest in technology. His mill was stacked with state-of-the art equipment and he built his own experimental still and wine press, with which he produced syrups and herbal wines of his own invention. Not for nothing was he Monda's favourite son. He died a much-loved figure in the 1950s, having lived long enough to fulfil his ambition of watching television. Maybe that's what killed him.

El Castillo

A new castle now dominates the town, and its history is very much that of the pueblo itself. As previously noted, in 1570 the Moorish fortress which had long stood on a crag above the town was demolished. Miraculously, a few ruins from the Moorish period have survived, though in a very poor state.

The site of the old castle remained derelict until the 1970s, when it was bought by an aristocratic German who began to rebuild the structure. Unfortunately, as the infernal red tape of Spanish officialdom wound interminably about him, he eventually abandoned the project in grand Teutonic exasperation and fled home leaving the work half done. The site, and the unfinished castle, then passed into the hands of a group of more phlegmatic English entrepreneurs, who completed the building and turned it into an hotel.

Should we be grateful? It sits on top of the town like an ill-fitting, ugly grey hat, and it has to be said that from a distance it is riveting for all the wrong reasons. The closer you get, the worse it looks. The ruined Moorish tower which is the most notable of the few remnants of the original structure stands outside the main complex, staring sadly away from it like a man who's friends have got disgracefully drunk at a party and from whom he wishes to disassociate himself entirely. No attempt has been made to restore a Moorish appearance to the new castle, at least on the outside, and it gives the impression of being constructed haphazardly from any available blocks of stone, thrown together at random as a child might toy idly with his Lego set. It has all the hallmarks of Architecture by Committee: a committee of deaf Albanians and blind Eskimos who did not understand each other's language, but loved each other's wine. Incongruous windows, designed to give visitors light and lovely views, suggest a nascent office block being eaten slowly by a prison. However, all these reservations are swept aside when, at the end of a bone-shaking drive up an access road obviously surfaced by the local garage owner and tyre franchisee, you eventually get inside. Here the advantage of the large, outwardly disconcerting windows is obvious. The Moorish flavour, such as it is, is far more obvious within than without and with fountains, quiet corners, an excellent swimming pool and superb cuisine the castle has undeniably become an ideal, if expensive, spot to stay.

Church of Santiago Apóstol

Monda's main church is, as you would expect it to be, in the main square, inevitably known as the 'Plaza de la Constitución'. Dedicated to Santiago Apóstol – St James the Apostle – it was built in that bumper year for church building, 1505, but like many another, it was in need of refurbishment and reconstruction within a century. It is hard not to escape the sneaking suspicion that in the rush to build a church in every parish in the years following the Christian reconquest, quality was often sacrificed for speed. The task of restoration fell to Diaz Palacios, and he set about it in the church's centenary year, 1605. In the almost four centuries since, it has been restored several times, but apart from the addition of two extra chapels in the early 18th century, the original plan has been retained. There are three aisles separated by rectangular pillars and semi-circular arches. The central aisle is covered by a vault, while the other two have normal roofs.

Calzada Romana

Calzada is a word meaning causeway, or roadway, and a stretch of an ancient Roman path is still hidden away in Monda, but very easy to find. Take the old Coín road away from the town, and on a corner, just before you reach the modern bridge over the river, a path winds away to the left. Park the car and follow the path on foot, and very soon the dusty trail becomes a stony track leading down to the waterside. Clearly a bridge once existed at this point, but time and floods have swept it away. As you meander along these uneven stones that once connected small and remote communities, it is hard not to wonder if the mountain dwellers of two millennia ago had particularly flexible and adaptable feet. If the stones are uncomfortably irregular now, after two thousand years of erosion and the tramp of countless travellers, how much more rugged must they have been when they were still new and freshly laid. The fields on either side of the pathway are still farmed, but the internal combustion engine has made moving from town to town much quicker and easier, and the old road has been tucked away in the weeds and forgotten, except by the few who seek it out simply to walk upon it, and feel the weight of its years.

Many brief guide books will tell you that very close to this spot is the *Puente del Arroyo de la Teja.* This is the last remaining Roman bridge in Monda and is on the Coín road, roughly a kilometre and a half from the town. However, its precise location is elusive. Should you attempt to find it, you are in for a pleasant walk, but likely to have nothing to show for it after a couple of hours.

Calvario and Monolito

Some monuments are odder and less immediately logical than others. 500 metres along the Monda-Coín road, close to the pathway which leads to the *calzada Romana,* and on the opposite side, is a hill topped by a very curious construction indeed. The whitewashed, triple-towered brick Calvary was erected in the 1770s at the instruction of Juan de Cózar Gallo y Torrecilla. It stands about twelve feet high, and each of its three towers is topped by a wrought iron cross. In the centre is an arched alcove which may once have contained a religious statue, but which is now empty. The brickwork is rough and unimpressive, though much of this may be due to erosion and the constant reapplication of the whitewash. What makes the positioning of the shrine interesting is that the area in front of it has been paved with stones set in a circular pattern, and was once used for threshing. Perhaps the monument to the Lord's suffering on the cross was intended to bring His blessing to the harvest. Threshing is today left to machinery, but the *Calvario* continues to receive its regular coating of whitewash and serves not only as a place of local pilgrimage, but as a useful and very visible landmark for travellers.

The Sierra de las Nieves – Monda Entrance

Monda has its own access to this beautiful natural park along a trackway that is just about manageable for most vehicles. Take the old Ojén road out of the village and two kilometres into your journey you reach the entrance to the gorge, which the modern road now dominates. From the old arched bridge, turn right and the track will lead you bumpily into the heart of the park.

There are two things to notice on the road before you cross the municipal dividing line into Istán. The first, one kilometre along to the left, is an elaborate system of hill terracing which is certainly of Moorish origin. There does not appear to have been a settlement allied to the fields, and the workers would probably have walked to the site across the mountain from Monda, two kilometres away.

Five kilometres beyond the terracing is one of the oddest and most surprising sights in the area: an industrial 'factory chimney' forming part of an associated rural complex. The chimney, looking for all the world as though it has been magically transported from some smoke-filled northern English valley, was most probably used in the processing of limestone. The 'factory' stands squarely on the division between the limestone and sandstone rock formations, and probably produced lime in large quantities for building and agricultural use. Its former glory is gone, but the complex is still lived in and used by a number of poor farmers. A row of telegraph poles leads to the main road, but they are bare and wireless. The electricity has been cut off, but the relentless advance of technology is clear from the roof of the associated living quarters, which carry a set of solar heating panels.

The track leads ultimately to a junction just inside the municipal district of Istán. From here the views of the mountain landscape are truly stunning. From this junction a left turn will take you to Istán. The alternative route, to Tolox, is only for the brave. (See Tolox.)

Chapter Nineteen

Ojén

Historical Background

OJÉN, WITH A LITTLE OVER 2000 PEOPLE, has roughly the same population as Benahavis, and like Istán it remains relatively unspoiled in spite of its accessibility. It stands beside the Almadán stream above the valley of the río Real at a height of 650ft, hemmed in by the Sierra Blanca and the Sierra Alpujata which have long been known as rich sources of talc, nickel, iron and lead. Today it straddles a modern road, with the newer and more affluent half rising into the hills and looking down, and the older part crouching in the valley and doffing its cap.

There is very little available historical data about the town. Its Arab founders must have wondered what on earth they were doing there, since they called it *Hoxán*, which may be translated as 'rough' or 'bitter' place. That is not a description which would spring to the mind of the modern-day traveller, and it is to be wondered why the Arabs apparently disliked it so much, or stayed in spite of their apparent antipathy.

But stay they did, and they even built a castle. In the 10th century, during the caliphate of Abderrahmán III, the caliph fought a battle outside its walls against the ambitious rebel leader, Omar ben Hafsun. The caliph was victorious, and celebrated his victory by erecting a mosque. It was all he could think of at the time.

Because of its distance from the sea, Ojén survived the Christian reconquest in reasonable shape and its Moorish inhabitants were allowed to remain. That all ended in 1569 during the widespread Morisco rising, when the castle and virtually the whole town were burned down. Today, the only vestiges of the old castle are to be found high up on an escarpment. The mosque inevitably disappeared beneath a new church, the *Iglesia de Nuestra Señora de la Encarnación*, completed around 1670.

It is difficult to believe, as one looks at the quietly dozing towns in these sierras, that in the early part of the 19th century they were in the vanguard of Spain's nascent industrial revolution. Chiefly responsible was a young entrepreneur named Manuel Agustín Heredia, who was born in La Rioja in 1786, but made his home in Málaga. His big chance came during the Spanish War of Independence. Under the protection of the guerillas who infested the

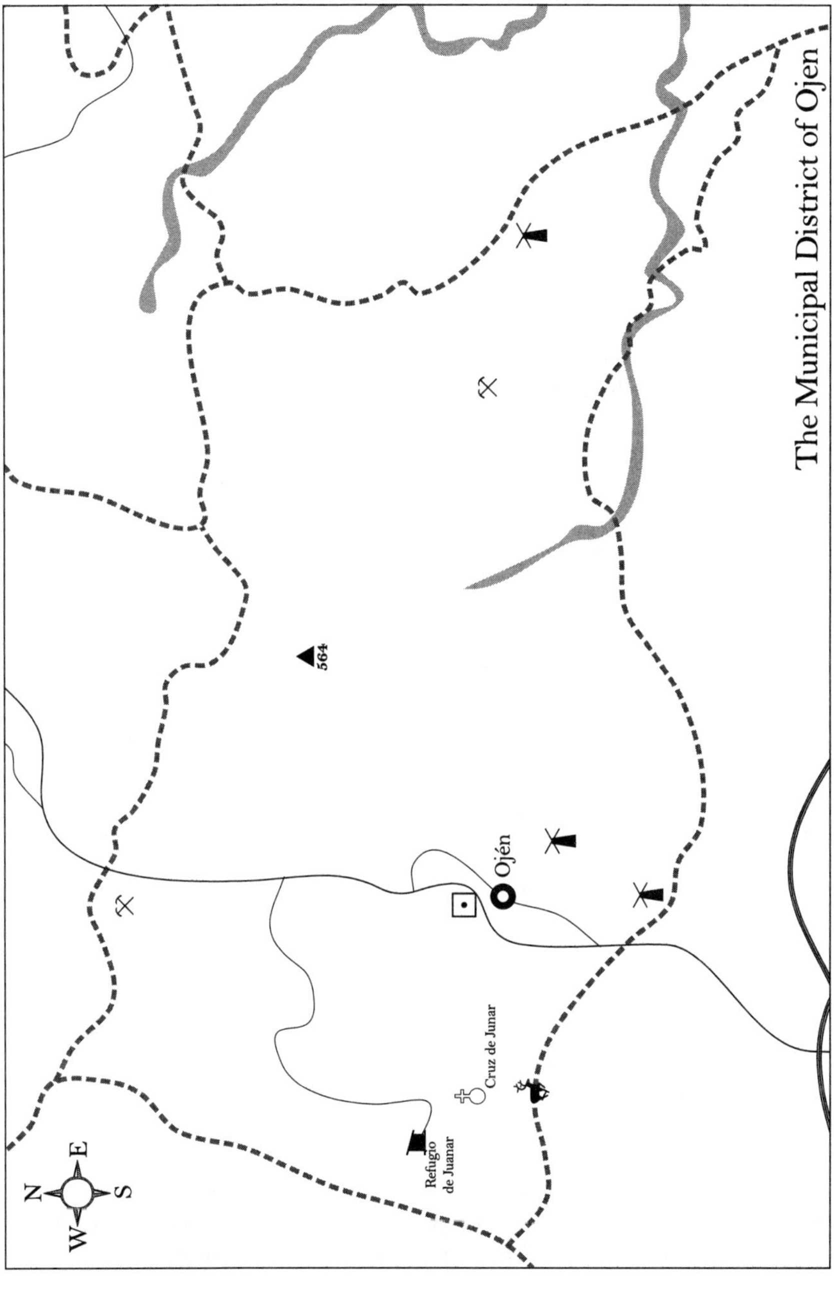
The Municipal District of Ojen
564
Ojén
Cruz de Junar
Refugio de Juanar
N
E
S
W

mountains, he took control of the graphite mines in Benahavis and the hills around Marbella. In no time at all he had virtually exhausted the deposits and incidentally made himself a huge fortune. After 1825, he cast his net a little further and set his eyes on the iron mines of the Sierra Blanca.

It was in 1828 that he set up two important foundries – *El Angel* and *El Concepción* – beside the rio Verde, between Marbella and Ojén, making use both of the river water and the abundant supplies of firewood in the mountains. The ore was good, but very hard, and so he developed a method of refining it in two stages. If the industrial revolutions of Europe in the 19th century can be called the birth of the modern age, and their factories its maternity ward, Heredia was the unlikely midwife who delivered it to the hills of Andalucía. He went on to become perhaps the most important Spanish industrialist of his time, being involved in the foundations of Málaga's textile industry in partnership with the Larios family, and also of the Bank of Málaga.

Before this, though, Ojén did have a name for itself among the cognoscenti for the production of the anise drink, *aguardiente.* Although its manufacture no longer plays a major part in the town's life, the drink is still popular in Spain, and it is common to see Spaniards taking a glass with their morning coffee.

In a bid to attract the more discerning and affluent tourist, the village now has its own wine museum, and mountain tours for lovers of nature can also be arranged.

The Pueblo

An excellent view of Ojén can be had from the modern highway which leads from Marbella, over the pass to Coín, but to begin your exploration of the town, park your car close to one of the many ventas on the old main road which cuts it in two and walk down into the pueblo. As with Istán, the streets are narrow and cobbled and well served by strategically located fountains. A rough and bitter place? What astounding earthly paradise did its Arab founders leave behind them?

The older part of Ojén, the part below the level of the old road, is like a prim spinster who locked her few treasures away in her bottom drawer to await the return of a man who went to war and never came back. A drinking fountain, dated 1905, is dedicated to the benevolent Mayor, Don Pedro Fernandez Sanchez, who was responsible for its erection. One can imagine that the day of its inauguration was among the most exciting the town had seen in centuries, and that generations of children have learned of it since at their mothers' knees.

Within minutes of the start of your walk you will reach the small but pleasant *Plaza de Andalucía* and the parish church. As noted above, the church was completed in 1670. Today it bears a plaque lamenting the horrors of 'bad and barbarous war'. It is a noble sentiment, but there is a lurking irony in the fact that it adorns a building which owes its existence to the brutal destruction of another.

Ojén

The patron saint of Ojén is Dionisio Areopagita – Dionysius the Areopagite. It is a name guaranteed to stop the casual reader in his or her tracks. Dionysius the *what??* It sounds like a sexual deviation, a synonym for a balloonist or the brand name of some patented super-glue. In fact, the word is derived from Areopagus, a low hill to the northwest of the Acropolis in Athens, which was the meeting place of the city's earliest ruling council of aristocrats. Dionysius, we may therefore assume, was a strong committee man. His story is, however, somewhat confusing. According to the Bible (Acts 17.34), he was one of a mere handful of Athenians to have been converted to Christianity by St Paul while the new religion's first great evangelist was in Greece. Tradition holds that he became the first bishop of the city, but with so few candidates to choose from, this cannot be considered a major triumph. In the 9th century, Dionysius somehow became identified with St Denis of France, but Denis was born in Rome and died a martyr's death at the hands of the Romans in Paris around the middle of the 3rd century AD. Saints are famously ubiquitous, but Dionysius/Denis was obviously carrying the tradition too far.

For the people of Ojén the two are certainly one and the same for, while revering Dionisio Areopagita as their patron saint, they ascribe to him a version of a story told in the 9th century about St Denis. Dionysius, they say, was condemned to death by the Romans. As they marched him to the place of execution, his guards grew weary of the walk, and since their charge was due to die at the end of it anyway, decided it was a pretty pointless exercise and promptly decapitated him. Stung by their unchivalrous action, the condemned man petulantly picked up his head, wiped it clean of blood, replaced it on his shoulders and walked six kilometres before dropping dead. The immediate cause of death is not recorded.

The original story as told by the 9th-century abbot Hilduin about St Denis merely has his man being led by an angel after his decapitation from Montmartre to the abbey church, which now bears his name. The Spanish are a dramatic people, and clearly prefer the Hollywood version. Dionysius/Denis is invariably portrayed in religious iconography as some kind of music hall ghost with his head, if not tucked underneath his arm, at least in his hands.

Calle Cuevas

Though Ojén is quiet and still, life is stirring where it is least expected. A sign on the southern corner of the plaza alerts the visitor to the existence of caves, and they are not hard to find. Walk down the helpfully named *calle Cuevas* and sure enough, it will lead you to a group of caves close to a spring where, it would seem, some enterprising residents of Ojén have made bold plans. The first cave is deep, and a wander into its depths may well reward the intrepid. Sadly, its entrance is so liberally strewn with rubbish that all but the most dedicated troglodyte will be instantly discouraged.

It is in the other adjoining caves that real evidence of activity is to be found. They are, to be accurate, grottos rather than caves, and their floors have been neatly tiled. In one there is a raised platform which is clearly intended for use as a stage. The stage and the cave are so small that the chances of it hosting a major rock music festival or theatrical extravaganza are slim, but it would be ideal for intimate cabaret under the Andalucían stars.

But where is the army of workmen toiling to bring the dream to reality? One of the great, enduring mysteries of southern Spain is the enigma of the missing workmen. Everywhere there is evidence of projects underway. The shells of half completed buildings, road rollers standing ready to roll roads, caves being turned into cabaret bars. Yet they are invariably deserted. No clanging hammers, no chattering drills, no stooping navvy rewarding the prurient with a glimpse of builder's cleavage. They stand silent and empty; half-formed and apparently destined to remain so for eternity. It is both oddly comforting and strangely eerie.

Castillo de Ojén

Returning to the old main road from the lower reaches of Ojén, it soon becomes clear that something is missing. Where is the castle? We know the Moors built one, but there appears to be no trace of it. Tantalisingly, the bar, which tempts you to cross the road and wash away the dust of the day with a cold beer, is called *El Castillo*, and it stands at the foot of a steep hill called *Paseo de Castillo*. One need not be Sherlock Holmes to sniff the lingering scent of a clue. A walk up *Paseo de Castillo* will bring you to *calle de la Torre*, proving conclusively that you are hot on the trail. Actually, the Spanish sun will already have told you that, but here is confirmation. Continue your walk up the hill, sticking to *Paseo de Castillo*, or switching to *calle de la Torre* as you choose, and eventually you will find a field imprisoned behind a strong wire-mesh fence. Within it are remnants of walls and in one corner the stunted remains of a tower. It is difficult to imagine these few weathered stones as a mighty Moorish castle, and how they must have looked at the time of Abderrahmán's mighty battle with Omar ben Hafsun. Now they give refuge only to beetles, mice and spiders. If a picture is worth a thousand words, how many millions of words echo silently in a sight like this? Its very banality is eloquent testimony to the careless ravages of time.

But let us not give way to melancholy. We have one advantage over the Moors. A short walk back down the hill is the bar *El Castillo*, and colder beer than they could ever have imagined.

Refugio de Juanar

The name of Larios is a venerable one in Spain, inextricably linked to a popular brand of gin. If it is true, as Yorkshiremen insist, that 'where there's muck there's brass', then it is surely true that where there's drink there's gold. Provided, of course, that you are a producer of it and not a dedicated consumer. Less well known is the strong connection with the important textile industry which flourished in Málaga from the mid-nineteenth century. Whether from cotton or gin, the Larios family is among Spain's wealthiest, and the *Refugio de Juanar* was at one time their sumptuous private hunting lodge. Among their regular guests was King Alfonso XIII. His father, Alfonso XII, died of tuberculosis in November 1885, leaving his wife Maria Cristina pregnant with the son he never saw. Alfonso XIII was born on May 17th 1886, and was immediately proclaimed king under the regency of his mother. He reigned until the advent of the Republic in 1931, becoming disastrously associated in his latter years with the dictatorship of Primo de Rivera.

Although earning much respect for his qualities as a soldier and his devotion to humanitarian causes, he was unpopular, and a frequent target for assassination attempts. It must have been a great relief for him occasionally to escape to the safety of his wealthy friends' estate and instead of dodging the bullets, get some sort of therapeutic revenge by aiming a few of his own at the goats, deer and partridge.

The refuge lies within the nature reserve of Serrania de Ronda, which sprawls its way across 23,000 hectares, with trails winding to Ojén, Istán and the Sierra Blanca. Shooting at the wildlife is not compulsory, even during the hunting season, and those who simply want to walk and enjoy the stunning scenery will find it exhilarating. Ibex, wildcats, eagles and more abound in the mountains, and the refuge's *mirador*, just two miles away along a rather bumpy track, provides a truly staggering view of Marbella and the coast, 3,000 feet below. When the air is clear, the hills of Africa are also visible.

The palace, for such it surely was, eventually came into government hands and was turned into a state-run hotel. It remained so until 1984, when it was virtually given away to its staff, who, to make the whole thing legal, 'purchased' it with a symbolic but small amount of money. It is now extremely popular with visitors and rates three stars in hotel guides. Strangely, standing as it does on the foundations of a hunting lodge, and still a favourite haunt of hunters, it has one unbreakable rule: No dogs.

To reach the refuge, take the road from Marbella to Ojén, and 3km beyond the latter a turn-off to the left will take you to your destination. It is impressive and inviting. In the winter, visitors can sit and dream of its glorious past in front of a roaring log fire. The restaurant specialises in game found close by in the *Reserva Nacional de Serrania de Ronda*: partridge, rabbit, venison, quail and mountain goat.

If you are feeling adventurous, energetic or both, you might wish to take the track which you encounter approximately one metre before you reach the welcoming haven. Leave the car and wander through the chestnut and pine trees until you come to the olive grove of Juanar, planted in the distinctive red earth so rich in iron oxide. A little way beyond is a recreation/picnic area in which you will find benches and wooden tables. The path winds on for about 300 metres until it brings you to the *mirador.* To the right rises the *cerro del Juanar,* and there is a footpath behind a metal fence which will take you directly to the summit. Take a deep breath and begin, but be ready for a tough climb. The path is extremely steep, and easily lost. It rises almost perpendicularly for 300 metres to the highest point of the sierra (1,180 metres). Marking the spot is an iron cross on which you will no doubt lean heavily as you look down on yet another incredible view of the coastline.

Most of the people who come this far do not do so to visit ruins like the *Cortijo de Juanar* complex. They come because they are hikers. Tracks lead across the hills and down to Istán, offering the jaded and reasonably ambulant a healthy green alternative to sea and sand, if not to sun. However, the always controversial Mayor of Marbella, Jesús Gil – a man not noted for the athleticism of his build or pursuits – has plans to build a cable car to link this mountain sanctuary to his famous town.

Minas de Penoncillo

Gil's cable car will not be the first. As we have seen, iron has been mined in the hills of Málaga province for centuries. This particular mining complex stands on the border between Marbella and Ojén, on the main road. In its heyday, the ore which was mined here was taken to the coast below by cable car, and although mining has long since ceased, the remains of the terminus can still be found standing on the beach at Marbella. (See Marbella)

The area has also been heavily quarried for limestone, and there is little left to see which would interest the industrial archæologist. Walking around cannot be recommended, although some indication of its former industrial glory can be seen in the various pits scattered across the landscape.

Monda

Above: Architecture by Committee – the new castle at Monda.

Left: Calvario (Monda).

Below: Monda or Rhondda? – 'Factory chimney', *Sierra de las Nieves Nature Reserve.*

Ojén

Decorative tiles on the mirador.

Ojén – patchwork of narrow streets.

zarra.

ermitage church of
uestra Señora de Fuensanta
izarra).

Pizarra

The palace of Conde de Puerto Hermos.

Municipal Museum, Pizarra – part of Gino Hollander's collection.

Tolox, clinging to the hillside.

This narrow passage may be all that remains of Tolox castle.

Tolox

Balneario de Fuente Amargosa.

Torremolinos

Casa de los Navaja – a maiden aunt lost in the disco.

Chapter Twenty

Pizarra

Historical Background

HOYA MAY BE TRANSLATED IN NUMEROUS WAYS: pit, ditch, depression in the ground, grave, seedbed, dimple. It is also the word for a river basin. Hence, *Hoya de Málaga*, the name used to describe the fertile valley land around the great Andalucían city.

7 kilometres to the north, Alora is probably the first of the true mountain pueblos, but the last of the villages lying in the *Hoya* is Pizarra. It is situated 30 km upriver in the Guadalhorce Valley, lying prostrate at the foot of the 350m *Sierra del Hacho*, as though its first inhabitants had trekked long and far and, confronted by the mountain, simply did not have the energy or will to go on. They pitched their tents, put up their houses and stayed. The village church is 82m above sea level, and that was as high as they wanted to go until they went to Heaven. Long afterwards, when they had well and truly got their breaths back, they placed a cross and a statue of an open-armed Christ, the Sacred Heart of Jesus, on two of the highest of the surrounding hills. The Christ is inescapably reminiscent of the larger and more famous statue standing above Rio de Janeiro. Travellers passing by night do not go on their way in blissful ignorance. After dark, the statue is illuminated. In its comforting shadow, comedy and tragedy, joy and pain spin in their eternal orbits. There is the base of another cross, lost among uncaring weeds and brambles beside a hillside footpath on the outskirts of the village. No-one tends the memorial. Its inscription is almost illegible, and soon it will completely disappear. It was raised to commemorate a murder on that spot in 1937. The murderers, it says, were Marxists, and the victims died in defence of democracy. The cross that once stood on the base has been deliberately broken off and is now gone. The break appears to be comparatively recent. Perhaps it was done after the death of General Franco in 1975, when those who felt differently finally felt able to vent their feelings. The cross was not replaced. Either the desecrators had strong support in the village, or no-one cares any more. The war was long ago. Many people died. Many people were murdered. Maybe it is better not to speak of such things. There is today to be lived and, if it is God's will, tomorrow.

Pizarra is still very much a farming community, taking full advantage of

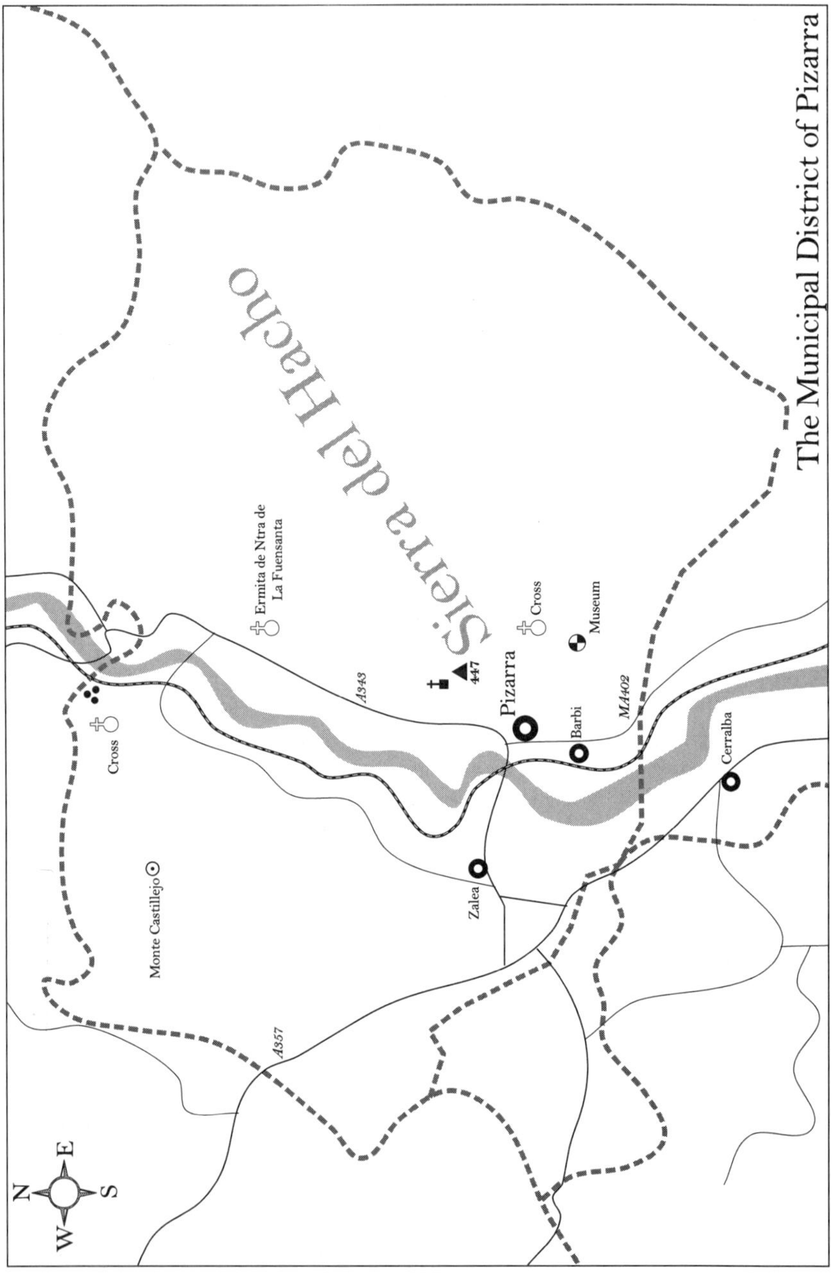

The Municipal District of Pizarra

the wet and fertile *vega* (the word means simply, 'fertile plain'), which is watered by the motherly, if occasionally irascible, river. Citrus fruits are the main crops, although olives are grown extensively on the lower hills.

The all-conquering motor car, and the improved roads built in its homage, have put Pizarra within comfortable commuting distance of Málaga and, as we have seen, with Alhaurín de la Torre, that can be the kiss of death or the breath of life to unassuming rural pueblos, depending on one's point of view. If we see urban development as a form of rejuvenation, then the first two spots of adolescent acne have already erupted. Within the last thirty years two new settlements have appeared on the western face of Pizarra – Zalea and Cerralba. These are creations of the Franco era, and were intended as model farming villages. Alas, they were born out of their time. In the 1960s, around the kernels of the original villages, heroic attempts were made to terrace and irrigate the lower hills. Today most of the land lies abandoned and untilled. Zalea and Cerralba have forgotten how to farm.

If Pizarra does eventually get swallowed by the voracious Málaga machine, it can trace the roots of its doom to the day in 1859 that the railway arrived on its doorstep asking if it could build a station and stay. Before that, the villagers were good at farming and rural pursuits, but hopeless at history. True, the Romans were thereabouts, and had founded the town of Barbi in the area. This is now lost, and the name lives on only as that of the world's best-selling plastic doll. Two thousand years of human development and technological advance in a nutshell.

A strong Christian Visigothic community must have maintained some kind of continuity into the Moorish era, since the remains of a Mozárabe church have been found. 'Mozárabe' was the name given to Christians who lived in parts of Spain under Moorish control, and implied no allegiance to the Moslem faith. Contrast this comparative tolerance and freedom of worship with the plight of the Moriscos – Moors who found themselves in Christian areas as town after town fell during the final years of the Reconquest. Their presence was tolerated, when it was tolerated at all, only if they openly rejected Islam and embraced, or at least professed to embrace, Christianity.

The Moors showed little interest in the area and established no settlement worthy of the name. Development had to wait until 1483, when the Christians took control of nearby Alora and decided that Pizarra was a place which could use a few more people. They seemed oddly reluctant to come, and could only be persuaded by the bestowing of a grant. With this carrot dangling beneath their noses, 100 settlers made their way to the foothills of the *Sierra del Hacho,* led by the determined Don Pedro Romero de Figueroa, who intended to make a go of it. The fact that this was virgin territory on which the pioneers hoped to write a whole new chapter was reflected, either deliberately or with unintended irony, in the very name which they chose. *Pizarra* means 'slate', or 'blackboard'.

If they had dreams of glory, they were slow in being realised. It was a hundred years before they got around to building a proper church, and Pizarra was never more than a small attachment to Alora until 1847, when, more than three and a half centuries after Don Pedro led his pilgrims to the Promised Land, it was granted independence.

Even so, it was not the thriving, robust community that Don Pedro had envisioned, and one extremely large and very visible reason may well have been the infamous *peñasco,* a huge rock which hung over the town looking for all the world like a gigantic bomb waiting to be dropped. The rock was estimated to be more than 5,000 cubic metres in volume, and to weigh almost 3,000 tons. Pizarra was not a place for the nervous, and its unfashionable reputation begins to make sense. One person who snapped his fingers in the face of danger was the Conde Puerto Hermos, who came, bought land cheaply, and built a palace. In 1922 the palace was host to the biggest event in the entire history of the town: a political conference. Unless, of course, you were one of the old men sitting quietly in the square reminiscing. Most of them still rated the coming of the railway higher.

Many failed attempts were made to remove the rock over the centuries, but its mocking threat was not finally eliminated until 1988. Some years before, nervous residents had reported dangerous cracks appearing in its sides. Not surprisingly, this resulted in grave apprehension and probably increased sales of hard hats. Technicians and rock experts were called in, and it was decided that the rock had to go. A great hole was dug beneath it, and 175 kilos of explosives were strategically inserted into the condemned monolith. 125 kilos went into specially drilled holes, while the remaining 50 kilos was crammed into natural fissures. Shortly after four o'clock on the afternoon of March 28th 1988, the plunger was pushed, and the great *peñasco* of Pizarra, which had watched over the village like a stern Victorian father since it was born, was blown to smithereens which rained down into the waiting pit. A menacing ogre it may have been, but surely a few eyes were moist that day, and not simply from the billowing clouds of dust which blew across the village square.

The destruction of the rock had cost two million pesetas, and when the dust settled, traces of gunpowder were found on its shattered remnants – relics of a less successful and certainly cheaper attempt.

The town's population today is around 6,500, and its main attractions for tourists are the annual Flamenco Festival which is held from July 25th–29th, the fiesta of *Nuestra Señora de la Fuensanta* (August 14th–18th), and the one-day festival on October 7th in honour of the Virgin of Rosario.

The Village

We would normally use the word *pueblo,* but here it just does not feel right. Village is hardly better, for the same reason. Both words have a ring of the ancient about them. Pizarra is less than five hundred years old, and the only real building took place in the 19th century. Many of the buildings are pleasing, particularly those in the main street, which were probably constructed around the same time as the *Palacio de los Conde de Puerto Hermos.* (see below)

In spite of these reservations, there is a certain tranquillity here which makes a short visit enjoyable, and the car can be parked safely and easily between the church and palace, directly outside the police station and the town hall.

Church of San Pedro

Since Pizarra in its present form was a creation of the Christians after 1483, there is no trace of Moorishness in its character. No large castle was built, and no mosque. Had there been, then the Church of San Pedro might be considerably older. An existing mosque would undoubtedly have been destroyed and a church raised in its place. As it was, without the incentive, the job was always put off for another day. Excitement and anticipation ran high in the community in the 17th century, when the Church of San Pedro finally made its appearance, but only as a nave. The workers then went off for a siesta, and did not return for a hundred years. Shaking the sleep from their eyes and dusting themselves down, they then built a tower on one side.

A main feature of the church is the life-size wooden Crucifixion – the work of the Sevillian sculptor, Francisco Buiza. The four stained glass windows depicting various saints are modern, and lovers of completeness, or simply fair play, may wonder why the apostles Mark, Luke and John are represented, while Matthew is ignored.

There are some 18th-century statues of St Joseph and the Virgin, and a painting of St John the Baptist from the 17th century. The latter, since it is contemporary with the building of the church, may well have hung on its walls since the day its doors were thrown open to admit the very first member of its first congregation.

The church, like Pizarra itself, seems small and afraid of showing emotion. On its outer wall is a niche containing a statue of the Virgin. The image is behind a pane of glass, and the window is protected in traditional style by an iron grille. Such a shrine would normally have at least a few candles burning before it, but not here. A notice asks the faithful not to light them because of the dangers of fire and of cracking the glass.

Palacio de los Conde de Puerto Hermos

As noted above, the Conde de Puerto Hermos turned his eyes on Pizarra during the 19th century, and accumulated enough land to build an impressive palace as the outward sign of his power and prestige. The three-storey building, large and square, is pierced by a tower and surrounded by a high wall with a fine-looking mock gateway.

Its finest moment came in 1922, when it was chosen as the setting for the *Conferencia de Pizarra*. War was raging in Spanish-controlled Morocco, and politicians and soldiers gathered at the palace in an attempt to find a military and/or political solution to the problem. The long history of Spain's involvement in Morocco is far beyond the scope of this book, but in July 1921, the Moroccan scholar and leader Muhammad Abd el-Krim defeated a Spanish force sent to quell a planned rising, and established what he called the Republic of the Rif. The conference at Pizarra made little progress. It is hardly to be wondered at, since the chief military delegates were General Dámaso Berenguer and Admiral Juan Bautista Aznar, who found it impossible to keep order in Spain itself during the years before the founding of the Second Republic, let alone in the colonies. It was five years before a combined French and Spanish force of more than a quarter of a million men brought Abd el-Krim to his knees and exiled him to the Indian Ocean island of Réunion. After that, what remained of Spanish Morocco was quiet for a decade, until Gen. Francisco Franco used it as his base to attack the Republic, and bring about the bloody and divisive Civil War.

The palace is still a private home, and is not open to the public. It is well signposted in the little town, and is now surrounded by neat, tidy streets and a pleasing section containing the police station and the church of San Pedro. (See above.)

Municipal Museum

It is not every Spanish village which can boast its own museum. The reader might be forgiven for assuming that this must be nothing but a collection of rusting farm implements and worn-out sandals thrown together like a car boot sale, but not so. The museum is located close to the Casablanca Tunnel on the Málaga road, just 1km outside the village itself. There are certainly farm implements among its exhibits, but it also boasts a large collection of Roman and other artefacts of considerable interest. The story of how Pizarra came to have this little jewel in its crown is an odd one.

The basis of the collection was amassed over more than twenty years, beginning around 1962, by an expatriate American artist, Gino Hollander, who lived and worked in the area. Eventually he decided to return to America, and take the collection with him. Sadly, he failed to seek official permission to do so, perhaps because he knew that it would be refused. The export of historic artefacts is carefully controlled. The collector had a daring plan. He would smuggle his treasures out. This, of course, was easier said than done. A substantial collection of archæological finds is not an extra bottle of wine. It will surprise no-one to learn that the plan failed dismally, and that the American was caught red-faced and red-handed.

The municipal authorities were justifiably proud of their coup, and were left wondering what to do with their unexpected legacy. The answer was obvious. Pizarra had its museum. The collection and the farm came into public ownership in 1991. The estate was initially known as the Hollander Museum, but this was subsequently abandoned in favour of the rather grander title of the Municipal Museum of Pizarra.

Pizarra has bold plans for its Municipal Museum. It is situated in an extensive but long neglected cortijo – *Cortijo de Casablanca* – associated with the mansion, which stands on the hill above it. The house, by the way, is confusingly pink. Abundant cacti fill the roadsides leading to the farm. This is another clue to the relative youth of Pizarra. The cactus was an import from the Americas and did not exist in Spain before the discovery of the New World by Columbus in 1492. Is it simply coincidence that it should be so ubiquitous in the New World, being simultaneously created in the *hoya de Málaga* by Don Pedro Romero de Figueroa?

Drive into the farm complex on a slow day, when you are perhaps the first, or even the only, visitors, and your immediate impressions are likely to be ones of mild confusion. There is a bar-restaurant fronted by a pleasant, well-kept garden, and signs directing you promisingly to the museum and the souvenir shop. Follow them, and you will see a number of solidly restored farm buildings standing beside others which are dilapidated but in the process of regeneration. An old, rusting mechanical thresher stands forlornly outside one of those which has yet to be given its injection. A tired, patient donkey is tethered to a rail, as impassive and unmoved by your presence as a guard on duty at Buckingham Palace. One of the restored buildings has been transformed into clean, modern *servicios* (toilets) for the hoped-for crowds, yet immediately to its left is a rubble-strewn courtyard surrounded by the roofless skeletons of other, and so far less fortunate, buildings waiting their turn to go under the surgeon's knife. At its centre is a circular stone cattle feeding trough half submerged beneath a pile of rocks.

But where is the museum? Wandering back in the direction of the restaurant, your movements may be watched by a girl standing at the open door of the room designated as the souvenir shop, where ceramics and shawls – even that 20th-century necessity, the 'been there, seen it and done it' T-shirt – are on sale. 'You want the museum?' she will ask.

You do. She will dive inside the shop, return with a bunch of keys, and lead you a few yards to the closed door of what you will soon discover is the resurrected shell of what was once (to do a fine building no justice whatsoever) a cowshed.

This is the first of two rooms which house the museum's exhibits, and although the museum itself no longer bears Hollander's name, it has been retained for this part of it. This is *Gino Hollander's Room.* There is an entrance fee. Currently (1998) this is set at 300 pesetas for adults, and 200 pesetas for children under fifteen. Suddenly, this quirky semi-restored *cortijo* complex takes on an entirely new dimension. The old barn may long to be something in the city, but it is not ashamed of its rural past. The feeding troughs have been cleaned up and given a lick of paint, but they remain as a convenient centrepiece; a neat dividing line in the centre of the room, around which Hollander's collection has been arranged, in roughly chronological order. Iberian, Roman and Moorish pottery, Roman columns, coins. There are explanatory notices beside each one, but these are only in Spanish. This may not be the disadvantage it first appears. Visitors are handed a small, duplicated leaflet giving a very brief description of Pizarra and its museum. The English version speaks of the Phœnicians and others leaving 'their deep prints in an open, modern and jealous society of its past', and ends with an invitation for us to 'reflect over our latest history'. Perhaps you are better off with the Spanish version after all.

It is an eclectic concentration of Andalucía's history. Glass cases containing ancient pots, tools and the fascinating bits and pieces of lives too long gone to be within our comprehension, are separated by wagon wheels, wooden roof awnings, cupboards and rural benches, little more than a century old. The tour of the room begins to the left of the entrance, and ends full circle on its right with a selection of wooden farm machinery which, though it certainly belongs in a museum, is probably identical to other machines still being used in remote areas.

While you browse, the soothing but incongruous sounds of Gregorian chants play softly from the barely concealed hi-fi system. No doubt it seemed to someone like a good idea at the time, but until musical historians resurrect the sound of Roman revelry, or the plaintive strumming of the Iberian troubadour, it is probably one embellishment which the museum can do without.

From Gino Hollander's room, the guide will take you around the corner and unlock the door to room number two. This one is dedicated to Agustín Clavijo, and is given over mainly to Spanish furniture and household items ranging from 15th-century chests to an early 20th-century bed and bedside table. On the table is a solid, old-fashioned radio set. Mercifully, it is not switched on and tuned to a concert of Gregorian chants.

Around the walls is a selection of Hollander's paintings. His style ran from the uninspired representational portrait to the kind of action painting so memorably produced by Tony Hancock in his film, *The Rebel.* Art is the perfect subject for furious intellectual debate. Since all æsthetic appreciation is ultimately subjective, everyone's opinion is as valid as the next. If one critic declares a pile of bricks, or a dead sheep preserved in a glass case to be stunning masterpieces, while another denounces them as self-indulgent infantile absurdities, you simply side with one or the other. You either see the King's new clothes or you don't. Great art bypasses the mind and speaks directly to the soul, but no two souls hear the same words. Nevertheless, it is hard not to conclude that Gino Hollander was a better collector than he was a painter or smuggler.

The cheaply duplicated leaflet calls the Pizarra civic museum, 'a first class touristic and cultural complex with easy access, car park, gardened zones, restaurants, shops ...' It is not that yet, but the authorities are working hard at it with some success. There is enormous potential at *Cortijo Casablanca.* The museum, in spite of its faults, is a minor miracle. And when you finally finish your tour, the restaurant is waiting with excellent food and cooling drinks. Sit on the verandah and enjoy the garden and the views across the valley. Only one thing occasionally shatters the tranquillity. At the bottom of the garden is the railway line, and from time to time trains screech and rumble invisibly past. Invisibly, because the line is at the bottom of a gully, which shields the trains from view. It is all eerily reminiscent of Arnold Ridley's famous old play, *The Ghost Train.*

As with so many similar places of interest around Spain, the museum's opening times are curiously arbitrary. You won't get in before ten o'clock in the morning, and if you arrive after two in the afternoon, you will have to wait until four, when the doors are thrown wide again until 8pm. That is, unless you turn up on a Monday, when it is firmly closed all day.

Almost directly opposite the museum you will see an abandoned road which leads around to the back of the village. It is on this road, shortly before it crosses a small stream, that you will find the previously described base of the broken cross erected in memory of a murdered nationalist.

Roman Town of Barbi and Eras de Zalea

The Roman town of Barbi does not exist. Not anymore. Not even as a recognisable pile of stones or a broken wall on a windswept hill. There is strong evidence that a town of that name was established close to Pizarra, but at some point it was deserted and what was not looted and carried away was simply swallowed up by time and nature until it vanished like a mirage.

It is not given to every seeker after lost towns to find a Troy. In that lottery, Heinrich Schliemann came up with all six numbers and the bonus ball and earned the admiration and the tight-lipped envy of generations of those who had to bear the disappointment of screwing up their worthless tickets and tossing them into the fire.

Barbi was no Troy. It was just another Roman hill town, but its name hangs in the air, calling to us. It is stubbornly determined to be rediscovered and remembered, and as we drive the hills we catch tantalising echoes in the wind.

Drive out of Pizarra towards Málaga, cross the rio Guadalhorce and the rio Grande, and make your way towards the new settlement of Zalea. Turn left on to the grandly named *Camino el Lobo* (Wolf Road), which is scarcely more than a dirt track, and you will soon begin to hear them. After a while the road forks. Go left and you will pass a *vivero* (garden centre) and the red house of the *Finca las Tinajas. Tinaja* is a term for an earthen jar. Earthen jars are associated with Romans. Almost unbidden, our detective instincts are springing to life.

There is a hunter's wind hissing through the pine trees; whispering, sighing, and then suddenly letting out a long, exuberant laugh. But it is a friendly, not a mocking laugh. Visitors are welcome. Come one, come all. Come and solve the riddle if you can. The wind is a fairground conjurer, and the hills are the thimbles on his table. Which one hides Barbi? Now you see it, now you don't.

To the left is a likely hill. Others before us have singled it out for attention. Its sides are defended by a barbed wire fence, but its strands are widely separated and it is easy to scramble through. We park the car and begin our climb.

It is steep, but not steep enough to make the climbing difficult or uncomfortable. The first thing which draws our attention is the stones. There are stones everywhere, strewn across the surface like the studding on a biker's leather jacket. Tiny pebbles to large rocks, and many more than seems natural.

The top of the hill is flat and self-contained. A perfect place for a Roman town, a Visigothic village, an Iberian settlement. On the way up we see what might be the hidden remnants of a defensive wall, or simply a trick of the contour aided by our imagination. One mystery catches our eye. On the summit, an area has been cordoned off and protected by more barbed wire. Why? It seems to contain nothing but trees and undergrowth. Surely there must be something more? At another spot, some of the larger stones have been heaped together, but for what reason? The pile of stones is recent. It might have been made yesterday, or last week. There is no evidence that they have been used to surround a camp fire, and the hill is mercifully free of human refuse. If it were not for the mysterious barbed wire and the neatly stacked stones, we might be the first visitors to this hilltop in a thousand years. The warm wind laughs again, like a wise old uncle watching children at play.

Then we see something among the rocks and pebbles and stones. Hiding like a chameleon, afraid to show its face, is a shard of pottery, and then another, and finally the unmistakable corner of a Roman roof tile. It is not enough for us to cry a triumphant *Eureka!* to the heavens, but it makes us feel good. If Barbi, or any other town, once filled this hilltop with people, it has gone like Brigadoon, the mythical Scottish village which reappears for a single day once every hundred years.

But that is the stuff of fantasy and whimsical Broadway musicals. The wind may whisper and whistle and laugh, but it does not sing. All that the gods are prepared to give us are our tile and our few shards of pottery. A reward or a maddening tease?

The Roman town of Barbi does not exist. Not anymore.

Unless, of course, its bones lie at Eras de Zalea. This fortified Iberian settlement, dating from the 3rd–1st centuries BC, has been selected by some as the site of the lost town. Roman records certainly mention 'Barba', but this is generally thought to relate to Singilia Barba, another Roman town some 25km to the north.

However, during the later Visigothic period, a Roman Christian community became associated with the name 'Barbi', and this community would appear to be responsible for the Mozárabe church described above.

Eras de Zalea can be found on the high ground at the junction of the Guadalhorce and Arroy de Casarabonela, opposite Pizarra itself. The site was identified in 1967 and was immediately considered a likely contender for the lost town in view of the fact that it was located on the old Roman Málaga-Alora-Ronda road. A second major Roman road ran parallel to this one, directly through Pizarra and on to Antequera and Córdoba.

Pick a card, any card. The Barbi mystery remains unsolved.

Ermita de Nuestra Señora de la Fuensanta

This hermitage is located just a kilometre north of Pizarra, and was built in the 18th century on the site of the old Mozárabe church. The word Mozárabe is a corruption of the Arabic, *musta'rib*, which means 'arabicized' or 'would-be Arabs'. This was true to a point. The Mozárabe adopted Arabic culture and language, but otherwise remained steadfastly Christian. They were a distinct and occasionally influential section of Moorish society, who were ruled by their own officials and inherited the Visigothic legal system. Mozárabe enclaves – today we would probably call them ghettoes – were common in the larger Arab cities. Significant and wealthy communities existed in Seville, Córdoba and Toledo.

Mozárabe churches were well established. The sect had its own bishops, founded monasteries, and translated the Bible into Arabic. They finally settled, mainly in the north, and the horseshoe arch and vault became a familiar feature of their architecture, which we now associate strongly with Islamic Córdoba.

The original Mozárabe church, which pre-dated the *Ermita de Nuestra Señora de la Fuensanta*, was carved directly into the rock. A good off-road vehicle will take you out of the village and up to the shrine, but those without the advantage of four-wheel drive should be prepared for a tiring climb of maybe twenty minutes to half an hour. The building is still beautifully maintained, and its freshly painted red and white facade make it almost a caricature of the picturesque. The shrine itself is small; no more than eight feet wide and perhaps thirty deep. It is rectangular, with a simple altar surmounted by an unflamboyant image of the Virgin, in front of which are six bare, functional benches and a couple of chairs. A crucifixion hangs on the left-hand wall, a statue of Christ on the right. Beyond that there is nothing. Pizarra seems determinedly modest in all things.

The living quarters to the left of the shrine are occupied, and the visitor may be surprised to see members of the family seated in the sunshine outside, surrounded by cats and dogs, or hanging out their washing on the line. A flight of steps will take you down to the level below the church building.

Here there is an area which is being used for the growing of vegetables. Curiously, there is hemlock growing here too. No sinister purpose is implied, though it would be wise to think twice before accepting drinks from strangers.

Beneath the church are several great arches, suggesting that it was built above an access bridge which has now been incorporated into the fenced courtyard area in front of the shrine.

A special fiesta is held in the Virgin's honour each August. The image is paraded around the vicinity of the church to the irresistible sounds of Flamenco music.

Monte Castillejo

It would be facile but nonetheless true to say that there is hardly a hillside in Andalucía which is not haunted by the ghost of its past. In the case of Monte, or Cerro Castillejo, in the north west corner of the Pizarra municipal district, this was once literally true. True, that is, if you believe in the existence of wraiths and spirits. It is on a spur of land 300m wide, 800m long, and 200m above sea level.

The hill takes its name from a Moorish tower – the last trace of the small fort which once stood on its summit. It was an eerie place, that the people of Pizarra resolutely refused to pass by after nightfall. They whispered darkly that it was the lair of an evil spirit that would grab any unwary traveller and drag him screaming and unshriven to the netherworld.

In 1643, a young soldier, Andrés Carrasco, who had been born in the village, returned home weary of war after fighting valiantly in the army of Philip IV. He had done well, rising to the rank of Second Lieutenant, but he had had his fill. Friends, family and neighbours turned out to welcome him, and a great feast was held on a farm outside the town. When it was time for him to leave, they rallied round and begged him to wait until morning. To pass by Monte Castillejo at midnight would mean certain death, or at least instantly whitened hair.

Carrasco had faced certain death a thousand times. He was a soldier, and he was not about to be frightened by ghosts. In any case, he strongly suspected that the stories were lies spread by people who wished to discourage prying eyes, though what kind of nefarious activity he believed to be taking place on the dark hillside is not clear. Against all advice he set off home, and as he passed the dreaded spot, a shadow approached him out of the gloom. His sword was obviously useless, so he confronted the wraith with a holy relic which had been given to him by a Belgian nun, and which he never left home without. The ghost was unperturbed. Relic, shmelic. It explained to Andrés that it was the spirit of a priest who had died in sin, and that all it wanted from the people of Pizarra was a few prayers and orations so that it could rest in peace.

On reaching the village, Andrés told the story, and immediately prayers were offered for the cleric's just repose. Sure enough, the presence vanished and was never seen again. From that point on, the inhabitants of Pizarra, whenever they passed by Monte Castillejo, would stop and offer a prayer, and then, for reasons which will strike a chord with every Spanish villager, but which baffle the rest of us, toss a knot into the branches of a tree. The tree, with its curious foliage, eventually became know as 'The Cleric's Broom' – *la retama del clérigo.*

Chapter Twenty-one

Tolox

PROFESSOR J. R. R. TOLKIEN, author of that classic tale of wizards and elves, *The Lord of the Rings*, once said that for anyone not burdened by the knowledge of their literal meaning, the words *cellar door* were among the most mellifluous in the English language. It is certainly true that certain words, even languages, strike the ear as either particularly attractive or particularly ugly. Opinions differ, but generally speaking the English tend to find French 'romantic', German anything but, and Japanese positively manic.

The sound and look of a word colour our imaginations more than we know. A foreign traveller in Spain coming across names such as 'Sevilla', or 'Córdoba' for the first time might, even if he knew nothing of the towns, feel that he wanted to visit them. The names *look* right, and pronounced properly, they ring with the lost glory of Spain. But *Tolox?* It is a harsh, unattractive word which, when pronounced in the English manner with the accent heavily on the first syllable, sails perilously close to an expletive. The derivation of the name is unclear. The obscure and little-used Spanish word *tola* means 'bush', so it may be that it is connected in some way to the abundant vegetation on the spot, but this is mere speculation. In any case, the name almost certainly has Moorish origins. Whatever images the word conjured up to those who gave the village its name are difficult for us to recapture. We see and hear its abrupt discordancy and are reminded of the invented names of patent medicines and purpose-built industrial estates. Our traveller would see it and drive carelessly on.

Which is a pity; for Tolox is a tranquil place of much charm, a million miles from belching factory chimneys and 20th-century jargon. It lounges like a resting shepherd at the end of a side road leading from the C–344 Málaga-Ronda highway close to the rio Grande, and its fame, such as it is, is today founded on the *Balneario de Fuente Amargosa*, the medicinal spa of the Amargosa spring. Except for dedicated film buffs. They know it for its association with the actor, Antonio Banderas, who remains proud enough of his family's origins to visit it occasionally with his American actress wife, Melanie Griffiths. It is also, as we shall see, the home of some of the oddest traditions in Andalucía.

Historical Background

Tolox is perched on a defensible spur of land between two rivers, the rio de

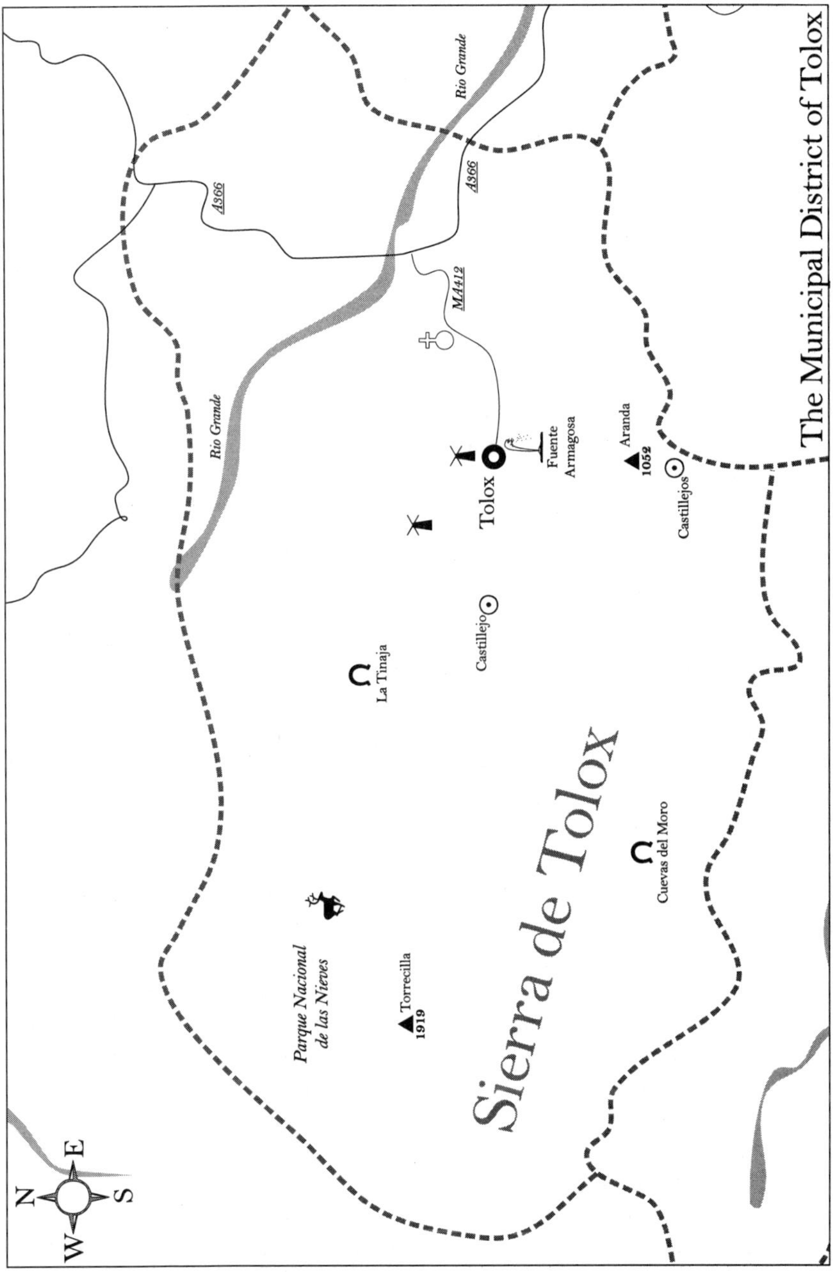
The Municipal District of Tolox
Sierra de Tolox
Rio Grande
Rio Grande
A366
A366
MA412
Tolox
Fuente
Armagosa
Aranda
1052
Castillejos
Castillejo
La Tinaja
Cuevas del Moro
Parque Nacional
de las Nieves
Torrecilla
1919
N
E
S
W

los Caballos and the rio de los Horcajos (respectively 'Horse River' and 'Fork River'), which meet at the village and combine to form the modestly named rio Riachuelo ('Stream River'). Here, the hillside is so steep that the houses seem like photographs nailed to a vast green wall, and the law of gravity appears to be flouted, if not repealed. The limestone hinterland of this particular municipal area was certainly inhabited in Neolithic times; the abundance of natural caves in the then nameless *Sierra de Tolox* making it a perfect home for our troglodytic ancestors. The Romans may have known about and made use of the mineral waters which are today piped into the *Balneario de Fuente Amargosa*, but the pueblo itself was undoubtedly a Moorish creation.

It is known that between the years 917 and 921 it formed part of the independent, Christian-leaning Moorish kingdom of Soleimán, son of the celebrated Omar ben Hafsun. Soleimán's short-lived enterprise came to an end when he was ousted by Abderrahman III, who raised an *aljama* (mosque) on the ruins of the destroyed church and castle, thereby setting a pattern which Spain's Christian reconquerors were to adopt with enormous gusto over the coming centuries.

The castle had probably been refortified by the time that Captain Sancho de Angula snatched Tolox back in the name of the Catholic Kings in 1485. Although the Moorish population, by and large, pragmatically embraced Christianity, becoming *moriscos*, his victory was not a prelude to universal peace and harmony. In a story which may be apocryphal, but which nevertheless vividly highlights the tensions which existed between the Christian and Moorish communities in the turbulence of the sixteenth century, a squabble between two women in Tolox escalated first into a riot, then into a tragedy, and finally found its way by a tortuous route into local folklore and custom. It happened at Christmas in the year 1539. The daughter of the Arab Mayor and the maidservant of the local Christian priest arrived simultaneously to make use of the communal baking oven. They were making *rosquillas* – traditional ring-shaped cakes for the coming festivities. They argued about whose dough should go into the oven first, and the baker took an executive decision in favour of the maid. At this, the Mayor's daughter flew into a rage and shrieked loud curses, including one that the priest should choke on his cake. Within moments a magnificent fracas broke out – Moors on one side, Christians on the other. Flour and sugar filled the air like a sweet, choking fog. Hair was pulled; fists, feet and flour flew in all directions. The shrieks became deafening. This might have passed and been quickly forgotten; an entertaining diversion for passers-by and an exhilarating workout for those who took part. But these were restless times. There had already been a number of risings and rebellions by the simmering Moors in other *pueblos* in the hills. The curses and the threats were taken very seriously. So seriously that the Christian population evacuated their women and children under cover of darkness, while the men took up strategic positions to await an expected reprisal by the Arabs. The Moors, for their part, planned to take revenge on the Christians at Midnight Mass (known in Spain as the Rooster Mass, *la Misa del Gallo*), but arrived to find the church locked and empty. In the resulting confusion the Christians came out of their hiding places and attacked, but were severely beaten – the survivors fleeing north for safety to Alozaina. The Moors then vented their anger by setting fire to the church. The rebellion was finally put down when the Christians returned with reinforcements from the fort at Alozaina. The fort, incidentally, still stands. Alozaina today is a beautiful, award-winning village of 3,000 souls, but since it falls outside of Málaga province, a detailed description of the fort and the village's other attractions must wait for another book and another time.

Over the years, the legend of the great flour fight grew, and by means which are not readily apparent, it became twisted into an odd courtship ritual which the young men and women of Tolox acted out each year at carnival time.

It was now the men who threw the flour at the young women of their choice. An aspiring swain would go to the house of his hoped-for sweetheart armed with a bag of flour. If he was in luck, a door or window would have been left invitingly open and he would 'break in' and hurl the flour at the girl and any other women hiding inside. Much innocent, if messy fun would be had, and the girl would be his for the asking. If he arrived to find the door locked, it was a signal that the girl was not interested, and he would slink sadly away, leaving the flour abandoned in the street to mark his sorrow.

The tradition, after having undergone yet another transformation, still continues. Shrove Tuesday, the final day of the annual Tolox carnival, is known as *Dia de los Polvos* (Day of the Powder). The flour, now symbolically represented by talc, is once more back where it belongs – in the hands of the ladies, who throw it with wild abandon and deadly accuracy not only at young men who take their fancy, but at any man within range. Sadly, an unchivalrous streak has manifested itself in recent years and men have taken to arming themselves similarly and striking back, turning the whole thing into a frenzied free-for-all which begins immediately after midnight and continues without let-up well into the afternoon. In this the tradition is almost back to the original riot, and few emerge from the streets of Tolox on *Dia de los Polvos* unscathed. Tradition or not, what red-blooded woman could resist the opportunity to get away with criminal assault on the menfolk on at least one day each year?

As a result of the conflagration sparked by the original fight, the *moriscos*, those who were not executed, were expelled and moved on foot into the mountainous hinterland where they were left impoverished to scratch out whatever kind of living they could. Tolox was left in ruins and all but abandoned.

The area remained relatively unpopulated until 1571, when King Felipe II decided that it should be revived and re-stocked with loyal subjects. Obviously the tenacious *moriscos* had still not entirely learned their lesson and were still causing problems. Their mood was not improved by the offers of free land given to potential Christian settlers, who snapped eagerly at the bait and came by the dozen from Córdoba, Huelva, Galicia and Sevilla. Inevitably, the pot boiled over again. On December 8th 1609, while the privileged 'Spanish' Christians were celebrating the Feast of the Immaculate Conception, their church was surrounded by angry *moriscos*, who imprisoned them inside. One member of the congregation somehow managed to escape and made his way to Alozaina to ask for help. His story and the plight of his friends appears to have provoked little interest or sympathy, and only a handful of men agreed to return with him to sort the belligerent Arabs out. Being so few in number, they needed a cunning plan, and it was not long in coming. The small group of volunteers set off towards Tolox making as much noise as they could: shouting, ringing bells, and flashing lights. By so doing, they reasoned, the Moors would think that a large army was on its way and immediately retreat in disorder. At this distance the plan seems not so much cunning as daft, but according to legend it worked. The *moriscos*, who had long memories, fell for it and scattered in panic. Their retreat did them little good. The area was put under virtual martial law, and an inquisition set up under Fernandez Villamar. Its findings and recommendations were predictable, and as a result, the *morisco* population disappeared from the mountain communities.

The story sounds suspiciously like a garbled version of the aftermath of the flour fight seven decades before, but no matter. Tolox needs little excuse for eccentric celebration. On December 8th each year, the event is celebrated with the *festividad de la Inmaculada Concepción*, a pious name for a festival out of the nightmares of anti-noise campaigners. In essence the population, especially the young, take to the streets ringing bells and attempt to make as much racket as they can. This licence to let off steam is known as *la cencerrada*. In this context the word simply means 'to make noise', but it has a second most peculiar meaning which sheds a strange light on the often cruel humour of the Spanish. What other nation could invent a word specifically intended to refer to the custom of making fun of a woman on the first night of her second marriage? Indeed, what other nation could invent the custom?

In common with others, the village fell under French occupation during the War of Independence. The invaders held it from 1810 to 1812, when the people of the pueblo received orders from the General-in-chief of the Campo de Gibraltar, Francisco Javier de Abadía to rise against them. The rising was so successful that the people were able to eject the French before the regular troops arrived. Abadía must have wished that war was always so easy.

The village finally began to attract the attention of health-conscious outsiders with the opening of the *Balneario de Fuente Amargosa* complex in 1871. (See below) Whether over-indulgence in the waters had anything to do with the curious affair which set the village buzzing in 1886 is open to doubt, but the bizarre story bears retelling.

Doomsday cults are increasingly common as we approach the millennium, but they are nothing new. They had a venerable pedigree even by the late 19th century, when a certain Padre José (Father Joseph), who had previously confined his preaching to the oratory he maintained in Mangas Verdes, took it upon himself in an idle moment to announce the imminent end of the world. Calling loudly upon sinners to repent and prepare to meet their doom, he went hither and thither across the hills, carrying his disturbing message to pueblo after pueblo. Most paid him little attention, but his words apparently caused panic among the people of Tolox. This was not assuaged when a *toloxeño*, Miguel Soto Marín, vowed that he had seen the infant Jesus with a clock in His hands which, in addition to the accurate time, bore on its face the words *Mundo! Mundo!* (World! World!). This admirably terse message he instantly interpreted as confirmation of Father Joseph's prophecy. To cap it all, he had also had a visit from the Virgin Mary, who had been dressed entirely in black and had appeared deeply troubled. The Virgin, he said, had asked for the people to gather outside the gates of the cemetery to pray for two hours for the soul of the son of a prominent citizen named José del Río. Del Rio's son was buried in the cemetery, but his soul was languishing in Purgatory. Only the mass prayers of the faithful would save him and send his soul safely to Heaven before the fateful hour. The unkind might see the all-too-human hand of José del Río in the rush to save his son from damnation rather than the supernatural one of the Blessed Virgin, but a father must do what he can.

Micaela Merchán, another inhabitant of Tolox, had a better idea. Declaring that she was acting under divine inspiration, she gathered a large crowd of people at her ranch beside the rio Verde and lit a huge fire into which food and live pigs were thrown as appeasing sacrifices to the anger of God, whom she clearly believed to be neither vegetarian nor Jewish. Then she encouraged everyone to strip naked and dance around the fire. If this was truly the end of the world, there was no reason why it shouldn't be fun. The following morning, Guardia Civil investigators found her land liberally scattered with shivering nudists who had no memory of what had happened. That, at least, was their story, and in view of the world's stubborn refusal to end, they were determined to stick to it.

As a result of this all-enveloping mass hysteria, 1886 became known in Tolox, perhaps satirically, as the Year of the Enlightened Ones (*el año de los iluminaos*).

The Pueblo

Halfway between Ronda and Málaga, there is a turn off beside the rio Grande. Take it, and after driving less than two kilometres you will find the *ermita de San Roque*, from which the pueblo of Tolox can be clearly seen. San Roque is the patron saint of the village, and is favoured with not one, but two annual fiestas which take place respectively on May 2nd and August 16th. Tolox may be a peaceful place, but *toloxeños* appear to love noise. In addition to the manic *festividad de la Inmaculada Concepción*, there is the equally raucous *cojetá* associated with the festivals of San Roque. During the *cojetá* the air is filled with thousands of exploding skyrockets (*cohetes*).

The streets are narrow, so park on the edge of the village and walk over the old pack horse bridge to a stretch of the town walls which is bisected by a long flight of stairs and some simple municipal gardens. On entering any mountain town or village, the diligent seeker after traces of Roman or Moorish occupation instinctively makes for the highest ground. In Tolox, this is like climbing a spiral staircase to Heaven. As you pass through one impossibly steep street after another, the heads of curious and clearly pitying *toloxeños* will turn as they sit wisely on their doorsteps in the shade. It is difficult not to be reminded of favourite scenes from fondly remembered Westerns, where the mysterious stranger rides slowly into town while a hidden orchestra plays sinister music and all eyes fall upon him. But the interest is not unfriendly. A cheerful *buenos dias*, or *buenas tardes*, depending on the time of day, will invariably be returned, and you can pass unmolested on your way, leaving them to shrug and mutter *'loco'* in your wake.

The highest point on the spur is an area called *Rinconadas del Castillo* (Castle Corners). This, as the name clearly implies, was the site of the long-vanished castle and the old Arab district. The fact that this is situated a mere 313 metres above sea level – more than a thousand metres below the Tolox municipal district's highpoint, Torrecilla (1,919 metres) – gives some idea of the steepness of the region.

Rinconadas del Castillo can boast nothing more magnificent now than the parish church of San Miguel, which dates from the 16th century. It is a simple building: a nave and two arches leading to two aisles and entered through two unpretentious brick doorways. The tower is not contemporary with the main building, and was obviously added sometime later. Around the church there is a network of tight streets and alleys which have swallowed the castle like some absorbent blob from outer space. The analogy is unfair, because the village, in spite of its clinical and somewhat ugly name, is far from blob-like, but the absorption is virtually total. As you wander among the huddling houses like a mouse in a maze, only one remotely castle-like feature is to be seen – an arched gateway and passage, short and anonymous, which may well be the sole surviving piece of *el Castillo*. If so, it is tempting to wonder whether ghostly feet still shuffle through it on winter nights when the centuries swirl together in the mountain mist.

Notwithstanding the disappearance of the castle and all that went with it, this part of the town still retains the feel of a Moorish village, and it is a good place to take in some fine views of the valley below, including an old mill complex.

Leave *Rinconadas del Castillo* and walk back down into the town square, the *Plaza Alta*, where you will find the *junta* building, which houses a small museum devoted to old working implements and machines used in the making of bread, furniture, olive oil, esparto work and so on. The collection, which was opened to the public in the early 1990s, goes by the grand name of the

Museum of Popular Arts and Traditions. The collection is basic, but worth a brief detour if the building is open. Standing in the silence of the room and staring at tools worn smooth by generations of hands merely strengthens the impression that walking the streets has already produced: that of a place isolated by time, location and history. The other interesting building on the *Plaza Alta* is the *Casa Inquisición.* The place that once inspired dread in the hearts of heretics and suspected heretics has a fine late 16th/early 17th-century facade and is now in private hands. There is an amusing irony, almost as absurd as the famous *Monty Python* comfy-chair Spanish Inquisition sketch, in the fact that the House of Inquisition is today an ice-cream parlour.

But like other enterprising mountain villages, Tolox has hopes of using its long-neglected past to propel it into a hopefully prosperous future, one where the jingle of coins in the pockets of tourists echoes more loudly around its hills than the bells on the necks of its goats. To this end, the *ayuntamiento* has embarked on an ambitious scheme to renovate and refurbish the museum. It remains to be seen how much this will reinforce or diminish the timeless feel of the original. Conveniently, the local tourist information office is located in the same building.

Fuente Amargosa

It is easy to find the famous *balneario,* or spa, which collects and uses the water from the Amargosa spring. As you approach the village, turn to the left and drive up the valley alongside the river bed. You will pass the Hotel Balneario, and a little way beyond that you will see the spa itself – a long, low building squatting at the foot of the mountain from which the miraculous waters flow – 15,000 litres of them each day. Close by is the entrance to the *Parque Nacional Sierra de las Nieves.* A statue of a wild goat, a *Capra hispanica,* looks down on the scene, reminding one and all that this is hunting country. The surrounding hills are among the few places where the goats still exist in their natural state. Being constantly shot at is the high price they pay for their continuing presence.

The waters of the Amargosa spring are particularly renowned for curing breathing difficulties and disorders of the kidney. The casual visitor, poking his head in the door out of simple curiosity, is likely to be handed a glass of the salty and, to be honest, foul-tasting medicine by a white coated attendant, while serious *balnearistas,* who have come not, as you may think, to bathe, sit patiently on the verandah, clutching the number they have taken from the supermarket-style queuing machine on the wall, and waiting to be called.

If bathing is not their object, what is? The answer is bizarre. They have come, in effect, to be gassed. The nitrogen-rich water is kept at a constant temperature of 21°C, and gives off a mildly radioactive gas. The word sends a shiver down most spines, and the majority of us would run a mile from the invisible vapour. But not those who have faith in the Amargosa spring. The upper rooms of the spa building contain rows of chairs facing a series of pipes out of which the gas given off by the water is sprayed directly into the mouths and noses of those who have queued patiently to pay for the privilege. To receive the full benefit, they say you should have yourself fumigated in this way for 15 consecutive days. At last a *different* idea for an adventure holiday! You are always welcome, though, to try a one-day sample.

The present building was constructed in 1867, but it was four years before the spa was ready to receive its first clutch of patients and volunteers. On May 11th 1871, the waters were declared fit for public use by royal decree, the doors were thrown open, and the unsteady stampede began. The first *agüistas,* as the intrepid pioneers became known, included some who made the journey by horse from Coín and galloped away with lungs as good as brand new bellows, shouting and singing the praises of the miraculous spa.

Word spread quickly. In 1880, the Amargosa waters won a gold medal at the *Exposición Provincial de Málaga.* The reader may be as surprised as the authors to learn that spa waters compete for medals, and one wonders whether the judges are required to be suffering from some specific ailment, and whether they drink, bathe in, or subject themselves to Amargosa-style gassing when judging their effectiveness. Whatever the case, in 1883 they were at it again in Madrid, though this time Amargosa could only manage bronze.

Close to the spring, and built at the same time as the spa, is the one-star 60-room Hotel Balneario. Like the spa itself, the hotel is open only from mid-June to mid-October each year, and is occupied almost exclusively by those who have come to seek respite from bronchial and respiratory ailments. Like many another hotel, its darkened corridors echo each night to the sounds of laboured heavy breathing. For once they have a prosaic, unromantic origin.

Parque Nacional Sierra de las Nieves

The most popular route into the *Parque Nacional Sierra de las Nieves* is clearly signposted on the Ronda-San Pedro road. The majority of it is within the municipal district of Tolox, and is dominated by the Sierra de Tolox. Its highest point, Torrecilla, is invariably snow-covered during the months of January and February, and it is this which gives the park its name of *Sierra de las Nieves* (Mountains of the Snows). On clear days, the icy peaks can be seen as far away as Gibraltar.

The road, or more accurately track, which leads into the park from Tolox doubles back on itself and leads the traveller eastwards towards Monda. Follow the road for 10 kilometres and at *Puerto de las Golondrinas* you will find the ruins of what was once an extensive farmstead.

4 kilometres or so along the minor road which takes you into the park from the Fuente Amargosa, is a track approximately 500 metres long leading off to the right. At the end of it is a small plateau 840 metres above sea level, bearing the ubiquitous name of *Castillejo.* This would clearly suggest that

there was an early settlement here, but if so, nothing remains. It is remarkable how often mere names and folk memory prove more lasting and resilient than bricks and mortar and stones.

There are a fair number of caves in the area, and many have been recorded and explored by the Málaga caving society, the GESM. Certainly the most important of the caves is the one known as *La Tinaja*; a word derived from *tina*, meaning a large earthen jar. Though the name probably describes the shape of the cave itself, Neolithic ceramics were found within it. The largest of its chambers is 300m long, and the cave entrance can be found 5km up the rio Horcajos from the village.

Those with a solid, reliable off-road vehicle, a sense of adventure, and several hours to spare, could do worse than to drive into the park and follow the network of tracks which criss-cross it, linking Istán, Tolox and Monda. Frequently, in the course of this book, views and scenery have been described as 'stunning', 'incredible', 'breath-taking'. Wherever such adjectives have been used, they have been used with justification, but this leaves the authors with a problem. What words are left to describe the truly exceptional views awaiting the determined as they penetrate ever deeper into the mountains? There are times when the sheer scale and magnificence of the panorama is overwhelming.

From the coast, you can begin your journey from the Istán end. About a kilometre from the village, on your way into the park, you will pass a natural spring bubbling from the limestone rocks. The spring appears to have no name, but its clear, fast-flowing water is as tempting as an ice-cream stand in the baking heat of the Andalucían summer. Two viaducts channel the water away to Istán and the rio Verde.

Drive on into the sierra, and you will soon find yourself in a schizophrenic landscape where dreamlike beauty and the jagged shapes of nightmare co-exist in an uneasy alliance. Several years ago, a devastating fire swept through the hills. Witnesses who watched the forest burn from the safety of the coast described the conflagration as being 'like a volcano'. Now the blackened, twisted stumps of dead trees cover the hillsides like madmen frozen forever in some silent, manic dance. But around and among them the grass and the flowers are blooming again. It is a sobering reminder not only of the destructive force of Nature, but also of its astonishing powers of recovery. Though the bulk of the park lies within the municipal boundary of Tolox, it also takes in part of Istán and Guaro. Close to the spot which marks the junction of all three, a stone obelisk has been raised bearing a plaque dedicated to the memory of Juan Garcia Aguilar and Manuel Quintana Gallego, who, it says, gave their lives in defence of the values of the *Parque Natural* in July 1994. No further details are given, but the timing suggests that the men died fighting the raging flames.

Ironically, just yards away is a sign erected by the *ayuntamiento*, announcing work to repair damage caused by the floods of 1989. Here in the wild sierra, Nature is as fickle as she is fierce.

There are other signs along the way. Some are more useful than others. For example, at one point there is a stern warning that it is forbidden to circulate in the hills using *medios motorizados*. The unwary, caught without an adequate dictionary or phrase book, might well tremble. *Medios motorizados?* What does that mean? Half motorized things? What are they? Whatever they are, people have been circulating in them and it has the park keepers fuming. They are determined to stamp it out. But it's too late to turn back now. Just pray that your vehicle is not half-motorized and plough on.

The true translation is prosaic, yet more puzzling, for in this context the word *medio* means not 'half', but 'method' or 'medium'. In other words, the sign appears to prohibit exploration of the park by motorised vehicles of any kind. Do not worry that you are about to be arrested by the Guardia Civil. So long as you stick to the recognised paths, and do not attempt some spectacular off-road stunt driving in your four-wheel drive or on your Harley Davidson, you will be fine.

Although the country is wild and comparatively remote, it is far from being an uninhabited wilderness. It is, as we have noted, a hunting reserve, but hunters, hikers and four-wheel drive enthusiasts are not the only human presence. There are still a few isolated farms, and the remains of innumerable lime kilns.

The trail across the mountains from Istán leads eventually to the junction of the Monda-Tolox track, a spot known as *Puerto Blanco.* Turn right for Monda, left for Tolox. The stretch to Monda is the shorter and easier. A drive of perhaps ten to fifteen minutes brings you to the well preserved but obsolete old arched road bridge, which is now overshadowed by the modern bridge of the new highway.

The more adventurous should turn left instead and head for Tolox. This trail is longer and in a far worse state than the Monda stretch. Nevertheless, it is safe enough if you drive sensibly. The first signs that you are approaching the village are both a little incongruous. A grassless sports/football ground has been built well outside the village on top of a hill. Its oddly isolated position surely means that only the hardiest or most fanatical will make the climb without motorized – *perhaps half motorized?* – assistance to watch or take part in its activities. To encourage them to do so, benches and picnic spots have been provided along the way.

The second sign looks even more out of place. A large and impressive hotel, blindingly clean, of pink and white stone and shimmering windows, stands haughtily on another hilltop, defying you to ignore it. This is the *Cerro de Hijar* refuge, built in the early 1990s at a cost of 140 million pesetas, 40% of which was donated by the Department of the Environment. At this point the dirt track ends. The road from Tolox to the doors of the hotel has been tarmacked to facilitate the arrival of its guests; guests anxious to sample the mountain air, the breath-taking scenery, the soul-reviving wilderness. But there is something wrong. The hotel is silent. The car park is empty, and the doors are firmly shut. From a distance it looks clean and fresh, but closer inspection reveals wood beginning to rot, paint beginning to peel. *Cerro de Hijar* is a beautiful ghost, but a ghost which never lived. Along with the aptly named *Hotel El Cerrado* (Hotel Closed) in the *Montes de Málaga* natural park, it is an embarrassing white elephant, thrown up in the heat of touristic enthusiasm, only to stand empty and unused while the authorities dilly-dallied and wondered what to do with it. The gardens which were intended to surround it have not been planted, and as late as the summer of 1998 it had no electricity. None of its 45 beds had been slept in, and its 120-seater restaurant had never served a meal. Eventually, if it can be arranged before the termites and the mountain goats take up permanent and irreversible residence, the lights will be fixed, and the running of the hotel will be put out to tender. Applicants will be expected not only to have a solid background in hotel management, but a strong commitment to the environment and the preservation of the sierra. They will have to set up an information service, be responsible for the sale of books and souvenirs, and to organise suitable activities within the park. They will be required to provide guests with guided tours through the mountains on foot, horseback and by vehicle. It is an impressive plan, full of good intentions and bright ideas. And while it fizzles and sizzles inside the bureaucrats' heads, the refuge of *Cerro de Hijar* bakes in the summer sun, soaks up the winter rain, and echoes in the night to the sound of its own exasperated sighing.

But if this is merely a mirage, a promise of rest and refreshment which mocks the hungry mountain traveller with silent laughter, at least the dust and the bone-shaking are behind you. Suddenly you are bumping along no longer. The road is smooth. The sierra roller-coaster ride is over and you can coast into Tolox exhilarated and ready for a cold drink and a few reviving *tapas*.

The *Parque Nacional Sierra de las Nieves* is an area not only of spectacular beauty, but also of great ecological importance. Both flora and fauna are impressive. Moving among the rare pine trees which cover the slopes, you may, if you are very lucky, spot mountain cats, mountain goats, and even the occasional Egyptian mongoose looking lost and searching for sand. The river abounds with trout and barbel. Any reader who wishes to experience the dirt-track journey through the sierra but who does not own or have access to a suitable vehicle should note that organised trips are available from Marbella. The journey is made safari-fashion in small open-backed trucks and jeeps, so be prepared for a bumpy ride. Anyone interested should contact the Marbella tourist office for current information.

Castillejos Aguila

In the southern extremity of the Tolox municipal area, very close to the junction with Monda, is the 1052m mountain peak of Aranda. The route to this point is described in the chapter on Istán, since it is in the same general area as the *Fuente Amargosa* spa. The four-wheel drive enthusiast has the opportunity here to take the road from the spa into the national park towards *Puerto de las Golondrinas* (Swallow Pass) and on to the junction between the three municipal areas which is marked by the memorial stone also described in the same chapter. Here you can park your car and explore on foot the Moorish observation point known as *Castillejos Aguila* (Fort Eagle). It is at the south end of Aranda peak, and gives excellent views down the rio Verde valley to Málaga and the sea. The white limestone *Sierra de las Nieves* easily dominates the area and is in startling and beautiful contrast to the dullish red of its mainly sandstone surroundings. The derivation of words, and the means by which, once born, they grow and twist and constantly change colour and shape like linguistic chameleons, is a source of endless fascination. Although we have chosen to translate *castillejos* in this context as 'fort', the word *castillejo* literally means 'scaffolding'. One wonders by what intricate, labyrinthine thought process it has come to have its secondary modern meaning (in the phrase *castillejo de niño*), of 'go-cart'.

The small fortification acted as a lynch pin between Tolox and Istán and even today a rough trackway links the two Moorish settlements. However, readers should be aware that it is a dangerous drive even in fine weather, and should not be attempted under any circumstances during the rainy winter months.

Chapter Twenty-two

Torremolinos

Historical Background

TORREMOLINOS IS ANOTHER COSTA DEL SOL TOWN which owes its present-day vivacity, perhaps even its continued existence, to the tourism trade. Indeed, to many holidaymakers the terms 'Costa del Sol' and 'fortnight in Torremolinos' are almost synonymous, though the studious may well find its lively non-stop pleasure park atmosphere a culture shock they can live without. *Which?* magazine has no doubts. Its *Guide To Spain* gives it top marks for its restaurants, pubs and discos. Like Fuengirola, it has grown from a tiny watering hole into a thriving, bustling place of packed beaches, large hotels and non-stop night life, thanks to the influx of high-spending foreign visitors who have made southern Spain the No. 1 European holiday destination since the 1960s. Its indigenous population is now around 25,000.

But though Torremolinos has developed more in the last forty years than it did in the previous thousand, it does have a long history. Longer, in fact, than history itself, for prehistoric human skulls have been discovered in nearby caves, alongside arrowheads, pottery and bracelets. The limestone mountains behind the town abound with hidden caves and caverns. One of them, known as the Tapada Cave, yielded evidence of archaic Bronze Age inhabitation in the shape of a Bell Beaker burial of around 1500 BC. The cave must have been well concealed, since *tapada* derives from the verb *tapar,* meaning to cover or to put the lid on. Every visitor to Spain is familiar with the *tapas,* which are served in bars. These were originally tidbits – a piece of bread or small slice of meat – given free and placed on the top of the glass of anyone who purchased a glass of wine. Hence they were 'lids' – *tapas.* It is rare today to find a bar serving free *tapas* in the traditional way. Every bar has its own selection, from the plain and homely to the impressively elaborate, and though they are no longer *gratis,* they are usually cheap.

Just beyond the municipal boundaries of Torremolinos are some of Spain's oldest cultural archæological sites. *Cerro del Villar,* for example, was the site of an island city in the Phœnician period and many other Phœnician, Greek and Roman sites are to be found. Two thousand years ago the cliffs of Torremolinos were the last firm ground before travellers reached the outskirts of Málaga. The rio Guadalhorce disgorged into the

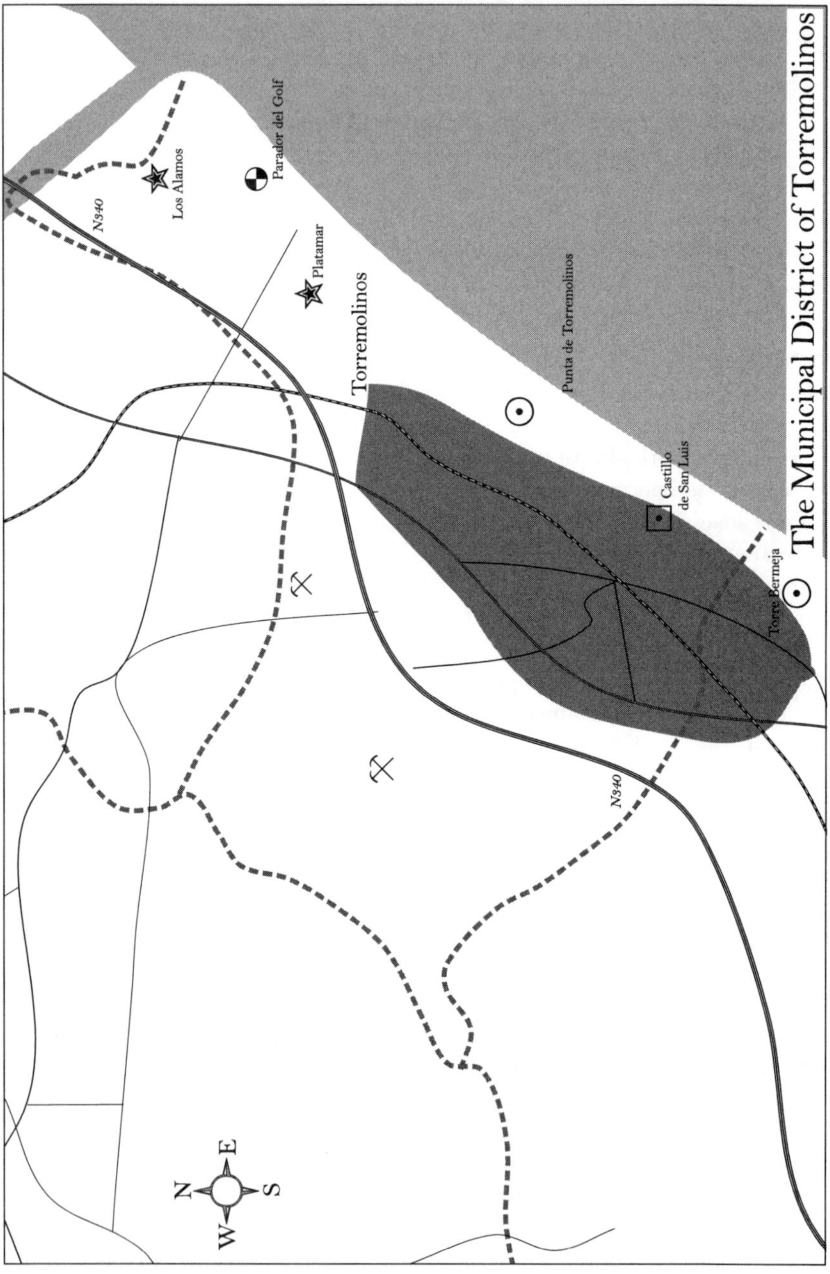
The Municipal District of Torremolinos
Torremolinos
Los Alamos
Parador del Golf
Platamar
N340
N340
Punta de Torremolinos
Castillo de San Luis
Torre Bermeja
N
E
S
W

mouth of an estuary 7km wide, which is today occupied by a large part of Málaga Airport.

After the departure of the Phœnicians and the Romans, who followed them as colonisers of the area, no mediæval settlement developed until the building of the tower in the 16th century. Progress remained slow until the arrival of mass tourism four hundred years later.

Torremolinos owes its name to the Arab tower which stands at the end of calle San Miguel. This watchtower is noted in the Ordinances of 1497 as *Torre de los Molinos* – Tower of the Mills. Dutch maps of the 1740s also give the name 'de Molinos' to this part of the coast.

The tower is recorded on a map as early as 1748. It was clearly an important landmark for mariners, heralding their imminent approach to the port of Málaga. It stood then proud and unchallenged on cliffs which today are lost in a cluster of high-rise developments, making it difficult for us to picture the scene as it was. The mills which gave the tower its name were nineteen in number, and surrounded it like a group of attendant children. They were powered by three streams which flow into the sea at *El Bajondillo* beach.

As late as the 19th century, Torremolinos was a rural community making its living from its host of water mills by grinding the wheat grown in the immediate area and in the fertile valley of the Guadalhorce river. An interesting glimpse of Torremolinos in its rural heyday has been left to us by Lady Louisa Tenison. She visited Andalucía in 1850, and was largely unimpressed (see Málaga), but Torremolinos, at least, caught her eye:

> At the extreme point of the Sierra (de Mijas) is the small village of Torre Molinos where, as well as churriano, most of the bread consumed in Málaga is made. Nothing can exceed the cleanliness of the houses here. The stream which flows through keeps several mills at work. The greatest care is bestowed upon the corn preparatory to grinding. It is carefully washed in running water and dried again in the sun several times before it is consigned to the mill. A man of the name of Parody has a very pretty villa here at which strangers can make arrangements to stay, and it certainly is a desirable place at which to spend a little time during the spring and summer months.

Interestingly, the name Parody (pronounced with the accent on the second syllable, and not like its English equivalent meaning a satirical skit) is not of Spanish origin, but arrived on the peninsula with the Maltese and Italian immigrants who came to Gibraltar after its capture by the British. Can it be that as early as the mid-nineteenth century wealthy inhabitants of the Rock, which had by then been in British hands for a century and a half, were already breaking out of its confines and settling up the coast?

In 1924, Torremolinos was annexed by its powerful neighbour, Málaga, and it was not until 1968 that it regained its status as an independent municipal district. For the first half of the decades that it spent as an unspectacular piece of the Málaga jigsaw, before the tourists came and changed everything, it was treated badly. During the 1930s many of its mills were forced to close when water was diverted from the mountain streams and springs to Málaga in order to feed the mother town's ever-growing population. However, a few remain, most notably *Molino del Rosario*, which can be found beside the *Torre de Pimentel*, and *Molino de Inca*. The latter, at least, appears to have some sort of a future. After restoration, it will start a new life as a reception centre, museum, historical archive and botanical garden.

And so, as the twenties ended and the thirties began, Torremolinos appeared to be in serious, perhaps terminal, decline. Its salvation might be traced, not altogether frivolously, to the arrival of a certain George Langworthy. If any man can be said to be the true pioneer of the English invasion of the Costa del Sol, other than Mr Parody of the very pretty villa, it is he. In 1930 he began to bring groups of English visitors to the property which he had bought and rechristened *Castillo del Inglés*. Far from resisting and resenting this foreign intrusion into their tranquil world, the people of Torremolinos took Langworthy to their hearts, calling him, inevitably, if unimaginatively, '*el Inglés*'. *Castillo del Inglés* was, in effect, the first tourist hotel on the Costa del Sol. Although the true tourist boom did not begin for another two or three decades, Langworthy's pioneering enterprise was undoubtedly responsible, in large measure, for Torremolinos being poised to play a major part in it when it came. It received its second boost as early as 1940. In that year a certain Enrique Bolín Bidwell rented a building known as *La Roca* – The Rock – and turned it into an hotel, which he opened to the public in 1941. Torremolinos was on its way, without knowing where and how far it was destined to go, like a blindfolded driver in charge of a powerful new car. The site of Langworthy's vanished seafront home is now fittingly occupied by an hotel (*Castillo de Santa Clara*) and a block of tourist apartments (*Castillo de Vigía*), both of which stand on a street which still bears the name of 'calle Castillo del Inglés'.

When the writer Marjorie Grice-Hutchinson knew Torremolinos in the 1950s, the straws were already in the wind. It was the last great lull before the fury of the storm. She was still able to describe it as a village and 'a maze of narrow cobbled streets and whitewashed houses perched high up on a cliff'. But she reported, without being aware of the impending cultural cataclysm whose quiet birth she was witnessing, that it had 'already been discovered by a group of English and American painters and writers'. According to Mrs Grice-Hutchinson, 'they enjoyed living in the old houses without "improving" them, and did little to spoil the atmosphere of the place'. Had she but known it, the 'improvers' were hot on their heels, and not merely with a coat of new whitewash.

Photographs taken in 1957 show beachside vegetable allotments and sugar cane fields where high rise apartment blocks and hotels now stand. Back in 1957, Torremolinos boasted only one first-class hotel. In addition there were four inferior ones and seven pensions, and that was that.

As noted above, in spite of its long history, Torremolinos is, as a distinct municipal terminus, a very recent creation, having been freed from its Málaga shackles and carved out of the surrounding municipal districts in the 1960s. Only thirty years before, it had been a small village situated on a rocky cliff beside the mediæval tower (*Torre de Pimentel*), consisting of no more than fifty households engaged almost exclusively in fishing and milling. Early photographs of the now heavily tourist-infested beaches show fishing boats pulled up on to the otherwise deserted sand.

Nina Epton, writing in 1968, noted with dismay its rapidly changing face in her book *Andalusia*. She spent only one Sunday afternoon there, but that was enough. The narrow streets had survived, but holiday chalets were already encroaching and the nights, once silent and lit only by a fisherman's moon, now throbbed to the lights and music of the clubs and discothèques. The first few tower blocks had also appeared. Torremolinos was up and on its way to the promised land, and its marching song was '*Y Viva España*'.

Torre de Pimentel

This still imposing square Moorish tower, the oldest free-standing building in the town, is at the end of calle San Miguel. The authorities have declared it to be a site of historic and artistic interest, which should assure its survival for some time yet. Though Torremolinos has changed out of all recognition during the past half-century, let alone in the five centuries since the end of Moorish rule, at least one thing has remained constant at its heart. Calle San Miguel is still its main artery, as it was once the principal road of the old fishing and milling community. The tower may have survived, but it looks uncomfortably out of place amidst its modern surroundings. A staid old man who has wandered by mistake into a throbbing disco and doesn't begin to know how to dance.

If he has a partner, it is the Molino de la Torre, the remains of which stand resolutely by its side and which have been converted into a restaurant.

Casa de los Navaja

From calle San Miguel, take a walk along *paseo del Pan Triste*, or climb the steps close to the *Torre Pimentel*, and you will find yourself in the area of town known as *el Bajondillo* – the Short Drop. 'Pan Triste' means literally, 'sad bread', but do not be alarmed, this is not the site of the bakery which turns out the dreaded and ubiquitous *Bimbo*. Once in *el Bajondillo* you will quickly find the sinisterly named *Casa de los Navaja* (House of the Jack-Knife). This building is considered to be of historic interest, but although it is built in a pastiche of the Moorish style, it actually dates from the early 19th century. If it looked garishly out of place among the fishing huts of the 1800s, it looks no less so now that it is in the shadow of tall apartment blocks. It is almost as though it was destined for another town but somehow mislaid.

Parish Church of Nuestra Señora del Carmen

This church can be found amid the many fine restaurants in the fishermen's district of *La Carihuela.* The tower looks a little large for so small a chapel, almost as though the plans for the two parts of the structure were drawn up by different architects with different ideas, or were once intended for two different buildings and got mixed up in a classic bureaucratic bungle. Nevertheless the end result is not unpleasing. The most notable feature of the interior is the glazed-tile altar piece depicting the seamen's favourite guardian, the *Virgen del Carmen.* It is a modern piece, dating from the 1970s – the work of the artist Ruiz de Luna.

Each July the Virgin leaves the church to be paraded through *La Carihuela* before large crowds of people who, as everywhere in Spain, manage to combine their unleashed religious devotion with a great deal of earthy festivity.

There are other fairs and fiestas in Torremolinos. While it maintains the tradition of setting aside days to praise and thank its old benefactors, it has not forgotten its new ones. The first Thursday in September each year has been designated *Día del Turista.* On the 17th of the same month its people are out in the streets again, celebrating the town's segregation from Málaga. It is almost like Liberation Day in the Channel Islands. September, in fact, is virtually a fiesta from start to finish. It ends with a bang from 25th to 29th, when the town's patron saint, San Miguel, is honoured with a *romería* (pilgrimage and picnic) which ends among the pine trees of *Los Manantiales.* In 1998, more than a hundred thousand people took part, making this particular *romería* the largest in Málaga province. A feature of every *romeria* is the elaborately decorated caravans in which many of the pilgrims ride, and the 1998 San Miguel extravaganza sported no less than 65. Everyone, it seems, wants to get into the act. Among those treading the path to the San Miguel chapel in the Manantiales woods, and merrily tinkling their cymbals, were the Málaga Hare Krishna community. What Saint Michael made of it all we can only imagine.

Those bored by chapels, or the idea of simply sitting and eating beneath the trees, can make instead for the largest aquatic amusement park on the Costa del Sol – 'Aquapark' – which is also in the area. You may think that as September drew to a close, the people of Torremolinos would be exhausted and too full to eat until Christmas at the very least, but that would be seriously to underestimate them. During the first quarter of October fish along this stretch of coast live in fear as Torremolinos holds its annual fish feast.

Los Alamos and Playamar

On the eastern outskirts of what is now the urban sprawl of Torremolinos, before the land drops down to the flat but fertile estuary of the rio Guadalhorce, a number of classical sites can be found. The most famous, *Cerro del Villar,* is just across the provincial border in Málaga. In antiquity, *Cerro del Villar* was an island in the mouth of a large river, and it was the site of an important Phœnician settlement. For a fuller description, see the chapter on Málaga.

But other Phœnician and later sites associated with the settlement have been found on the Torremolinos side of the old river bank. Among them was *Los Alamos* (the poplar trees) a little to the south. Excavations on the edge of the silted up estuary revealed a Roman industrial area with vats and graves, although the villa complex presumably associated with the site was not found. Sadly, the site's re-emergence was short-lived and it has now been lost to make way for a modern housing project.

Playamar, too, has fared badly. At first sight merely a piece of scrubland surrounded by high-rise buildings, it hides a Roman bath, which, if it has not already done so by the time of this book's publication, will probably be allowed to disappear in time due to development. Discovered close by on more waste ground in *La Carihuela*, but also in danger of destruction for the same reason, were Roman ovens for the production of amphorae. The proximity of the two sites suggests that they were once part of an industrial area associated with a villa estate and dedicated to the service of nearby Málaga and other places upstream in the great Guadalhorce hinterland.

It is almost certain that many more sites of archæological interest were uncovered in Torremolinos during the early years of its frenzied development, only to be rapidly concealed so that projects could proceed unhampered.

Bibliography

Primary Source

Mapa Militar De Espana
1: 50,000
1985 & 1997 Editions

Alora 16–44
Coin 16–45
Cortes De La Frontera 14–45
Estepona 15–46
Jimena De La Frontera 14–46
Malaga 17–44
Marbella 15–45
San Roque 14–47
Torremolinos 17–45

Theory Of Place Name Evidence
The Archaeological Museum Of Malaga
The Garrison Library, Gibraltar
Town Halls Of Manilva, Estepona, Marbella, Fuengirola, Mijas
The Archaeological Museum Of Benalmadena
Museo De Artes Y Tradiciones Populares & Museo De Bellas Artes (Malaga)
The Tourist Offices Of Estepona, Coin, Marbella, Istan, Fuengirola & Malaga
Municipal Museum Pizarra
Hotel El Castillo, Monda
Refugio De Juanar

Published Sources

Alonso, F. W. *Historia Antigua de Málaga y Su Provincia* Editorial Arguval 1994
Alonso, J. *Historia de Andalucia: Málaga* Byblos Fundacio Privada, Barcelona 1991
Baird D. *Excursions In Southern Spain* Lookout Publications 1991
Bellagarza & Ortiz *Istán* 1992
Blanco Sepulveda, R. *Un Modelo de Habitat Rural: El Lagar de los Montes de Málaga* Biblioteca Popular Málagueña 1997
Boyd, A. *The Sierras of the South* Harper Collins 1992
Cabrillana, N. *Moriscos y Cristianos en Yunquera* Editorial Arguval 1994
Churchin, L. A. *Roman Spain* Routledge 1991
Dodd J. D. *Al Andalus: The Art Of Islamic Spain* The Metropolitan Museum Of Art New York 1992

Epton Nina *Andalusia* Weidenfeld And Nicolson 1968
Fernandez, Cuevas & Valero *Por los Caminos de Málaga* Primtel Ediciones 1992
Gallego & Lancha *Malaga En La Leyenda* Editorial Arguval 1996
Gonzalez, D. C. *Tolox, Un Oasis en la Sierra* Editorial Mar y Luz 1993
Goodwin, G. *Islamic Spain* Penguin Books 1990
Grice-Hutchinson, Marjorie *Malaga Farm* c. 1956
Harrison R. J. *Spain At The Dawn Of History* Thames & Hudson 1988
Jacobs, G. *A Guide to Andalusia* Viking 1990
Keay S. J. *Roman Spain* British Museum Publications 1988
Marin, F. A. *San Pedro Alcántara* Ediciones de la Diputacion de Málaga 1979
Papilla Monge A. *La Provincia Romana De La Betica (253–422)* Editorial Graficas Sol, 1989
Preston, P. *The Spanish Civil War 1936–39* Weidenfeld & Nicolson 1990
Rodríguez-Sánchez, Juan Antonio *Historia De Los Balnearios De La Provincia De Málaga* Diputacion Provincial De Malaga 1994
Sanchez Bracho M. *Encuentro con Estepona* 1984
Souvirón, José Maria *Málaga* Editorial Noguer 1958
Thomas H. *The Spanish Civil War* Pelican Books 1986

Periodicals

Sur Village Guides, Sur in English

Index